Subject Matter

Subject Matter

Technology, the Body, and Science on the Anglo-American Frontier, 1500–1676

JOYCE E. CHAPLIN

HARVARD UNIVERSITY PRESS

Cambridge, Massachusetts, and London, England   2001

Library of Congress Cataloging-in-Publication Data

Chaplin, Joyce E.
  Subject matter : technology, the body, and science on the Anglo-American frontier,
1500–1676 / Joyce E. Chaplin.
      p.   cm.
  Includes bibliographical references (p.) and index.
  ISBN 0-674-00453-1
      1. North America—History—Colonial period, ca. 1600–1775.   2. Frontier and pioneer
life—North America.   3. Great Britain—Colonies—America—Social conditions.
4. North America—Race relations.   5. Colonists—North America—Attitudes.
6. Indians of North America—First contact with Europeans.   7. Imperialism—Social
aspects—North America—History.   8. Human body—Social aspects—North America—
History.   9. Science—Social aspects—North America—History.   10. Technology—Social
aspects—North America—History.   I. Title.

E46 .C48 2001
973.1'7—dc21   00-050028

For David

Contents

Tables and Figures

Acknowledgments

It has been wonderful to spend most of the last seven years working on the sixteenth and seventeenth centuries, and delightful to share the company of the many brilliant scholars who specialize on this period of history and on the history of science. With the completion of this book, I am sad to leave their company, but have the consolation that it gives me the opportunity to thank them.

Conversations with Margo Todd, Bill Sherman, Arleen Tuchman, Yoshi Igarashi, Teresa Goddu, and Michael Bess helped me conceptualize this project in its very early stages; Ian Moxon taught me my very small Latin. I presented sections or versions of the project to many helpful seminars and groups, including the Cambridge Seminar in Early Modern History; the Imperial History Seminar, Institute of Historical Research, University of London; the European Association for American Studies; the North American Conference on British Studies; the Centre for Reformation and Renaissance Studies, Victoria University in the University of Toronto; the Omohundro Institute of Early American History and Culture; the Columbia University Early American History Seminar; the Huntington Library, San Marino, California; the John Carter Brown Library in Providence, Rhode Island; and the history departments of the Johns Hopkins University, New York University, Northwestern University, Harvard University, the University of California–Santa Barbara, the University of Pennsylvania, Vanderbilt University, the University of California–Berkeley, and Stanford University.

I received financial support for this project from the University Research Council of Vanderbilt University, the Huntington Library, and the John Carter Brown Library. For reasons I still don't understand, Joel Harrington agreed to read all of the first, long, messy draft of the manuscript, and I can't thank him enough for his generosity with his time and for his extremely helpful comments. I also benefited from advice from readers of sections of the manuscript: Cathy Corman and Brian Delay patiently read and helped me with an early version; Katy Park, Paul Freedman, Dan Richter, Tim Breen, Michael Hunter, and Laurel Ulrich and her early American history writing seminar at Harvard University waded in during later phases. David Harris Sacks, Matt Ramsey, Michael McGiffert, Barbara Donagan, Fredrika Teute, Felipe Fernandez-Armesto, Karen Ordahl Kupperman, Margaret Jacob, and Paula Findlen read and commented on individual chapters. Beverly A. Straube of the Association for the Preservation of Virginia Antiquities and Catharine Macleod of the National Portrait Gallery, London, gave expert advice on, respectively, arrowheads and Elizabethan portraiture.

Aida Donald of Harvard University Press and the anonymous readers of my manuscript had tremendous enthusiasm for what I was trying to say, and I am grateful for their support of this book. I also thank the British Library; the President and Council of the Royal Society; the Houghton Library of Harvard College; the Huntington Library; the National Archives of Scotland; the Bodleian Library and the Museum of the History of Science, University of Oxford; Guildhall Library, the Corporation of London; the Worshipful Society of Apothecaries of London; the William L. Clements Library, University of Michigan; and the Public Record Office for access to their collections and kind permission to cite manuscript sources. The book's illustrations are reproduced courtesy of the Folger Shakespeare Library, the Pierpont Morgan Library, the American Antiquarian Society, and the Syndics of Cambridge University Library. The *William and Mary Quarterly* kindly permitted me to republish material I had written for an article in volume 54 of their journal.

Above all, I must thank Clint Chaplin and David Armitage for their constant support. Clint has not yet read this book but has always helped me with it, giving advice on computers and printers, expressing interest in all my ideas, and respecting my distinctly unfriendly work schedule. David has seen and assisted with this project at every stage of its being, from a verbal description I gave of it at a kitchen table in Providence, Rhode Island, to the final written incarnation. I will never be able to thank him enough, but dedicate the book to him to mark my debt and record my love.

Subject Matter

Noses, or The Tip of the Problem

If anyone could have the last word on the relationship between science and empire, it should be Francis Bacon, who after all wrote that knowledge is power. Bacon gave, furthermore, one of the best-known formulations of the belief that European arts and technology were the reasons for Europeans' superiority over other peoples. Bacon asserted that the people of the old world differed from those of the "Indies" not in climate or body but because of their *artes*, meaning the compass, gunpowder, and the printing press. In our age of globalization and attacks on concepts of race (which valorize technology and shrink differences between climates and peoples), Bacon's would seem to be a fairly shrewd insight. However unfair or temporary a benefit it may have been, Europeans enjoyed certain technical advantages that assisted their construction of overseas empires. But not everyone in the immediately post-Columbian world agreed with this assessment. Most Europeans saw only a correlation between their discovery of America and discovery of other new things without arguing causation from one to another. An engraving of 1600 showed these coincidences, with cannon, printing press, compasses, and a map of the Americas displayed among other new discoveries *(nova reperta)*. There was a long delay between 1620, when Bacon might have suggested a causal relationship between science and empire, and the eighteenth century, when Europeans would accept that connection. Further, the English who colonized America thought that climate and body made more of a difference than Bacon had admitted. And above all, there is no reason to believe that Indians agreed with any statements (Baconian or otherwise) about European superiority over them.[1]

In 1700 some Santee Indians of Carolina told the following story. When two Indian men emerged from a remote place where they had survived an illness (probably syphilis), their compatriots noticed that they no longer had noses. The Indians asked the two men "where they had been all that Time, and what were become of their Noses?" The men replied that they had been conversing with the "Great Being" who "had promis'd to make their Capacities equal with the white People in making Guns, Ammunition, &c. in Retalliation of which, they had given him their Noses."[2] Indian trader and naturalist John Lawson heard and recorded this story. It seemed to acknowledge the power of two famous elements in the conquest of America: guns and

Renaissance *nova reperta*. An accumulation of discoveries: gunpowder technology front and center, and aimed at a printing press; compasses to the left, by the clock in front of the map of the Americas. From Johanes Stradanus [Jan van der Straet], *Nova Reperta* (Antwerp, 1600), title page. Courtesy of the Folger Shakespeare Library.

germs. In addition, the story corrected (or updated) Bacon's contentions about European strengths by adding disease to the equation; in other words, European bodies as well as tools were stronger, making it hard to determine which was the more important factor. But the tale did more than relate a set of material circumstances; it also judged colonial ideology. The story may have been a joke that functioned on two levels: as a bitterly ironic critique of the native condition meant for intracultural consumption, but also as a story meant to elicit a response from Lawson. The joke was supposed to smoke him out: was he one of those colonists who thought that white people were superior because they had both noses and guns, that is, stronger bodies and better technology? Or was he a holdout, someone skeptical of these premises? It took considerable nerve for Indians to draw attention to any of their fellows' maimed bodies in front of a member of a group with whom they were in competition. The Santee's noseless bravado hints at the tremendously fraught relation between the body and power in early America.

Early modern science provides the intellectual context that shows why the inhabitants of colonial America, Indian and English, dwelled so obsessively and, ultimately, so divisively on bodies and technology. The character of the human body, and concomitantly the tools (such as guns) it might create and wield, determined the cultural roles different people were supposed to play in the English Atlantic empire. This book investigates the transatlantic argument on the connection between the natural and imperial worlds, an argument that explored the deepest consequences of European settlement in America. The problem for the historian is that the Indians who were in contact with the English were not able, before the 1660s, to generate written records of their commentary on the argument; although the English often quoted Indians, they hardly ever did so with the intention of giving their quotations with greatest accuracy.

In this study, therefore, which concentrates on English sources written before 1676, the aim of interrogating the English is to make as clear as possible what they wanted to say about nature in the new world and what they wished they could make America's natives say about it. This interrogation—of technology, the body, and science in the early English colonies—is meant to circumvent colonizers' continuing power to make us misunderstand (at the expense of Indians) what happened in America.

Approaching America, 1500–1585

Transatlantic Background

Did the English conquer America? Perhaps this should be a simple question with a straightforward answer. Two opposing traditions of interpretation in early American history have managed to agree, however, that the English were not conquerors—not really. First, emphasis on the settler ideology of creole whites has privileged the experience of plantation, that is, the planting of an Anglo-American people on land they said America's aboriginal population underused, an accusation that became reality after old world contagious diseases reduced Indian numbers. English settlers were therefore rarely required to fight for territory unless they did so against other Europeans or when native populations later regretted giving settlers any foothold. Further, the English rarely moved large groups of natives by force, in the manner of their Spanish contemporaries or United States descendants. They instead got down to the task of developing an Anglo-American identity and culture. Second, ethnohistorians have stressed that native Americans were rarely conquered outright. Military resistance and cultural continuity among natives demonstrated the limited power of English-speaking colonists to displace or subjugate Indians.[1] However many disparate elements of conquest appear in the history of early America—war, spread of an Anglo-American population, legal and linguistic conformity prejudiced against Indians, assumption of "native" status by people of European ancestry—conquest is still not a manifest event or series of events that colonial historians admit to their discussion. But the English themselves debated whether conquest was happening, and this is a debate well worth examining.

There were many dimensions within this debate, but the most revealing was an argument over nature: the composition of the material world, the technology to exploit material resources, and—above all—the nature of the human bodies that wielded the technology. To analyze these facets of the argument over English conquest, this book (the first of two volumes on science and empire in Anglo-America) examines early modern science and English colonization in North America and the Caribbean. *Subject Matter* is the first study to place the history of science at the heart of the early English colonizing process. In it I explain the violent struggle over North America and the Caribbean as a constitutive part of the history of the nation that established Europe's first "scientific" institution, the Royal Society. This study is not, however, a project in traditional intellectual history; it does not focus on how discovery of the new world affected old world patterns of thought. Instead, the book pursues a topic within cultural history that is of at least equal significance: the way in which contemporary European theories about nature influenced English settlers' relations with Indians during the initial formation of the British Atlantic empire. Understanding English views of the material world makes clear what Indians were up against; it also explains why English-speaking people of European descent are still considered prototypical "Americans," new natives of a new world.[2]

Two main assumptions have heretofore guided studies of the cultural encounters in early America and of the role of science in those encounters. First, the scholarship has stressed that the English sharply contrasted their understanding and use of the material creation to that of America's natives; second, it has emphasized that early modern theories of matter and bodies did not conceptualize biological difference between the English and other peoples, including native Americans. Instead, such racial ideas had to await the advent of "modern" science in the eighteenth and nineteenth centuries. The general historiography reflects both positions: that the cultural difference mattered to early English colonists, but a biological one seems not to have.[3]

My book questions both these ideas, which rely on selective reading of some remarks by English colonizers that catch the eye but are misleading. The English did not initially stress their technological superiority over Indians, yet they were quick to construct ideas of bodily differentiation. From the 1500s into the early 1600s, when the English thought and wrote about technology, they saw forms of equivalence between their culture and those of natives, and they exchanged information (for instance, about food) and tools (such as iron implements) with Indians. But when it came to making comparisons between bodies, the English saw nothing but separation and differentiation, mostly because of the high native mortality rates during epidemics. Hence the "subject matter" of this book's title: the English believed that they shared with Indians the task of subjecting nature to human control, but concluded that the truly inferior material entities in the Americas were the bodies of its native peoples, who were to be subjected to the English. In the second half of the seventeenth century, when slavery spread in the Caribbean, the English used both Africans and native Americans to identify their own bodies as optimally suited to rule America. From this tentative racial definition of hierarchy, which emerged in the mid-1600s, the English elaborated ways to denigrate Indians' mental and technical capacities, though they had initially admired them.[4]

From the 1500s through early 1600s, English accounts had not stressed a philosophical difference between European and native methods of regarding the natural world; instead, colonists had seen in native Americans their most contested opinions about the material creation. But once racialization of native bodies was under way in the mid-seventeenth century, settlers ridiculed Indian technology as little more than a compensation for corporeal frailty, and in the late seventeenth century began to present native views as negative examples that supported redefinition of European philosophy on nature. Scholars' insistence that English opinions on Indians were negative at the start, and were focused on cultural rather than physical prejudices, has made it seem that the English formed their beliefs only once—that is, well before they went to America. These scholars have not explicated responses to phenomena the English witnessed in America, especially the "Great Dying" that occurred among native Americans. The devastation was central to English colonists' most dramatic reformulation of opinions about Indian peoples. We have misunderstood the English colonization of America because we have misunderstood the fundamental ideas about nature the colonists brought to the endeavor.

Ideas about nature were the foundation of English colonization because they defined the terms by which the English believed in their conquest of America. To their minds, material forces explained displacement of the aboriginal population, a natural process that required less definitive use of military action than had been the case with the Spanish. A deeper reading of narratives of colonization permits better understanding of the role that nature was made to play in the English Atlantic empire. Just as Perry Miller drew our attention to a misunderstood body of literature, the religious ideas that some of the English (Miller's "Puritans") used to define their mission in New England, so this book examines ideas that nearly all of the English who wrote about the new world used to define their interests there. Neglect of English theories of nature has imparted a sense that the English understood their place in the new world in terms divorced from the natural world, as if the intellectual history of early America had to do only with politics and religion. It is especially remarkable that Miller had so little recognition of the significance of learning related to nature, even within New England's university-educated elite. Miller's contention that "the employment of nature as symbol or as doctrine was for the Puritan mind much more important than the choice of which particular system of physics was used to explain nature" has perpetuated an inaccurate view of colonists as indifferent to the specific and contentious meanings of matter and of nature in the new world.[5]

Early modern science was the foundation of colonization that cut across the differences among the many ventures that disparate English people put together in different parts of the new world. The texts that I examine in this book have not been neglected in the way that Miller's religious writings had been neglected; indeed, many of my sources are quite well known. But within these sources, the narrative strand having to do with the natural world has been ignored or, at best, interpreted elliptically or anachronistically. To tease out this narrative, my analysis must navigate around two historiographic difficulties: debates over the relation between science and empire, and definitions of the early modern inquiry into nature.

It is difficult to decode early modern connections between science and empire because the literature on modern imperialism has so enthusiastically propounded a connection. From the mid-eighteenth century onward, modern science explicitly supported empire, defining strategies for colonization, recommending systems to record and assess information about new territories, and supplying a vision of imperium over the material world. Science also distinguished between civil, rational invaders and primitive, credulous natives. Yet the science appropriate to these functions achieved stable definition only after European colonization had been under way for over two centuries; neither imperialism nor modern science was prefabricated to support the other, and both shared a pattern of unsteady, nonlinear development.[6] Nevertheless, insistence that "science" affected early colonization has pervaded environmental history, much of which has postulated a dramatic contrast between European and native American cultures: western views of nature are instrumental and native views are reverential. Variety among European or Indian cultures does not exist in this scenario, nor does complexity of cultural response.[7]

Although such studies explain much about the outcome of European advance into the new world—which resulted in an imperial exploitation of American nature—their interpretation is simplistic. They project backward onto early modern Europeans a view of nature that would not have been dominant. The Europeans defined "science" as any form of learning, not one unique to an empirical understanding of the material world. Bacon may have begun, in the early seventeenth century, to define a science that fits our popular notion—experimental, empirical, and with an instrumental view of nature—but, despite attempts to promote his vision, its implementation as a program started only with the founding of the Royal Society in 1660. Further, historians of science are skeptical that modern science has ever fulfilled a Baconian definition—or that Bacon or the Royal Society's founders ever intended it should. Enlightenment propagandists invented a modern pedigree for science meant to delegitimate other views of nature, thereby misdescribing earlier forms of inquiry and providing ample opportunity for historians of science to argue about the nature of any "scientific revolution," real or invented.[8]

This book reexamines what happened as the English colonized America and as theories of nature were being redefined in order to explore the connections between these developments without making an anachronistic argument about "science" and empire. English colonizers in the sixteenth and seventeenth century never had a stereotypically Baconian view of their actions, yet they did eventually use their technical capabilities to differentiate themselves from Indians and began to posit differences between their and natives' forms of intellection. To see how they did so, we need to begin with contemporary definitions of the natural world and possible knowledge about it.

It is not the case that early modern views of nature were less intellectually rigorous than modern science. The English did not praise Indian views of nature because they lacked learning and intellectual discrimination. Their ideas about the natural world had a learned foundation in *natural philosophy,* an amalgam of intellectual traditions that was eclectic in its multiple foci and methods of analysis. It was based on Aristotle's books of nature *(libri naturales),* and its students took most of their questions from Aristotelian examination of sensible matter, those material entities known to the senses. Natural philosophy would include ideas about the physical construction of the cosmos from earth to heavens, generation and corruption of living material, and animal (including human) life. Accretions to this Aristotelian base included Arabic science, ancient corpuscular theory, Neoplatonic or Hermetic views of nature, and newer empirical studies, such as those of Galileo, Vesalius, and Harvey. Natural philosophy's achievements were explained in canonical texts about nature. These ranged from ancient works such as Pliny the Elder's *Naturalis historia* to modern treatises such as Nicolaus Copernicus's *De Revolutionibus Orbium Coelestium* (1543). Medicine, the study of the human body, had a close association with natural philosophy; its assumptions about physiology, reproduction, disease, and death were included in the study of nature. Natural philosophy was not a secular pursuit; all European views of nature were religiously informed. Indeed, theology was the paramount *scientia* in the bundle of subjects that were collectively called sciences.[9]

Natural philosophers combined rational deduction from occult phenomena with empirical examination of visible criteria. Nature was a concatenation of animating forces, a web of analogies, sympathies, and antipathies. A *microcosm* (such as the human body) reflected the structure and meaning of the *macrocosm* or cosmos. Humans could understand the cosmos through discovery of its invisible orders and visible workings. Copernicus, for instance, used empirically derived findings to support mystical conceptions of the creation. Some philosophers described how natural magic (contemplation and subtle manipulation of natural forces) elicited further wisdom and functioned as an efficacious way to control matter. This magic did not, like diabolic sorcery, force nature against itself; rather, it utilized nature's own processes to achieve its ends. Distinctions between the empirical and mystical, or even between technology and magic, were not recognized. Individual thinkers might have emphasized one tendency above another, but they would not have praised one to reject the other. This was perhaps most apparent in alchemy. Assuming that all parts of nature were linked—from macrocosm to microcosm, from the pure elements (earth, air, fire, water) to matter formed of elements—alchemists searched for ways to transmute one form of matter into another. They believed in mystical metamorphosis but also investigated the composition of different materials. For this reason, many scholars now argue for a connection between early modern alchemy and the modern field of chemistry.[10]

Most men who called themselves natural philosophers had received some training at a university. At Oxford and Cambridge (as at continental and Scottish universities), education in natural philosophy followed the scholastic division among metaphysics (the nature of being or matter), physics (changes in matter), and mathematics (quantifiable changes). The curriculum therefore included the material now denominated physics, chemistry, and biology (animal and plant life), as well as the related fields of mathematics, geometry, astronomy, and cosmography, but also the theological questions implied in metaphysics. Medical training at universities included study of anatomy, physiology, and pharmacology. The new humanist curriculum of the late Renaissance would de-emphasize metaphysics in favor of subjects such as rhetoric, though there was little development of science at English universities compared to the flowering of subjects such as mathematics on the continent.[11]

Natural philosophy was a disciplined system of thinking whose highest levels were restricted to an intellectual elite, but it also translated into popular understanding. This was especially true once printed texts proliferated, particularly in years when censorship was lifted, as in England's interregnum. By the seventeenth century, popular literature on nature had a wide market and many entrepreneurs eager to serve it. The almanac was the clearest example of a popular English genre that discussed medicine and the physical environment. Works like almanacs conveyed classical assumptions about nature without elaborate exegesis of their provenance or of disputes between interpretations. Popular conceptions of nature thus functioned as an *educated* but not *learned* set of assumptions about the natural world;

these educated views, rather than learned discourse, were what informed writing on America. Many of those who published texts on America had received at least some university-level education or its equivalent at the hands of tutors. Most of those who could read these texts had at least some grammar school education or its equivalent in private instruction; the same would be true of those who circulated correspondence or other manuscript material on America.[12]

Three sets of ideas were especially relevant for colonizers: hypotheses about the physical nature of new territories, information about technology appropriate to the resources of new places, and assessments of the human bodies suited to these places. Such questions did not require occult knowledge about the material creation. George Peckham, in 1583, confessed his lack of application at "Universitie" (a formulaic humanist apologia), but he nevertheless described the climate, geography, population, and natural productions of North America in technical terms familiar to educated Europeans. Writers and readers accordingly formed a fairly broad population, as Robert Rich indicated in 1610, when he addressed the "*Reader*" of his *Nevves from Virginia* as "perhaps Learned, perhaps vnlearned." Discourse on nature in America was manifestly related to power, but it was not an elite discourse. Educated English people (who could perhaps read but not write) were included in, even co-opted by, the eventual claims of bodily and cultural superiority over Indians.[13]

How did such claims emerge? This book looks at three necessary components. First, the emergence of concepts of race, that is, an understanding of the human body that posited heritable and meaningful corporeal differences. This component reflected European interest in population dynamics, especially the rapid decline of late medieval population owing to the Black Death and Hundred Years' War, which prompted attention to the causes of physical weakness in some peoples compared to others. Authorities began to measure populations (as in London's sixteenth-century bills of mortality) and to explain why certain populations increased while others declined. This effort reached a stage of maturity with John Graunt's *Natural and Political Observations . . . Made upon the Bills of Mortality* (1662), the first modern demographic study. Second, Europeans began to identify technology as a distinctive part of their culture. This was related to development of a theory of property, associated with John Locke's *Two Treatises* (1690), that emphasized the role of human labor to define natural resources as property; labor mingled bodily energies with nature to demarcate what was owned by humans (because transformed by them) from what was wild. Last was Max Weber's "disenchantment of the world," the rejection of mystical views of nature in favor of a gaze that demanded distance between the mind that regarded the world and the material that it regarded.[14]

Although these intellectual transformations took place in the same era in which Europeans colonized America, no one has demonstrated a strong connection between the two developments. Hence in this volume I suggest that the three components received significant validation from the English experience in America. Long before Graunt analyzed London's bills of mortality, English colonists emphasized their own demographic rise compared to the decline in the native American population and began to argue that this revealed Indians' bodily inferiority even in their place of nativity. Further, the idea of America as a land of undeveloped resources that required colonists' bodies and *techne* to improve it formed an important bulwark of prejudice against Indian technologies. Finally, colonists at the end of the seventeenth century differentiated between their own and Indians' abstract definitions of the material world, identifying themselves against Indians' perceived ignorance and superstition. This was in contrast to earlier judgments that English and Indians were similarly prone to idolatry and magical practices.[15]

Demystifying nature, displaying bodily strength, and using technology all became measures of colonial power. Colonists began with the body, arguing that Indians were unable to propel much energy into nature because they had to spend too much time and effort on maintaining their frail, disease-ravaged bodies. Indians' lack of technology to develop nature, and their resulting lack of true property, were thus results of corporeal weakness, not of cultural difference. The *artes* that Bacon had thought more important than bodies were, settlers maintained, dependent on the body.

Subjection of matter and subjection of bodies: both topics framed the idea of English conquest of America, and both revealed the serious consequences of grounding empire in nature. This book examines English colonization in the years from, roughly, 1500 to 1700, but concentrates on the period from 1519 (when the word "america" first appeared in a printed English source) to 1676, when King Philip's

War and Bacon's Rebellion elicited conclusively denigrating opinions on Indians.

The three most prominent constructions of nature in English texts on America—as an intellectual framing device, as justification to explore or colonize, and as a mark of the educated character of colonists—correlated with the three phases of early English colonization: circa 1500 to 1585, 1585 to 1660, and (overlapping) 1640 to 1676. In the first phase, the English had few concrete accomplishments in the new world, but they envied Spain its American gold and silver and fantasized about getting quick results from minimal investment in American ventures. These fantasies revealed an obsession with mineral wealth that continued throughout colonization. At this time England was lamenting its loss of empire on the European continent and began to look west to regain power and glory. The shift westward required redefinition of English relations with France and Spain, as England's Protestantism challenged pre-Reformation alliances. Theories of nature suggested what England might acquire from the western Atlantic. During this initial approach to America, the English crown authorized explorers' voyages (those of Francis Drake, Walter Ralegh, and Martin Frobisher are the best known) and supported plans for American trading stations or mining camps, none of them successes.

The next two phases of English expansion were more successful. In the second stage (1585–1660), a minority of Englishmen began to propose American settlement, beginning with Roanoke and running through the lasting colonies in the Chesapeake, the West Indies, and New England. Colonization initiated a long debate over whether it was physically possible to get profits from North America or plant English people there. Could English bodies be mingled with American nature in order to make property and profits? Examination of the natural world answered these questions, and comprehension of what Indians had accomplished (the fruits of their labor, the numbers of their children, the vigor of their bodies) would show what was in store for the English. In the final phase of colonization (1640–1676), colonists had more confidence in their ability to survive, produce children, and extract benefit from natural resources in America. Their own numbers were rising, and their settlements extended over increasing territory. They at last contrasted themselves to native Americans, emphasizing perceived differences between their views of nature, use of technology, and bodily strength.

It is highly significant that the first English text to print the word "america" also pioneered interpreting nature in the new world. John Rastell's 1519 *Interlude of the Four Elements* was constructed as a play on "phylosophy naturall and of dyvers straunge landys and of dyvers straunge effects and causes." The play's characters (including Nature, Humanity, Experience, and Ignorance) discuss cosmography, the physical characteristics of the globe, and their cosmic significance for humans. Nature instructs Humanity in the construction of the heavens and earth as well as the division of the earth into different zones or climates. Later, Experience produces a map on which Humanity can see Ireland and the British Isles, then trace the "great Occyan," first crossed "this xx.yere," beyond which are the "new landes." The map continues westward, over Asia and Africa, then back to Europe. Rastell's play showed the concern to situate England on the world's changing map as old world alliances shifted and a new source of wealth and power shimmered in the west.[16]

The assumption that America was most properly comprehended in terms of its physical configuration appeared in many other accounts, such as *mappae mundi*. This was the pattern Martin Waldseemüller had established in 1507, in verbal descriptions and in cartography, and which Rastell used in his play. Some of the concern over geography registered the European shock of discovering a new continent (and new peoples) and of reassessing classical learning, which had not explained America. Other *mappae mundi* delineated particular features of the new lands, usually through astrology. The way in which a land was placed beneath the stars and planets explained much about its material resources and the character of its people. Was its climate warm enough to nourish gold within the earth or spices on its surface? Were its people and land of a temperate nature? What navigational routes to or around it were possible? Rastell's play revealed the significance of such questions to educated English people. He emphasized that his work was in his "moder tonge" rather than Latin, so that "all subtell sciens in englyshe myght be lernyd." Further, his work was meant to be performed and so made accessible to the illiterate, including women and servants.[17]

Of course, the Spanish had written the earliest accounts of America and did most to establish a genre of new world natural history which assumed that the material characteristics of the Americas were foundational, the first facts to be set out and examined. My study cannot systematically examine the connections and contrasts between Spanish and English analyses of nature in the New World (a subject that deserves book-length studies in its own right), but some Iberian precedents are worth noting. Gonzalo Fernández de Oviedo y Valdés's *Historia general y natural de las Indias occidentales* (1537), Nicolás Bautista Monardes's *Dos libros* . . . (1569), and José de Acosta's *De Natura Novi Orbis* (1589) began to assess information from conquered territories. Jealous of Spanish accomplishments in America, the English scanned Iberian accounts in order to learn how to catch up. Richard Eden, cosmographer and alchemist, translated many Iberian accounts into English in the 1550s, in the Marian era, when England was dynastically allied to Spain. Not only did Eden convey the concern over American nature contained in the Spanish texts, but also he introduced and glossed the texts with further commentary on nature. For instance, Eden inserted a translation of Vannuccio Biringucci's *Pyrotechnia* (1540) in his translation of Peter Martyr's *Decades of the New World* to balance a discussion of Indian riches with an explanation of how the earth formed mineral wealth. English accounts of America would follow this pattern; for example, both Thomas Hariot's *Briefe and True Report of the New Found Land of Virginia* (1588) and William Wood's *New England's Prospect* (1634) began with the natural world and then considered the people within that world.[18]

Nearly all English writings on the new world were, in some way, promotional, meant to encourage investment or migration, to flatter those who invested in American ventures, and to justify the actions and character of the people who had actually migrated. The earliest accounts were intended to entice patrons, especially the monarch. The efforts of natural philosophers were key to this design because these men were, in effect, expert witnesses on the new world's productive capacity. Eden had begun to define such a role for himself and other scholars of nature. He translated Oviedo's *Natural History of the West Indies* to emphasize the features of natural history not explained in Martyr's earlier *Decades*. In 1561 Eden translated Martín Cortés's *Arte de Navigar,* which not only explained the nature and significance of navigation for new discoveries, but also provided what was probably the earliest map of America printed in England.[19]

Study of geography and navigation especially applied natural philosophy to questions about America. As John Dee explained of arithmetic, one of its common uses was by "Marchant venturers, and Trauaylers ouer Sea." Geographical texts and maps were some of the most influential representations of the new world and of the European nations with aspirations to control people and resources there. Propagandist Richard Hakluyt the younger reminded his readers that Charles V had endowed a lecture on navigation in Seville on which all masters of ships to the West Indies were examined. Hakluyt pleaded with Queen Elizabeth's adviser Sir Francis Walsingham for the "erection of that lecture of the arte of navigation" in England after seeing the lecture on mathematics Peter Ramus had founded in Paris. Ramus "thought those sciences next after divinitie to be most necessarie for the commonwelth." Hakluyt asked Walsingham to approach the queen to endow two lectures in Oxford: one on mathematics, one on navigation (each would require £50 per year). Like Dee, Hakluyt saw mathematics as a melding of the theoretical and the practical: "How necessarie for the service of warres arithmeticke and geometrie are, and for our new discoveries and longer voyages by sea the arte of navigation is."[20]

These plans eventually bore fruit; interest in geography increased at England's universities from the late 1500s into the early 1600s, as did publication of geographical works intended for educated readers outside the university and court elites. Indeed, some believed that university learning did not provide the best resources for understanding new parts of the world. Robert Norman's treatise on navigation with the compass, *The New Attractive* (1585), argued the superior knowledge of ordinary seamen. He described himself as another Archimedes, though "being my selfe an unlearned mechanician." Norman also emphasized that navigators could learn all they needed through experience and by study of books in English and other "vulgar" tongues. Latin and Greek were not needed.[21]

The first natural philosopher to inhabit fully the role of technical adviser to new world adventurers was John Dee, whose interests included navigation, mathematics, alchemy, optics, and magic—among many other things. Dee's expertise in navigation (he introduced the astronomer's staff to England) was of particular interest to new world explorers. In fact, Dee acted as consultant to the Muscovy Company, which Michael Lok and Martin Frobisher petitioned for a license to search for a northwest passage to Asia. In 1576 Dee instructed some sailors in the "Rules of Geometry and Cosmography" at Muscovy

House in London. His efforts were supposed to underscore the practicality of Frobisher's and Lok's plan, but also to lend prestige to the project because of Dee's learning and status at court.[22]

Natural philosophers continued to fill these promotional functions through the era of settlement at Jamestown. It was nearly routine for early ventures to include some specialists, whether consultants at home or experts in the field, and England's mineral obsession guaranteed use of experts in mines and mining. Martin Frobisher's third Arctic voyage of 1578 included five trained assayers. Humphrey Gilbert employed the Hungarian humanist Stephen Parmenius on his 1583 voyage to America, as well as mineralogists and refiners. Richard Hakluyt the younger, in his *Discourse of Western Planting*, recommended that colonies employ "phisitions . . . Cosmographers, hidrographers, Astronomers." In preparation for the Roanoke venture, mineralogists and druggists occupied first and second places on a list of preferred occupations; another adviser recommended taking an engineer, traverse master (navigator), physician, surgeon, apothecary, and alchemist. The mathematician Thomas Hariot and Czech mineralogist Joachim Gans surveyed natural resources at Roanoke. Finally, the Virginia Company would send an array of technicians to Jamestown.[23]

Learned men were expected to describe the natural resources of the places they saw and help realize profits for the investors in new world ventures. Their learning also gave cachet to their patrons' interest, which was peculiar for the time, in the western lands. Eden played on the prestige of such patronage when he flattered William Cecil, secretary of state, with the assertion that he was with Cecil what "was Plato with King *Dyonisius,* Aristotle with greate Alexander." Still, natural philosophers' participation in early ventures to America had mixed results. Because profits from the earliest ventures were usually nonexistent, employment of alchemists was highly speculative and expensive. Nor did learned men always bear up under the rigors of shipboard life and pioneering. Among the few survivors from Henry Hudson's ship *Discovery* Thomas Woodhowse, "a Mathematition," was "put away in great distress" in 1611.[24]

Moreover, the English had significant doubts about their own learning and assumed they would have to learn about America from its natives. This promoted their early respect for Indian technǒlogy and Indian views of nature, a sympathetic response that was maintained through the first two stages of colonization. As I will argue in the next chapter, the English doubted that they had learning that made them superior to America's natives; they were too aware that they lagged behind their European counterparts in the science of mining, for instance, and they suspected themselves of impious idolatry when they managed to find reasons to admire their own handiwork. Martin Frobisher's three voyages to the Arctic in the late 1570s especially revealed this multivalent anxiety. The uncertainty of the English about their mastery over nature continued, even to the extent that they did not believe that firearms guaranteed them success when they began invading Indian communities from 1585 onward. As Chapter 3 points out, the English still relied on bows and arrows as weapons into the early 1600s. They even suspected that they might have to revert to these weapons in the mid-1600s, when supply lines between the colonies and England failed. Fetishization of gunpowder technology, which Bacon defined and subsequent scholars of imperialism have assumed, had not yet occurred among the English colonists.

While respect for Indian technology continued during this second stage of English colonization, admiration of Indian bodies did not. Chapters 4 and 5 show how colonizers looked more closely at American environments than explorers had done and began to analyze native physiognomy in order to discover what kind of humans could live in the places designated for colonies. When the English initially wrote about the new world and examined the peoples native to its hemisphere, they explained bodily variation in environmental and non-racial terms, using a broad discourse on cosmography and climate. First the English identified what climates America had; then they identified which human bodies could thrive in such climates.[25]

Later, more specialized medical theories did important work when they began to define differences between the English and the Indians as racial, as I argue in Chapter 5. While much scholarship on race and racism in early America has emphasized the representation of cultural differences that prefigured, paralleled, or conveyed racial ideology, less has been done on the emergence of belief in *physical* difference; scholarship on American exceptionalism has usually focused on the cultural dimension of colonial history without paying equal attention to the way English settlers constructed a corporeal identity for themselves. The settlers' physical identity was eventually comprehensible as racism, though scholarship on race has pointed to the science of the late eighteenth and nineteenth centuries (especially after Darwin) as the start of a truly biological definition of human types.[26] But long before the eighteenth century, English colonists articulated assessments of bodies as superior and inferior, particularly in response to disease. This book builds on the point, established by scholars of medieval and early modern Europe, that the body was the site for the construction of identity. Further, arguments for inherited differences that focused on African bodies provided a foundation for emerging ideas about race, that is, the belief that certain corporeal traits were specific to certain lineages. Racial identity was a logical if unintended outgrowth of English views of corporeal differences among the peoples (including Indians and Africans) in early America.[27]

Finally, in the last stage of English colonization (1640–1676), discourse on nature advertised the educational aspirations of long-term settlers and creoles, especially those in New England. (The Chesapeake and Caribbean, lacking universities, had to continue to import their learned men.) New England's college, Harvard, followed a curriculum that taught the medieval division of sciences (metaphysics, physics, mathematics) brought up to date with new texts and theories. Indeed, Harvard was on the cutting edge with its acceptance of Copernicanism, tutorials in a chemistry laboratory, and interest in corpuscular theories. New England's culture of learning—for its white settlers—influenced even those who did not attend university. Anne Bradstreet's *Tenth Muse,* a discussion in verse of topics that were divisible by four, began with the four elements, proceeded through the four bodily humors, then took on the four earthly monarchies that preceded the fifth monarchy of Christ. Interest in alchemy was also pronounced among New Englanders. John Winthrop, Jr., and George Starkey were the most noted alchemists. Starkey achieved an international reputation (under the pseudonym Eirenaeus Philalethes) after he moved to London. In parts of New England known for their religious unorthodoxy, belief in the transmutation of the elements remained noteworthy even into the early nineteenth century.[28]

Knowledge of natural philosophy became a way for colonists to claim intellectual equality with people back in Europe and superiority to Indians. As Chapter 6 points out, colonists feared to a large extent that their hybrid material culture—in which Indians learned sailing technology and the English grew and ate corn—made them look like versions of Indians. But if practical forms of technology did not differentiate natives from settlers, abstract learning did. The chemical arts, in particular, distinguished settlers from Indians, who had not given the English much information about potential mines in America, therefore (colonists argued) demonstrating their ignorance of what lay beneath the earth and within the elements. Chapter 7 describes the outcome of this effort to distance the English settlers from Indians. As negative opinions on the natives' use of nature began to predominate in the late 1600s, the English intensified their negative ideas about Indian bodies and further developed their criticism of native technologies. Warfare had encouraged the English to believe that the male Indian body was powerful and dangerous. Yet colonists quickly asserted that this bodily strength masked an inherent weakness that was always revealed in cases of disease. Further, they contended that Indians had to spend an inordinate amount of their technical energy to maintain the strength of their bodies. This artifice signaled the natives' misplaced creative energies, which curtailed their developing better technologies and greater understanding of nature.

Last, Chapter 8 explains the final step that undid the earlier work of establishing similarity between English and Indian. After 1662 (the date of the chartering of the Royal Society), native beliefs—real or supposed—were used to represent intellectual failure, as contrasts to the ajudicated separations between physics and metaphysics that were now to be the norm for natural philosophy. Learned men such as Robert Boyle were reconceiving matter as an inanimate object of inquiry for natural philosophy. The New England project to convert Indians to Christianity was tellingly linked to this new effort. John Eliot's *Indian Grammar Begun* (1666), for example (a work dedicated to Boyle), categorized Indian words not in genders or cases but according to whether they designated "animate" or "inanimate" things. That these categories reflected emerging scientific categories emphasized the perception that Indians had benighted notions of nature. In this way, New England's priority as a colonial center of learning privileged its role in transatlantic culture—not by fulfilling the religious errand its founders had envisaged but by arguing to England's premier learned organization that Indians had inferior intellectual abilities, with subsequent popularization of this devastating view of natives' mental capacity.

To understand these trends, it is necessary to reexamine the descriptions of colonization that English people wrote and to identify the limits of their reliability, especially regarding America's natives. In this book I question the tendency of poststructual theory to portray colonizers as components of a cultural or linguistic field of containment, rather than as agents whose creativity and intentionality are worth serious consideration. Following the lead of Edward Said's *Orientalism* (1978), such studies represent European description of non-European peoples as a hegemonic structure, a system of power coterminous with systems of language. Likewise, conquered peoples, at least as much as conquerors, lack the agency to redefine or manipulate their circumstances, and function only within the epistemic system that denigrates them.[29]

Different groups of scholars who are interested in early America have had very different responses to these poststructural challenges. The earliest period of English colonization—the late sixteenth century and first three quarters of the seventeenth century—has elicited the most divided opinions. Some literary critics have agreed that the earliest English texts on America can tell us little if anything about native Americans and their cultures. Following the lead of Stephen Greenblatt, scholars have assumed that English descriptions of the new world reveal only English constructions of power over America.[30] Ethnohistorians have also emphasized a cultural divide between Europeans and native Americans but have insisted that the written record can shed light on native experiences and identities. Even though these records are products of the colonizers and have imperialism written into and through them, their biases can be accounted for and filtered out. But if poststructural theory is too discouraging over the prospect of comprehending native cultures, ethnohistorians are possibly too sanguine that such comprehension is achievable, particularly for the earliest phases of encounter. Indeed, and in contrast to the pioneering work of James Axtell, the most successful examinations of Indians in or near the English colonies have considered parts of New France (where the sources are more plentiful) or have focused on the late seventeenth or eighteenth century. Otherwise, we have available only what the English said about Indians, whether they knew Indian languages or not—usually not.[31]

This is the case because we lack Indian texts for the earlier period. In the English colonies, writings by native Americans did not exist until the 1660s and 1670s, when they emerged in a context of heightened English attempts at cultural domination. The earliest to be identified is a land deed in handwritten Massachusett, dated 1664. Next came a 1665 Latin oration that Caleb Cheeshateaumauk wrote while studying at Harvard. A second Latin text, by a native man known only as Eleazar, was written in 1679 to honor his teacher, the Reverend Thomas Thacher. Both Latin essays probably had considerable coaching to shape them as apologies for their writers' barbarity and as statements of gratitude for English education. The earliest native text in English dates from King Philip's War, when a Nipmuck (possibly James Printer) wrote a defiant note in English and left it for colonial troops to find near Medfield in 1675. Texts in English and Massachusett thereafter proliferated, most of them oriented toward legal concerns, such as land transactions. (Sustained narratives by native writers began later, in the eighteenth century.) In this manner, Indians—at least those in or near New England—could finally use writing to explain themselves to the English, but not until a century after English colonization of America had begun.[32]

Concomitantly, English comprehension of native American languages was considerably retarded until the end of the seventeenth century. Early communication depended on gestures, pictographs, and the contributions of natives who had learned English, often as captives. Some early explorers tried to learn native languages. In the 1580s, Thomas Hariot developed a phonetic alphabet to transcribe southern Algonquian words. Subsequent colonizers, including John Smith, William Strachey, and William Wood, drew up short vocabularies. And Roger Williams produced the first large vocabulary and phrase book in his *Key into the [Narragansett] Language of America* (1643). But it was not until John Eliot learned a dialect of Massachusett, and preached and translated Scripture into that language, that there was any systematic attempt to render a native language comprehensible to English people, and to make Europeans' texts comprehensible to natives who were not fluent in English or Latin. Considerable misunderstanding, and high-handed attempts to dismiss Indian languages as simple or easily learned, characterized the earlier period. Thus Welshman Peter Wynne wrote in 1608 that, because southern Algonquian was like Welsh, he was able to serve as an interpreter at Jamestown. Other colonists admitted English ignorance of native languages. The John White who wrote *The Planters Plea* (1630) confessed that evangelization of Indians would proceed slowly "untill we may be more perfectly acquainted with their language, and they with ours." So far, White stated, communication was fit only for "trade" and those "things that are subject to outward sense." But this did not prevent commentators from describing what they thought Indians believed about spiritual matters and occult natural processes.[33]

It is therefore important to recognize that when the English appeared to be quoting natives, they were more likely engaged in ventriloquism. Ventriloquism was perhaps most apparent in the seal of the Massachusetts Bay Colony, in which a cartoon savage was made to beg, "Come over and help us." Here the intention was clearly propagandistic, designed to solicit funds, personnel, and other support for a puritan venture in America. This ventriloquist strategy characterized many English contentions about what natives believed, which could cast Indians in either flattering or unflattering terms. For example, the English marshalled Indians into post-Reformation debates over religion. Roger Williams said that the Narragansett believed the English came to their land because, in England, the trees were "too full of people"; this meant that the English population was too crowded and

Seal of the Massachusetts Bay Colony. Courtesy of the American Antiquarian Society.

had used too much wood, but it was also a play on the hangings that had resulted from European religious persecutions. The English also ventriloquized natives to assign them statements that made more sense within English debates over nature than they did within the conceivable field of Indian opinions. Ventriloquism could be a sign of English sympathy (a desire to stress cultural similarity), but that made it a no less inaccurate and manipulative way of representing native statements.[34]

We will never begin to comprehend what Indians may have been trying to say in the sixteenth and seventeenth centuries until we turn down the background noise, the static of cultural expectations and assumptions that the English put into their accounts about their early colonization. It would be foolish to expect to recover transparent meaning from these texts, but it is equally damaging to give up on them entirely. It is extremely important to recover what Indian cultures and beliefs may have been like, but not with such eagerness that, in our haste, we accept what the English said about them as true. What we are looking at is the *process* by which the English constructed comparisons of themselves to Indians, using nature as a point of reference. By enlisting ideas about the material world to interrogate English narratives, historians can see more clearly the stages of this process. What I am proposing is in fact a structural analysis (*pace* poststructuralists), but an analysis only of the English, not of America's natives (*pace* ethnohistorians). This structuralist reading detects patterns in English accounts of colonization in order to reinterpret the nature of that colonization without allowing the English the power to put words in native Americans' mouths.

To detect pattern, this book recommends two strategies, *triangulation* and the detection of *absurd transcription*. Triangulation requires playing English texts about America against some other point of reference in order to achieve reasonable hypotheses about what occurred. Archeologists and historical linguists have recommended that historical texts, other information in the form of artifacts or linguistic inquiry, and the resulting analysis form the three points of an analytic triangle. In this book I use the English conceptualization of the natural world as the second point of the triangle, the other point of reference for narratives of colonization. Triangulation performs mostly negative work by establishing what Indians probably were not saying because the statements ascribed to them represent too well English concerns about America and the natural world; there is too much static for credibility. Conversely, the English sometimes performed absurd transcription. By this I mean that they may have accurately recorded true Indian statements because they believed them too ridiculous (absurd) to comment upon. But the English may also have been deaf (literally *ab-surdus*) to such statements' implications, which we can now see. This was especially the case with Indians' comments that they suffered more from disease after colonization, which should have challenged emerging English opinion that Indians were simply weaker and more diseased, and prompted recognition that natives suffered disadvantageously from newly introduced maladies.[35]

Triangulation and the search for absurd transcription require connections between fields in early modern history that have been considered separately. Scholars' premature differentiation of Europeans and Indians in the early modern era has assumed that a stereotypical prescientific "savage mind" predated the Columbian encounter; rather, I will argue, it was a product of it. The questionable separation of intellectual history and ethnohistory has been a particularly troubling legacy of the idea of the savage mind. Two of the liveliest literatures in contemporary historiography analyze early modern science and the experience of native peoples in colonization. But these were not distinct stories and should not have separate fields of inquiry. Leaving the new world out of English debates over nature makes it impossible to understand what happened in the formative period of English colonization. The interesting, if tiny, subfields of ethnophilosophy and ethnolinguistics have begun to blur the boundary between intellectual history and ethnohistory; but this interpenetration of disciplines is easier to accomplish with the materials from French Canada, where Jesuits were more interested in the task of translating Iroquoian and Algonquian languages and belief systems into written texts. Ethnohistorians of early English territories have no comparable materials from the period of early contact. They must deduce native beliefs from sources that heavily recoded whatever message natives might have been trying to deliver, and they have done little to examine English patterns of thought about nature (especially about the body) which could allow better decoding of these texts.[36]

One example of my decoding will be useful here to establish the method of analysis for the rest of the book. This is Thomas Hariot's *Briefe and True Report of the New Found Land of Virginia* (1588).

Hariot was a mathematician and natural philosopher; Walter Ralegh, who helped organize the Roanoke colony in the Chesapeake, was one of Hariot's patrons. In 1584–85, Ralegh took into his household two Roanok men, Manteo and Wanchese, from whom Hariot evidently learned some southern Algonquian. Hariot then went to the colony to analyze its land and people, taking extensive notes meant for a long study, though he in the end published only a "brief" narrative. In his account, Hariot wrote that the Indians believed that English technical devices such as guns were "rather the works of gods then of men," and that the English deliberately sent epidemic disease to them as if by "inuisible bullets." Here is a tidy bundle of assumptions: natives recognize that English technology is superior to theirs, and they react superstitiously to the new material conditions of colonization. Hariot's statements seem to support a *Heart of Darkness* scenario that can contrast either European evil with native innocence or European technology with native superstition.[37]

Indeed, this is the reading that Stephen Greenblatt has emphasized in his essay "Invisible Bullets." Greenblatt has interpreted Hariot's report as evidence of English desire to manipulate the superstition of the natives in order to control them. Natives' innocence about the natural world and of the means to control it was turned against them. In this way, Hariot's account was an instance of ethnographic experimentation on the natives, who enacted a part in a test of the hypothetical origins of political authority within the superstitious fears of a primitive people. Depending on one's cynicism, Hariot seems to have forced the natives to enact a morality play for the benefit of an English audience, without in any way conveying beliefs real to them. Or he pressed their real beliefs into the service of an old world argument over authority. They are at least translated freely, if not ventriloquized outright.[38]

But this reading ignores the sphere of speculation most appropriate to Hariot's background in early modern sciences and mathematics: how matter was constituted. Hariot was a rare example of a sixteenth-century atomist, someone who believed that matter was composed of discrete, durable particles. This was not equivalent to modern atomic theory with its different kinds of particles. Instead, proponents of what is more properly called the corpuscular theory drew on ancient writings and medieval commentary on Aristotle to reject the Aristotelian view that matter was simply a continuum, an indivisible extension of elemental stuff. Atomists believed instead that matter was formed of corpuscles; individual particles could not be subdivided, but the materials they constructed were divisible at points between the atoms. A concept of invisible bullets would therefore have been a lively and meaningful image for an atomist. Hariot's manuscripts indicate that he thought all natural phenomena were composed of particles that were hard, unalterable, and not apparent to human sight. His work on optics assumed that particulate matter, whether visible to the eye or not, was responsible for characteristics of light, such as refraction.[39]

Two other factors strengthen the case for an intellectual connection between Hariot's interests in America and in corpuscles. First, Hariot used atomism in other ways to make sense of the new world. As Amir Alexander has pointed out, Hariot represented colonists' entry into American territory as a penetration between the divisible parts of a seeming continuum. Second, Hariot elsewhere used "bullets" (by which he meant shot for cannon) as an image of the particles that made up the cosmos. In 1591, when he drew up a chart of the ground space needed to store cannonballs, he next made notes on the more abstract question of the arrangement of discrete particles as they extended to form matter. Throughout his papers Hariot referred to corpuscles and used images of small circles or dots; they were his preferred way of representing the material world, whether in words, diagrams, or even his doodling.[40]

This was, at the time, a highly unorthodox view and one associated with atheism and pagan error, especially in the writings of Epicurus. Early corpuscular theory tended to imply that matter had always existed and would always exist, as if it did not need a divine creator and caretaker. Helkiah Crooke, for instance, in his 1615 examination of human anatomy, decried the "beastly *Epicure*" who believed that bodies were "made by chance and fortune, out of a turbulent concourse (forsooth) of a number of Atomies or Motes." Even the corpuscular theory of disease, an extension of Greek atomism, was suspect. The idea of preexisting matter was at odds with Christian faith that God had made something (*the* creation) out of nothing. To question this tenet was heresy. Many in Ralegh's circle, and especially Ralegh himself, were accused of atheism: denial of the existence of God and the immortality of the soul, and belief in the cosmic continuity of matter. For this reason, Hariot was mocked when he died of nicotine-induced cancer of the nose. A fellow mathematician recounted that Hariot's natural philosophy asserted *"ex nihilo nihil fit"* (nothing comes out of nothing), but "a *nihilum* killed him at last: for in the top of his nose came a little red speck (exceeding small), which grew bigger and bigger and at last killed him." The references to both a "nothing" that proved deadly and the tiny specklike nature of the original seed of Hariot's demise were jibes at Hariot's atomism, popularly conceived. As with the Santee, loss of a nose invited a joke at the expense of the noseless and his beliefs.[41]

The suspect status of corpuscular theory might explain another odd feature of Hariot's statement—its use of the word "bullet." During the early modern period, "bullet" usually meant a cannonball, a large metal projectile. Small projectiles for firearms were usually called "shot" or "balls." Hariot elsewhere stuck to this distinction. Calculating the movement of fired projectiles, for instance, he referred to "a bullet of Iron" that was twenty-four inches in diameter. In what appears to be a list of things to bring to Virginia (probably intended for a later journey, never attempted), Hariot included powder and "shot" along with "Books of voyages," pen, pencil, paper, and copper plates to make engravings. But the word "bullet" lent itself better to metaphor than did "shot," and it was the generic term for a gunpowder-propelled projectile of any size. Other English natural philosophers used the term to make metaphorical statements about the cosmos. Balthazar Gerbiers's 1649 lecture on cosmography stated that "if a Canon bullet should descend two hundred leagues in one houre, it would be more then fifteen yeares ere it could arrive to the superficies of the earth." In contrast, the human heart could, by "faith," ascend the heavens in a "moment." Did Hariot use the word "bullet" when he quoted Indians in order to ascribe a similar metaphor to them? Did he mean it to convey belief in unseen but real particles—like infectious corpuscles? Everything about the statement is elusive, probably deliberately so.[42]

The highly contested and dangerous nature of corpuscular theory helps explain why a statement about natural phenomena being formed of distinct particles appeared as a quotation from a native American. It is interesting that Hariot's statement about invisible bullets resembled another he made about native beliefs, this second one about the resurrection of the dead. The Roanok supposedly told Hariot that reincarnation had happened to some Indians, and it was part of their explanation for the status of the English as supernatural beings; the colonists "were men of an old generation many yeeres past then risen againe to immortalitie." This impious assertion of human resemblance to Christ's condition was, even more obviously than atomism, anathema to orthodox Christianity. It did not surprise many of the English that pagans held heretical beliefs. All things American signified absence of true religion, as when another man in Ralegh's circle, accused of denying the immortality of the soul, had been seen to "teare twoe Leaves out of a Bible to dry Tobacco on." Association among America, atomism, and heresy may have incited accusations against Hariot that he did not believe in the resurrection of human bodies at the end of the world. An informant of John Pickering, Lord Keeper of the Great Seal, related the "vile opinion" that Hariot and others held, "Quia mortui non mordent," that the dead do not bite (were never restored to life). It was as if Hariot's recounting, without denouncing, stories of Indian bodily resurrection before the final trumpet meant that he himself had indulged in heterodox speculation against Christian doctrine.[43]

In the cases of invisible bullets or resurrected bodies, it is not clear that Hariot related actual native beliefs. Here, as elsewhere in the early English settlements, comprehension of native languages was lacking. Although Ralegh had brought Manteo and Wanchese to England to provide information about their language and country, there is no evidence that they taught anyone much Roanok. While Hariot recorded several Roanok words in his published account, he wrote down only one full phrase, "KECOW HIT TAMEN," which appears in his manuscripts. The phrase meant "What is this?" a minimal device to prompt Indian informants to tell their names for things, which Hariot then put into his account. Further, it is possible that Hariot gave Ralegh the wrong translation for the expression "Wingandacon," which had been thought to be the name of the Roanok's country. Someone else told Ralegh that the phrase meant "You weare good clothes"—a flattering admiration of English appearance. This does not evidently correspond to any such Algonquian meaning, however; if Ralegh consulted Hariot, he got the wrong translation, and if he did not ask Hariot about it, then he had a puzzling lack of confidence in his expert's linguistic ability. Hariot even admitted that he could not convey to the Roanok the abstractions of Christianity "for want of perfect vtterance in their language"; his grasp of Algonquian was evidently not up to a discussion of abstract questions about the natural

and supernatural properties of the world. It is possible that he ventriloquized dangerous hypotheses about matter through informants
who would appear exotic to his readers, and therefore appropriate
bearers of heterodoxy. It is also possible that Hariot was relating
Indian statements that he was not sure about and did not wish to
comment on, however fascinated he might have been to discover
transcultural vindication of his beliefs. Further, Hariot and others
may have unwittingly primed their subjects: who knows what
Manteo and Wanchese had heard discussed in Ralegh's household
and then related to other Roanok?[44]

We can never know the actual content of whatever Roanok statement Hariot was quoting. In the end, what we might glean is that,
when Hariot reported Indian portrayal of matter as hard, invisible
particles, he was not necessarily making fun of his informants or contrasting them to Europeans. In other ways, he saw or wanted to see
similarity between Indians and Europeans. Hariot wrote that the Indians thought disease might result from astral phenomena, specifically
an eclipse their "Astrologers" reported, or a comet visible just before
one epidemic. This belief resembled contemporary European theories
that the heavens portended sublunary suffering, and Hariot's willingness to use the word "astrologer" in relation to Indians showed respect for their ability to observe the natural world. The quotation
about invisible bullets appears to be more complex when read within
Hariot's full intellectual universe. Previous interpretation has denied
the statement intellectual purchase except as a reflection on savage
mystification of nature; Hariot's statement is made to speak only to an
imperialist. The interpretation denies the possibility that the quotation also spoke to a natural philosopher who was representing contested hypotheses about matter.[45]

Whatever his motives, Hariot identified, even before Francis Bacon,
the two elements of colonization—bodies and technology—that
would continue to fascinate everyone, although he complicated the
comparison between European and Indian bodies that Bacon would
assert and that John Lawson and his Santee storytellers would continue to ponder. Because later commentators would also relate that
Indians believed Europeans had brought new diseases to America
(and that natives had different beliefs about resurrection of the human body), it is not certain that Hariot only ventriloquized the
Roanok. More likely his was an absurd transcription, one repeated by

other colonists throughout the seventeenth century. If the English asserted that Indians who died in epidemics were simply weaker than the English, they had to ignore both European theories of infection (such as the heterodox idea of infectious corpuscles) *and* Indian statements that they had been healthier before the arrival of the English, to which colonists were deaf. Their selective interpretations naturalized their emerging control over American territory. At the very least, Hariot's and Lawson's narratives hint that Indian interpretations of nature and responses to colonization were innovative, profound, witty, and ironic: they were complex and important in ways that we have never before comprehended. But native testimony was not to dominate the narrative that the English were composing.

Hariot's report on Roanoke summarizes most of this book's themes: the uneasy comparison between Englishmen and natives (including their military technologies) discussed in Chapters 2 and 3; the emerging contrast between English and native bodies (especially in relation to disease) that is the focus of Chapters 4, 5, and 7. What Hariot could not have foreseen was the ominous differentiation of English and native technical capacities and intellectual abilities analyzed in Chapters 6 and 8. The English had not begun their colonizing enterprise with the conviction that their ideas about nature were superior to those of Indians, but they began to believe this *because* they colonized America and found reasons to claim that learning about nature distinguished Europeans from non-Europeans. The foundation of this belief was not, however, response to Indian technology or views of nature, though these factors would ultimately take on a life of their own in the last half of the seventeenth century. Instead, views of Indian bodies that used discourse on nature to propose a profound physical difference between the English and the Indians were the starting point for denigration of America's natives.

Nature always seems an irrefutable quantity—this was why the English kept coming back to it in order to argue for their superiority. Representation of nature was fundamental to the English imperial project, and the proof was in the human bodies that lived and died in America. But colonial contentions about Indians, disease, and mortality were flawed, requiring suppression of evidence that the English enjoyed an unfair advantage in introducing diseases to which they were more resistant than Indians. Nature did not tell the English that they were destined to conquer America; the English made nature seem to say this. Perhaps this is what Hariot and the Carolina Santee—three noseless witnesses to the post-Columbian world that spread tobacco and syphilis to more people—were trying to explain.

Technology versus Idolatry?

An important shift in English expectations of Indians appears in two images that follow the same format but convey different implications. John White painted the first picture around 1585 while he was governor over the ill-fated Roanoke colony; Theodor de Bry engraved it for his 1590 edition of Hariot's report on Virginia (the first part of de Bry's monumental *America*), which is the version shown here. The second is an adaptation of de Bry's engraving made for Robert Beverley's *History and Present State of Virginia* (first published 1705; this image is from the identical 1722 edition). There are several differences between these two images, but one very revealing detail is the objects placed in the child's hands. In the earlier picture, they are an English doll in Elizabethan clothing and an armillary sphere, an instructional and decorative representation of the globe and heavens; in the later picture, they are an Indian rattle and an ear of corn. This is curious. It would seem to make more sense had the first picture, painted during early contact with Indians, shown natives with articles of their own manufacture. It is as if the English had initially been eager to place European objects in native hands, but later they were just as eager to take these things away.

In fact, this is exactly what the English did. Their first response had been to assume that the natives might be similar to them in their tools and technical capacities. This was not necessarily a positive assessment; it meant that the English assumed Indians would have the same

Two views of Indian technical abilities: Theodor de Bry versus Robert Beverley. In the top image, the girl carries English objects; in the bottom, the boy carries native produce. From Thomas Hariot, *A Briefe and true reporte of the New Found Land of Virginia* (Frankfort, 1590), table 8, an engraving of Theodor de Bry based on a watercolor by John White; Robert Beverley, *The History and Present State of Virginia* (London, 1722), table 6. Courtesy of the Folger Shakespeare Library.

deficiencies and failings. The initial Anglo-Indian encounter took place during an era of intellectual indecision: doubt over whether humans (pagan or Christian) could keep their technology separate from idolatry of the things they created, and lack of commitment to defining sciences and technology as practices unique to Europeans. To give natives opinions useful to these questions, the English ventriloquized them within ongoing arguments over matter and technology, even though natives would have had little knowledge of (let alone interest in) such questions.

At the start of colonization, the English only uneasily used their technical abilities to define imperial goals. They did make some grand claims about their technological prowess. Read alone, such statements seem like evidence of cultural confidence; but placed within the broader range of things the English said about themselves, the boasting was as much nervous and defensive as it was confident and instrumental. The English were not sure they could make their country into a source of learning and of colonial power. A number of talented and ambitious men in England wanted to use their *artes* to establish control over America, but the talent and ambition simply did not add up. England remained backward, compared to the continent, in two key areas: mining and metallurgy, and cartography and navigation, both practices deemed essential for new world ventures. Richard Eden accordingly scolded his countrymen for their ignorance of metals and of "Cosmographie," which impeded English colonization.[1]

The backwardness of the English guaranteed that they would not make significant progress either in natural philosophy or in colonization during the sixteenth century, but their deficiency had important implications for their views of America and its natives. The English were willing, for instance, to entertain radically new ideas about the natural world and about America. This intellectual flexibility was significant for the early connection of science and empire. Three factors illustrate the simultaneous underdevelopment of English expertise and openness of opinion. First, early modern science included mystical views of the creation and embraced the practice of magic, thereby establishing points of similarity with other peoples who had magical traditions. Second, the Protestant Reformation's iconoclastic destruction of objects that invited worship encouraged the English to question whether pride in their technology was a form of idolatry. Third, the English experience in the American Arctic was a formative episode that encouraged fundamental reassessment of the globe's physical environments and the human place within them; these concerns over climate and body would appear again and again in English accounts. This early experience showed the convergence between speculation about America and speculation about ways to understand and use nature.

Eclecticism and mysticism still strongly characterized English views of nature. John Dee, for instance, had no difficulty seeing unity within his varied roles as adviser on colonial navigation, astrologer to Queen Elizabeth, annotator of the English translation of Euclid's *Geometry,* and conjuror of spirits. Nature and the supernatural were interconnected. In his preface to Euclid, Dee stated that mathematics formed a third state of being "betwene thinges supernaturall and naturall"; numbers expressed a connection between the tangible things people saw in nature and the mysterious construction of the cosmos known only through divination and magic.[2]

But in the early modern period, those who were interested in the sciences had a new desire to police their mysteries. Magic was a particular problem. Christians had always wanted to differentiate natural magic, in which a person could discover nature's own properties and perform remarkable acts, from the black arts, which used knowledge supplied by demonic forces. Still, these were difficult boundaries to maintain, and they underwent constant challenge in early modern Europe. Religious reforms and sociopolitical turmoil made witchcraft such a troubling practice that traditions which resembled it, including natural magic, were on the defensive. Many feared that the ignorant could fall into error concerning magic; conversely, practitioners whose arts were not diabolic could be misunderstood, either as agents of the devil or as deceivers of the innocent. Dee was careful to explain that while Moses had been a magician, his art was from God, not the devil. But Christopher Marlowe was reported to say "that it was an easy matter for Moyses being brought up in all the arte of the Egiptians to abuse the Jewes being a rude & grosse people," and "that Moyses was but a jugler, & that one Heriote [Hariot] being Sir W Raleighs man can do more than he."[3]

The issue of idolatry connected debates on religion to debates on natural philosophy; the radical Protestant program smashed religious art, and natural philosophers attacked the anthropocentrism that misled inquiry into nature and worried over the pagan heritage of the classical texts. Fear of idolatry created anxiety over many abstract human creations such as poetic imagery, the immortality that fame might confer on humans, and any magic that seemed to worship objects. Scholars have pointed to these early modern debates over the proper relation (or separation) of humans, nature, and the supernatural as the starting point for the disenchanting of the world. This took its best-known form in Francis Bacon's identification, in *The New Organon* (1620), of mental constructs that impeded knowledge. The idols of the tribe, of the cave, of the marketplace, and of the theater all contributed to confusion, error, and dogma.[4]

Concern to understand material things elicited new attention to investigation, description, and verification. People in the sixteenth and seventeenth centuries began to value experience as part of learned inquiry into nature; they also began to reassess travelers' testimony as a foundation for knowledge about the world. Scholars have noted these trends without connecting them, but the earliest English explorers of America contributed to both developments, demanding that their travel narratives be taken seriously as evidence about the new world. They talked of "experience" or "experiment" (meaning something known by the senses) in America and used the word "discover" to explain how they would determine the nature of unknown parts of the globe. Interest in experience and discovery showed explorers' confidence that inquiry into nature might have practical uses and that those at home would take seriously their testimony about America.[5]

But indecision over human technical capabilities played interesting havoc with early English explorers' sense of purpose. Mastery of nature was the goal of civil peoples. Both classical and Christian exhortations to control nature expressed ways for humans to deal with its central fact, its materiality. Aristotle had defined *techne* as human ability to transform nature into new material forms, lack of which intimated barbarism. To order nature was also the duty of Adam's postlapsarian heirs, who got their bread by the sweat of their brow and brought forth new generations in sorrow. Nature's painful materiality reminded humans of their difficult position on a cosmic divide between the physical world of bodies and degenerate matter and the incorporeal world of souls and providential order.[6] Praise of *techne* and worries over idolatry were not opposing cultural forces, ranging secularism versus piety, but were connected tendencies that formed the basis of doubt for the English over their status as technical creatures.

Were America's natives the same kind of creatures? The English tended to think they were. But explorers also tentatively differentiated themselves from natives in two ways: by suggesting that some bodily differences were inherited rather than caused by climate, and by arguing that native magic had no effect on Christians. The first point built on contentions that significant bodily features were inherited, a minority opinion that was strongest in its assessments of African peoples, whose stigmatization became a model for some statements about America's natives. The latter supposition (about magic) was at this point the only technological difference the English saw between themselves and natives. Indeed, the English assumed that the natives they encountered were otherwise intelligent and educable, an important admission that the traits the English labeled incivility and idolatry were mutable. Belief that native magic was only partly efficacious therefore separated pagan from Christian techniques but did not reject either magical practice or native intelligence. It was a tentative and nonsecular differentiation that presaged the later and more sweeping distinctions. These hypotheses—that some bodily differences might be inherited and that the English were immune to native magical practices—were informed by anxiety of the English over their similarity to pagan Americans and appeared throughout early assessments of America, especially the Arctic region they called Meta Incognita, where, as we shall see, English faith in the human ability to control nature ebbed and flowed in surprising ways.

English writers who first reported on exploration recorded their nation's exploits in ambivalent terms. They were eager to define a nascent imperial identity that depended on the ability to control nature, but feared that sinful pride in such an ability would negate any benefit of an overseas empire. Maintaining a division between human abilities and divine powers was of particular concern. It was difficult to praise the endeavors of mortal English explorers while avoiding impious hyperbole—or idolatry.

To complicate matters, the English were not at all sure which technologies would help them in America. Spain already claimed some of the richest parts of the new world: what was left and how might it be used? Some English accounts maintained that America still embodied the golden age, in which plenty was available with minimal human effort. Visions of Spanish gold reinforced a sense that America was a golden world—but perhaps beyond the English grasp. Spanish dominance held sway over most of South America, with the exception of Guiana during the brief English ventures there under Elizabeth and James I; it continued in parts of the Caribbean, including Florida, Spain's beachhead in North America. Francis Bacon's *New Atlantis* (1627) reflected the fear of Spain's dominance over the Atlantic world. When the emissaries in Bacon's story receive a message from the Atlanteans, it is written in Hebrew, Greek, Latin, and Spanish, the last the only modern language in Atlantis's diplomatic culture.[7]

Other accounts promised that America needed little human effort to bring forth riches. According to Arthur Barlowe's 1584 description of the Outer Banks, its natives were "such as lived after the manner of the golden age" and its "earth bringeth foorth all things in aboundance, as in the first creation, without toile or labour." Ralegh maintained that tropical Guiana's native Tivitiva used only "that which nature without labor bringeth foorth," and enjoyed a physical setting of plains interspersed with groves set down "as if they had been by all the art and labour in the world so made of purpose." But Ralegh could not help exaggerating, and some of his descriptions blurred the distinctions between art and nature. While the natives "use neither planting nor other manurance" they could "build very artificiall townes and villages." And, though the countryside of fields and groves was not the product of artifice, the deer would flock to riverbanks "as if they had beene used to a keepers call."[8]

Perhaps to distinguish English effort from Spanish serendipity and Indian error, early narratives of exploration boasted that English technical prowess guaranteed overseas glory. English authors remarked that their (hypothetical) empire would exceed those of the ancients because of their superior technology. Richard Eden recounted in 1555 how the inventions of "this our age" would "exceede" those of "the Auncientes," for "what of theirs is to be compared to the Artes of Printyng, makyng of Gunnes, Fyre woorkes, of sundry kyndes of artificial Fyres"? This too would be Bacon's contention about the "*artes*" peculiar to modern empire.[9]

English commentators described how the deification of inventors was a model for those who discovered new territory. In the preface to a work on exploration, for instance, Thomas Hacket stated that "none are more to be commended . . . than those who wer the first inuenters and finders out of Artes and Sciences, wherwith mankind is beautified and adorned, without the which giftes he were but naked, barbarous and brutish." Bacon specified that lawgivers and inventors had in the past been deified, as with the human prototypes of Ceres and Bacchus. In New Atlantis, the people were reported to keep "statua's of all principal inventors. There we have the statua of your Columbus, that discovered the West Indies: also the inventor of ships: your monk that was the inventor of ordnance and of gunpowder," as well as inventors of printing—in other words, those humans who had made all the advances specific to the modern age.[10]

Explorers' efforts were important not least because they challenged ancient (and therefore pagan) concepts of the globe and prompted unusual hypotheses about humanity and nature. English ventures to the far north were key in this regard. Historians of English colonization have neglected or misunderstood the voyages of Martin Frobisher and John Davis; these expeditions, much more than Roanoke, are the "forgotten" ventures of colonial America. Important precedents were set in the icy north that explain subsequent English expectations about America and its natives. Most significant, those who funded and wrote about Frobisher's voyages were putting three things on trial: English skills with mines and metals, the possibility of planting English people in the new world, and (the best-known aspect of the venture) the existence of a northwest passage to Asia.

To answer questions about such things required speculative leaps, and English voyages to the north indeed blended creativity with desperation. Analyses of the human place within the world relied on *cosmography*, a classically based theory that divided the world among sublunary zones—temperate, torrid, frigid—that had different properties because different astral bodies affected them. Plants, animals, minerals, and people differed according to climate. Extreme climates were hazardous if not fatal for humans; tropical and Arctic regions were not expected even to have inhabitants. Warnings about hot regions were at least softened, however, by assertions that these places offered vegetable and mineral abundance that compensated for the discomfort of farmers and miners. Africa and India were therefore supposed to be places where gold, spices, and dyes naturally occurred. The extreme north had no such advantages: it simply extinguished life. John Rastell asserted that, beyond Iceland, "so cold it is / No man may there abyde." Nor did things improve much in subarctic climates. Northern peoples were supposed to be torpid and barely able to gain a living, let alone progress toward civility. In contrast, warm zones were associated with cultural refinement as well as material abundance; the sun not only engendered plant life and precious minerals but also made humans more lively than sluggish northern folk. The need to defend their reputation as northern people helps explain why the English were so concerned with climatic theory.[11]

The Spanish had, in any case, already laid claim to the new world's warmer zones. The English had been skimming off Iberian wealth through piracy in the Caribbean and Latin America, but this was a dangerous and limited strategy. Robert Thorne the younger therefore explained to Henry VIII in 1527 "to which [new] places there is left one way to discover, which is into the North: for that of the foure partes of the worlde, it seemeth three parts are discovered by other Princes." And, as Thorne pointed out, "this your Realme is thereunto neerest and aptest [to the north] of all other," and "as all judge, *Nihil fit vacuum in rerum natura:* So I judge, there is no lande unhabitable, nor Sea innavigable." Roger Barlowe also argued to the monarch that "by the waie of the meridian there is a grete parte discouered by the Spaniards, so ther resteth this waie of the northe onelie for to discover which resteth onto your graces charge." But Henry was reluctant to invest in westward ventures.[12]

Only under Elizabeth did the English accept that they would have to settle for—and perhaps settle in—America's less promising north. They thus participated in the post-Columbian debate about what the world, with its hitherto unknown parts, was really like. Classical assertions about the globe had by no means survived intact the early era of exploration. José de Acosta wrote that the discovery of America had proved "two great wonders": that the ocean was crossable and that humans could live on the equator and even below this dreaded line, in the supposedly desolate antipodes. Indeed, discovery of equatorial populations may have been as great a shock as discovery of the Americas. Accounts of population in the far north seemed as remarkable, and the English may have been stimulated by these narratives and by a sense that they were continuing explorations begun by the Norse. Olaus Magnus's *Description of the Northern Peoples* (1555), which recounted medieval narratives, focused on Scandinavia but also referred to Iceland and Greenland. Magnus's texts explained how life in a cold climate was possible because domestic animals, especially reindeer, provided food, clothing, and transport. Peter Martyr's *Decades* also noted that cold regions were inhabited by living creatures even in winter; this was known by experience, contrary to the false "coniecture" of the ancients. Nevertheless, the polar regions were so barren that its scattered populations had to keep moving to get enough food.[13]

To encourage investment in northwest voyages, the English had to continue to adjust the long-standing pessimistic assessment of the cold north, a task that required them to give backhanded praise to the region's residents for their arts and technology. Indeed, accounts of the Frobisher and Davis ventures were unusual in their admission that natives of North America were no longer quite at a level of Stone Age technology. But early English accounts of the north simultaneously related that native artifice (including practices that seemed religious or magical) reminded the invaders of their own uneasy attitudes toward human artifice; their apprehension registered contemporary English doubts over human ability to mold nature and over admiration of the artificial that verged on idolatry.[14]

The very attempts to navigate the north and discover a northwest passage represented a willingness to forsake contemporary understanding of the globe. Fourteenth-century reports that people (the Baffin Eskimo, ancestors of the Inuit) had invaded Greenland from the west had supported speculation about a new world connection to Asia, from where the invaders might have come. But there was no evidence that it was possible to sail into the icy reaches of the Atlantic, still less any account of a marine route through or around North America, nor any promise that the navigationally ignorant English were best qualified to find this or any route. The English resorted in part to reasoning their way into a northwest passage, but it is significant that they were willing simply to sail out and observe the world. Frobisher and Davis were going to put the North Atlantic on trial. Their reports would be proof, an indication that hypothesis and practical experience were beginning to coalesce in the art of navigation. As one assessment of Cabot's voyages put it, Cabot had "manifestly approved" that the seas northwest of New France were open to navigators; similarly, Frobisher would "make full proofe thereof." The English believed that their navigations carried on European discoveries of the new world, beginning with Columbus's westward venture, continuing with Magellan's voyage through the earth's southernmost sea route, and culminating with a projected English voyage around the northern extremity of the globe, an accomplishment to accompany Francis Drake's circumnavigation of the globe in 1577 and 1578.[15]

If Iberian exploration in the early sixteenth century had shattered the ancient idea that the equatorial and antipodean regions were uninhabited, the English had the distinction of pointing out the same about the northern Arctic at the end of the century. Eden emphasized that the English had voyaged to "the frosen sea" and its "innumerable landes and Ilandes vnknowen to the Antiques, euen vnder and farre within and beyonde the circle Artike, where they thought no lyuynge creature coulde drawe breath." George Best asked "what hath the Spaniarde or Portingale done by the southeast and southweast, that the Englishman by the northeast and northweast hath not countervailed the same?" Humphrey Gilbert argued that "whereas other Cosmographical workes doe but shew us things already knowen and treated of, this Discoverie doeth tend to a very profitable and commendable practise of a thing to bee discovered."[16]

And if the Spanish had found gold in the south, so the English

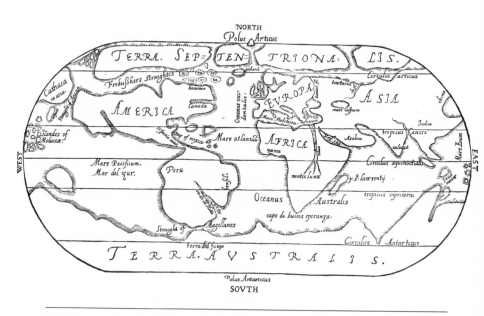

Map of Meta Incognita. From George Best, *A True Discourse of the Late Voyages of Discoverie* (London, 1578), based on the work of surveyor James Beare. Courtesy of the Folger Shakespeare Library.

might find it in the north, against all assumptions that heat generated precious minerals. To pursue this goal, the English poured energy and resources into the American Arctic. Frobisher made three journeys (1576, 1577, 1578) to Meta Incognita, particularly the Countess of Warwick Sound, between 62 and 63 degrees latitude. During 1577 and 1578, at seven different sites, Frobisher's men dug out over 1,500 tons of what they thought was gold ore and shipped it back to England. John Davis followed Frobisher with three Arctic voyages in 1586 and 1587.[17]

Those who planned Frobisher's mission regarded the crew members as guinea pigs whose fate would demonstrate whether North America (albeit a very cold part of it) could be inhabited by English people. In addition to dropping some felons in Friesland, Frobisher was to "leave some persons to wynter in the Straight [Frobisher Bay], givyng them instructions how they maye observe the nature of the ayre and state of the countrie." The venture's backers also planned a permanent Arctic settlement, a "hundred man colony" described for the final venture in 1578. Indeed, this 1578 voyage was the largest and most elaborate Arctic expedition that would take place until the twentieth century, with an astonishing 397 men on 15 ships—the largest fleet in the history of maritime exploration. (Table 1 details the skilled personnel on Frobisher's three voyages.) Frobisher's mining camp on Kodlunarn Island was site of the new world's first Anglican sermon and of its first English building with a mortared foundation. Both the religious service and the stone house indicated considerable cultural and material investment. The English also realized that they needed to use materials not familiar in England but necessary in a colder climate. Archeologists on Kodlunarn Island have turned up fragments of tile with a green glaze characteristic of German stove tiles. Stoves were not commonly used in England at the time, but they were deemed essential in the Arctic.[18]

To support his unlikely project, Frobisher depended on expert advice. John Dee and William Borough (one of the Muscovy Company's navigators) gave instruction in navigation; their dual efforts show that the venturers wanted to hear from both practical technicians and learned philosophers. Noted instrument maker Humphrey Cole provided the navigational devices for the first voyage (including a globe, armillary sphere, universal dial, astronomical ring, and level) and repaired the instruments for the second voyage. Tests of the ore back in

Table 1   Skilled personnel on Martin Frobisher's three voyages, 1576–1578

	1576	1577	1578
Assayer	0	3	6
Miner	0	9	148
Pumpmaker	0	1	1
Instrument maker	0	1	0
Geometrician	0	0	1
Minister	0	0	3
Surgeon/asst.	1	4	4
Shipwright	0	0	4
Carpenter/cooper	4	7	9
Smith	1	3	4
Tailor	1	1	1
Shoemaker	0	0	2
Fisherman	0	0	2
Cook/grocer	2	2	3
Baker	0	1	5
Trumpeter/musician	1	6	4
Total*	8	37	193

Source: William W. Fitzhugh and Jacqueline S. Olin, eds., *Archeology of the Frobisher Voyages* (Washington, D.C., 1993), 241–250.

Note: Mariners' and military skills not included.

*Adjusted for the cases of double-skilled persons: 1576, 2; 1577, 1; 1578, 4.

England required yet another set of experts, usually foreigners. First John Baptisto Agnello, then Jonas Schutz and Burchard Kranach, tested the ore, though they would ultimately disagree over its value and be backed by different factions, until the whole enterprise fell into lawsuit and recrimination.[19]

In the meantime, the importation of skilled workers to mine gold ore and service the mining camp evidenced a serious effort to exploit and live in the far north. Frobisher's first two expeditions had brought modest numbers of skilled men, mostly to repair the wooden ships and containers. But the numbers of skilled workers increased steadily, the largest increment represented in miners, with a lesser but still interesting increase in assayers and other metallurgists. They left behind signs of their activities in the fragments of assaying vessels (crucibles and cupels) still found on Kodlunarn. The final year of mining required three tons of miners' tools and between three and eight furnaces for making assays. Indeed, the planners believed that invest-ment in skilled workers would pay off in the long term, even beyond 1578. A Dr. Burcot who contracted to serve on the third venture was required to train another man to "go suche a vioage agayne." The other skills represented in the 1578 voyage were surprisingly diverse, and made sense only if Frobisher and his backers meant the final venture to be a nearly self-sustaining operation, and the beginning of the permanent fort the planners envisioned. The two shoemakers and one tailor sent in 1578 were therefore intended to make or repair shoes and clothing on Kodlunarn; the two fishermen and five bakers likewise helped two cooks and a grocer serve the large crew with a va-riety of foodstuffs. More surprising are the three ministers and four musicians. They, and the six trumpeters who came on the second voyage, provided order, comfort, even pleasure to a crew that spent several months in an alien environment devoid of other European in-habitants.[20]

It would be interesting to know more about Inuit reaction to the mining camp and its working, praying, and music-making residents, who reported that the natives watched what they did. It is possible that some peaceful interactions took place (despite two skirmishes, Inuit kidnapping of five Englishmen, and Frobisher's abduction of four Inuit). George Best, who accompanied the 1577 voyage, wrote that the Inuit "delight in musicke above measure, and will keep time and stroke to any tune which you shal sing," a tantalizing indication that English musicians amused a bicultural audience. Further, the men of the second voyage made "a columne or crosse of stones heaped uppe a good heighth" where they said prayers on their arrival. The Inuit evidently observed this activity, and thereafter used the cross (which was on a hill) as a site from which to summon the English with a flag. Finally, Frobisher drew up detailed "Orders" for the company during their stay in Meta Incognita that resemble nothing so much as the better-known *Lawes Divine, Morall and Martiall* (1610) of Jamestown, including prohibitions on individual trade with the na-tives. If this had to be spelled out, workers were not so afraid of the Inuit that they shunned them voluntarily.[21]

The Frobisher expeditions therefore showed a surprising attempt to transplant English people and technology to an unlikely corner of the new world. Efforts to grow grain in the north were meant to demon-strate the region's unexpectedly temperate nature; descriptions of this activity repeatedly used the words "trial," "prove," and "experience." One of the final tasks of the last Frobisher voyage was to sow some grain and peas to see whether the crops took, the results to be assessed by the next expedition. In similar fashion, Parmenius evaluated the flora in Newfoundland and claimed that "this soyle is fitt for corne: for I founde certayne blades and eares" that would, "by manuring and sowing," produce edible grain. The council of the Newfoundland Company instructed John Guy that "experience [was] to be maid how our Seedes graine corne pulse will growe and prosper in those parttes." Guy predicted that the "ground" in Newfoundland would "prove verie well" and noted that his crew would set a "triall of wheat and Rie" in it. As late as 1622, an English crew "did for a triall and experiment thereof sowe some small quantitie of corne" in Newfoundland. While the Arctic experiments seem especially far-fetched, the English after all went north during the summer and marveled that it was "daie alwais, without darknes or eny night." Hence they reasoned that constant exposure to the sun during one season might offset the climate's cold. Best argued that the summer sun was unceasing, "which maketh to the great increase of sommer." The English even cheered themselves by using the "Little Ice Age" to emphasize similarity between the new world and old. The ice that one northbound crew encountered in 1607 was explainable, they said, because that was the year "when the extraordinary frost was felt in most parts of Europe."[22]

Expectation that precious metals could be found in the Arctic took shape within this speculative context and relied on the language of proof and trial. The English argued that the hotter climates that enriched the Spanish were unsuited to their own temperate nature; "how muche better shall it be for us . . . to possess goold & Sylver in health of boddy." Maurice Browne asserted in 1582 that America's northwest was "the most richest place for gold, silver, and pearle, as also for all frutfulnes of the soyle." Frobisher's attempts to mine gold ore were therefore part of this highly contested speculation. Several assayers in fact rejected the initial ore sample of 1576. Only the mysteriously sanguine Agnello concluded that it contained gold. When questioned why others had failed to find gold in the ore, Agnello replied *"Bisogna sapere adulare la natura"*—one must know how to flatter (coax) nature, perhaps a reference to alchemy. This statement satisfied Michael Lok (the most powerful investor and adviser) and

Frobisher, and led to the mining of 200 tons of ore in 1577, then of a stupendous 1,300 tons the next year.[23]

Such was the eventual English familiarity with the Arctic that, on Davis's second voyage, the natives were "making signes that they knewe all those that the yeere before had bene with them"; on the third voyage, the Inuit greeted the English "after the old maner, with crying Ilyaoute." Even people in England grew familiar with the Inuit. Frobisher took four captives back with him, one man from his first journey (taken to London), and a man, woman, and infant from his second (who went to Bristol). All were sketched or painted in a "unique pictorial documentation" of American people; John White executed a set of watercolors of the captives, and the court painter Cornelis Ketel did full-length oil paintings (now lost) of the two adults. Further, Calichough (the second male Inuk) demonstrated his kayak and bird dart on the river Avon in Bristol in October 1577 and then carried his kayak through the crowded streets. For those who did not see the captives, Bristol chronicler William Adams recorded their arrival.[24]

These Inuit disconcerted the English. Accounts of Frobisher's voyages and exhibition of Inuit captives gave modern proof of the scattered, astonishing tales Magnus had recounted about northern inhabitants. But it was one thing to have expected to meet Asian migrants passing through the north and another to meet people who lived there. Indeed, Frobisher's first crew was astonished that they had an audience for their efforts in the Arctic, which Best reported was "habitable" by people and animals. The people lived in a veritable desert, one where agriculture itself was impossible—something incredible to Europeans. In such surroundings, established opinions about raw nature and its transformation made little sense. The English puzzled over how the Inuit managed to stay alive in their region, and how they so quickly adopted European technology. Lack of sustained contact with the natives of Newfoundland, before 1612, created a continued context for puzzlement, especially as the English tried to make sense of the increased presence of European technology among the Abenaki, Beothuk, Micmac, and Montagnais, without the increased presence of Europeans.

The English learned that the natives of the north were familiar with outsiders and with trade in metal goods. Long-distance trade in copper and small amounts of meteoric iron existed in many parts of

North America before sustained contact with Europeans. Further, the Norse voyages to Greenland and Newfoundland had introduced European tools to natives of the northern parts of the Americas in the twelfth and thirteenth centuries. Excavation of Norse artifacts from Indian sites in North America (including fragments of wrought and slag iron), and from Inuit sites on Greenland (including pieces of chain mail and Inuit carvings portraying Norsemen), has indicated that some new world peoples retained objects they had acquired from or modeled on foreigners long past the era of first contact. Natives' eagerness to acquire hard metal items from Europeans who returned to America after 1500 may demonstrate not that Indians and Inuit were reacting to unfamiliar materials, but that they wanted to get more of what they had already used.[25]

The Frobisher voyages also encouraged speculation as to how people—including the English—might adapt to severe climates. One explanation by George Best, scholars have argued, resembled later definitions of race. Best's intention was to counter English fears of the north; he therefore attacked the environmental interpretation of human physical differences and argued that humans could maintain physical continuity even in severe climates. He pointed out that people had different appearances despite living in (or migrating to) a particular climate. Best's key examples were that Africans remained dark in northern climates and Afro-European children still retained a dark complexion. Climate did not explain these phenomena, so Best cited the scriptural curse placed on Ham to interpret Africans' darkness as an "infection" that continued through their lineage. While this explanation may seem to resemble racial descriptions of humans, Best was indifferent to the biology of physical differences and their generational transmission. Further, because Best's goal was to persuade Englishmen to sail into the icy north, his argument for the fixity of human characteristics (elliptically constructed with reference to sub-Saharan Africa, an extreme climate better known to Europeans than the Arctic) must be read within this context, and not as a statement easily applied to other non-Europeans. It might best be construed as whistling past the graveyard, which the tropics and Arctic might very well have been for the English.[26]

For this reason, many English believed that Arctic areas could not be inhabited year-round. The eleven convicts condemned to colonize southern Greenland (part of Frobisher's assignment for his second voyage) refused to cooperate. One man preferred jail, and the others proved so obstreperous that Frobisher set them loose in Cornwall. When the English built their stone house on Kodlunarn, Edward Fenton (one of the ships' captains of the third voyage) called it an "experiment" to "prove what the vehemencie of winde and weather would do therwith this winter." Dionyse Settle concluded that the Inuit could not make "houses, or apparell" to "withstand the extremitie of colde" and that they migrated north to hunt in summer, returning to southerly "Winter stations" that must exist, even if the English had not seen them. These were of course assessments that recognized the limits of English technology, which could not have enabled construction of houses and clothing for an Arctic climate. After several episodes of contact, the English finally realized that the natives could live year-round in the Arctic and began to admire their way of doing it. Best commented that the Inuit were excellent fishermen and hunters; lacking wood and textiles, they made boats and sails from the skins of their prey. By the time of Davis's first voyage to the north, his crew bought kayaks from a group of native men, as well as "their clothes from their backs" that were so well sewn for the climate that, he said, "we were fully perswaded that they have divers artificers among them."[27]

Such was the emerging admiration for Inuit crafts that the English sometimes praised them inappropriately. Fenton referred to "raine deere" (probably caribou) that he saw, suspecting that, like the Norse, the Inuit had domesticated deer. Eventually, the English did not find it impossible to imagine that European-style technology could result from native arts. When Thomas Ellis described Frobisher's third voyage, he related that the English found a box of nails in an abandoned village in Greenland. This showed, Ellis concluded, that the natives "had either Artificers amongst them, or else a trafficke with some other nation." Ellis obviously hoped for proof of a northwest passage, but could not eliminate the suspicion that the natives might make such objects on their own. This was an almost unique statement about the probability that the peoples of the western Atlantic produced and crafted iron. (Ellis did not state the most likely hypothesis, that the nails were collected from driftwood.) As puzzling to the English was the presence of objects made from copper (including personal ornaments) and from meteoric iron, including needles and projectile points. Meteoric iron had spread with Eskimo migration eastward, from North America to Greenland, but it is possible that the Norse had left forged iron artifacts that natives then carried or traded to the northwest. The Baffin Eskimo/Inuit were at the center of these two trajectories, which makes it difficult to determine when different forms of iron arrived in what is now the Canadian Arctic. It is still a puzzle. Several iron blooms (round lumps of forged iron) found on Kodlunarn at first appeared to date from the Frobisher era. But carbon-14 analysis has given dates from the twelfth or thirteenth century. Norse settlers, who were in Greenland from roughly 1000 to 1500, might have supplied the blooms, which then moved west with native migration or trade; alternatively, the blooms might have been forged in Frobisher's era with much older wood, which would have left carbon traces of its earlier time. In either case, the late sixteenth-century Inuit were witnesses to, and becoming participants in, a technology that was no longer at the Stone Age level.[28]

Gradually, the English understood that some metal artifacts in the north had been acquired from Europeans, through trade or salvage. This realization dawned especially during exploration of Newfoundland, where English contact was more prolonged than in the Arctic. John Guy specified that one Newfoundland village (which the people had fled, leaving the English free to rummage) contained not only a brass kettle but also fishhooks, a lead sinker, and "a French basket," which were all evidently used for native fishing. Natives adapted some European artifacts to their own use; this same village had a tent covered with "a sayle, that they had got from some Christian." The English also believed that, in cases where the natives had as yet no European-style technology, they had only to be given the appropriate tools and supplied with examples of products they could make. When Frobisher's last Arctic expedition departed, the Englishmen left behind their mortared stone house. This they "garnished" with "many kindes of trifles, as Pinnes, Pointes, Laces, Glasses, Kombes, Babes [human figures] on horsebacke and on foote." Likewise, the men of Davis's 1596 expedition gave nails and knives to natives, assuming the former could somehow be adapted to use in a climate where wood was not a common building material, perhaps as points for arrows or harpoons.[29]

Native adaptation to cold climates remained perplexing, however, and not all English hypotheses about northern technology reflected a sneaking admiration. The climate of the Arctic was simply too extreme, and the English ability to envision human subsistence there too limited. Settle, for instance, was astounded that the Inuit did not use anything with a "roote"; their whole subsistence, even building materials, came from "beastes, flesh, fishes, and fowles." This was incredible to people who came from a culture dependent on farming and grazing. The Inuits diet seemed even less civilized than that of other hunting peoples because they "eate their meate all rawe," plucked up grass to eat without "salt" or "oyles," and would suck "yce" rather than drink water. In no way did they cultivate or cook the rawness out of nature, as expected of humans capable of artifice.[30]

After Settle and others in Frobisher's crew decided that northern Americans practiced no significant European-style arts, some next speculated that the natives might instead be witches or monsters. Best concluded, even as he praised Inuit crafts, that the people "are great inchaunters, and use many charms of witchcraft," as if this technology trumped all the others. After capturing an old woman—"eyther a Diuell, or a Witch"—Frobisher's men "had her buskins plucked off, to see if she were clouen footed." This is one of the few English eyewitness accounts of America that identified its people with the mythical monstrous races. This radical speculation was countered, however, by the careful autopsy and postmortem report that Dr. Edward Dodding performed on the Inuk Calichough, who died in Bristol in 1577. Dodding found the man's body in no way extraordinary and described the causes of death as universal signs of human mortality. Dodding did remark on the cultural and emotional peculiarities of Calichough, such as the man's "uncivilised" refusal to have his blood let and his female companion's ability to maintain that she was not "disturbed by his death." But he did not support opinions like Best's that human bodies varied significantly from one another. The Inuit woman's subsequent death likewise elicited description rather than speculation. Further, that her unweaned infant was given to an English wet nurse indicated belief that the Arctic Americans were similar enough to the English to warrant one suckling the other. Thus the wide range of speculations about human difference expressed in the context of Arctic voyaging: that differences were carried through inheritance (Best), or characterized by inhuman monstrosity (Settle), or superficial when compared to cultural variation (Dodding).[31]

In a sense, the English had no way to order the phenomena they saw in the Arctic; hence their wild hypotheses about gold mines and cloven-hoofed humans, but also their desire to create fixed categories for bodies and technologies. John Janes's observations during Davis's 1586 voyage used technology as Best had used the body: to limit comparisons between the English and other peoples. Some Inuit technologies were familiar. Janes found "stones layed up together like a wall," encountered domesticated Inuit dogs, and saw wooden sleds "like ours in England." But other materials were disturbing; the stone wall had a human "skull" on it and another stone structure, "like an oven," contained "many small trifles, as a small canoa made of wood, a piece of wood made like an image, a bird made of bone, beads having small holes in one end of them to hang about their necks" like idols or charms.[32] Janes's descriptions encapsulated the contrast in opinions about the Inuit: they had excellent techniques to manage their environment, but they also depended on sorcery. The objects Janes found fit into one or the other category. Construction with stone to store meat, domestication of animals, and use of sleds all resembled European accomplishments. But the stone constructions were decorated with human skulls and filled with talismans. Technology slipped into idolatry; artifice intersected with pagan backwardness. In the account of Davis's second voyage, these suppositions were rendered as conclusions: the natives had "images" which they wore and placed in their boats, "which we suppose they worship. They are witches, and have many kinds of inchantments."[33]

In part, negative assessments of the Inuit reflected a sense of their own technological failure on the part of the English. None of the three aims of Frobisher's ventures had been fulfilled. The mineral obsession was particularly ill served; the tons of ore were worthless. Further, Frobisher had not made "some discoverie of the passage for Cathai," nor would Davis. And Frobisher had failed to "plant C[hristopher] Fenton and the c. [100] men to inhabit in that new land" as his promoters had required. They blamed Frobisher's fear that "Fentons deede therin woulde dashe his glorye," underscoring their belief that such a deed was possible. The three voyages had required £19,300 in investment; most of the money was lost, along with two ships, about twenty-two boats and pinnaces, and twenty-four English lives. Nor could the English keep these embarrassments secret. Spain monitored all three voyages, and King Philip's spies in England sent him specimens of ore and a map of Frobisher's strait; one spy even managed to go along with and stay undercover during the third voyage. The smuggled ore was assayed in Spain and declared worthless, evidence of English backwardness in relation to mines and America. English dependence on foreign experts had been most shamefully revealed by the fact that no one in England had the skill to challenge Agnello or to referee Schutz's and Kranach's quarrels over assays. Indeed, the assays had very likely yielded results only because silver-bearing elements were used in the procedures and because someone might have slipped gold into the samples. Small wonder that the English were thereafter reluctant to invest in American ventures; the next attempt, Humphrey Gilbert's fatal venture to America in 1583 (for which planning began in 1579), was disastrously underfunded, and this would remain the pattern through the barely surviving colony at Jamestown.[34]

Meanwhile, the English knew nothing about the most important trial of their skills and tools. Five castaways from Frobisher's third voyage owed the Inuit their lives when their own technology failed them. The explorer and ethnologist Charles F. Hall learned of their fate when, in the winter of 1861–62, he tried to find Sir John Franklin's lost expedition of 1845–1848. The people north of Frobisher Bay (who knew nothing about Franklin) told Hall of some white men who had lived on Kodlunarn. The name of the island in fact derived from the Inuktitut word for "white men," *qallunat*. Gradually, Hall realized that this story related events not from the nineteenth century but the sixteenth.[35]

On Kodlunarn, Hall was told, the five Elizabethan castaways were unable to keep from freezing in their stone house. The Inuit took them into their houses built of snow and fed them. When the weather allowed, the men built a small ship from wood their expedition had left behind. Some of the Inuit helped them clear out a ship's trench and were paid in bits of iron, which they used for arrowheads and knives. In spring, the castaways launched their ship down the trench and attempted to sail out of Frobisher Bay, but they had not waited long enough; some Inuit said that their ship was smashed by ice and they perished, others claimed that they had returned, but with parts of their bodies so badly frozen that they soon died. Hall visited Kodlunarn Island and carried away "Frobisher relics" along with notes on the natives' oral history. Hall's main informant, Ookijoxy Ninoo, supplied details that mirror the English written records. She related that the *qallunat* came three times: "first two, then two or three, then many—very many vessels" close to the two (1576), then three (1577), then fifteen (1578) ships that had indeed come. Ookijoxy Ninoo's account of the numbers of Englishmen seized during the second voyage, and the numbers of Inuit kidnapped by the English, also paralleled sixteenth-century written accounts. Still, Hall's record is problematic. He wryly observed that small payments to the Inuit yielded a flood of items from Frobisher's era, despite earlier claims that they had no such things. He also posed leading questions, prompting his informants about what he wanted to hear.[36]

Whatever the variation, Inuit accounts related what Frobisher's crew already knew: the five men were probably deliberately abandoned. Frobisher was running low on supplies; even without these five mouths to feed, the crew barely avoided starvation. The abandonment was carefully obscured in the records of the voyage, probably to avoid lawsuits, that great transhistorical constant. Indeed, it was long assumed that the Inuit accounts of the five castaways described the five Englishmen kidnapped in 1576. Only details about how the five men built and launched their ship made it clear that they used a mining trench that had not been in place until 1578. Hence the English never knew the extent of their fellows' ingenuity in digging up timber and other stores cached on Kodlunarn and crafting them into a vessel of some integrity, if not ice-breaking strength. Nor did the English learn that Inuit technology had been essential to survival during the winter, though they might well have suspected it. The English might have been pleased, however, that the Inuit could not use all the technology they had left behind. An abandoned anvil, for instance, proved useless to any Inuk and was eventually left perilously close to a sea cliff or simply pushed into the sea. Frobisher's men would also have been interested to know that the Inuit had imitated their patterns of worship. Ookijoxy Ninoo related that her people performed devotions at a stone monument Frobisher had erected—perhaps the cross of 1577—and she sketched a picture of herself doing just that. Inuit ritual adaptation of an English religious monument showed cultural parallels in forms of worship which would continue to give the English pause. Despite the Reformation, the English (albeit uneasily) used material symbols in their religion, thus exhibiting their similarity to the non-Christian cultures they were invading. Neither technology nor idolatry was unique to either people; however much Janes and the other English decried the talismans they observed in the Arctic, they managed to provide the Inuit with another one.[37]

English experience in the Arctic continued to influence perceptions of other native Americans. In part this was because of the publicity that the dramatic Frobisher ventures received. Indeed, Dionyse Settle's account of the second voyage was the "first piece of American exploration literature to be translated and circulated widely in European countries." John White's images of the Inuit were reproduced in de Bry's *America*, which also had wide circulation and whose illustrations conveyed ideas about America to the illiterate. Whatever the failures of the Frobisher expeditions, they were considered important efforts, ones that could be used to defend their participants. When Dee fell into disgrace under James I, his published refutation of charges that he was a necromancer included a list of his published and unpublished works, including writings on navigation into the north which he had assisted. The Arctic was an arresting test case: the English would apply their speculation about its natural productions, its people's technological abilities, and their bodies to other parts of America.[38]

Anxiety over their status as toolmakers persisted among the English through the early 1600s, especially the fear that colonizers shared the worst native tendencies toward idolatry. Certainly, any statements that the natives thought their invaders godlike must be read within the anxious context of the post-Reformation propaganda war over America, which imparted stern lessons about the error of any form of anthropocentrism, let alone deification of mere mortals.

In early modern England this concern was particularly evident in discussions of portraiture, which maintained that as God had reproduced his image in humans, so humans could reproduce images of themselves. Such images might have a talismanic force to remind the viewer of the power of the viewed; mimesis mirrored divine creation. Images of Queen Elizabeth (the first monarch to reign over transmarine settlements) expressed these goals. Elizabeth's iconic properties demarcated an English empire: they encouraged men who ventured forth in England's name and warned trespassers away from English territory. Thus when Frobisher fitted out ships for his first Arctic expedition, he paid for translating the queen's letter to foreign "princes" into Greek and Latin and for limning the letters and "culleringe the quenes Majesties pictures therin."[39]

Images and tokens of Elizabeth were also meant to impress native people. A 1563 silver sixpence (with the queen's portrait) was in the twentieth century unearthed near Roanoke; a hole had been made in the coin with a steel drill, evidence that it was used as a piece of jewelry—perhaps by an Indian who received it as a gift. The armillary sphere placed in the Indian girl's hand in White's image from Roanoke also indicated the royal presence in America. This sphere was a token of the Boleyn family, one that Elizabeth took up in her campaign to defend her mother's, and thus her own, honor. A badge in a religious book that had belonged to Anne Boleyn showed an anchor and a celestial sphere interlinked. The image represented constancy: the celestial heavens were fixed in place by God, while an anchor fixed a ship to the shore. The sphere appears in Elizabeth's "Ditchley" portrait, attributed to Marcus Gheeraerts the younger (ca. 1592), in which Elizabeth wears it in the form of a jeweled earring. Another sphere appears in Elizabeth's "Rainbow" portrait of circa 1600–1603 (also attributed to Gheeraerts), this time embroidered on the queen's sleeve. As a symbol of royal female constancy, the armillary sphere was an excellent token for White to bestow on a land called Virginia in honor of a queen who had struggled to prove her legitimacy and chastity. Further, the sphere's cosmographic function represented the navigational learning that carried English people to America.[40]

Other Elizabethan icons were transposed to America. When Drake's circumnavigating crew left Nova Albion (California), they erected a post displaying an English sixpence so that "her Highnesse Picture, and armes" could claim the shores of the Pacific. The queen bestowed a miniature of herself on Humphrey Gilbert before he departed for America. Gilbert's token was a small metal anchor which the queen (whose portrait was set into the anchor) appeared to grasp with her hand; an inscription read, "We are protected under the holy anchor" *(Tuemur sub sacra anchora)*. The Boleyn-Tudor anchor signified a queen's constancy to her subjects, especially bold mariners. Further, this monarch appeared to reach beyond her frame and her motto, emphasizing the supernatural properties of her image and the uncanny ability of a human artist to imitate nature.[41]

That such artifice could deceive the eye was an uneasy commentary on human perceptual ability: if people could create such images, how could they also be fooled by them? What was art, and what idolatry? Frobisher had left lead manikins in the stone house on Kodlunarn Island to show the Inuit what English people looked like, but not to *be* them. The lead toys were tokens, not talismans. The English pondered this distinction further in relation to images of the new world's natives. Several artists had represented the Inuit kidnapped during Frobisher's first voyage. On the second voyage one native man was shown images of the first captive Inuk, "both as he was in his own, and also in English aparell." The Inuk marveled and spoke to one of the images, "for he thoughte him no doubte a lively [living] creature." When the image remained silent and the man was told that the subject had died in England, the English concluded that he must think "we coulde make menne live or die at our pleasure," the human ability to represent the body standing in for the divine ability to give or take away life.[42]

Whatever the Inuk really thought, the English themselves believed that only God could make humans live or die. It was left to Ralegh to identify the problem with this crafting of talismans and delight in human artifice. Ralegh recorded how, among the natives of Guiana, he "shewed them her maiesties picture which they so admired and honored, as it had beene easie to haue brought them Idolatrous thereof." Though he probably meant to flatter the queen, Ralegh went a bit too far and made a statement that Protestants should not have accepted. The idolatry of pagans was a reminder that any worship of the queen's image had to remain in the realm of metaphor, not actual practice. English propaganda about bringing Protestantism to America militated against carelessness in this regard; the English were not to slip into papist error. The Hungarian Protestant refugee (and Newfoundland colonist) Stephen Parmenius, who had witnessed central Europe's wars of religion, represented the English mission to the new world by ventriloquizing a "sad" America who had been misinstructed by the French and Spanish:

> They make me raise altars to mortal men
> And pray to silent idols or to trees,
> In madness honouring I know not what
> Catholic deity.[43]

If, in Ralegh's example from Guiana, the Indians were surrogate English subjects (worshipful of Her Majesty but prone to the sin of idolatry), other portions of the literature of exploration directly criticized the English for too-confident search after the things of this world. Despite the persistent association of America with wealth, especially mineral wealth, the English literature of the 1500s conveyed an undercurrent of dissatisfaction with the materialist ambitions of colonizers—even before English colonies existed. A commonwealth tradition that emphasized the good of the realm alongside the wealth of its private citizens appeared in the writings of a surprising array of authors, both Catholic and Protestant. Thomas More's *Utopia* (1516) ironically assessed the mineral wealth of the western Atlantic. The Utopians had such contempt for gold and silver that they used it for chamber pots, badges for criminals, and chains for slaves; infants played with gemstones and pearls. John Rastell (More's brother-in-law) lectured in 1519 that the "commen welth" was more important than personal gain. The world's riches "Lyeth of the grounde by goddes sendynge / And by the labour of pore mennes handes . . . though thou ryche man have therof the kepynge." Richard Eden, a sometime-Catholic and Marian apologist, lamented the loss of an age of "innocencie" when "men thought it crueltie by breakynge the bones of owre mother the earth, to open a way to the courte of infernal Pluto." Parmenius hoped that in an English America "Freedom and the use / Of talents will not be repressed by wealth." Instead, "Mother Earth / Will yield to all, from little effort, rich / Provisions." Cosmographer William Cuningham likewise cautioned that those who pursued the "gatheryng of Plutos corne" were like the lifeless objects created by humans: they were "rather Images, and pictures of men" than real beings. Admission that some material images remained lifeless restated ambivalence over the human condition: partly in control over matter but ultimately subject to its mortality.[44]

Commonwealth disapproval of American riches matched some natural philosophers' disdain for the gross alteration of nature needed to gain wealth, as through mining. Alchemists maintained that humans could achieve understanding of the metaphoric as well as natural relationships that defined the cosmos. An occult philosopher not only manipulated natural phenomena to determine how they worked; he also reasoned from what was visible and, with God's assistance, he learned about nature's invisible properties. This was how an alchemist could make gold; he was reproducing nature's own efforts. (So Agnello had said of Frobisher's ore: one needed to coax it.) Such a procedure was preferable to mining, which brutally tore gold out of the body of the earth. Even while recounting Iberian descriptions of America's mineral wealth, Eden thought it "a thynge vndecent" to talk of so much gold without considering how it was naturally generated.[45]

The desire for "Plutos corne" was a particularly contentious point for new world explorers. Envy of Spain's mineral resources in Central and South America informed most English interest in the new world through the 1500s. Ralegh's description of Guiana assumed that the country represented a golden age as well as a land of gold: there, riches as well as ordinary livelihood could be got with little or no effort, thus negating the line between nature and artifice. At the emperor's court, all ordinary utensils were made of gold and silver, and the household was adorned with "statues of gold which seemed giants"; "there was nothing in his countrye, whereof hee had not the counterfeat in gold." Not only did counterfeits masquerade as nature, but also living beings became like the statues in the imperial court. During the ritual called El Dorado, men were coated with white paint, then with gold powder, "untill they be al Shining from the foote to the head, & in this sort they sit drinking by twenties and hundreds." Ralegh played to the fear that all this gold might fall to Catholics, and Indians to Catholic command. He wrote of his hot pursuit of a party of Spaniards, one of them a gold refiner who left behind his "Indian basket," which held "quicksiluer, saltpeter, and diuers things for the triall of Mettals."[46]

Fulminations against mineral wealth thus warned the English not to forget higher reasons to colonize America and to reject Spanish models for doing so. One 1590 assessment of Anglo-Spanish diplomacy cautioned against any peace or "amitie which they [the Spaniards] haue gained by gold, by their water imperiall, drawne from the hardnesse of iron." Caution echoed, too, in Ralegh's account of Guiana, in which he denounced how the "Indian Golde" of Spain "purchaseth intelligence, creepeth into councels, and setteth bound loyalty at libertie." Ralegh also worried that English intrusion into Guiana would harm the land and its people. He characterized such ventures as rape, violent seizure of a land and people denominated feminine; the region was virgin because it lay on the Amazon River and was associated with the maiden warriors of Amazonian legend. Ralegh talked of the prospect of "the passage into the golden partes of *Guiana*," but warned that the country "hath yet her Maydenhead." The land was not yet "spent by manurance, the graues haue not beene opened for gold, the mines not broken with sledges, nor their Images puld down out of their temples." Ralegh knew that such actions would outrage not only nature but the people of Guiana as well: "If wee should have grieued them in their religion at the first, before they had beene taught better, and haue digged uppe their graues, wee had lost them all."[47]

The English feared that they might support natives' sins as well as destroy their virtues. Indians' bodily adornment warned of shared error. Self-love and misapplication of technology could turn the human body, the image of God, into a mere object. This Christian prejudice informed most descriptions of native body painting, tattooing, decoration of hair, and wearing of talismans. One account related that the native men of Dominica painstakingly removed all their facial hair, pierced their ears and lips, and "cut their skinnes in divers workes." Still, this line of criticism condemned universal human sin, and made the natives equal to the English in their potential for impiety. John Bulwer, in *Anthropometamorphosis* (1653), considered this prospect at length. Bulwer used the bodily deformations and decorations of non-European peoples to prove the "Pedigree of the Nationall Gallant," a depraved type whose sins provided the "Anacepheloisis of the whole Book." The frontispiece showed God and Nature (the latter flanked by Adam and Eve) sitting in judgment on humans who had altered their bodies and were thereby "guilty of *high Treason* against *Nature*." Here fashionable Europeans mix with non-Europeans in body paint and tattoos; a native American is shown with a feathered headdress. Bulwer identified human folly by contrasting "man" to the beasts; he is the only creature who is always "by displacing himselfe . . . losing his place" as king of creation.[48]

Human sacrifice was the ultimate debasement of God's image and, on this point, the English were eager to differentiate themselves from Indians; whatever their own sins, the English did not sacrifice one another in the name of religion (religious persecution notwithstanding). The English were convinced that Indians not only treated their own bodies with vain idolatry but also used bodies as objects of sacrifice. The Virginia Company instructed the colony's governor to capture native priests, "these murtherers of soules and sacrificers of God's images to the divill."[49]

The English nonetheless managed to confuse rather than instruct Indians as to the proper stance toward material things. Like Frobisher's men, who built and ceremonially used a stone pillar, they were not always aware that their actions might mingle religion and technology or obscure the object of worship. When George Waymouth's crew brought some eastern Abenaki on board ship in 1605, the natives watched what the sailors did, including when the men on night watch sang with their hands lifted upward. The Abenaki thought at first they were worshipping the moon, or perhaps the rising sun; if the English never bothered to explain their transcendent deity, the Indians would be none the wiser. John Ellis likewise erred when he imitated Inuit gestures, pointing to the sun, then striking the chest as a salutation, which Ellis did until the Inuit "beganne to trust him," perhaps because he was acknowledging some divine power they recognized, though, as Janes wrote of the people Ellis was greeting, "We judge them to be idolaters and to worship the Sunne."[50]

Whatever mistakes the English might make about native religions, encouraging native belief that the invaders were divine was out of the question. If the English welcomed such worship, they were worse than their worshippers. It was easy for the English to deride Indian idolization of other Europeans, particularly Catholics. Peter Heylyn observed that, although Caribs had first thought Spaniards were "immortal" beings, they were wise enough to test their idea by holding some Spaniards' heads underwater until they "knewe their mortality." Unlike Catholics, who were asking for such treatment, Protestants had to prove their consistently non-idolatrous behavior. The horror over native belief in English divinity appeared in Francis Drake's report of Nova Albion, where the English feared that the Indians (perhaps the Miwok) thought them gods. When the women wept and tore the flesh of their cheeks, "we perceived that they were about a sacrifice" in which the human form was an object of ritual abuse (and the mistaken object of worship). The English "used signes to them of disliking this . . . and directed them upwardes to the living God, whome onely they ought to worshippe." The Englishmen also took care to "eat and drinke in their presence, giving them to understand, that without that wee could not live, and therefore were but men."[51]

At this point the invaders were probably performing not for the natives but for God, lest He see and condemn the Christians for setting themselves up as idols. Indeed, some commentators insisted that, at worst, Indians were only as bad as Europeans used to be. Somewhat misinterpreting Drake's account, Bulwer noted that Roman matrons had lacerated their cheeks in grief, "which in some part of *America,* they doe in sign of joy," thus "disfiguring the Face, which is the picture of the Face divine." Other accounts continued to warn the English against exploitation of native error. As the puritan Roger Williams pointed out in 1643, the Indians might idolatrously paint their faces, but Europeans sold them looking glasses to assist their wicked self-adornment.[52]

These examples show that the English were not yet certain that human bodies were intrinsically (rather than superficially) different, nor that their technological abilities made them substantially different from Indians. Like the natives, they believed that physical objects and people were invested with spiritual force (portraits were talismans, humans were images of God), and they feared that they too might be duped into forms of idolatry—in which objects or bodies were improperly worshipped. These fears informed the earliest English ventures, especially those of the late sixteenth century. By the early seventeenth century, colonizers were somewhat more confident that they did not suffer from the same errors as pagans, and indeed felt less guilt over exploiting Indian ignorance of their own symbols. When Christopher Newport erected a cross at the falls of the James River, inscribed with his own name and that of the king, the Powhatan who watched asked him what it meant. Newport glibly asserted that the two lengths of the cross signified himself and their leader, also named Powhatan, now united in amity. It is hard to believe that earlier explorers would have published an account of their lying about a symbol of Christianity.[53]

Thereafter, the strongest fears over idolatry existed in New England's puritan colonies. Two early seventeenth-century episodes, at Plymouth and Salem, have received much scholarly attention, though really they are belated postscripts to the story. The Pilgrims had long been horrified over activities at an English trading post at a small elevation the natives called Ma-Re. Led by Thomas Morton, the English traders here at "Merry Mount" not only lived with Indians (including women) but also introduced pagan English customs such as maypoles. After the Pilgrims expelled Morton and extirpated the trading post, they renamed the place Mount Dagon, after the Philistine idol whose ultimate fate—thrown down as an abomination—reminded latter-day iconoclasts of their duty. In this instance, however, it is not clear whether the heathenish English or the pagan Indians were the Philistines. In similar fashion, a 1630s controversy in Salem and Boston over flying the Cross of Saint George (England's national standard) resulted in the decision not to use the flag, which, like all saints' symbols, puritans found popish and superstitious. The flag was not flown until Governor Edmund Andros of the Dominion of New England enforced it in the 1680s.[54]

If the English thought idolatry was a common human failing, they were careful to distinguish between their own and Indian forms of magic. At no point did the English postulate that native magic lacked power, but they could not believe that the conjuring of non-Christians could be anything but demonic. In other words, the English believed in magic but criticized certain forms of it. Without knowledge of God, native sorcerers had to resort to black arts; sorcery (as in the Arctic) proved the native inability to derive magic from true principles of nature. William Strachey made this distinction when he said that Virginia Algonquians disdained "the inbredd motions of Nature yt self, with such headlong, and bloudy Ceremonies, of Will, and Act." Simple native technology showed ingenuity, but more elliptical strategies to control matter were devilish and contrary to nature.[55]

English observers maintained the efficacy of native magic but denied its power over themselves. John Davis concluded that the Inuit had "many kinds of inchantments" but could not enchant him. When one man threw "diverse things" into a fire, he wanted Davis to stand in the smoke, though his fellows refused to do so themselves. Davis therefore pushed another Inuk into the smoke, then ordered one of his crew to stamp out the fire and throw the charred wood into the sea, "which was done to shew them that we did contemne their sorcery." (Perhaps indifference rather than theatrical contempt would have been more convincing.) Roger Williams made clear that he feared the impiety, if not the efficacy, of native superstition; he said of Indian ceremonies, "I durst never bee an eye witnesse, Spectatour, or looker on, least I should have been partaker of Sathans Inventions and Worships, contrary to *Ephes.* 5.11," which admonished Christians to "have no fellowship with the unfruitful works of darkness, but rather reprove *them.*" Williams feared God's displeasure, not the devil's magic. He and Davis saw some similarity between English and Indian recognition of demonic forces, but they differentiated between the targets of native magic: pagans might be affected, but never true Christians.[56]

This was, accordingly, a distinction not between secular and superstitious comprehensions of the world, but between Christian and pagan practices. The English could not define Indian magic as other than sinful; the mystical elements of Christian natural philosophy were not available to unbelievers. Descriptions of Indians along these lines were an early sign of separation between European sciences and "native" ways of thinking. If humans were prone to sin, some of them nonetheless had a greater tendency to resort to desperate forms of manipulating matter. In this way, the English tentatively differentiated between non-efficacious and real forms of technology, a categorization that would in the end denote magic as more superstition than science. The distinction was an incoherent one until the late 1600s, but its possibilities in the meantime hovered over Anglo-Indian interactions.

Even as the English began to differentiate between neutral and wrongheaded technologies, they had confidence that humans everywhere were tool-making and tool-using creatures. Indeed, the first English ventures were heavily invested in the prospect that a high level of skill and very specialized forms of technology would be the best methods to reap new world profits. Most of the first expeditions were, like Frobisher's mining camp on Kodlunarn Island, militarily fortified "factories," that is, sites for intensive production of a few raw materials, perhaps supplied by trade with the natives. Mineral wealth, such as the Spanish had found in southern parts of the new world, was the ultimate prize, and the mineral obsession led colonizers to employ scores of mineralogists, as with Frobisher's ventures. Roanoke had the attentions of Thomas Hariot and Joachim Gans, the Czech expert in making copper. Hariot claimed that some coastal rock was "by the triall of a minerall man, founde to hold Iron richly," and that the local copper was "founde by triall to holde silver"; a crucible fragment recovered from Gans's workshop shows traces of copper.[57]

Unqualified hopes for mining and other technical activities ended in Jamestown. Officers of the Virginia Company at first funded a high percentage of technical experts and military personnel. While the soldiers were idle or made trouble, the experts at least yielded mixed results. The colony found no mines, but a glass factory established in 1608 (excavated in 1949) seems to have produced some glass from Virginia materials. The factory used German and Polish experts who came with the second crew sent to the colony and by 1610 were described as busily making glass. A second glassmaking operation was under way in 1621. The search for mines continued throughout the seventeenth century, though without the expensive importation of experts.[58]

Perhaps because the English had such hopes for America's products, the first settlers tended, if anything, to assume too much about native ability to use and transform nature. In the Arctic, after all, the natives accomplished more than the English had thought possible. The early narratives on temperate areas similarly defined the natives as handy and resourceful, probably because it reassured the settlers to believe that the people they would meet would be helpful to them and were capable of entering into trade with the English as producers of commodities and consumers of manufactures.

English accounts accordingly stated that the natives had technical skill and could describe the cosmos in abstract terms. One typical account, from 1593, admired "certaine round pondes artifically made by the Savages to keepe fish in, with certaine weares in them made to take fish." Likewise, John Nicholl had "greate admiration" for a "Garden of Potatoes" in St. Lucia with a bank constructed "so equally, that [it] made us thinke some Christians had made it for a strength to save them from the Indians." William Bradford confessed his capture in a Wampanoag trap meant for game; though Bradford spied part of the trap and tried to avoid it, "as he went about [it], it gaue a sodaine jerk vp, and he was immediately caght by the leg." The Indians' trap was "a very pretie devise, made with a Rope of their owne making, and having a noose as artificially made, as any Roper in *England* can make." James Rosier described how the Abenaki made bread and, somewhat less convincingly, how they made butter and cheese from the milk of reindeer and fallowdeer, "which they have tame as we have Cowes." This was either a wonderful example of Englishmen's willingness to ascribe their own arts to the American natives, or an attempt to project the Nordic-reindeer relationship on non-Arctic regions. Rosier also stressed that the Abenaki gave "names for many starres, which they will shew in the firmament." Roger Williams later rhymed, "The very *Indian* Boyes can give, / To many *Starres their* name, / And know their Course, and therein doe / Excell the *English tame.*"[59]

English belief in Indian astronomy showed conviction that America's natives might be able to acquire the highest of European skills: the use of technical instruments and writing. The early accounts agreed that the peoples of North America and the Caribbean lacked written language, and scholars have emphasized the Europeans' sense of superiority in this regard and their claim that Indians mystified books and writing. But the English did not argue that the situation could not change. Even the earliest narratives indicated that natives quickly learned the nature of written representations. John Dee helped Frobisher interrogate Calichough about the location of gold in his country; the man evidently pointed to a place on a map, a gesture Dee and Frobisher took seriously as a designation of a potential mine. When Frobisher tried to recover the five men lost during his second voyage, Settle reported that some Inuit "made tokens, that three of his five men were alive, and desired penne, ynck, and paper" so that a message from the men might be carried back. The Inuit "knewe very well," Best concluded, "the use we have of writing." Gabriel Archer noted that some Micmac sketched in chalk an outline of their coast, a written map that was an abstract representation of the world. And White's putting a navigational device in the hand of a Roanok child in his illustration showed a faith that natives could learn some of the most prestigious forms of old world learning, including celestial knowledge and scientific instrumentation. Knowledge of pen and ink might develop into use of these things; marks that indicated geography might become markings of the alphabet; toys might become tools.[60]

The English did note deficiencies in native technology, but usually thought these could be remedied once they showed the natives new ways to utilize natural resources and gave or sold them better tools. Especially in the late 1500s, when most ventures to America were meant to discover opportunities for trade, the English calculated that Inuit and Indians would be good consumers. Human desires were universal, even if human commodities were not yet. Richard Hakluyt predicted that the chilly "Esquimawes" would crave coarse woollen cloth and rugs. Frobisher's crew had put this expectation into practice when they left behind English manufactures "to allure & entice the people to some familiaritie against other yeares." Thomas Hariot concluded of the Roanok that "although they haue no such tooles, nor any such craftes, sciences and artes as wee; yet in those things they doe, they shewe excellencie of wit." George Peckham noted that the natives "withall shalbe taught mecanicall occupations, artes, and lyberal Sciences"; indeed, it was the colonists' duty to see them "brought from brutish ignoraunce, to civility and knowledge, and made them to understand how the tenth part of their land may be so manured and emploied, as it may yeeld more commodities to the necessary use of mans life, then the whole now dooth."[61]

Some later colonizers continued to advocate this task, particularly in regions where the English desperately needed Indians' help to stake out a claim against the Spanish. Robert Harcourt advocated in 1613 that the English should bring tradesmen to contested Guiana to "teach the people of that Countrey" their crafts. Education seemed also to be the point when John Smith demonstrated to Powhatan leader Opechancanough how a compass worked, gave a "discourse of the roundnes of the earth, the course of the sunne, moone, starres and plannets," and presentated the compass to Opechancanough. Smith, the perennial show-off, probably wanted to dazzle his captor with a memorable gift in order to save his own life. But his giving the device to Opechancanough after demonstrating its properties resembled White's putting an armillary sphere in an Indian girl's hands: a sign of English superiority over the Chesapeake natives, but also an assumption that they were educable.[62]

As English settlements took root in the early 1600s, however, a new uneasiness over the technical abilities of the natives began to emerge. The English finally had gained some experience and skills (such as expertise in navigation) which they had lacked when they first approached America and now no longer had to rely on foreign experts. Settlers were more confident that they could survive in America without native assistance and less eager to see the Indians become handy with tools—indeed, more likely to see such handiness as a threat. Their apprehensions began when they discovered natives who had acquired European tools before the arrival of English settlers. Hence Thomas Ellis's fear that iron nails in an Inuit box might indicate that another European trading nation had beat the English to the Arctic (even as it could alternatively promise a trading route to Cathay). Given English resentment that Catholic competitors had monopolized the southern new world, suspicion that the same might happen in the north was maddening. At Dorchester, Massachusetts, in 1631, a man who was "digginge the fondation of his house" found "2: peeces of Frenche monye one was Coyned 1596." That Catholics' money lay in the "fondation" of the puritan colony was puzzling, even troubling.[63]

The English likewise feared that the Indians would gain technological understanding faster than they acquired trading dependency on or loyalty to the English. An account of Bartholomew Gosnold's 1602 voyage to New England exemplified this apprehension. Gosnold was greeted by six Micmac who came out in a boat to the English ship. As the boat came closer, the crew could see that it was in fact a Basque-style "shallop with mast and saile, an iron grapple, and a kettle of copper." The leader of the six wore "a waistcoat and breeches of blacke serdge, made after our sea-fashion, hose and shoes on his feet." So European did the Micmac seem that they were "supposed at first to bee Christians distressed." (These were the natives who sketched a map of their coastline for the English.)[64]

Worse was the native habit of appropriating European tools, either from viable English towns or from abandoned settlements and shipwrecks. Some of these incidents resulted from differences over trade practices. To the English, trade was a mutually agreed exchange of goods; for many Indians, it involved an initial phase of gift giving in which one party might simply take the things they wanted as gifts. In the north, Davis reported that the natives "brought us Seale skins, and sammon peale, but seeing iron [tools], they could in no wise forbeare stealing: which when I perceived, it did but minister unto mee an occasion of laughter, to see their simplicitie." Gabriel Archer dismissed one native group as "very theevish," perhaps registering that native adoption of European tools seemed illicit, either literally or metaphorically.[65] Certainly, Indians were adept at salvaging stray European commodities, continuing the pattern that had begun with Norse settlements. Arthur Barlowe observed that people in Florida had metal tools left from a twenty-year-old wreck of a European ship; they had even prised out the ship's nails and spikes to use as implements. John Nicholl was outraged that the natives of St. Lucia had benefited from three Spanish wrecks; "much of the goodes these Indians had saved with their Boats, and hid it in the Woodes," enough to fill a forty-ton bark. During explorations of the country around Plymouth, Pilgrim men found Indian houses with "a great Ketle, which had beene some Ships ketle and brought out of *Europe,*" and "an English Paile or Bucket."[66]

Native appropriation of old world tools began to look threatening; it seemed that Indians were gaining new technology faster than the English were establishing settlements, and, in the case of salvaging wrecks, it seemed that the natives were benefiting from European failure and loss. Hence the suspicion among the English of native "theft" of their material culture and their willingness to interpret native acquisition of tools in terms of competition if not violence. Perception of threat appeared in an English account of a castaway Catholic friar on Dominica. The friar claimed he had been spared death only because he "did shew the Savages how to fit them Sayles for their Cannoas" using cloth salvaged from shipwrecks. The English realized that they too had left castaways, who might be forced to give up whatever tools they had, or demonstrate their uses, to natives who might capture them. The men Frobisher left behind, and five other men earlier kidnapped by the Inuit, were the first such example, and the lost colonists at Roanoke the largest number. There were probably more such instances than are recorded, plus other Europeans left behind, as with French, Spanish, and Basque peoples who joined native groups. From the perspective of colonizing leaders, that European people and their goods might melt into America was horrifying. A Pilgrim exploring party was disturbed when they dug up an Indian grave only to find that the body had a European's skull with "fine yellow haire still on it, and some of the flesh vnconsumed." The body was buried in "a Saylers canvas Casacke" and "cloth breeches," but also with some native goods and "the bones and head of a little childe." They guessed that "it was a Christian of some speciall note, which had dyed amongst them, and they thus buried him to honour him; others thought, they had killed him."[67]

Even if people were not abandoned, materials and constructions might be. Frobisher left behind a house, mining trench, cached wood and charcoal, and probably many stray tools and scraps—plus the trade goods and lead figurines. The Inuit received some items in trade, and later helped themselves to remaining supplies. An iron arrowhead and wedge found at Inuit sites might have been given to the natives; the Inuit themselves reported burning coal from English caches, and they scraped grit from European tiles to polish their brass ornaments. Ralph Lane left behind a fort and town at Roanoke in 1586 without time to pack up all the movables. Gosnold abandoned a house he had built in Maine, and the Virginia Company's Fort St. George (on the Kennebec River in Maine) was likewise left to the natives. Archeological evidence has shown that Indians did move into abandoned English settlements and that European items spread, as gifts or in trade, even into areas that had not been in contact with settlers. Three Virginia examples attest to this. Part of a human figure from a German bronze candelabrum was dug up in King William County, a bronze mortar inscribed with the year 1590 was found in a field near Richmond, and a Catholic bronze seal matrix was discovered near Smithfield. Any of these items (especially the last) might have been traded by natives in contact with the Spanish further south, but the first two might have been left at Roanoke, or perhaps originally given to coastal Indians there.[68]

Such incidents seemed to raise a terrible possibility for the English: if Indians could gain European tools and learn European skills, colonists themselves might be superfluous; a new America with improved methods of extracting natural resources might take shape in native hands, not English ones. Materials from abandoned settlements, like those at Kodlunarn or Roanoke, could be seeds for a hybrid North American culture, a combination of American native cultures and European technology, sans Europeans. Rather than see Indians' hybridity as evidence of intercultural harmony, colonists tended to regard it as a sign of competition, appropriation, and danger, an assessment that increased over time.

Fear that Indians might get the upper hand led to prohibitions in the early 1600s against supplying them with tools or technical skills. Many such restrictions had to do with weapons or other technology that might threaten military security. After being cast away on St. Lucia, and furious that the natives had plenty of salvaged Spanish goods, Nicholl forbade his men to sell them any "Sworde, Dagger or Hedgebill." The Virginia Company specified in 1609 that Indians could not buy weapons or indeed "any thinge of iron that may be turned against" the English. The company also forbade any settler to teach a native any "arte or trade tendinge to armes in any wise, as smithey, carpentry, or of such like." Such arts were not even to be "used in their presence, as they may learne therein." William Bradford reported on the dangers of a breach in this policy. He maintained that Plymouth's adversary, Samuel Morton, had provided his Ma-Re Indian allies not only with guns but also with expertise in repairing them. Morton and his associates gave or sold the natives screw plates so they could make screw pins to replace broken parts on their guns. "O, the horribleness of this villainy!" Bradford wrote. "Could they attain to make saltpeter, they would teach them to make powder," and the natives would be released from any trading dependency and free to make war on the godly English settlers. Bradford, like Ellis in the Arctic, was too complimentary of native *techne,* but his paranoia shows continued English fear of underestimating native artifice.[69]

By the early 1600s, the English no longer welcomed all signs that Indians resembled them. The situation was still a long way, however, from

Robert Beverley's crafting of primitivized Indians when he altered John White's earlier portrait of Indians holding European objects. In White's day, the English had several ways to portray native arts and beliefs as backward, whether as magical, idolatrous, or credulous. But these critiques still represented an anxiety the English had about themselves, and a suspicion about universal human error. English praise of human ability was likewise inclusive. The English believed that all humans craved the best technology, even as they needed to remember that their arts only dimly resembled those of the divine creator. They were therefore unsurprised that natives wanted their tools, and welcomed opportunities to give manufactured items to them in order to open trade or secure alliance; nor was native propensity to worship idols unfamiliar, as it was a sin to which even well-meaning Protestants were prone. Only forms of magic divided English and Indians.

Even during war the English were surprisingly willing to see Indians as comparable to themselves and to use icons to bridge cultural differences. When Massasoit warned of a "plot of the Indians of Massachusetts against us," the Pilgrims sent out a war party that killed the chief conspirators. Miles Standish brought back the head of the ringleader, writing, "And [it] is set on the top of our fort, and instead of an ancient [war banner] we have a piece of linen cloth dyed in the same Indian's blood, which was hung out upon the fort when Massasoit was here." The Pilgrims' blood-red ancient, contrasted to their disdain for the red cross of Saint George, showed the precision of their abhorrence of idolatrous symbols, and their willingness to employ Indians' blood and body parts as symbols of their military power. The English also used military technology to measure cultural commensurability. Warfare marked the next stage of English-Indian interaction, after the earliest phases of sporadic contact gave way to prolonged encounter. English suspicion that the natives would prove to have minds of their own, and have the ability to approximate or appropriate colonists' military and other technical abilities, was proved correct in the early to mid-1600s. Above all, the bloody Pilgrim flag indicated that even if the English were like Indians in terms of technology, they might be different when it came to their bodies. Comparison and then differentiation of bodies would guide the next two phases of English interest in America: invasion and then settlement.[70]

PART TWO

Invading America, 1585–1660

CHAPTER THREE

No Magic Bullets:
Archery, Ethnography,
and Military Intelligence

Heads, whether severed (like Plymouth's grisly effigy) or attached, continued to focus English settlers' comparisons of themselves to Indians. In 1617, the seventeenth-century encyclopedist of travel narratives, Samuel Purchas, cited testimony from Virginia that some of the Englishmen at Jamestown had adopted the Algonquian hairstyle, in which the hair on the right side of the head was removed. The Indians had such coiffures, Purchas claimed, to emulate the devil; the colonists were thereby "imitating salvages, and they the Divell." While Purchas reiterated English suspicion of transcultural idolatry, his description revealed colonists' new attention to specific technologies that they and Indians might share. The hairstyle in question was a custom of the Algonquian adult male, who closely sheared the right side of his head to prevent his bowstring and arrow shaft from being caught in his hair, which could spoil his aim, to say nothing of tearing off his scalp. The Algonquian archer left a token lock of hair on the right side of his head or a roached tuft down the center, the famous scalp lock that became a prize of war. The deity called Oke (Purchas's "Divell") had this hairstyle, appropriately for his divine function as personification and protector of warriors, those mortals who wielded bows. It may have been this feature that interested the men at Jamestown. The local Powhatan often attacked them with arrows, and they sometimes had nothing but arrows to shoot back. In contrast to the scholarship on modern empires that has mythologized gunpowder technology, early English settlers had no such delusions.[1]

By the late 1500s, the English were buckling down to the task of gaining American territory in which to set up colonies. They had to determine with greater precision how Indians used nature and with what tools. These tools included weapons, and curiosity about native warfare indicated English awareness that gaining a foothold in North America might require fighting its inhabitants. Skirmishes in the late 1500s and early 1600s, the Anglo-Powhatan Wars that began in Virginia in 1609 (reaching a peak during the Indian attack of 1622), and New England's Pequot War of 1637 all reminded settlers that the American frontier was a militarized one. Because so many of the early ventures were done on the cheap, colonists were rarely in a position to mock natives' weapons as outdated or outlandish. Indeed, when they began colonizing America, in the late 1500s and first four decades of the 1600s, the English were at an interesting moment of historical incompletion: they still carried bows, and hence their military technology was not fully differentiated from that of the people they invaded. Even as warfare emphasized the cultural distance between invader and invaded, it pushed them together in terms of technological similarity. Both sides initially carried bows; for a few decades the English would carry bows and firearms, as did Indians. Finally, each had a technology of war based on firearms.

Notwithstanding some lingering scholarly affection for the old premise of European technological superiority, most recent work has emphasized that English monopoly of firearms in America was a short-lived phenomenon and a dubious point of strength. The English (unlike the Spanish) were never able to control—let alone prevent—trade in European weapons to Indians.[2] Furthermore, it is noteworthy that the period during which the English managed to keep firearms out of Indians' hands correlated exactly with the years when they also failed to establish permanent colonies in America. Monopoly guaranteed nothing. In any case, natives rapidly acquired guns in all the English settlements. In late 1609, two years after the founding of the first permanent English settlement at Jamestown, the Powhatan had firearms. It is not clear that the earliest versions of firearms were a significant advantage to the English anyway. This was especially true of clumsy matchlock muskets, which required the shooter to push a piece of lighted cord into an open pan of gunpowder. The flintlock was better because its flint struck a spark to ignite the powder, but this smooth-bored weapon was much less accurate than the rifles developed in the eighteenth century. Further, Indians had only bows at a time when the English still valued archery; as the status of archery among the English declined, that of firearms among the Indians rose.[3]

As they watched these transitions, the English began to construct an ethnography, that is, a systematic observation of Indians that in many instances dwelled on their technology. Modern ethnography began to coalesce out of the travel narratives Europeans produced as they traversed an increasing area of the globe. Scholars have been slow to recognize that many of these early observations were constructed in the context of military confrontation and with the aim of supplying military intelligence. This was particularly true of English ventures to America. Early English expansion depended on low-level military aggression coupled with a desire for trade; both behaviors encouraged interaction, albeit a competitive one, with the natives. In these contexts, the religious commentary on native idolatry was of less interest than were secular characteristics. Proximity to natives determined which perspective took precedence. Purchas's fear of idolatry was paramount in his description of native appearance, but many colonists conceived of their wary hosts as people whose quotidian weapons, dress, physique, and movements gave clues to future battle or exchange.[4]

The cultural interface between natives and English in North America therefore almost always involved war, and war provided the main opportunity for ethnographic observation. If the earliest English assessments of Indians posited their potential friendliness and handiness (while warning about the idolatry and vanity that might afflict both peoples), later observations presented similarities that were pertinent to invasion. This type of ethnography sought, above all, to make native warriors seem less fearsome by making their unusual features familiar. Most scholarship on war in North America has ignored its ethnographic significance, instead examining its strategic consequences or arguing for its evidence of English loathing of Indians. For its part, work on the early modern literature of war focuses on Europe itself, especially the conflicts in the "school of war," the Low Countries (1567–1659), or, for England, experiences in France, Ireland, and Scotland.[5] And the main thrust of recent scholarship on early modern ethnography has been to assert that such observations stressed differences between the European subject and the objectified native. Studies of early modern Europe have emphasized the significance of binary contrasts and the horror of inversion to conceptualization of cultural difference; scholarship on early colonization has likewise used the concept of "otherness" to explain the encounter between Europe and America. This poststructuralist criticism argues that the main result of ethnography was not comprehension of nonwestern cultures but exposition of the linguistic and symbolic concerns of Europeans themselves, and of their desire to construct terms of containment and debasement for non-Europeans.[6]

This critique of ethnographic writing does not, however, exhaust the meanings we can glean from early descriptions of America, and it especially overstates "otherness" as the category essential to imperialism. In part, this difficulty arises because much of the work on the ethnography of new world colonization has stressed the Iberian model, particularly Tzvetan Todorov's construction of absolute cultural contrast which (as J. H. Elliott has emphasized) is not easily transferred to early English observations of Indians. In the English case, the relation between early ethnography and colonial warfare shows colonizers' desire to see themselves as comparable to natives. Usually this idea of comparison is taken to indicate sympathy for aboriginal peoples. Indeed, Richard White's idea of a "middle ground" has proved irresistible and is now misused and overused to express all manner of peaceful cultural hybridity. But White's definition of the middle ground was precise and not meant to conjure up forms of cultural exchange that were easy to perform and existed in a permanent steady state. People in the middle ground had made an uneasy bargain to suspend some of their cultural differences in order situationally to avoid self-defeating violence.[7] Few English colonists who lived along the frontier wanted to make this bargain; they wanted to have their cake and eat it too, to be *like* the enemy but not *as* him. In this manner, colonists styled themselves as counterparts of Indians, not so as to express sympathy with them, however, but to fight and kill them.

For effective battle between two cultural groups to proceed, there must be some basis (real or imagined) of mutual intelligibility. The literature on war in the English colonies, which emphasizes strategy and antipathy toward Indians, has failed to elucidate how English determination to overcome revulsion at cultural strangeness was meant to facilitate military advance by reassuring Englishmen who had to face Indian warriors. As Inga Clendinnen has shown, war between Atzec and Spaniard halted in 1521 because of a lack of this "essential mutuality." But warfare between North American Indians and the English was continual, the common mode of interaction. On the surface this would seem to suggest cultural incomprehension; but, while warfare indeed indicated antipathy, it by no means implied incomprehension, which might have prevented any continued interaction, however violent.[8]

If imperial warfare elicited some self/other definitions, the English apparatus of contrast was not yet constructed of stable binary opposites. Like other European observers of America, the English presented a temporal theory of ethnographic difference that traced the progress of humans through stages ranging from barbarism to civility, with particular reference to the tools specific to these stages. This schema could have established another binary contrast (barbarous/ civil) that favored Europeans, or it might have encouraged those who enjoyed civility to look upon others as potentially civilizable, though otherwise inferior. But historicized views of cultural difference, and the ethnography that supported them, often swerved into a lament for the primitive virtues (especially military valor) lost when humans advanced toward cultivation. This positive view of "wild" peoples was a species of nostalgia, an essential element of English colonization. The English believed that they had progressed from savagery to civility but did not necessarily believe that all their new acquisitions—especially the new gunpowder technology—were signs of cultural advance, and they worried over losing the military vigor that had once promoted their freedom.[9]

To extract ethnography from their invasion of America, the English emphasized that archery provided a material basis for comparisons between themselves and Indians, and they used classical texts on the Roman invasion of ancient Britain as a model for this assessment. Their ethnographic texts described native Americans in order to improve the efficacy of English military ventures. But they also functioned as a nostalgic critique of human culture as firearms began to replace bows in English warfare and as the English became invaders of a distant place, just as they once had been a distant people invaded by Romans. Their nostalgic fantasies about revival of ancient virtues were of a piece with the Arcadian and pastoral fantasies of Tudor and Stuart England. The ethnographic texts of Julius Caesar and of Tacitus, especially, represented Rome's barbarous northern foes as people whose savage desire for liberty underpinned their military strength. The English took this image of savagery and extended it across the Atlantic, repeatedly stating that they and native Americans shared a cult of the male warrior, a mythology that relied on Englishmen's perception that they once had been, as the Indians still were, forest-dwelling archers. They thereby created an imperial identity for themselves, one that represented Indians nostalgically as versions of their ancient, savage, and valiant forebears. The expectation of military similarity was all the stronger because English national mythology elevated archers—Robin Hood and his men, the yeomen of Agincourt—to heroic status. Bows and arrows were important measures of Englishness, as well as the literal defenders of English men and women. That Indians defended themselves with bows did not, therefore, make them seem backward to people who had better access to firearms. And in this manner the English made a point of pride out of the technical backwardness that had otherwise allowed the Spaniards to show them up in the Americas.

Englishmen other than Purchas understood one cultural meaning of Indian coiffures, as technology to facilitate archery. This might help explain the asymmetrical haircuts worn by Englishmen in Virginia. It is possible, as some settlers at Jamestown maintained, that the fashion had begun with Englishmen who had returned from the earlier Roanoke colony. (It became a fashion among some men at court, and either remained so or was revived with the Jamestown colony.) This may indicate a craving for the exotic among Londoners. But the original imitators had been in one of the last English colonies whose settlers took bows with them to America. If they had to fight Indians using their own weapons, they might also choose to adapt other forms of defensive technology toward this end, for similarity to the enemy meant strength against him. Indeed, soldiers often adopted clothing, words, and habits of the countries in which they campaigned. Invaders stressed the customs that affected physical appearance rather than hypothesizing the underlying bodily differences between themselves and others. Fascination with the enemy's appearance (and weapons) thus operated as a pre-racial assessment of alien peoples; the English in America continued to scrutinize Indians' bodies without yet concluding that they were intrinsically different from their

own. This was a highly gendered comparison, specific to English constructions of masculinity and of war, that would contrast to later settlers' concern with women and procreation.[10]

Archery is therefore interesting as a permeable barrier between self
and other, especially during the early years of English invasion of and
settlement in America, when positive views of Indians might have
been harder to maintain, yet still colonists could not help but see Indians as technologically adept. At several stages in its generation, the
Anglo-Indian frontier was perceived as a symmetrical formation, pa-
trolled on either side by opponents with, more often than not, the
same weapons and similar appearance.

Before 1600, colonists' nostalgia over archery registered an accurate
understanding of England's long history of military aggression; after
1600, the sentiment was at odds with trends in modern warfare and
was meant to apologize for the technological backwardness of the
colonies. English expansion commenced well before the military revolution that would associate modern empires with firearms. England's
imperialism began with the twelfth-century invasions of Gaelic territory, matured during the fourteenth- and fifteenth-century attempts to
conquer France, and took its final form with the sixteenth-century re-
invasions of Scotland and Ireland that led up to the colonization of
America. At each stage, the English longbow played a key role. This
weapon was a "self-bow," a carefully shaped stave of wood (usually
yew) which was strung to create the tension that propelled an arrow
forward. Each bow was about the height of the man who drew it,
so that the English spoke of shooting "in" a longbow—the archer's
body framed within the drawn string and compressed bow. England's
yeomanry—peculiarly well fed compared to other European peas-
antries—generated armies of men who had the strength and energy to
acquire expertise with Europe's most physically demanding weapon.
Indeed, since excellence with a longbow required constant and body-
warping practice, the best archers were professionals. Drawing a
longbow was equivalent to lifting sixty to seventy pounds while keeping the muscles steady enough to aim with precision. The skeletons of
two archers recovered with the Tudor warship the *Mary Rose* reveal
deformities in the spine and forearm, which were, respectively,
twisted and enlarged under the repeated stress of firing arrows.[11]

That bowmen had been England's glory in its wars with France was a particular point of pride, one that continued to influence military policies in the early modern era. For example, no fewer than five plays that celebrated the 1415 defeat of the French at Agincourt were performed just after defeat of the Spanish Armada in 1588. Praise for the English archers who had defeated the French, culminating with the successful invasion of France, marked Shakespeare's 1590 history *Henry V;* the theme was repeated in Michael Drayton's 1627 epic poem "Battaile of Agincourt." Until the end of the sixteenth century, archery remained the basis of the militia and the longbow continued to measure manliness within local English society. Both guns and bows were used in tandem in the Wars of the Roses; Henry VIII's 1513 army of invasion into Europe relied on archery in the form of no fewer than 5,200 bows and 240,000 arrows. Longbows remained standard equipment on Tudor warships, which had cannon but also companies of archers to assault an enemy crew after ordnance had inflicted initial damage to a ship. Other Europeans praised English skill at archery. Giovanni Botero commented that different nations were known for their prowess with particular weapons, as "the Parthians with their steele-bowes, the English with their long bowes, and the Spaniards, in the new world, with horse and hargabuse."[12]

The English longbow enjoyed its greatest written defenses during the 1500s in the context of Tudor conquest of the kingdoms of Britain and Ireland. As England refigured itself as a Protestant and colonizing nation, it defined its role within a struggle, first European, then global, to control people and territory. Early modern English imperialism repeated and expanded the earlier incursions into Gaelic territory and invasions of France. In the wake of these violent accomplishments, Tudor policy identified borderlands, especially Gaelic ones, as regions whose people were in need of English law and Christian civility. England thus identified itself as a fighter against Catholic Scotland and Ireland, while it began to bring these places (as it had done Wales) into a larger nation poised for oceanic expansion.[13]

Innovative activities, such as conquest and incorporation of the three kingdoms under a crown and parliament centered in London, were nevertheless represented as a defense of English tradition, including archery. The courtier and royal tutor Roger Ascham did most to connect archery and empire. In *Toxophilus* (1545), Ascham gave the first modern English description of archery. In part the book was a practical guide to the archer's equipment—the longbow and its string, headed and fledged arrows, shooting glove (for the hand that held and released the string), bracer (to strengthen and protect the forearm against the friction of the bowstring)—and to modification of the shooter's body. Ascham described, for instance, how the emperor Leo had commanded his "archers in war to haue both theyr heades pouled, and there berdes shauen leste the heare of theyr heades shuld stop the syght of the eye, [and] the heere of theyr berdes hinder the course of the strynge"—an indication that coiffures designed to facilitate archery were not unknown to the English.[14]

Attention to the proper training of the archer indicated Ascham's other concern, the imperial virtues of archery. Dedicated to King Henry, figured as defender of English Protestantism, *Toxophilus* stated that "the [holy] Boke and the Bowe" would preserve England against "the Scot, the Frencheman, the Pope, and heresie," a modern and imperialist extension of the idea that archery was England's traditional preserver. Ascham also observed that Wales had been "wylde, untylled, unhabited, without lawe, iustice, ciuilitie and ordre" until it was ordered by the English, who would soon do the same in Scotland. Because Ascham was the princess Elizabeth's tutor, it is probable that he nursed her up in this aggressive Protestant anglocentrism.[15]

Even if England's consolidation of its empire over Britain had begun before the military revolution, its modern overseas expansion did not. It is therefore striking that, in their modern attempts to gain (or regain) transmarine territory, the English still did not construct an imperial identity around the new technology of war. They refused to see the bow as an outdated technology, and instead used it as one strategic form of attack alongside cannon. Henry VIII's invasion of France in 1544, and the French retaliation, made him, briefly, defender of two borders, the Scottish frontier and the southern coast of England. On both fronts he used a mixture of archery and gunpowder. This was true for his daughter's defense against the Spanish Armada some four decades later; both the fleets sent out to the Spanish ships and the ground troops at Tilbury had longbows. Continued reliance on the bow in these newly ambitious circumstances perpetuated national mythology about the English archer.[16]

But archery was a declining art, even under Henry VIII. His 1541 statute to encourage men to practice with bows was designed to prevent further decay. Elizabeth repeated such laws, as would James I. King James famously countered puritan bans against sporting on the

Sabbath by insisting that no one was to be barred, after divine service, "from any lawfull Recreation; Such as dauncing, either men or women, Archerie for men." Grammar schools promoted archery too; shooting with bows was perhaps the only outdoor activity that schools organized in the Tudor-Stuart period. As Thomas Elyot asserted in his educational treatise *The boke named the Governour* (1531), "shotyng in a longe bowe is principall of all other exercises." If these measures show that officials continued to support archery, they also reveal a lack of popular interest—which was what necessitated regulation. Indeed, archery was the subject of class friction. Men of the lower classes were expected to devote themselves to this time-consuming exercise that kept them away from other pastimes, and archery regulations constituted a source of revenue through collection of fines. Further, lower-class men were less likely to use bows to hunt, as hunting was increasingly restricted to the aristocracy. Ascham may have claimed that archery was the proper pastime for "all the gentlemen and yomen of Englande," but this was one of the few grounds of similarity. The lower classes were not to divert themselves with any other of the gentry's and aristocracy's sports. This was especially the case for bowling, a popular game but one that King James wanted "the meaner sort of People" to stop playing. Statutes and pleas to motivate archers thus show that the upper classes used bows willingly for sport, and the lower classes unwillingly to prepare for war. Without regulation, most people would have preferred the less strenuous pastime of bowling. In sum, the terms by which archery was to be shared were contested.[17]

Until the seventeenth century, archery regulations had a predominantly practical aim. On land, archery was a standard part of English military preparation until 1595, when muskets replaced bows in the Elizabethan trained band; hunters would continue to use bows well into the 1600s, and serious arguments for archery's military use persisted until Gervase Markham's *Art of Archerie* (1634). But over the course of the seventeenth century, archery became a sport. (In 1628 John Winthrop reported that his son Wait accidentally shot an arrow "full amonge the children" who were watching the game.) Membership in the old companies of Fletchers and Longbowstringmakers of London did not significantly decline until the seventeenth century, because sportsmen filled the demand no longer met by soldiers. As Charles Cotton put it in his 1674 guide to English sports, archery "hath been necessary for a Commonwealth, but was "now laid aside by *English* men for fighting, there being found out more dextrous and speedy ways to kill and destroy one another." Nostalgia over Agincourt continued at least into the late eighteenth century, but without the serious contribution it had once made to discussions of warfare.[18]

Archery's associations gradually became ceremonial. Legends of England's patron saint had inspired the 1537 founding of the Fraternity of Saint George, an archers' association that was England's first sporting society. The fraternity was renamed the Artillery Company of London in 1612 (then relabeled the Honourable Artillery Company by Charles II), and carried the myth of England's ancient archers forward into the Civil War and Restoration. Boston's Ancient and Honorable Artillery Company, founded at the start of the Pequot War in 1637, was modeled on the London company, to which several New England members had originally belonged. The Royal Company of Archers (still the monarch's official guard at Holyrood Palace, Edinburgh) was founded during the second half of the seventeenth century as a self-consciously backward-looking group. Nostalgia also informed William Wood's 1682 *Bow-mans Glory*, written in the wake of the Popish Plot and Exclusion Crisis. Pointedly recalling a better age, Wood described a Tudor archers' ceremony that included a procession of "green men clad in Ivie, with Clubs on their Necks" as well as a ship "from the *Indies*" that was accompanied by "two Indians or Blackmores." Here was a jumble of exotica: traditional English archers, European wild men, and undifferentiated non-Europeans.[19]

After 1600, such archaism only made sense in America. The backward-looking American colonies were unlike contemporary Ireland, where the military revolution was already over and the likelihood that the English would celebrate the virtuous qualities of a bow-wielding Irishman was rather remote. Although the English had continued to carry bows in the Elizabethan invasions of Ireland, both sides began to rely on gunpowder during the 1580s, when ordnance and small firearms were common. By the rebellion of 1641, Ireland's war with England was little more than a story of fortification and siege with ordnance. Such was the reliance on gunpowder technology that shortages of materiel were disastrous. During the 1642 siege of Waterford, the Catholic Irish were so desperate for gunpowder that they dug up corpses of Protestants to boil down into saltpeter until they finally received supplies through the port of Dungarvan. Similar dependence on gunpowder would not develop in America until Bacon's Rebellion (1675–76) and King Philip's War (1675–1678) thirty years later. The English reliance on gunpowder in Ireland revealed fear that if the French or Spanish eroded English control of the island, a Catholic beachhead would exist at England's back door.[20]

If investment in supplies for American colonies was made to minimize expenditures, the English crown took no such chances closer to home. Elizabeth, who had lost money on the Frobisher venture, was now warier about America. She paid for a small stock of gunpowder for the Roanoke colony, but no more; in contrast, from 1558 to 1570 she had Berwick-on-Tweed in Scotland refortified at a cost of £130,000, about half of England's total revenue for a given year. The only American region that began to approximate such heavy investment and dependence on gunpowder was the Caribbean. There, as in Ireland, the English were cheek by jowl with Catholics, their competitors for control of the native people and land—in the islands as well as in Central and South America. The Indians along the Amazon accordingly grew more adept with fortification and siege than did natives in North America. As a Portuguese commentary on Dutch and English settlements put it in 1623, if one European party was to be ousted, "Indians have to be the sappers by whom the entrenchments and diggings have to be made together with all the labour of the fort." In North America, such investment in ordnance and fortification was not made until the close of the century; instead, colonists lightly fortified their settlements and kept small stocks of firearms and ammunition rather than a battery of cannon. Paradoxically, this scarcity encouraged colonists' contemplation of primitive virtues; what seemed a cultural luxury was a military necessity. The English in the penny-pinching settlements could exploit the rich field of nostalgia over archery to defend their archaism.[21]

Some English narratives had associated technology with imperialism and guns with conquest, a connection that implied a historicized view of civilization. English authors (such as Richard Eden and Francis Bacon) had remarked that their empire would exceed those of the ancients because of their own superior technological development. English narratives on America also expressed some prejudice against non-western military technology and sometimes presented the bow as a stigmatizing mark of technical inferiority and military insignificance compared to gunpowder and fortifications. But the so-called military revolution was slow, uneven, and accompanied by doubt. Parts of Europe (including Britain) were relatively backward compared with more innovative places such as Germany, Italy, and Spain. A comparative paucity of firearms was therefore not the unique attribute of native Americans or others outside Europe.[22]

Further, the English continued to debate the virtues of gunpowder technology even as they adopted it. They worried that use of the powder made them like Asians, Muslims, and Mediterranean Catholics. Did their technological borrowing make them less English—or more so because they could better defend themselves and their culture? Eden took an optimistic view: "Seeyng that nowe our enimies the Turkes, and other Infidels, haue the vse of these deuylyshe inuentions (as they name them) it may be thought requisite for vs, agaynst suche deuylles to vse also the lyke deuylyshe inuentions, lest refusyng the same . . . we shoulde wyllyngly suffer the kyngdome of the deuyll to triumphe ouer vs." Still, that the English took up firearms in an era when they were coming into contact with so many other cultural forms and outlandish objects was unsettling. The best-known example of this xenophobia was repugnance over tobacco. King James decried that "fashion" made English smokers imitate "beastly *Indians*" and become "like Apes, counterfeiting the maners of others." The satirist Samuel Rowlands also concluded, "We shew our selues the imitating Apes / Of all the toyes that Strangers heades deuise." The use of the word "gunpowder" to label the Catholic plot against King James in 1605 continued the English association among gunpowder, foreignness, and treachery. As prelude to his discussion of the Gunpowder Plot, John Swan's *Speculum Mundi* (1643) concluded that, of all weapons, "gunnes be most devilish."[23]

Some military analysts argued that firearms could never entirely replace longbows. Early muskets were less accurate than bows, were harder to use in wet weather, and shot fewer projectiles in a minute than bows. An able archer could shoot up to ten arrows per minute, and could maintain accurate shot up to two hundred meters, while it took several minutes to reload a matchlock which was accurate to only about one hundred meters. (Crossbows were slightly better; they shot four bolts per minute.) Before the development of better flintlocks or snaphaunces around 1650, portable firearms were difficult to maneuver (except in predictable terrain and under optimal battle conditions). For these reasons, John Smythe's *Certain Discourses Military*

(1590) gave the most enthusiastic praise to the bow since Ascham. Others were not convinced. Sir Roger Williams, military expert and veteran of the Low Countries, flatly stated that bowmen were "the worst shot used in these daies," and Smythe's strongest critic, Humphrey Barwick, also scoffed at archery as hopelessly outmoded. But in an unpublished retort to Barwick, Smythe maintained that "our manner and use of shooting in our sort of longbowes was a verie peculiar guifte of God given unto our nacon." He also pointed out that even Asians, who had developed gunpowder and guns, prized bows and arrows, "knowing the excellent effecte of their archery." Strategists also recognized that technology was rarely the only or decisive factor in battle. In a chronology of events appended to his accounts of New England, John Josselyn noted that in 1647 "the *Tartars* [had] over-run *China*," despite their cultural backwardness (including reliance on bows and arrows) and small numbers.[24]

Extremists like Smythe, who refused to see any advantage in firearms, were nevertheless regarded as cranks. A more reasonable position was to assess the different virtues of bows and guns and determine a useful mix of the two weapons. This could cut costs (bows were cheaper), but because an archer required more training, it was wise to supplement the dwindling numbers of effective archers with easily trained musketeers. In emergencies, moreover, bows were welcome. When Londoners were alerted to the danger of Spanish invasion in 1588, and ten thousand men were ordered to be armed and ready, many of them were given bows and arrows rather than firearms. Knowledge of the enemy might also encourage preference for a certain mix of weapons, in order to conserve precious shot or archers' muscles, as needed.[25]

Careful observation of enemies, or even potential enemies, was a notable element of foreign and military policies; military intelligence might be significant for the outcome of a battle, campaign, or siege. Strategy necessitated knowing as much as possible about the enemy: how many there were, what tactics they tended to use, their placement in the field or behind fortifications, and the way they were armed. Sir Roger Williams, in his canonical work on war in the Low Countries, stressed the significance of "intelligence." Conversely, it was important to prevent the other side from learning too much of one's own strengths and weaknesses. Edward Cooke specified the need to keep the enemy in the dark; even flight should be carried out in a confusing manner "that your Enemies may have no intelligence of your meaning." Such admonitions regulated the way in which Europeans could disguise themselves from one another, using their familiarity with one another to recode their behavior in order to deceive.[26]

But what about non-European enemies? How could an unfamiliar culture be comprehended in order successfully to confront it in battle?

In order to begin to understand what an alien people might be like, the English looked at their past, especially the period of England's greatest backwardness. This was the era when it had been colonized by Rome and converted to Christianity, changes that pointed up ancient Britain's military weakness, barbarism, and pagan heritage. It was only when England began to acquire a modern empire, however, that it examined with care the period when it had been part of Rome's ancient empire. Tudor-Stuart study of the classic texts that described the Roman colonization of Britain reveals this interest in the nation's archaic beginnings; these key texts were Caesar's *Commentaries* (ca. 51 B.C.E., first printed 1469) and Tacitus' *Germania* (98–99 C.E.) and *Agricola* (written slightly after *Germania*), first printed between 1470 and 1480. Study of these texts, and especially translations from Latin to English, showed an intention to distill the imperialism of an old Mediterranean world into lessons for the English themselves. The first English translation of Caesar's *Commentaries* made this abundantly clear. John Tiptoft's posthumous edition of 1530, translated at some point before 1470, restricted itself to "as much as concernyth thys realm of England sumtyme callyd Brytayne," leaving out the material on Germans and Gauls. In similar fashion, Elizabethan authors adapted *Germania* and *Agricola* to national histories. Whereas Sallust was overall the most popular ancient author in the Renaissance, the first half of the seventeenth century saw more European editions of Tacitus than of any other Greek or Roman historian. Under James I, there was even wider reading and citation of Tacitus than under Elizabeth.[27]

Reading Caesar and Tacitus was more common than might be expected. Both authors were in the grammar school curriculum, part of the instruction of older boys, to be sure, but considered too elementary for university study. Indeed, Caesar, especially his military writings, was "nearly always required" in upper grammar school for boys aged fourteen and above. Elyot's *Boke named the Governour* recommended Caesar (along with Sallust) "for the exquisite ordre of bataile"; Caesar's *Commentaries* were "studiously to be radde of the princes of this realme of Englande and their counsailours," for Caesar could give "necessary instructions concernynge the warres agayne Irisshemen or Scottes: who be of the same rudenes and wilde disposition that the Suises & Britons were in the time of Cesar." Elyot, like Tiptoft, wanted the English to contemplate their historical distance from their wild forebears, and from their wild neighbors who should, as the Britons had been subjugated by the civil Romans, be subdued by the civil English.[28]

The cultural differences between civil and savage peoples were significant to the military exchanges between them. Tiptoft's selections from Caesar stressed the impact of novelty. The Romans gained advantage because of "the maner of the[ir] artyllary whyche the Brytons had not bene accustomyd to see"; from the other side, "the noueltye of Battell of them of Brytayne the Romayns were a ferde." The *Commentaries* also first noted that the Britons painted themselves blue to be "of more terryble counteynaunce in Warr." Clement Edmonds's 1655 translation of Caesar, which included the German sections that Tiptoft had ignored, emphasized "the fiercenesse of thier looks," which "conceived such a fear" among the Romans. Of the German Harlii, Tacitus (here in Richard Grenewey's 1598 translation) concluded that they would "use black targets [shields], and die their bodies with the same colour, and choose the darkest nights to fight in, striking a terror" into the enemy, "the eyes being first ouercome in all battels." Tacitus also explained that Suebi chiefs knotted their hair up on the crowns of their heads to appear taller and thus "to seeme to the enimie more terrible." This was an early example of ethnography that sought to express the bizarreness of the enemy in order to prevent surprise, terror, and military rout. Edmonds's edition of the *Commentaries* noted that Caesar "never undertook any expedition, but he first received true intelligence of the particular site and nature of the Country, as also of the manners and quality of the people."[29]

These detailed observations revealed a studied ambivalence toward humanity's advance to civility; people whose way of life—or war— was still wild had an arresting vitality. Tacitus' texts were especially noteworthy in their nostalgia. The "Germans" of his account are opposite to Romans: rude, dirty, bloodthirsty in war, yet hardy, simple, uncorrupted by luxury and vice. Tacitus found these savage warriors valorous, despite their lack of settled culture and material refinement.

Their focus on war made them heroic; "to get that with the Sweate of thy browes, which thou maist winne by the losse of thy blood, they hold as an idle & slothfull part."[30]

Admiration of the primitive functioned as criticism of early modern European culture. For instance, it softened representations of the wild man, the hairy and dangerous figure of European myth. Still shaggy and equipped with clubs or bows like their medieval ancestors, Renaissance wild men were nevertheless domesticated; they had wives and children and exhibited a noble character that shamed debauched town dwellers. English poetic evocation of wildernesses, Arcadias, and pastoral pursuits widened the fantasy of escape to either a rural place or simpler time, away from the court, the city, the corrupt age. The English could draw further nationalist inspiration from Tacitus' *Agricola,* which extolled the virtues of the barbarous Britons in imagery similar to that bestowed on Germans. Like the Germans, Britons were forest dwellers who loved liberty above civility. Roman-acculturated renegades left the rural life, and "by little and little they proceeded to those prouocations of vices, to sumptuous galleries, and bathes, and exquisite banquettings." Because of their ignorance, these things they "termed ciuilitie, being indeede a point of their bondage." The uncivil appearance of ancient British warriors became an element of modern discussions of England. Peter Heylyn scoffed at etymology that derived "British" from "Brutus," declaring that the country got its name from "*Brit:* signifying painted, and *Tayne* signifying a nation"; the painting had been done "to make them shew more terrible to the enemy."[31]

It was comforting for the descendants of Britain's unbathed and painted natives to think they had ancient, autochthonous virtues that could awake in moments of crisis. It was probably not accidental that tales of Robin Hood—whose liberty-loving bowmen also dwelt in a forest—revived during the Wars of the Roses and the English Civil War; both were eras of sociopolitical fragmentation that made English people yearn for triumph over evil and adversity. Within the contexts of medieval battles, let alone Sherwood Forest, archery was not only a practical pursuit but also an endower of sturdy virtue. The fact that a longbow took considerable strength to draw, whereas a gun could be shot by a young boy or (perhaps worse) a woman, contributed to a sense that archery was the proper military art of men. Both Ascham and Smythe emphasized the manly exertion the bow required. Ascham said of archery that it was an "honest" pastime for the mind and "holsome" for the body; it kept men from effeminate exercises such as music and vicious ones such as gambling, which were like "Sirenes, and Circes" to Englishmen. Smythe too deplored the men who "have given themselves to effeminacy and forgetting of all use of their bows and archery and other exercises military."[32]

England's men thus defined themselves according to a historical definition of cultures, ranging from wildness to civility, and promoted a militarized and masculine sense of their national power. Exploration of America gave new opportunity for comparisons among types of cultures, weapons, and men. Toxophilite Smythe compared himself to, of all people, Bartolomé de las Casas. Las Casas had defended the Indians of New Spain against the Spaniards; so too did Smythe find it "as allowable for me to write in favor of my owne native country" and its long-standing military arts. Smythe was responding to critiques that longbows were weapons only of people as backward as Indians, or England's Celtic enemies. Smythe rejected Barwick's contention that the English "haue the like estimacion of the longe bowe as the Irishe haue of their darts, the Dansker of their hatchets, and as the Scotch-men haue of their speares: all of which are more meeter for sauadge people." Defense of the bow, and exploration of Britain's savage past, provided ammunition against hasty dismissal of savage virtues, which necessitated a strange, opportunistic identification with Indians.[33]

How many English people would have had some knowledge of these debates over the bow and over primitivism versus civility? It would be wrong to assume that these were elite concerns. The statutes that promoted archery would have been common knowledge among adult Englishmen. Further, the fact that Caesar and Tacitus were recommended for grammar schools rather than university meant that knowledge of their texts circulated among many literate and semi-literate men, not just an intellectual elite. Indeed, as literacy rates among men rose, as more Latin texts were translated into English, and as the percentage of the population that went to university increased, popular knowledge of Caesar, especially, spread to some surprising individuals. Both William Shakespeare and Jamestown's Captain John Smith (neither one a man of great learning) drew from Caesar to establish some understanding of ancient Rome and of the comparative perspective that knowledge of ancient history gave to an understanding of modern England.[34]

There are indications as well that positive representations of archery were available to (indeed possibly generated by) the illiterate. Stories of Robin Hood, for instance, became increasingly popular among the unlettered during the sixteenth century. This was pointedly represented in John Rastell's morality play *Interlude of the Four Elements* (1519), when the character Ignorance lures Humanity to a tavern, where they drink and sing songs about Robin Hood until rebuked by Studious Desire. (Benjamin Franklin would, two centuries later, make a similar comment about "common people in their alehouses [who] sing the twenty-four songs of Robin Hood.") The culture of archery was indeed common, but therefore a source both of national nostalgia and of denigration of the lower orders.[35]

Nor were the elite the only witnesses of what the peoples and weapons of the Americas were like. Commoners in England's cities had occasional glimpses of native Americans. The Inuk Calichough had demonstrated his kayak and bird dart in Bristol; some Indians in London canoed on the Thames in the fall of 1603. The English also incorporated America and Indians into their sense of themselves as archers. At London's Finsbury archery fields, a mark or target at which sporting archers shot was named "Princes of America," probably after Manteo and Wanchese, the Roanok who lived with Ralegh before they returned to America in 1585. The American princes remained in evidence within the English metropolis; the mark at Finsbury formed a geographic and cultural target.[36]

Just as Indian archers went to England, so English archers went to America. The first stage of colonization (in the 1570s and 1580s) promoted use of bows and arrows since these were the final years when these weapons were part of the recommended artillery of English soldiers. The strategic advantages of archery were in fact well suited to the military needs of early exploration. Archers were useful on shipboard, where they could assault people in other vessels without the danger an explosive weapon posed to the flammable ship; bows and arrows were also useful in small-scale skirmishes on land, such as the English had with American natives. To some extent, the English at first underestimated native archery, though only to elevate their own art rather than argue the superiority of firearms. George Peckham claimed in 1583 that "the peculiar benefite of Archers [with] which God hath blessed this land" of England "will stand us in great stede amongst those naked people." Richard Hakluyt the younger, in his

1585 report on the colonies, had guessed that "archerie prevaileth much against unarmed people," and that the English could make shields of wood or horn as adequate protection "against the darts and arrowes of Salvages." Hakluyt also recommended archery over firearms because "gunpowder may soone perish, by setting on fire." And the longbow's great apologist, Sir John Smythe, argued that the weapon was, if anything, too powerful against Indians. "Some, per-adventure, will say that the Spaniards without longbows but with crossbows, harquebus shot, and other weapons have conquered a great part of the West Indies." But "those Indians were simple people that went naked and had no use of iron nor steel." Hence Smythe's assumption that longbows would have been overkill.[37]

Bows and arrows were standard equipment for English voyages to America down through the 1580s; their use in England declined more rapidly than in the western Atlantic. (Table 2 provides some comparisons.) The first Frobisher voyage to the Arctic stocked sixteen bows and twenty sheaves of arrows among the usual ordnance and small firearms. Armaments for the hundred-man colony intended for the Arctic included another sixty bows and over four thousand arrows. Archery was effective in the Arctic, where the flat and unwooded terrain made arrows an excellent weapon. In two engagements with the Inuit, both sides shot arrows at each other. In the second skirmish, the natives "fiercely assaulted oure men with their bowes and arrowes,

Table 2 Bows as a percentage of portable weapons

Country	Year	Purpose	Firearms	Bows (percent of T)
England	1558	Militia units	46	82 (64%)
	1559	Royal Navy stores	1,000	3,000 (75%)
	1577	Ship *Triumph*	250	50 (17%)
	1577	Ship *Victory*	200	40 (17%)
America	1576	Frobisher voyage	25	16 (39%)
	1585	Roanoke supplies	400	150 (27%)
	1622	Virginia (from Tower)	1,300	400 (23.5%)

Sources: Lindsay Boynton, *The Elizabethan Militia, 1558–1638* (London, 1967), 65–69 (1558); M. Oppenheim, *A History of the Administration of the Royal Navy and of Merchant Shipping in Relation to the Navy* (London, 1896), 155 (1559, 1577); David Beers Quinn et al., eds., *New American World: A Documentary History of North America to 1612* (New York, 1979), 3:274 (1585), 4:195 (1576); Susan Myra Kingsbury, ed., *The Records of the Virginia Company of London* (Washington, D.C., 1906–1935), 3:676 (1622).

who wounded three of them with our arrowes." Such encounters demonstrated that bows and arrows could be used in America, but would need to be repaired or replaced there. Richard Hakluyt the elder specified that the crew bound for Roanoke should include smiths to make "pikes heads" and "arrow heads," as well as "Fletchers, to renew arrowes," and "Bowyers also, to make bowes there for need." When an adviser to Ralegh drew up a list of weapons for the 1585 voyage to Roanoke, he included four hundred "harqbuses" but also "150. long bows." It was perhaps one of these bows that an Englishman used two years later, when he shot "a wild fire arrowe" and killed a Roanok man. As late as 1627, Smith recommended that ships going abroad should carry "arrowes trimmed with wild fire to sticke in the sailes or ships side shot burning." Even if they did not expect to use these arms against natives on land, colonizers had them just in case.[38]

Despite early assertions of the superiority of their technology, by the 1590s the English admitted that they feared the natives. Certainly their accounts relate that Indian culture seemed terrifyingly unfamiliar. The English felt compelled to describe native military practice as brutal and bizarre, even though these contentions sat uneasily with other claims that the natives were weak, cowardly, and mystified by English weapons. Arthur Barlowe emphasized that the natives in the Chesapeake would carry "their Idoll" into battle and that "their warres are very cruell, and bloodie." Yet Barlowe had written that the Indians "tremble thereat for very feare" if the English so much as fired a harquebus, even before he claimed that the natives were used to cruelty and bloodshed in their own wars. Captain John Smith did the same a few years later, when he said the Powhatan were "well armed, with Clubs, Targets, Bowes and Arrowes," but came to battle daubed with paint, singing, and bearing their "*Okee*" or idol.[39]

Military intelligence therefore encouraged reports on the natives that outlined all possible dangers and that separated merely alarming behaviors such as the use of war paint from truly deadly factors such as native weapons. The elder Hakluyt warned Sir Humphrey Gilbert in 1578 that "nothing is more to be indevoured with the Inland people then familiaritie," which would "discover," among other things, "all their strengthes, all their weaknesse." Instructions dating from 1582 or 1583 specified that one expedition's artist must "drawe the figures and shapes of men and women in their apparell as also of their manner of wepons." When George Waymouth's crew abducted several Abenaki, they were pleased that they had also managed to seize two canoes, bows, and arrows, the whole lot "being a matter of great importance for the full accomplement of our voyage." Efforts to detect natives' movements and intentions continued throughout the colonial period. The Pilgrims sought the people of Massasoit, the strongest Indian leader near Plymouth, "to know where to find them . . . as also to see their strength." Edward Williams recommended in 1650 that the Virginia colony employ Indian spies and "make use of their intelligence."[40]

To render the bizarre familiar, many commentators compared Roman-colonized Britain with English-colonized America. The English were, relative to Indians, what the Romans had been to their British ancestors. The stage theory of cultural advance informed this opinion and made imperialism seem handmaid to civility. As Robert Johnson put it in 1609, in elliptical praise of the Virginia settlement, "Wee had continued brutish, poore and naked Britanes to this day, if Julius Caesar with his Romane Legions (or some other) had not laid the ground to make us tame and civill." In his writings, Captain John Smith three times identified himself with Caesar the soldier and commentator; Smith wanted "to weild a weapon among the Barbarous" as well as "a Pen" at home. In 1622 Edward Waterhouse declared that the English could take Virginia just as the Romans had taken "*Great Britayne,* of which *Tacitus* sayes, *Ita dum singuli pugnant uniuersi vincuntur*" (thus while they fight individually they are collectively conquered). A note attributed to Smith explained how Caesar had guarded against the "Panique feares" that could seize his army upon first seeing an array of the enemy, and proposed that staged "smale skirmiges" would show soldiers "by litle and litle that neither their enemies wer[e] invicteable nor more valient [than] themselves." But the note twisted the comparison to make it appear that the greater task of an imperial conqueror was to *elicit* panic among barbarians. So Smith, as presumed interpreter of Caesar, wrote that "if our first discoverers" in the West Indies had been "as heedfull and wise to maintaine those Indians in theis kindes of Panique . . . as Caesar was to disengage his soldiers from them; wee might to this daye, have wrought more amongst them by the Beating of a Drumme, that [than?] now wee can by the fieringe of a Canon." Novelty might go stale.[41]

It is striking how willing the English were to dwell on their savage past, and to admit a resemblance between themselves and Indians, based on the stages that carried humanity through history. In this serial view of history, the bow acted as a historical marker. Indeed, the English thought that they had acquired the bow rather recently. Misinterpretation of British stone or flint arrowheads promoted belief that ancient Britons lacked bows and arrows. The English explained these objects as natural or supernatural productions—the work of the earth or of elves. Not until the end of the seventeenth century did the English observe that British non-metal arrow points resembled those of native Americans, and were neither strange stones nor "elf shott." The mistaken assumption that the bow was a recent arrival in Britain reinforced the sense that Britain had been a backward imperial outpost long before it acquired an empire of its own. What is even more striking is that the English believed Indians to be technically superior to the Britons conquered by the Romans because Indians, unlike the ancient British, confronted their invaders with bows and arrows. John White underscored this point in the images of Picts that he appended to his illustrations of the natives he had seen at Roanoke in the 1580s. None of the otherwise quite warlike Picts had bows and arrows, thus suggesting to White's viewers that the British had perhaps acquired archery after the Romans conquered them. White's lesser-known image of a Roman soldier wielding a bow gave a flourish to this point. But the English reassured themselves that they had made up for lost time: Ascham had claimed that modern English archery exceeded that in "the empire of Rome."[42]

Colonizers who described North American bows and arrows generally admired them and sometimes paid the ultimate compliment by comparing them to their traditional longbows. John Brereton said of one New England group that their copper arrowheads were "very workmanly made." In 1603 Martin Pring noted of the Massachusett that their bows were five or six feet long (hence like English longbows), but with strings "bigger then our Bow-strings." Their arrows had three feathers, "as closely fastened with some binding matter, as any Fletcher of ours can glue them on." Two years later, James Rosier examined Abenaki "bowes and arrowes, which I took up and drew an arrow in one of them," thus revealing his ability to judge from experience how a good bow should draw. The bow carried an arrow 100–120 yards and was "much like our bowes," though without nocks (indentations in the wood) for the string. One witness to the attack on

Fort Mystic in the Pequot War of 1637 specified that, when the first Englishman to enter the Indian fort was shot with an arrow, his assailant had "drawne [the bow] to the head," as did English bowmen.[43]

Everywhere the English went, they saw weapons similar to their own. In Virginia, George Percy admired Powhatan archers, who had stone arrowheads "made artificially [cleverly] like a broad Arrow: other some of their Arrowes are headed with the ends of Deeres hornes, and are feathered very artifically." The terms of comparison were clearly English ("like a broad Arrow") and pitched to an audience that could visualize what Percy meant. Smith recognized other native technology related to archery when he reported that the English were visited by three or four men "extraordinarily fitted with arrowes . . . and shooting gloves." Similarly, he commented that a Chesapeake warrior had a leather "vambrance" (or bracer) that protected the forearm against friction from the bowstring. Smith also wrote that the natives "bring their bowes to the forme of ours," using, like Percy, the English as a point of reference and similarity.[44]

Similarity was not equivalent to safety. Martin Frobisher was hurt in 1577 when an Inuk shot him in the buttocks. When John Nicholl's party was castaway in St. Lucia, Indians with bows drove them off the island even though the Englishmen had firearms; at one point, Nicholl confessed, "we could not get our match in the Cocke [to light the gunpowder] for pulling the Arrowes out of our bodyes." John Smith too was struck (without serious injury) in 1607, just before he, despite being armed with a pistol and his men with muskets, was captured by bow-carrying warriors. A set of 1606 orders for the Virginia Council warned against allowing native guides to carry firearms for the English soldiers: "if they Run from You with Your Shott which they only fear they will Easily kill them [the settlers] all with their arrows." This lesson was demonstrated on the unfortunate Eustace Clovell, who was shot with six arrows, ran back to Jamestown crying "Arme Arme," then took eight days to die. The day before Clovell's mishap, the Powhatan had not found an Englishman to shoot so killed one of Jamestown's dogs and "shott aboue. 40. arrowes into, & about the forte."[45]

Small wonder that the English represented the Indian archer as an admirable, if fearsome, figure. Surprisingly small details of native appearance made their way into English accounts of America, even down to the characteristics of native coiffures. Europeans were accustomed to recognizing status, regional background, gender, and occupation from hairstyles. Colonial encounters provided another arena to observe and classify human appearance. In the single image of a North American Indian rendered by an unknown artist (or artists) who accompanied Francis Drake to America in the 1590s, the depicted archer has his hair elaborately pulled back over his right ear while a large lock protrudes from the back of his head. This is in contrast to the artist's images of Caribbean men, whose hair hangs straight to their shoulders. John White portrayed a casually proud lord of Roanoke who leans on the bow in his right hand while his left hand rests on his hip—a classical posture that emphasizes the gendered view of archery.[46] John Smith too gave flattering descriptions of native warriors. Smith described how one band's "chiefest" man, with elegant near-carelessness, held an "Arrow readie in his Bow in one hand" then took up a "Pipe of Tobacco in the other." The Susquehannock whom Smith met were "like Giants to the English"; the tallest man was particularly imposing and armed with arrows headed with a "christall-like stone . . . an inch broad, and an inch and a halfe or more long." Smith also noticed the warrior's hair: "The one side was long, the other shore close with a ridge over his crowne like a cocks combe." John Underhill used archery to praise his adversaries in the Pequot War; they were "men as straight as arrows, very tall, and of active bodies."[47]

Although some English boasted that these stalwart men feared firearms, others were careful to specify exactly why this might be. The encounter between the Pilgrims and the Wampanoag was an interesting case in which English settlers gave nuanced assessments of native fears. Edward Winslow wrote that "our peeces are terrible vnto them," but he elsewhere determined that it was more the intentions of the English than their equipment that alarmed the Indians. The Pilgrims learned that several native villages had been plundered for slaves by an Englishman, Thomas Hunt, which left the remaining people "ill affected towards the English." Squanto, who became a significant ally and translator for the colony, "was one of the twentie Captiues that by *Hunt* were carried away, and had beene in *England* . . . and could speake a little English." One old woman whose three sons had been enslaved had never herself seen an English person until a party of Pilgrim men came to her village. Winslow lamented that she "could not behold vs without breaking forth into great passion, weep-ing and crying excessiuely." The Englishmen further admired "the vallour and courrage" of two old men, the only people "remaining aliue" of their village, yet "with shrill voyces and great courage standing charged vppon vs with their bowes." Fear of the English meant not awe of the objects they carried, but fear of their threat to turn Indians into saleable objects; the Indians' courage depended not on modern firearms but instead on bows and "vallour."[48]

Algonquian archer (with characteristically asymmetrical hairstyle) from "Histoire naturelle des Indes" (Drake Manuscript, ca. 1590), MA 3900, fol. 090. Courtesy of the Pierpont Morgan Library, New York.

By the Jacobean era, however, defense of the bow was as much nostalgic as practical. The decay of archery was apparent among settlers of this era, not least among Jamestown's infamously lazy residents. When Ralph Hamor reported in 1614 that he had found them "bowling in the streetes," their preference for bowls over bows indicated a disinclination toward the work of growing food as well as toward the sports appropriate to their status. Indeed, in light of growing English ignorance of archery, it is interesting that some of the English observations on native bows were, if anything, too flattering. Northeastern Indian longbows were not, in fact, as powerful as traditional English longbows. James Rosier's observation that an Abenaki bow could shoot 100–120 yards should have indicated that it was weaker than an English longbow, which, in the right hands, could shoot an arrow well over 200 yards (though a replica of the "King Philip's bow" in the Peabody Museum at Harvard, which approximates a weapon

Roanok archer. From Thomas Hariot, *A Briefe and true reporte of the New Found Land of Virginia* (Frankfort, 1590), table 8, an engraving of Theodor de Bry based on a watercolor of John White. Courtesy of the Folger Shakespeare Library.

from the 1670s, casts an arrow about 170 yards, closer to the strength of an English bow). Perhaps Rosier knew he was not a good archer, and gave the bow the benefit of the doubt rather than assume his shot indicated its real strength. It is possible, therefore, that by the seventeenth century, English observers were not very good judges of archery; alternatively, they may have thought it best to assume that Indian weapons were more powerful than they seemed. Better safe than sorry.[49]

Significantly, colonizers' arguments for archery made a virtue of scarcity. American ventures were underfunded and underequipped until the 1620s; thereafter, many Englishmen continued to be surprisingly undertrained in modern military techniques, and even the better-supplied puritan colonies suffered from the erratic nature of English transatlantic shipping and could not maintain supplies of powder and shot. One of the most commonly used cannons, the culverin, required fourteen pounds of gunpowder per shot; each musket required somewhat less than an ounce, but repeated gunfire might rapidly deplete supplies. Shortages severely impeded English incursions into Virginia in the 1620s. When the Virginia Company begged for arms in 1622, James I obliged with old stores from the Tower of London: 1,300 firearms (all near obsolescence), 400 bows, and 800 sheaves of arrows. Virginia seems to have been a rickety enterprise supported by antiquated materiel.[50]

Such plans reeked of desperation, as they had in London in 1588. Giving untrained men longbows was only slightly more efficacious than stockpiling rocks for them to throw. (It was not the same species of desperation, however, as the Irish manufacture of saltpeter from corpses.) Employing native allies as archers was a better plan. For this reason, when the Chickahominy agreed to ally with the English in Virginia in the 1610s, the English required them to supply three hundred to four hundred "bowmen to aide vs *against the Spaniards.*" But such bowmen might turn against the English. At the start of the Pequot War, several Englishmen who had headed out to do farmwork were ambushed by natives. Three of the men were killed with arrows, despite being armed with muskets and swords. To save face, the English reverted to assertions that Indian warriors used magic as well as weapons. Roger Williams said that when the Pequot heard of an English amphibious assault, they were reported to "comfort them selves in this that a witch amongst them will sinck the pinnaces by diving under water and making holes etc. as allso that they shall now enrich themselves with store of guns." Mocking Indians' sorcery may have reassured the English about the reality of their gaining gunpowder technology—or fighting with good bows and arrows. In 1642 officials in Connecticut ordered the three principal towns to prepare, within ten days, ninety coats "basted with cotten wooll and made defensiue ag[ains]t Indean arrowes."[51]

That settlers relied on defensive and outdated equipment left them open to European suspicion that America's natives were an unworthy enemy who could easily be subdued. Certainly this perspective influenced David Lloyd's parody of John Smith's writings, *The Legend of Captain Jones* (1659). Lloyd ridiculed Smith's pretensions to be a new Caesar who conquered formidable peoples: "This Brit; / As Caesar did, could he have writ, what comments had he made?" The implication was that Smith's braggadocio was beneath a real Caesar. But Smith/Jones knew no better than to boast that he had defeated the savage kings of "*Crotona*" (Roanoke) with his sword, "*Kil za dog*," despite their being "arm'd with darts and bowes, / And arrowes fadome long, well barb'd with bone . . . which pierc't through steel and stone." Throughout the mock epic, Smith/Jones defeats various barbarians who use weapons as quaint as his own canine killer (Indians with bows, Irish with swords, Africans with elephants), but he is, significantly, defeated by other Europeans, as when Spaniards capture him during a naval battle. To a certain extent, Smith had asked for it. He repeatedly overstated his case in his detailed descriptions of exotic battle; that an illustration in his *Generall Historie* showed him with a curved blade (falchion) that resembled a Turk's scimitar also gave credence to suspicions that he preferred outlandish battle with cultural inferiors. Perhaps to counter this kind of scoffing, the Pilgrims "sent to *England*" some native arrows headed with brass and horn as evidence of their trials.[52]

Settlers had a critical audience in America as well. This was painfully apparent when the Narragansett sent Pilgrims a bundle of arrows tied with a snakeskin. Squanto interpreted this as a sign of hostility, to which the English sent back a snakeskin filled with shot. (That they had shot to spare indicates their superior military preparation.) These not-so-invisible bullets the Narragansett refused to accept, either rejecting the objects as a declaration of war, or rejecting combat with warriors who did not have real weapons or did not know proper military etiquette. The English indeed misunderstood some ritual having to do with bows. When Indians gave them weapons, colonists tended to see this as a helpful, practical gesture, or as tribute—the laying down of arms before a superior. They did not understand that such gifts might have asserted alliance, the sharing of weapons against common foes. Further, John Smith's representation of the Susquehannock man who balanced bow and pipe saw this inaccurately as evidence of the man's agility and coolness in the face of the enemy. Rather, the man was probably offering two options: war or peace.[53]

Differences in the tactics of battle presented a greater cultural impasse than difference in weapons. Most Algonquian forms of battle were meant to maximize moments of personal valor while minimizing casualties. Hence the frustration and fear at Jamestown's constantly being shot at by invisible Indian archers. New Englanders noted during the Pequot War that some Pequot refused to keep formation and fire arrows as they faced musket fire, as European soldiers were expected to do. John Underhill encouraged "our Indians for to entertain fight with them. Our end was that we might see the nature of the Indian war." This involved "[ex]changing a few arrows together after such a manner, as I dare boldly affirm, they might fight seven years and not kill seven men." Even Underhill's Indian allies preferred this less mortal way of war. After one victory, he reported that "Our Indians" were appalled by the casualties; they "cried Mach it, mach it; that is, It is naught, it is naught, because it is too furious, and slays too many men." Still, it would be wrong to assume that military differences meant total incomprehension. When Nicholl's men were being shot full of arrows on St. Lucia, their assailants added to the terror by "naming us by our names when they hit us."[54]

Perceptions of similarity between invader and invaded grew stronger as both began to share a material culture and a related method of war. The native transition to firearms has attracted much scholarly attention, but change did not take the Indians directly from arrows to bullets. In an intermediate step, the English supplied more and harder forms of metal for arrowheads and sought local supplies of metals. The trade in metals interested the English because it was part of their mineral obsession. The silver and gold of Potosi and New Spain were the ultimate prizes, but base metals were welcome as well. English settlement of the Amazon sought "gold and silver Mynes"; in the meantime, the English dug a quantity of earth on the Amazon's north side, which they thought could be made into steel. Colonists avidly observed natives' metal weapons and ornaments and recorded their statements about mineral wealth. Robert Rich said of Bermuda in 1610 that there was "Iron promist, for tis true, / Their Mynes are very good." John Pory claimed of Damaris Cove in New England that "within an infinitie of rockes may be intombed abundance of rich minerals, among which silver and copper are supposed to be the cheife."[55]

If precious metals were hard to locate in North America, its natives had created an intra-American trade in copper for ornaments and arrowheads, on which they grafted Euro-Indian networks that distributed hard metal materials and (eventually) tools. As mentioned earlier, these exchanges had begun with the Norse and continued with Frobisher's and Davis's Arctic ventures; a recently recovered iron arrowhead from Kodlunarn shows signs both of European manufacture and of native reworking. Thomas Hariot noted that Roanoke's natives got copper from "inhabitantes that dwell farther into the countrey," a trade the English supplemented. Ralph Lane wrote that, in Roanoke, the Algonquian chief Wingina obtained enough English copper to pay mercenary bowmen in the amount of "seuen, or 800." Later, Jamestown colonists claimed that the Powhatan could "monopolize" inter-Indian trade in "all the Copper brought into *Virginia* by the English." The English learned, however, that natives could not work iron as easily as copper, unless the iron was already cut into usable forms. Without smiths' tools and knowledge of forging, large pieces of iron could not be converted into objects such as arrowheads. The 1590 report on the abandoned Roanoke site specified that iron weapons and bars remained on site, an indication that European competitors had not been there, but also that natives—other competitors—had technological limits.[56]

Slowly, the English modified their association between Indians and minerals. Nicholl thought that native St. Lucians were giving conflicting accounts of gold in the mountains; he suspected that they lied about mineral wealth to draw the English away from their ordnance and then attack. In early Maryland, colonists admitted that they had not learned what minerals the land held, even though the natives were otherwise helpful. When the English began to assert that natives were treacherous guides to locations of mineral wealth, they began to differentiate between colonial and Indian understandings of nature. Indians did not know how to work with hard metal, nor did they seem to know where to find precious metals. Their expertise with copper and with fragments of meteoric iron or salvaged wrought iron seemed less promising once they demonstrated no further knowledge or skill.[57]

The English began to suspect that they would need to rely on their own experts to find the locations of mineral wealth. John Harvey, an early governor of Virginia, promised England's secretary of state in 1630 that he would tour the colony in search of likely mine sites. Circa 1634 a "Mr. Yong" petitioned to take a mineral expert to the colonies with him. This required special permission, as the man in question, Alexander Baker, was under remand "concerning conscience." Still, Yong argued, Baker's release to go abroad was needed, as he was a "Cosmographer, and hath skill in mynes, and distinguishing & trying of mettals." English testimony on mines helped promote areas that did not otherwise invite settlement. Thomas Temple claimed to discover a mine in chilly Newfoundland in 1659. These efforts never yielded much wealth, though lead mining and iron forging later achieved some success in New England. The English had to import most hard metal items to use and to trade with Indians. The earlier idea, that natives might provide as much metal in trade (and at the ends of their arrows) as the English could send back, lost its power.[58]

By the early 1600s, however, European metal goods had several points of entry. Trade routes from the Spanish and Dutch, as well as English, brought new commodities to the natives, who spread these goods into regions where Europeans had not yet ventured. John Pory reported that the people in northern New England were supplied by English traders "with peeces, shott, powder, swords, blades, and the most deadlie arrow heads." The "giant" Susquehannock whom John Smith met already had metal knives and hatchets. Smith believed that the people around the Chesapeake Bay got their "peeces of iron, and brasse" from the Susquehannock, who presumably got these things from the French. When a Pilgrim scouting party met Massasoit's brother Quadequina, the man "looked vpon our messengers sword and armour . . . with intimation of his desire to buy it." Smith said of the 1622 Powhatan attack on the English that it was not "because they [the English] were Christians: but for their weapons and Copper, which were rare novelties." Roger Williams noted that the Narragansett associated hard metal with the English, calling their colonial neighbors "Chauquaquock," or "*Knive-men,*" meaning bearers of knives or swords. Ferdinando Gorges decried Maine's disorderly fishermen, who sold swords and arrowheads as well as firearms, powder, and shot to the natives. When Massachusetts authorities arrested Indian trader Thomas Morton at Ipswich in 1643, they confiscated letters he was carrying, as well as "arrowe heades taken about him."[59]

Firearms followed metal through colonial frontiers. The Indians began to use guns just at the point when the English began to use guns exclusively. Indeed, the transition to the new weaponry took place as a contest, real and implied, between bows and firearms. The contest was sometimes a reciprocal exchange of information. When he met the English in 1607, for example, Powhatan was "desirous to haue a Musket shott of[f], shewing first the maner of their owne skirmishes." Sometimes, natives tricked the English into demonstrating their firearms. The Pilgrims were thus duped when some Wampanoag "desired one of our men to shoote at a Crow, complaining what damage they sustained in their Corne by them." In 1623, when Massasoit attended the wedding of Plymouth's governor, William Bradford, he came in a party "with their bows and arrows—where, when they came to our town, we saluted them with the shooting off of many muskets and [exhibited] training our men." One could have such an exchange, however, only if the men on both sides had sufficient confidence in themselves. A contest revealed the technical limits of different weapons and of their handlers. The English recognized, for instance, that Indians' aim was better because native men tended to practice archery—not least to hunt food—more often than colonists practiced their shot. Edward Johnson, whose narrative of the Pequot War made fun of native warriors, nevertheless related that they were "very good marks-men."[60]

The English therefore worried over a negative outcome in open competition; they preferred to be the gatherers of military intelligence, not the hapless objects of others' surveillance. The Virginia Council in 1606 instructed settlers that "whensoever any of Yours Shoots before them be sure that they be Chosen out of your best Markesmen for if they See Your Learners miss what they aim at they will think the Weapon not so terrible." Two levels of competition, between humans and between implements, were clear in a Virginia shooting match of 1607. English and native men gathered, set up tar-

gets, and tested themselves and their weapons. One Indian man astonished the English when he shot an arrow into the "Target a foote
thorow, or better: which was strange, being that a Pistoll could not
pierce it." Because the English were determined that the contest not
end this way, they set up another target of steel and invited the Indian
marksman to try again. The shot went home but the arrow shattered
on impact and the archer showed "great anger." The outcome was
still ambiguous: the Indians had proved their ability to shoot accurately and even to pierce objects that were bullet-proof. Further, the
natives might well have concluded not that the visitors had better
technology, but that they could simply stack the deck. Indeed, to prevent Indian knowledge of the limitations of firearms, the English
sometimes refused to demonstrate their guns. In captivity, John Smith
"broke the cocke" of his pistol rather than reveal to Powhatan the
awful truth that it could not shoot as far as an arrow could fly. These
were indications that information about firearms, and not just the
equipment itself, was part of an uneasy frontier exchange. The English in northern Virginia were irate that Dutch and Swedish settlers
had hired themselves to Indians to teach "our arms and fights."[61]

For their part, the natives were careful not to release their weapons
to the English unless this maneuver gave them some advantage in
trade or alliance. Theirs was in fact an accurate realization that the
invaders could turn native bows against their makers. In 1612 one
canny man managed to exchange an arrow without its head for an
English knife. Nor did the natives let their weapons fall into English
hands. When the English raided a hastily abandoned Newfoundland
village, they found only one arrow; another foray yielded no arms,
only miscellaneous tools and clothing of little importance to the residents. On occasion the Indians did give their weapons to the English,
and the English seemed to welcome them. Smith reported that the
Susquehannock gave "for presents" their bows, arrows, swords, and
shields (along with beads and tobacco pipes); the Massawomec presented the English with "bowes, arrowes, clubs, targets," and food.[62]

There are signs as well that English and Indian equipment was interchangeable; one side could easily adopt the weapons of the other.
One report of an exchange of arrows during Frobisher's second voyage remarked that the Inuit were busily "gathering up those arrows
which our men shot at them, yea, and plucking our arrowes out of
their bodies," either to shoot them back or to hoard their metal heads.

The thrifty Inuit archers were rivaled by the English settlers who inhabited the besieged first fort at Jamestown. Archeologists have discovered stockpiles of over one hundred native arrowheads in and around the fort, some of them buried with Jacobean artifacts. The latter discovery points to the colonists' mix of technologies and their eagerness to shoot back whatever was shot at them. When Virginia received King James's castoff military stores from the Tower of London, colony officials decided, revealingly, to store the bows and arrows in the Bermudas. They believed that, if these weapons fell into native hands, Indians would quickly turn them against the settlers and might learn to make hard metal arrowheads. The colonists evidently did not think they could not have used the bows themselves, or may have thought they could use the local variety if need arose before the Bermuda supplies could be sent back.[63]

Firearms were nevertheless reaching the natives, who quickly learned how to use them. Despite bans on selling firearms to Indians, such sales accelerated as European colonization of North American progressed. Indeed, the trade in firearms and related supplies was a competitive one, in which the Dutch and English especially jostled for control and profit. Within a decade of permanent settlement, both English and Indians possessed bows and arrows, guns and bullets; the proportions may have varied, but neither side lacked a particular kind. The presence of these weapons across the frontier indicated a transitional era during which both natives and Englishmen went back and forth between using bows and guns. By this time, assertions that firearms mystified Indians were suicidal. During the Pequot War, Lion Gardiner commented that the Pequot would rush the English "to the very mussells [muzzles] of our peices"; in the same war, John Higginson concluded that "it hath been a common conceit but is in truth a dangerous errour, Indians are afrayd of pieces."[64]

In the meantime, colonizers' fascination with native archery continued and became more complicated than mere military intelligence. For instance, the English began to identify the place of bows and arrows within Indian ritual: weapons might be shown to the foe as a sign of imminent battle, placed in graves with fallen warriors, or offered to the gods. As both Indians and English moved from bows to firearms, they also converged on a shared method of war. Anglo-Indian battle would rely predominantly on firearms (though not so much on ordnance, which colonists usually intended for rival Europeans), but without the mustering and volleys of shot that characterized action with muskets in Europe. Instead, skirmishing and individual shooting predominated. In this manner, the English were no longer observing similarities they had with Indians but were creating them.[65]

Celebrations of autochthonous simplicity would continue in colonial America—from the religious focus of seventeenth-century Puritan jeremiads over the lost virtue of the founding generation to the calls for non-importation that preceded the American Revolution. Like nostalgia over ancient military vigor and defense of liberty, these statements registered an Anglo-American concern over the civilizing process. By the 1700s and 1800s, such ambivalence openly noted white Americans' status as creatures who combined elements of old and new worlds, of refined culture and tonic primitivism; Natty Bumppo and Daniel Boone became the new figures of Tacitean fantasy and critique. Some of this nostalgia pointed again to the bow, though with a less practical thrust than when Europeans had still used that weapon. In parts of New England, "to draw a long bow" meant by the late 1700s to tell a tall tale, an instance of verbal rather than physical prowess. The ironic view of primitive valor nevertheless died hard. During the first year of war between the United States and Great Britain, Benjamin Franklin recommended that the Continental Army "add Bows and Arrows" to its stores because "those were good Weapons, not wisely laid aside." Franklin listed the by then moldering reasons why bows were superior to muskets. He then concluded with a beautifully ambiguous phrase about the strength of English archers during "one of our Battles against the French in Eduard the 3d's reign," momentarily forgetting that the unified entity implied by the possessive "our" no longer existed. Creole Americans had a selective and nostalgic patrimony: they wanted to be like the English or like Indians, as they pleased.[66]

People on both sides of the Anglo-American frontier were changing, recognizing possible similarities while insisting on their differences. English and Indian adopted new forms of technology even as they respected old cultural forms. Native men kept their scalp locks, though having long hair on both sides of the head was less of a problem with firearms. The scalp lock retained importance as a prize of war, something the English would themselves recognize. By the mid-seventeenth century, a native warrior might bring down an enemy with a European firearm, remove the scalp with a European metal axe or knife, and then receive a colonial bounty for the scalp. (By the late eighteenth century, there are even examples of white colonists who scalped one another.) The path from native scalp lock to white scalping traces the progress of colonization, in which technologies crossed cultural lines, were reinscribed with new values, persisted in new contexts, or were volubly lamented in their passing. What is significant about this English phase of colonization—or, more accurately, invasion—is that change and exchange were accomplished with little desire for intercultural harmony, as had been the stated intention of Hakluyt's and Hariot's plans to give Indians tools and teach them crafts, to build on their well-developed sense of artifice. In contrast, using the same weapons as the other side and decoding the enemy's behavior were meant not to facilitate cooperation but to make sure that battles were coherent enough to yield a recognizable result.[67]

Indians had good reason to seek out new and alternative methods of warfare: the English wanted American land and wished to depict themselves as naturally suited to own, develop, and propagate over the land. Colonizers wanted not just a small foothold in America but a large claim to it, and a claim that would physically exclude Indians. The military interface of the initial encounter helps explain, for example, why the English had little interest in intermarriage. Military intelligence created a situation in which Englishmen regarded Indians in gender-specific terms: as men against whom they could test their manliness. The American frontier resembled the Irish frontier, where the English were similarly disinclined to let women and intermarriage complicate the picture of martial and cultural opposition. Thus the English colonies took initial shape in a zone of military encounter, where Indians and English may have allowed their cultures selectively to bleed into each other so that they could get on with the task of shedding each other's blood. Despite their enthusiasm for battle, the English soon began to read American nature in ways that de-emphasized Indians' martial prowess and pointed to reasons to believe them physically weak, virtually melting away from the places the English wanted for themselves.[68]

CHAPTER FOUR

Domesticating America

Military action continued to inform colonists' understanding of their place in America. In the 1670s, Nathaniel Bacon claimed that English troops would be helpless before an array of rebellious Virginians because of "the Country or clime not agreeing with their constitutions." John Bradstreet echoed this opinion ninety years later when, in 1759, he lamented to Charles Townshend that the British saw "great loss of Troops by sickness in Florida and West India Islands." Bradstreet wanted to "Raise a Regiment of Foot in America," a troop of up to one thousand creoles, its officers "the Sons of the best Families in the Several Provinces." These plans suggested a pan-colonial identity among English settlers that, like archery, could simultaneously express Anglo-imperial and new world identities. Unlike military or other technology, however, this characteristic existed within the very physical constitutions of the colonists. Discourse on nature (like military intelligence) thus decoded the unfamiliar in order to promote English control over America. This chapter will focus on how the English interacted with American nature, sometimes referring to Indian methods of interaction; the next chapter will focus on English interaction with Indians themselves.[1]

The English were finally finding the colonizing strength particular to their nation: their bodies. If other nations had had greater navigational prowess, better ability to discover mines, and swifter military control over native populations, the English could make up for lost time by planting themselves in America and breeding there. Prefiguring the Lockean argument about property, colonists suggested that it was their bodies that guaranteed overseas possession, both by creating a population that demonstrated territorial dominion and by generating many hands to improve "wilderness" through labor. Recent work that has interpreted arguments for English bodily affinity to New England as precursors of "American" identity is therefore misleading; the arguments were not unique to New England but expressed an English identity that underpinned all colonial endeavors.[2]

If military invasion was a quick way to claim territory, it lacked the definitiveness of settlement of the land, as Richard Hakluyt had argued in his pivotal *Discourse of Western Planting* (1584). Peter Heylyn likewise concluded that a small *"Fortress* is more fit for sudden use, and a *Colony* for continuance."* During the first decade of the 1600s, the (barely) surviving Jamestown colony hinted that the English might maintain dominion in America. Subsequent plans to colonize Bermuda and New England took firmer shape, and, during the 1620s and 1630s, more settlements had more success, from Plymouth down to Barbados. As the English catalogued their accomplishments, they defined an affinity between themselves and American environments which promised that they could domesticate America instead of themselves being transformed by it. Authors as diverse as John Smith, William Bradford, John Winthrop, and Richard Ligon all constructed narratives that identified the English physiology as their nation's peculiar asset in the project of colonization.[3]

Discussions of the new world carefully considered its effects on English people, continuing the speculation on climates and bodies that had informed Frobisher's Arctic ventures. The English described corporeal change in three ways: inherited, formed by custom, or induced by climate. Adaptation to climate (or physical environment generally) was the most widely accepted explanation of human differences. Colonizers would, however, emphasize custom to downplay the effects America's climate might have on them. Inherited and significant differences, belief in which underpinned later ideas of race, did not much interest commentators in the early modern period. They thought that inherited resemblance was typical only of smaller populations, such as families, perhaps villages, and occasionally provinces—but not the larger national populations that would later be the units of racialist analysis. To a considerable extent, this was because theories of nature stressed an underlying universal human similarity: monogenetic creation and descent from the primordial parents. Customs that altered appearance (such as Pictish war paint or Algonquian hairstyles) therefore operated with climate to create most of the visible variation among peoples. Only in the case of Africans' dark complexions would the English talk about differences peculiar to certain lineages, as George Best's earlier discussion of the Arctic had done.

Cosmography was the science that examined the human place within the world, building on ancient inquiry into climates; early modern analyses of population raised newer questions, especially those related to gender and procreation. As John Rastell's *Four Elements* had shown, cosmography made the new world comprehensible; Richard Eden said that his "affeccion" for "the science of Cosmographie" inspired his interest in accounts of America; William Cuningham called cosmography the "Art for all mens use." Descriptions of the human place in the cosmos referred, above all, to climate and constitution or complexion. These were contemporary terms for environment and human physical condition. The world's different climates (temperate, torrid, and frigid) affected the constitution or complexion, thereby creating human variation. As Eden explained in 1561, "the miraculous mouinges of ye Planetes, Starres, and heauens" caused "the varietie of times and dyuersitie of all naturall thynges, by naturall causes." Each climate contained plants, animals, and minerals peculiar to it. Forces indirectly linked to the planets (such as the nature of water or soil) also influenced earthly regions. Building on cosmography, medical theories described differences among human bodies, which varied naturally according to gender and climate. Many English commentators on America favored the Hippocratic method to explain bodily change as the result of environment. The internally derived characters of bodies were, for the moment, of secondary concern.[4]

Emerging studies of human population, precursors of demography, showed how groups of humans might move, increase, or decline—questions of particular interest to colonists. The first attempts at population theory came in the wake of the dramatic population decreases during the Black Death and the Hundred Years' War, when Europeans worried about rebuilding their numbers. The English were likewise concerned whether they could propagate, as well as survive, in America. Some of this fear reflected the fact that much of the new world lay farther north or south than England, but the hemispheric difference was on the whole more compelling than latitude; that is, all of America (not just its geographic extremes) was seen as a place alien to European bodies and not conducive to increasing their numbers. In their descriptions of their population in America, the English were determined to overcome these apprehensions.[5]

Concerns about reproduction of English bodies in America begged the question of how corporeal form could be transmitted over the generations. Colonizers stressed the role of gender in a way that both recognized and downplayed inheritance. If men were the warriors who fought for colonial territory, women were the breeders of new colonists and nurturers of English constitutions in their children, whatever the climate around them. To make these points, the English focused on what they believed to be the natural differences between the sexes. Recent scholarship has been careful to observe that gender is a social construction of sexual difference that refers not merely to the biological facts of sexual reproduction but also to customs and opinions about men and women that are unrelated to procreation. But this constructivist definition of gender has misled us about how the English actually thought about sexual difference. That is, most scholarship has not discussed nature and culture simultaneously, in the way the English thought about sex difference. Instead, recent studies have privileged the cultural understanding of gender in order to convey the arbitrariness of its decisions. This chapter follows contemporary logic (nature spoke; humans followed), not to argue that the English were right, but to reveal how they used nature to authorize unequal social roles in the colonies, an authorization in which gender was a subordinate part of larger interpretations of the creation. Theories of nature presented colonial dominion as natural, grounded in a material reality that could not be questioned. Colonists above all wanted to believe that English behavior and mores could soften the impact of an unfamiliar climate; women especially were responsible for maintaining the Englishness of creole infants.[6]

Arguments that English bodies had an extraordinary ability to reproduce abroad and to withstand foreign climates guided plantation building: Englishness could domesticate outlandish things. John Parkinson's 1629 treatise on gardening admitted that although most "English flowers" were "never naturall of this our Land," the white and red roses of national history were "the most ancient Standards" and could "therefore" be "accounted naturall." A generation later, John Josselyn drew up a typology of the plants and animals that could be transferred between old and New Englands. Josselyn's method imitated José de Acosta's earlier attempt to categorize American animals as to whether they "differ in kind, and essentially from all others, or if this difference be accidentall . . . as we see in the linages of men." This last phrase reemphasized the reluctance to typologize human variations as essential rather than superficial, accidents of climate or birth. But English strength overseas was no accident. The proof was in the body.[7]

According to natural philosophy, the human body mirrored cosmic construction and functioning, both as it was fixed in one place and as it was subject to movement and change. Colonization of new climates might exacerbate bodily change and suffering, but would not introduce the body to a fallen humanity; no one was "at home" in any physical setting in the way Eve and Adam had been in paradise. That God had ordered humans to "increase, multiply," and fill the earth with their progeny had doomed people to wander and to labor either on the land or in bringing forth children. As people migrated, tilled the earth, and raised new generations, their and their children's bodies were in constant flux.

Aristotelian texts taught that humans were composed of the four elements: earth, air, fire, and water; the bodily humors—black bile, blood, yellow bile, and phlegm—correlated with the elements. The Galenic tradition also related the elements to the humors and elaborated a theory of the qualities (the elements' hot, dry, wet, or cold characteristics) and the faculties (principles of alteration that the soul caused within the body). Humans' elemental composition reminded them that they were prisoners of their material bodies until God called back their souls. The body's fallen nature was evident in its continual state of imbalance. No one had a perfect balance among the four humors; illness manifested the naturally imperfect human condition. Each body was also adapted to the material entities peculiar to its native region. "All the inhabitauntes of the worlde," Richard Eden wrote, have "suche complexion and strength of body, that euery of them are proportionate to the Climate assigned vnto them."[8]

Heat was the great catalyst of life and of variety, and was both

prized and feared. Life was possible only because of heat and moisture, and the human body therefore had a middle temperature in order to maintain these qualities as long as possible. As the body aged, it
became colder and drier until it died. Bodily heat resembled and was
affected by climatic temperature. John Winthrop concluded that God
"nourished" the puritan colony in Massachusetts just as heaven's heat
and moisture nourished humans ("tanquam calore & rore coelesti").
Heat also explained sexual difference: men were hotter than women,
their bodies stronger and quicker; hence their capacity for politics,
war, and heavy labor. Women were cooler, therefore weaker, less decisive, and better fitted for domestic tasks; their relative coolness also
allowed them to nourish infants in utero, relying at least in part on
male seed to spark generation. Men were therefore associated with
fire, yellow bile, and anger (the choleric emotion); women were associated with earth, black bile, and melancholy. As Anne Bradstreet put
it, "What differences the Sex, but only heat?" Too much heat, however, was not good even for men because it burned up their essential
moisture, hastening death.[9]

Because all matter was composed of the same elements, all earthly
entities (including humans) were more or less related and their
changes owing to climate superficial. This was why alteration in humans was conceived of as complexionate—idiosyncratic, temporary,
and no challenge to a fundamental similarity among all persons, who
still had the same physical and spiritual composition as their common
ancestors, Adam and Eve. Eden asserted, quoting Saint Paul, "that
GOD made of one bloudde, all nacions of menne." Heylyn added,
"Men thus one by originall, are of diuerse complexions of body, and
conditions of mind, according to the diuerse climats of the Earth." Di-
versity was situational. Nor did material alteration proceed toward
any final and permanent change. It was the metamorphosis of Ovid
rather than the evolution of Darwin.[10]

Humoral imbalance drew particular attention as the proximate
cause of unusual body types and temperaments; hence the terms
"choleric" and "phlegmatic" for raging and impassive individuals, respectively. The best-known humoral condition was melancholy, an
excess of black bile that made the body colder and drier. Great external heat could elicit this condition (the body became colder in self-defense), as might factors that decreased the body's internal heat. Because it affected temperature, melancholy adversely affected sexual

differences. It could make a woman barren and prone to brooding, even to unnatural intellection. Helkiah Crooke claimed that because melancholy men were too hot inside, they burned fat and sweated prodigiously, becoming drier and weaker, like old men. Africans were melancholy because their climate's extreme heat forced an interior coldness; only in cooler seasons would their organs warm up enough to make generation possible.[11]

Just as individuals had characteristic constitutions, human populations had national complexions. Descriptions of national temperaments tended to be chauvinistic; such had been the case beginning with the ancient Greeks, who stressed that their middle temper (optimal humoral balance) befitted their position in the middle of the world at its most temperate latitude. Modern Mediterraneans insisted that they had the climate ancient philosophers had considered optimal; northern people such as the English retorted that they too lived within a temperate zone and, if anything, their cooler surroundings made them tougher than effeminate southerners. But classical theory assumed that peoples of very cold or very hot climates were uncivil, dull of wit, and deformed of body. They were preoccupied with survival and could never build a civilization of consequence; paradoxically, the people who most needed technology to modify their environment were least likely to develop it. Further, adverse climate prevented the density of population necessary for economic and political might. These attitudes had informed English reaction to the Inuit, who, according to Dionyse Settle, had "no capacitie to culture" their "barren and unfertile" land. In such circumstances, artifice was desperate, which was why the Inuit acquired astonishing tools and resorted to witchcraft. Poverty likewise fostered bodily endurance. Thus Heylyn said that the Irish were "patient of cold & hunger" beyond what an English person could stand.[12]

In relation to Africa, European notions of extreme climate and physical hardiness had the most insidious consequences, particularly to justify chattel slavery and forced migration. As Europeans who were captured and enslaved in the Near East and North Africa knew all too well, slavery was not a condition reserved for non-Christians and non-Europeans. In part because of this threat of enslavement, Europeans constructed arguments that Africans were naturally fitted to heavy labor, torrid climate, and low social status. Europeans thus proclaimed Africans' aptitude for slavery based on their perceived resistance to physical hardship (including disease), an argument that was just as important as the themes of skin color, paganism, and barbarity that previous scholarship has stressed.

Sub-Saharan Africans were thought to live in a climate that barely sustained life. William Cuningham thus concluded that Africa's heat and wild beasts prevented population growth. Under these conditions, Africans were supposed to become insensible of pain and deprivation. Robert Burton cited ancient authorities on "a nation in *Africke,* so free from passion, or rather so stupid, that if they be wounded with a sword, they will only looke backe" to identify the cause of a slight sensation. When the English later imitated Iberian use of enslaved Africans as colonial labor, they too used arguments about bodily durability to explain their actions. One tract concluded that American "plantations are best arrived on & managed by bodily labour, & the said Negroes & Infidill being a people strong & able" were prime candidates for the work. Further, Africans were supposed to thrive in climates on the same parallel as their native land, such as in the West Indies. Europeans, weaker than Africans in any case, were even more so in hot climates. Because the English and the Dutch assumed that heat would sicken them, they hoped that Muslim pirates in the Mediterranean would not think them worth enslaving.[13]

Illness was the most feared form of constitutional variation, though its causes remained uncertain. Contemporary medical writing portrayed most maladies as the result of bodily imbalances, often of the humors; a disease was a bundle of symptoms that manifested a particular imbalance. But commentators debated the reasons for imbalance. It might be internally caused by the *naturals* (Galen's qualities and faculties), propensities or flaws within a body. Other diseases resulted from the *non-naturals* (diet, exercise, temperature, sleep, excretion), external factors that triggered bodily change. Aristotelian ideas about climate and Hippocratic notions about the body's synchrony with geography and astrology both supported this second line of thought. An anonymous physician wrote circa 1680 about the fevers cinchona cured that they were caused not by the humors but by a "sominim febrile" from the "Atmos-sphere." Though the two hypotheses—bodily propensities and external stimuli—could compete, they were also related; certain bodies were more likely to respond poorly to miasma, exotic diet, hot climate, and so on.[14]

Two other views of disease informed these hypotheses. First, it was common to interpret illness as a moral judgment. This was another way that human character became apparent in complexion; temperament encouraged illness, or behavior created bodily imbalance. The supposedly American disease of syphilis was frequently interpreted in this manner. Early reports linked syphilis to the natives' sodomy, cannibalism, and general debauchery. Second, some doctors and scholars of nature hypothesized that diseases were independent, invasive entities. Although this idea had roots in ancient corpuscular theory, it was not widespread and, like atomism generally, carried the stigma of atheism. Most commentators remained satisfied with the concept of a disease as the manifest symptoms of imbalance or dysfunction, and could explain contagion without the need for corpuscles; disease could spread simply through the general quality of the air or water. Observation of diseases eventually recognized as infectious (such as syphilis) and interpretation of microscopic evidence (by the late 1600s) of small organisms gradually strengthened the idea that a disease was an invasive entity carried in particles or animalcules. But this view did not appear in the English colonies until the 1720s. Earlier, colonists maintained that environment had the greatest impact on the body, with behavior and moral status able to induce or check the climate's power.[15]

But climates themselves might change, like the rest of nature. Europeans suspected that the earth's postlapsarian state guaranteed physical degeneration. A lost golden age of material harmony and plenty had given way to harsh conditions and moral turpitude. People were not as long-lived as before the Deluge, when the earth was fresh and not plagued by bizarre celestial events such as comets and eclipses. Exploration of America encouraged speculation about other changes in nature. José de Acosta, who hypothesized a lost geological connection between Asia and America (through which America came to be populated), prompted other speculations about changes in geography and human history. The English suggested, for instance, that their land might once have been attached to Europe, a handy way to assert old English claims to French territory. Anne Bradstreet echoed this idea in her *Tenth Muse*, where she wrote that because of flooding, "*Albion* (tis thought) was cut from *France*."[16]

Human populations too could change, through either growth or migration, and early forms of demography indicate some of the most revealing ways the English looked at colonies. Such speculation extolled the command from Genesis to multiply so that Christians might outbreed heathens and bring more of the globe under the dominion of the gospel. Other statements on population functioned as Protestant incentive for all adults to marry and raise families, or as Counter-Reformation encouragement of Catholic family life. The vague earlier suppositions about the globe and population thus took on narrower political functions to promote certain nations and peoples. As part of the advice-to-princes literature of the late Renaissance, political theorists recommended ways to get and maintain a large population for economic and military strength. John Dee explained the art of "stratarithmetrie," calculation of the numbers of men needed to combat a given enemy force, which itself relied on accurate intelligence about the enemy. In time, observations like these fed into the corpus identified as mercantilism, which sought to maximize the wealth and power of the state.[17]

Thomas Hariot made the earliest mathematical analysis of population growth and the first connected to colonization. Hariot calculated the number of people who could "inhabit the whole world" and the number who could "stand on ye face of ye whole earth," two quite different questions. He answered the first by estimating increase through the generations. He assumed that a man and a woman could have a child every year, with male and female offspring alternating; these children would begin to breed at twenty years of age. Hariot began with a pair he described as "Man/wife/woman/husband" and charted the numbers and rate of increase over the subsequent generations. In this he took for granted quite a lot that nature would not have allowed, but Hariot's only restraints on breeding were cultural—prohibitions of incest. He declared that "a man shall not marry" his mother, father's wife, wife's mother, father's daughter, or mother's daughter. That Hariot paired his calculations with estimates of biblical generations showed his awareness that humans functioned culturally rather than mathematically. Adam and Eve had therefore not managed to produce the abundance of living descendants which Hariot had estimated a man and woman would generate in a mere 240-year period.[18]

Hariot's second question, how many people could literally stand on the face of the earth, was a matter only of mathematics. He made "suppositions" about the size of the globe, then calculated the ground space of the earth. He concluded that, if 6 million people could stand within a square mile, then 42,490,552,800,000 could stand shoulder to shoulder on the earth's face. In contrast, Hariot concluded that the carrying capacity of the earth was only 7,081,758,800. This was a nightmarish proto-Malthusian image. Hariot brought his estimate of the total population capacity of the earth closer to a practical case when he calculated the number of people who could stand within England itself. This figure connected estimates of population with images of the national power of a large population. He stated that "there may stand in England 300,000,000,000. persons," and concluded that "therefore theyre place of standing must be allso three times greater than England." Hariot had been overseas and seen a country where the multiplying English might find a new place to stand.[19]

Europeans believed that to "stand" on land represented territorial domination. Queen Elizabeth's "Ditchley" portrait (with its armillary sphere) monumentalized the way that England's monarch ruled her domain. In this image, the queen's feet are firmly planted on her kingdom, specifically Ditchley in Oxfordshire. Her skirts are drawn back, the better to expose Elizabeth's instrument of dominion: her body. The same is true of the frontispiece to Thomas Hobbes's *Leviathan* (1651), in which another gigantic figure stands over the landscape, this one constituted by the bodies of the individual subjects who recognize and therefore legitimate rule. The human body thus stood for England in two senses: it symbolized the nation, and it populated territory as a mark of national dominion.[20]

The first systematic theorists of population and its political implications were Jean Bodin and Giovanni Botero, who, unlike Hariot, published works on the topic. Both men influenced English writers; in 1606 Bodin's *Six Bookes* and Botero's *Greatness of Cities* were translated into English. Books 4 through 6 of Bodin's work examined population: the regional character of people, the factors that increased their numbers, and reasons why they might migrate. In ancient Rome, Botero observed, authorities sent the poor to colonies, where conquered lands were distributed to them. Censors (who calculated the people's numbers and policed their mores) could determine the numbers available for work, war, or colonization; Bodin said they could also "expell all drones out of a commonweale." Like Bodin, Botero examined reasons for population growth and extension, and recommended policies to encourage both, but his analysis had stronger implications for people planted in colonies. Botero argued that a city's greatness lay not in its own physical size but in "the multitude and number of the inhabitants and their power" to make wealth and war. Colonies had in fact increased Rome's population, as plants multiplied when "transplanted into an open ground"; the Romans chose "a number of poor citizens and sent them into colonies, where, like trees transplanted, they might have more room to better themselves both in condition and commodity, and by that means increase and multiply the faster."[21]

Bodin and Botero initiated widespread discussion of population dynamics, not least among colonizers. The Huguenot poet Guillaume de Salluste, Sieur Du Bartas, wrote *Les colonies* (1578–1584) to examine the diffusion of people since the Deluge and their subsequent physical and cultural variations. Du Bartas echoed the theme that humanity was doomed to wander: "no Race / Perpetually possesseth any place: / But, as all Tennants at the High Lords will." His epic was significant to Protestants who migrated to preserve and spread their faith. Josuah Sylvester, who made the first complete English translation of Du Bartas, presented King James with a manuscript of *The Colonies*. In his *Historie of the World* (1614), Walter Ralegh commented on the rise and fall of different ancient populations, and assessed the presumed longevity and fertility of the ancients by analyzing factors such as diet, wet-nursing, and age at marriage. Ralegh cited Botero and Bodin, and Hariot's figures on population might have helped Ralegh construct the chronology he appended to the work. Robert Burton's *Anatomy of Melancholy* frequently used Botero and Bodin, as did Heylyn's *Cosmographie in Four Books*. William Bradford showed familiarity with Bodin's *De Republica,* and John Winthrop quoted Ralegh's *Historie of the World* in his journal of early Massachusetts; Anne Bradstreet's *Tenth Muse* was deeply indebted to Du Bartas, and Indian missionary John Eliot owned a copy of the second edition of Heylyn's *Cosmographie.* Other commentators did not display this level of familiarity with population theorists but agreed with some of their tenets. The connection between population and wealth, for example, was widespread. Thus one adviser on colonies stated that "there is nothing that advances a trade more then a populous and well governed inhabitation."[22]

Like Hariot, commentators on population and colonies held that marriage and reproduction were the most important causes of a large population. Though human fertility depended on optimal physical conditions, including adequate food and absence of virulent disease, most writers tended to downplay medical variables and assume that fertility was a human constant. It was custom that influenced the birthrate. The best age for matrimony was one consideration, as was devotion to one spouse. Medical theory did not encourage early marriage, as sexual intercourse could stunt procreative capacity if it took place before full development of the generative organs. Further, Christian morality questioned whether frequent and indiscriminate sexual relations necessarily increased the birthrate. Moderate sexual activity with one lawful partner should engender the greatest number of healthy children.[23]

Intercultural comparisons encouraged Europeans to spread themselves over the globe. Botero concluded that the world's population should be differently distributed over the earth. He believed that human population had peaked three thousand years before he wrote and would not substantially increase, for "the fruits of the earth and the plenty of victual doth not suffice to feed a greater number." This meant that, until optimal distribution of people occurred, certain populations might feel materially deprived. The cruelest wars were fought for "the earth food, and commodity of habitation." Warm climates, by encouraging population growth, had the bloodiest altercations over resources. Botero thus believed that the southern parts of the new world had the worst wars over subsistence. In the Caribbean and South America, "the people chase and hunt men [as food] as we do deer and hares." Native Americans were driven to devour children and even infants torn from the womb. Similar scarcity elicited barbarity in West Africa, where desperate people sold their own children to "Moors," who sold them in turn to the Portuguese for "their islands," or to the Spanish "for the New World." In contrast, European population was fortuitously curbed by factors such as barren soil, epidemics, and natural disasters; these hardships spared Europe the problems of immoderate growth.[24]

Epidemics were nonetheless reminders of the European population's fragility, best demonstrated during the Black Death. Between 1346 and 1350, plague had killed at least a third of the population, which recovered only slowly. Between 1350 and 1500, nearly 1,300 English villages were deserted. Robin Hood ballads were popular in the late fourteenth century, when mortality and social instability prompted nostalgia and fantasy. After a brief respite, plague recurred in the sixteenth and seventeenth centuries. In 1587–88, for instance, England's death rate was 29.5 percent above the average trend; in 1625–26, it was 43 percent above. Epidemics could thus erode national power: land and labor would be underemployed, government and ecclesiastical services curtailed, and community density and cohesion eroded. As Burton wrote, "See that *Domesday*-Booke, and shew me those thousands of Parishes, which are now decaied, Citties ruined, Villages, depopulated."[25]

The memory of epidemics was woven into the history of early English colonization. Plague in London in 1582 may have delayed Humphrey Gilbert's departure for Newfoundland. John More's 1593 table of historical events recited the inroads of plague and the sweating sickness in five notable outbreaks from 1486 to 1579. In this last year—when Frobisher, Drake, and Gilbert were busy in the new world—the plague was at Norwich. Recurrence of the disease in the 1620s and 1630s paralleled expanded colonizing activities. New England, the colonial region that would become proverbial for its natural increase, drew many of its settlers from East Anglia, hard hit by medieval plague (half the people had died). The medieval new town of Boston never recovered from the Black Death; its population dropped precipitously from its fourteenth-century zenith and continued to suffer out-migration. Boston in New England would transplant and revive Saint Botolph's weakened church. That the Black Death bulked large in colonists' imagination was evidenced in their persistent labeling of Indian epidemics as "plague" when that disease was unlikely to have been present. Plague had, moreover, significantly altered the way the English would think about their population, as it created the bills of mortality that gave John Graunt data for his pathbreaking 1662 demographic study.[26]

As analyses of population complicated the scriptural destiny of humans to spread over the earth, they were anticipating the Lockean view of humans as creators of property. The most important aspect of this transformation related to land and its produce; labor turned raw nature into a cultivated landscape and artificial objects, things whose transformation demanded the law and civil society that were lacking in non-European regions. If Locke argued that, in the beginning, all the world was like America, Hariot had made this point nearly a century earlier when he claimed that Roanok use of land had small effect on the new world's productive capacity and on the reproductive capability of the current population. As Heylyn reiterated, sub-Saharan Africa and North America seemed to have scattered populations that neglected the lands over which they roamed. English labor, male and female, would increase the fruits of America and increase the population who consumed those fruits.[27]

Accordingly, early population theory presented two modern views of humanity's place within nature, both of which challenged classical learning. First, the attention to population inserted new Atlantic worlds into the comparative framework that had stressed geographical differences, especially north-south differences. The proliferation of comparisons between hemispheres as well as among latitudes explained how some peoples achieved population success despite climatic hardship. Second, early population theory contended that the natural history of humanity was essentially one of dramatic changes. Growth, decline, and migration all undercut the stasis that was the optimal achievement of human health and cultural adaptation. For this reason, early modern commentators were keen to understand the changes that accompanied migration, or eager to deny that some alterations took place at all. As Geffrey Whitney asserted in his emblem book of 1586, "No forren soile, hath anie force to change the inward minde." Ralegh concurred that, while the stars might affect the body, they could not change "the mindes of men immediately." But what about the immediate effects on the body?[28]

To some extent, the belief that humanity was destined to wander normalized English intrusion into America and its strange climates. England's own people, after all, were descended from their island's blend of invaders and invaded. Anne Bradstreet began her poem on America with a description of the Saxon, Danish, and Norman invasions of the mother country; Roger Williams concluded that "few *Nations* of the World but are a mixed Seed, the people of *England* especially[:] the *Britaines, Picts, Romanes, Saxons, Danes* and *Normans,* by a wonderfull providence of God being become one *English* people." This past could be a model for English colonization of America. Edward Williams recommended settlement in the Carolina barrier islands to act as "an inoffensive Nursery to receive an infant colony, till by an occasion of strength and number, we may poure our selves from thence upon the Mayneland, as our Ancestors the Saxons from the Isle of Tanet into Brittaine."[29]

The English believed that America had also been repeatedly invaded and that they were only its most recent colonists, just as the Normans had been their most recent conquerors. Indians themselves could not have originated in the Americas. The idea of a separate creation of humanity—in which Indians would be native to the new world just as Europeans were native to the old—was heretical and not widely debated until the Enlightenment. Instead, colonizers discussed monogeneticism and post-Noachic dispersal of peoples. Not that there was any agreement on what line of Noah's descendants had settled America. Some commentators, following Acosta, speculated that Indians had come from Asia; Josselyn stated that New England's Indians were "judged to be of the *Tartars* called *Samonids.*" Others hypothesized that Indians had come from Europe, via the Israelites expelled from Jerusalem, or the scattered Trojans, or from medieval migrations like those led by Brendan or Madoc. From these theories, the English concluded that the denizens of the new world were not true aboriginals but migrants whose territories might subsequently be invaded by others.[30]

The history of Spanish America reminded the English that the new world severely tested both invading and conquered populations. The Black Legend taught that the Spanish had all but annihilated the peoples of the Caribbean and prepared the land for resettlement. This criticism reminded the English to shun Spanish-style cruelty but also reinforced a sense that America's natives were delicate. According to Heylyn, America had been populous "before the arriuall of the *Spaniards,*" whose wars and demands for labor had destroyed the Indians. In Puerto Rico, Spanish greed had "consumed" both "*Natives*" and mines, the former dying out as they were forced to extract gold. On Jamaica alone, the Spanish had killed six thousand people, and the survivors so despaired that women aborted their children rather than see them live as slaves. George Gardyner likewise wrote that the Bahamas had "no Inhabitants" left because they had been "a harmless simple people, and therefore the easier taken and carried away by the Spaniards." In Puerto Rico, "the Natives here and at *Jameca,* have been totally destroyed by the Spaniards."[31]

The English portrayed enslaved Africans as new natives of the Caribbean, hardy subordinates who succeeded frail Indians. When Daniel Elfrith described the West Indies in 1631, he warned English ships' captains of places where they might be attacked by Indians or slaves, whom he perceived as settled in the landscape and hostile to English outsiders. Sailors needed to "take heed of the Indians" in Dominica, and those who went to a small island near Trujillo "must haue a gaurd because their are Some Slaues which plant uppone that Iland" within musket shot of river traffic. Drake's sack of Santo Domingo had killed or frightened away most of the Spanish, the city being left to "*Negros, Mulatos,* and other *Strangers,*" meaning non-Indians who, like Spaniards, failed to persist.[32]

The English wondered whether they were made of sturdier stuff, but took heart from their recent demographic upsurge. Scholarship on English colonization has wrongly emphasized that the English felt burdened by excess population. The secondary literature has stressed negative perceptions of population growth, including fear of under-employment and vagrancy. While some Elizabethan commentators did argue that England's population had rapidly increased under the Tudors, this was not a universal opinion, nor were its proponents convinced that England thereby suffered. Indeed, population growth often supported colonizers' propaganda, which rejoiced that England had people to spare. Complaint about the ill effects of population growth was in fact a luxury, a sign of England's new prosperity and power.[33]

England's fertility prophesied its colonizing future. Bishop (later Archbishop) George Abbot made the influential summary "*Anglia, mons, pons, fons, Ecclesia, foemina, lana,*" meaning England was a land of mountains, bridges, fountains, churches, women, and wool—abundant material resources, true Christianity, and women, the key to population growth. Abbot was widely quoted, as in Heylyn's 1621 *Microcosmus,* and his ideas were refurbished when the English began to think about carrying their fecundity overseas. An ivory diptych dial (a device to calculate position on the globe, made circa 1600) now in the Museum of the History of Science, University of Oxford, shows a map of England and Wales. A motto encircling the map echoes Abbot: "Of These Thinges Followinge, This Famovse Ile Is Fuel [Full], Movntaynes Fovntaynes Bridges Chvrches Women & Woll." The object showed the present geographic location of the English and (like Hariot's calculations) intimated domination of territory beyond. George Peckham exulted, "It hath pleased God of his great goodnesse" to preserve English "people" both "from slaughter by the sword, and great death by plague, pestilence, or otherwise." In contrast, Spain "dooth not greatly abounde with people." Colonial promoters Edward Hayes and Christopher Carleill agreed that both the Spanish and French lacked the English assets of "peace & people."[34]

If the English were burgeoning, the globe offered them ample space. Burton insisted that "a great part of the world is not yet inhabited as it ought"; Asia, Africa, and America could support "many Colonies." The underused land needed *people,* the real cause of wealth and plenty. An account of the Pequot War declared that the English were destined to rule the land, not only as "the first Discoverers" and "Planters" of New England, but also because they were "large and capable of innumberable people" whose progeny had "encreased, by a facultie that God hath given the Brittish Ilanders to beget and bring forth more children than any other nation of the world." Looking at Plymouth, John Pory agreed that "God has prospered our nation . . . he hath caused us to multiplie and increase exceedinglie." Emigration of superabundant population was therefore a project of national interest, not the mere dumping of people abroad. Richard Whitbourne insisted that "transplanted" people "deserue wel of the State." John White defined a colony as "a societie of men drawne out of one state or people," the terms "societie" and "state" indicating the cultural and political connections between old and new worlds.[35]

But the English were wary that transplantation might threaten their individual bodies and therefore the corporate body of a new settlement, which made it important to identify which parts of America suited English people. Early reports on the new world had perhaps incautiously advertised its alien qualities and had associated Indians with the monstrous races of ancient and medieval legend, initiating fears that the Western Hemisphere was unfriendly to Europeans. Eden glossed one of his translations by emphasizing that the Indies had "contagious ayre and extreme heate," and that in the new lands the stars were "placed in other order" than in Europe. He also observed that America "altereth the formes and qualities of [European] thynges" such as wheat and cattle. The idea that much of America was fairly warm (based on initial reports on the Caribbean) caused additional worry. Heat would enervate settlers and could threaten gender and reproduction. A hot climate made a man's body cooler (in self-defense) and a woman's hotter; the sexes then took each other's roles, men cooing over babies as Amazonian women wielded bows. Thus Helkiah Crooke said that "they that have travailed into the new world do report that almost all the men have great quantity of Milke in their breasts." Meanwhile, the darker women of hotter climates had scantier menstruation and therefore less generative capacity.[36]

Early English accounts of America likewise stressed its unusual features, much as Frobisher's nervous crew had checked the Inuit for cloven hoofs. Crossing the North Atlantic on his way to Massachusetts, John Winthrop noted that the Pole Star appeared lower and the moon smaller than in England; that birds appeared everywhere, even though there was no land in sight; and that if the wind blew, "we had still colde weather, & the sunne did not give so muche heate as in England." Landfall presented new dangers. America's native products might poison European bodies suited to different foods and medicines.[37]

The English were therefore concerned to designate physical continuities between North America and England. George Peckham, in his 1583 account of the new world, stressed that the recent discoveries were in latitudes between thirty and sixty degrees, where the English found "all thinges that be necessarie profitable, or delectable for mans life" in a region "neither too hotte nor too colde." The elder Richard Hakluyt assured settlers that they needed neither "to pass the burnt lyne nor to passe the frosen Seas" to find wealth in America. Propagandists also proposed a geographical affinity between Britain and North America, particularly the parts in the same latitude. In 1559, William Cuningham saw the eastern projection of North America as evidence that America was an island parallel to the island of Britain and the distance between them not so far as that between Iberia and South America. Peckham stated that North America's "Countrey dooth (as it were with arme advaunced) above the climats both of Spayne and Fraunce, stretche out it selfe towards England onlie. In manner praying our ayde and helpe" as depicted in "Mercators generall Mappe." Personification of America as needy neighbor accompanied depiction of ventriloquized native Americans as suppliants to the English. In order to hear the gospel, Hakluyt wrote, "the people of America crye oute unto us their nexte neighboures."[38]

The personification of geography most often described America as England's sister or daughter. (Sometimes England was a "Nurse" to the colonies, but it was more common to claim a blood relationship.) William Vaughan explained that Newfoundland was "*Great Britaines Sister,* or *Britanniol*"; another observer said that Virginia and New England were "Sister Lands." Richard Whitbourne claimed sisterhood among Newfoundland, Britain, Ireland, Virginia, the Summer Islands, New England, and Nova Scotia. Maternal imagery asserted an unequal bond between England and its colonies. One of Bradstreet's poems was a dialogue between "Old England" and "New England," a mother and daughter who in 1642 pondered joint action against religious unorthodoxy and war. If England was a true mother, John White argued, it was a "grosse errour that Colonies ought to be Emunctories or sinckes of States; to drayne away their filth." "Those whom we send out," White asked, "are they not our owne flesh and bones?"[39] Images of consanguinity not only helped colonists envisage themselves entering a familiar land but also checked metaphors that presented America as a potential bride or object of rape. To see Indians as neighbors and their country as a sister land emphasized friendly and even intimate relations, though not sexual ones. Indeed, insistence that English people were unusually fecund assured colonists that they did not need spouses already acclimated to America.

Just as American territory was domesticated, presented as fit for English people, so the bodies of its natives were described as falling within the normal lineages of humanity. The three explanations of bodily difference—climate-induced, inherited, and acquired through custom—were brought selectively into play. Reluctance to admit that American climates might turn colonists into monsters was one way to deny that new world peoples were bizarre, let alone part of the monstrous races. The English instead claimed that it was custom that created Indians' distinctive appearance, that custom was, in fact, a "second nature" whose effects were nearly indistinguishable from those of the real thing. Commentators especially focused on female actions that altered the malleable infant body. This idea of acquired characteristics, and the emphasis on women's power to effect them, showed that commentators found it hard to distinguish between sexual generation and human culture: both inscribed the body, but each had a different implication for the continuity of lineage. But the English downplayed inheritance further; arguments that Indians descended from a cursed lineage (as was said of Africans and Jews) were, for instance, never dominant. Scholars have paid a great deal of attention to these arguments, thus following the early modern fascination with patriarchy without fully explaining parallel ideas about how a (male) lineage might be subverted, particularly by women.[40]

Two vying theories explained reproduction: the Aristotelian view that male seminal fluid operated on female matter to form an embryo, and the Galenic theory that male and female fluids together underwent coagulation and metamorphosis. Helkiah Crooke's 1615 *Microcosmographia* hewed to the Galenic line. "Perfect generation," Crooke wrote, required copulation between two humans who belonged clearly to the male and female sexes, both of whom emitted seed. Because male and female seminal fluids were derivations of blood, "consanguinity" implied some resemblance to both parents or their ancestors. Following Hippocratic tradition, John Bulwer credited male seed with the power of generation and the female womb with having the proper nutritive capacity for the seed of men. Bulwer believed that male seed was stronger than female (men could generate offspring with animals but women could not), but that a human womb was essential to create human offspring. Hippocratic and Galenic theories could therefore account for a child's resemblance to one or both parents; both also fit environmental views which stated that external factors such as diet and climate could affect fetal development and modify inheritance from parents. Bulwer noted, for instance, "Children are not alwaies answerable to the Parents in every respect."[41]

But early modern views of generation were moving toward theories of greater continuity of type. Once William Harvey hypothesized (in 1651) that human females—like avian females—must produce eggs, theorists had an important way to represent the transmission of fixed human types that survived environmental effects. After late seventeenth-century microscopy confirmed the presence of human gametes, the notion of species fixity gained more power. The preformationist debate would also strengthen notions of racial fixity, especially during the eighteenth century.[42]

Inheritance nevertheless admitted of several competing possibilities. People realized, for instance, that mothers could transfer disease independent of paternal influence because they gestated infants within their own bodies and because childbirth usually shed and mingled the blood of mother and child. Crooke speculated that measles and smallpox, *"which are wont once in a mans life,"* resulted from an impurity in the mother's menstrual blood. This was why the two diseases could not be caught from the air; people got them only once, rather than repeatedly, as with other diseases. Crooke further explained that inheritance of disease took place not directly, through the blood of the parents, but through the "seede" that was a distillation of parental bloods. "These seeds containe in them potentially the Idea, formes and proprieties of all the partes" of the body and its peculiar frailties, meaning that for some theorists the seeds of disease existed as facilitating factors, not infectious entities.[43]

Settlers who were reluctant to accept that the new world's effects would be present from birth could use ideas about inheritance to modify Hippocratic and Aristotelian theories, which specified that fetuses and neonates could absorb local qualities. Early in the history of colonization, some had speculated that American nativity would produce radically different individuals—Indians, say, rather than Europeans. One Paracelsian text, reprinted in London in 1590, argued that the stars of a person's nativity could create a propensity for syphilis, the disease most closely associated with America. More often, however, and in contrast to Iberians, the English cited proximate rather than astral causes for creolization. Either way, English migrants faced the possibility that, in America, they would become a different people, and would be parents of different people.[44]

In this way, commentators gave neither climate nor inheritance a dominant place in determining bodily character, and their focus on women's customs revealed suspicions about female power over reproduction. Crooke explained that macrocephalics had elongated heads because midwives shaped them in infancy. Those who had been shaped by "custom and constraint" could then beget "children with long heads naturally." John Bulwer, in *Anthropometamorphosis* (1653), agreed that the so-called monstrous races were products of human custom. Infants, born more or less alike, were willfully bound or molded into unnatural shapes. Bulwer credited Indian parents, midwives, and even children with creating native Americans' various types of heads and noses. This included heads that were shaped like dogs' or were pushed toward the chest, features that modern European explorers had discovered to result from custom rather than nature. Denial of the monstrous races was intended to narrow differences between peoples while highlighting female error. Bulwer's point was that Europeans were idolatrously vain, like everyone else, but the sin was strongest in Christian women. In Persia, eunuchs molded infants' noses; in America, fathers sometimes shaped their children's heads. But in Europe, women (particularly midwives) did the deforming. A dedicatory poem to Bulwer's work abhorred the "hagge Midwife" who "models every Part" of a child until "shee be known / To spoile the child's braine, to delight her own."[45]

Custom might also explain skin color, a hypothesis that showed skepticism that climate created complexion. Bodin acknowledged that variations in skin color occurred even within the same climate; therefore something else must be at work. In America, for instance, complexion resulted from culture. Martin Pring suggested that Norumbega's natives were dark "not by nature but accidentally." Gabriel Archer agreed that Indians' "skynn is tawny not so borne, but with dying and paynting them selves, in which they delight greatly." No less a moralizer than Bulwer excused native Americans' painting of their skin. This practice was "Universall, and without exception among the *West Indians,*" and Bulwer compared it to the use in modern Europe of cosmetics and patches, as well as to ancient Pictish blue

Natives painted against the cold. From J[ohn] B[ulwer], *Anthropometamorphosis: Man Transformed, or, the Artificiall Changling* (London, 1653), 460. Courtesy of the Folger Shakespeare Library.

woad. Neither comparison was flattering, but Bulwer as usual intended his ultimate sanction for Europeans, so they might reflect humbly on their savage origins and corrupt habits. For this reason, Bulwer reproduced John White's images of ancient Britons which de Bry had included in his *America*. As for the bedaubed natives of Seal Bay whom Drake described, they did "resemble devils. Yet they have some commodity by painting their bodies . . . to be the defence it yeeldeth against the piercing and nipping cold." As with Algonquian men's hairstyle, diabolic appearance made sense if it was the result of technology, not idolatry.[46]

Europeans explained Africans' appearance with less sympathy. Neither climate nor custom was a sufficient explanation; other causes, especially inheritance or providence, had to be operating. The old idea that a burning sun caused Africans' dark skin made less sense once Europeans encountered American peoples who lived on a parallel with Africa but were lighter—even those who lived on the equator. Eden's translation of Peter Martyr's *Decades* emphasized the "greate difference" between African and American regions within the same "paralelle," which Martyr initially ascribed to "the disposition of the earthe" (a local cause) rather than the similarity of the heavens. Martyr hypothesized that "varietie of colours proceadeth of man, and not of the earth," meaning that a custom or an inherited feature was at work. Heylyn broke off discussion of African appearance, saying that "the true cause of it and its speculation, I will deferre till I come to treat of *America*," parts of which had a comparably hot climate but paler people.[47]

Because climate no longer sufficiently explained external appearance, the concept of maternal impressions received increased attention. This doctrine specified that the moral, physical, or emotional state of a pregnant woman impressed itself on her child—a preparturient version of the female propensity to shape newborns. Bulwer remarked that it was "vehement imagination which possesseth the greatest force of hindering the matter of seed"; a woman might bear a child with a harelip if during pregnancy she saw, thought of, or ate a hare. Belief in maternal impressions indicated both anxiety over female power to affect generation (hindering the seed or semen) and unwillingness to ascribe profound physical difference to inheritance. Giambattista della Porta's *Natural Magick* (translated into English in 1658) was the most important text to comment on maternal imagination. He recounted Heliodorus' story of the Ethiopian queen Persina who bore a white child because she had stared at images of Perseus and Andromeda during intercourse. Della Porta recommended that modern mothers follow this practice to bear children in the likeness of certain images. To bear a child of a certain sex, however, della Porta recommended manipulation of the mother's body (as by taking certain positions after intercourse) in order to foster seed of a particular temperature. His instructions indicated the Aristotelian assumption that internal bodily differences could not be imagined into flesh and that sexual difference was lodged deeper in nature than complexion, even African complexion. Commentators like Burton followed this logic, relating that fair children could be engendered with the help of images, but that body temperature (and therefore temperament) resulted from the body's own processes of generation.[48]

Such statements both conceded and bounded female power and debated whether inheritance was the most powerful agent of bodily composition and mental disposition. George Best had speculated that Africans' color would not change even if they went to cold climates, and had hypothesized that an infection in the skin's pigment was passed along in their seeds of generation. Burton similarly insisted that wetnurses' influence on children was "non-necessary, remote, outward, adventitious, or accidentall," insufficient to alter what was engendered before birth. Heylyn scoffed at the idea, however, that human seed could generate different-looking people; those who concluded "the generatiue seed of the *Africans* to bee blacke" were "foolish." Any tortured learning that asserted a hereditary difference between Africans and others was inferior to the scriptural exegesis about a curse placed on Ham, Noah's cursed lineage. "Naturall Philosophie" had nothing to say about Africans' appearance, Heylyn maintained, which was due only to "Gods peculiar will and ordinance." Ralegh also questioned whether color (or size) indicated a significant difference in animals or people. If it did, "then were the *Negro's* . . . not men, but some kinde of strange beastes," a proposition he thought ridiculous.[49]

Bulwer disagreed and offered other explanations. Africans' darkness was due neither to the sun nor to a curse, but to at least one of three causes. First was "the inward use of certaine waters," an environmental cause more subtle than exposure to a tropical sun. Second was "by the power and efficacy of imagination, which produceth effects in the conception." (This cause reinforced Bulwer's suspicion of female imagination.) Third, dark skin might result from the gradual application of pigments, which "first by Art acquired, might be evidently maintained by generation." The second cause might influence the third: hereditary darkness resulted first from "an artificiall device" and was later "induced by imagination" when adults looked at and desired one another. Despite the excuses he gave for Indians' painting (as protection from cold), Bulwer offered none for Africans.[50]

As different explanations for pigmentation vied with one another, the debate tended to combine environmental and inherited factors. Explaining pygmies, Bulwer argued that if African heat could make animals' bodies contract, "why not also men?" But this explanation did not suggest that the sun operated on each generation; an idea of acquired characteristics underlay this and other hypotheses. Other commentators agreed that Africans were dark because they inherited bodily differences. John Josselyn, for instance, suggested that Africans had two layers of skin whereas Europeans had one, the upper a tawny color, the lower a dark azure, which together appeared black. Josselyn's explanation implied that this skin was inherited, though he did not try to explain its origins. What was important to him, and to other colonists, was a way to stress continuity of corporeal form. This had motivated Best to argue for inherited African characteristics; it helped reassure colonizers that entering a different climate would not change them. African lineage was a special case, but debates about it showed that, if they wished, the English might ponder its applicability to themselves and others.[51]

Discourse on nature helped the English imagine themselves as a powerful people who would triumph over climatic perils in North America and the Caribbean. Because they were fecund, they had population to spare for overseas settlement; because America could not transform them physically, colonists would retain English strengths abroad. They would, as Hariot's image foretold, stand on more land overseas, demonstrating their physical and political prowess. Like faith in technical ingenuity and military power, faith in bodily integrity was integral to English colonization.

Possession of transmarine territory required adequate dispersal of inhabitants to discourage competing claimants. Richard Grenville thus promised one of Elizabeth's advisers that Virginia would be "possessed and peopled" for the queen. A 1606 petition to Parliament restated this point to gain more support for the Jamestown colony than had been the case with Roanoke: "neither is it sufficient to set foot in a Countrie but to possesse and howld it, in defence of an invading force." John White believed that England should pay attention to the command in Genesis to "be fruitful, multiply," and spread proper understanding and worship of God over the earth. Robert Johnson claimed that English people had "kept and posssessed" Virginia because of their earlier discovery and because "their seede" and "of[f]-spring" had persisted there.[52]

The precise number of English people needed to make a colony a success was unknown. Some schemes still assumed a golden age scenario of plenty without work (or workers), while others hoped that, like Spaniards, the English could use Indian labor. A 1623 piece on the briefly revived efforts to colonize Guiana reported that settlers need "take no paines nor labour" because "the Indians both house them, worke for them, bringe them victualls, and theire Commodities for a small reward and price, either of some Iron worke or glasse beades." But this vision was fading, as the author admitted; if restrictions on English tobacco imports (which favored Virginia and Bermuda) were loosened, both Indians and "our owne countrie people" would grow tobacco.[53]

The English colonies therefore needed thousands of settlers rather than hundreds of specialized workers, as in Frobisher's mining camp. Though estimates of the numbers of colonists may seem low by later standards, the increase was nevertheless a significant shift. Daniel Tucker, an early governor of the Bermudas, estimated in 1616 that the islands were "sufficient to sustayne 4 or 5 thousand men, if we had cattle" to haul goods and clear land. The authorities in Massachusetts decided in 1633 to settle a plantation "at Agawam (beinge the best place in the lande for tillage & Cattle) least a enemy findinge it voyde should possesse & take it from vs." In this way, the English feared other Europeans as they feared natives: as rivals who could steal their accomplishments and benefit from their misfortunes.[54]

Not all natives were competitors; without good technology and large populations, they were less threatening. This assumption partly compensated the disappointment of the English at not finding dense native populations that intensively used nature and could therefore provide trade goods, labor, and tribute, as had been the case for the

Spanish. By the late 1500s, drawing on French reports about North America as well as the English voyages of reconnaissance there, the English concluded that they would be dealing with scattered "wild" people. Hayes and Carleill stressed that North America had weak and dispersed natives (no real military obstacle), though the lack of native cities would mean a lack of important economic centers to conquer and exploit. A Scottish commentator on the plantation planned for Cape Breton assured backers that the natives lacked "multitude, power, or airte [technology] to harm vs."[55]

Calculations of the size of Indian populations often functioned as military intelligence. When Ralph Lane reported as many as seven hundred Indians around Roanoke, he was both boasting about the region's populousness and registering some apprehension about being outnumbered. In this way, estimates of Indian population assumed that people were the real strength of a state, either to fight or to work. William Strachey referred to "the Inhabitants" around Payankatank, though he usually singled out the fighting men as the key to native populations. In fact, many estimates of the size of native towns listed only the number of warriors. Robert Evelin calculated Indians in the northern part of Virginia according to the numbers of bowmen, as Ferdinando Gorges did for New England in 1658.[56]

If the native population was small and scattered, this was perhaps evidence that America was not kind to living things. Indeed, commentators had a sense that America was raw, only superficially altered by human art. Spanish accounts of America had stressed, for instance, that its plants had shallow roots; Nicolás Monardes wrote that Spanish trees brought to the Indies had to be shallowly planted. The English repeated this belief throughout the seventeenth century. Josselyn said that as concerned "all *Indian* Trees and plants, their Roots are but of small depth, and so they must be set" or they would die. He also stated that New England's plants had "a more masculine quality," perhaps based on the long-standing belief that the Indies were hotter than the old world.[57]

People as well as trees were shallowly planted. Bacon contended that America had flooded since the Deluge, while the old world dried out and enjoyed more human cultivation. Hence America's population was thinner and more primitive than that of the old world, its land in a state of unfulfilled fertility. Strachey argued that Virginia's coastal land was only recently formed. The "Mould" or topsoil of the earth was shallow and lacked stones and pebbles, Strachey contended, "which must proceed through want of Tyme." Even the coastal natives "are conceaved not to haue inhabited here below, much more [than] 300. years." This boded ill for Virginia colonists, who would scrabble in thin, stony soil for a crop, with little useful assistance or advice from the residents, who were themselves relative newcomers to the region. Strachey hoped better of the up-county, which he thought must be older, more fertile, and rich in minerals because there "hath bene sufficient tyme for digestion."[58]

On rich soil or poor, colonists had to put themselves to work. Critics of Edward Hayes's 1592 proposal to set up trade with Indians pointed out that North America was unlikely to have commodities that the English could simply buy from the natives or scrape from the earth's surface. Northern America was neither desert nor Iberian cornucopia but, like Ireland, temperate and fertile in the normal way, with an agricultural base "that [will] bring forthe, butt yearely riches & that with Labour." This raised the question yet again of who would provide the labor, in the absence of peasants like the Irish. In response to these questions, Hayes revised his expectations and admitted in 1608 that the continental ventures would have to plant settlers, which should be done "in places temperat and well agreeing with our constitutions."[59]

Such places remained unknown. Some information could be gleaned from Spanish sources. George Wateson, who had been imprisoned in Spain in the 1590s, wrote a tract on cures for diseases "in remote Regions" which could prevent "Mortalitie incident in Forraine Attempts of the English Nation." Wateson studied diseases that killed the English in the southern latitudes Spain had colonized. In contrast, Hayes and Carleill concluded, "Cosmographers" were unfamiliar with the northern parts of the North American continent; only after the "Chrystyan Inhabitants" had watched and received information from "natife inhabitants" would it be known. Their statement conceded that the natives, however backward, were still the best informants, in the absence of information from other Europeans. This established an uneasy if initially pacific stance toward the natives. Colonizers such as Strachey made clear that harmony with the natives was preferred; "as for supplanting the savages, we have no such intent: our intrusion into their possession shall tend to their great good." English good was the main expectation, however, as colonists realized that sweeping away the natives would destroy vital information and assistance.[60]

The English regarded natives, above all, as measures of the land's habitability. Exploration of the Arctic had set this pattern, with commentators such as George Best and Edward Fenton referring to the Inuit as "country people," meaning native to the place and thus good informants about their country. John Brereton attested to "the holsomnesse and temperature of this Climat" in New England by arguing that the native people had "a perfect constitution of body, active strong, healthfull, and very wittie." And, indeed, the settlers found "the agreeing of this Climat with" them. Brereton's comments also relayed that the Indians were taller than the English, as John Smith noted of the Susquehannock; it was possible that America would similarly nourish the English, but they might in the meantime be puny compared to Indians. The natives also showed settlers how to use the land. When the Pilgrims scouted a place for their plantation, they looked for land that was "fit for the Plow, and [had] some signes where the *Indians* had formerly planted their corne." The Pilgrims also observed that the natives lived "where victuall is easiliest to be got" and would "not willingly drinke, but at a spring head," nonverbal evidence as to the best place for human settlement on and use of the land.[61]

Indian testimony also shaped English comprehension of the natural world the colonists were entering. John White (probably assisted by Thomas Hariot) supplied Indian names for the plants and animals he painted at Roanoke. Edward Topsell's early seventeenth-century manuscript "The Fowles of Heaven" retained White's derivation of Algonquian names for the eight "Virginea birds" in the compendium. James Rosier reported that he had "learned the names of divers things of them [the Abenaki]: and when they perceived me to note them downe, they would of themselves, fetch fishes, and fruit bushes, and stand by me to see me write their names." Likewise, William Wood listed Indian placenames in lower New England, including towns and rivers that still have these names.[62]

If colonists respected Indians' knowledge of America, they nonetheless outlined their own duty to bring the land to its climactic stage of cultivation. In this they followed the assumptions of population theory about the optimal distribution of humans over the earth. For instance, colonies required livestock to clear and plow more land, and

to provide manure to increase crop yield, which would sustain a
larger human population. Ralph Lane reported that the area around
Roanoke was "wel peopled and towned, though [only] savagelie" because it lacked "Horses and Kine in some reasonable proportion."
Richard Grenville likewise thought that cattle and more people were
needed to plant Virginia. The Pilgrims commented at several points
that their part of New England lacked people. It was a "pitty" to see
"so many goodly fieldes, & so well seated, with-out men to dresse and
manure the same." "The Countrey wanteth onely industrious men to
imploy," they added, "for it would grieue your hearts" to see "so
many myles together by goodly Riuers vninhabited."[63]

It was not initially clear that English livestock would thrive in
America, but just as Indians indicated how humans might live in
America, so indigenous animals gave clues as to the prospects for
livestock. Some portents were foreboding. John Swan's 1643 treatise
cited Samuel Purchas to argue that American dogs did not bark, that
the wolves were as small as European foxes, and that a creature called
the opossum carried its young about in a fleshy bag. None of this reassured husbandmen who wanted stock of good size and normal function, able to call to their young and nurture them in the expected way.
Even worse, in the Caribbean, large quadrupeds such as deer were
scarce, and likewise European livestock did not do well at the start of
island colonization. Early reports on settlements were therefore keen
to detect anything that might predict successful animal husbandry.
The Virginia Company attested that "the beasts of the Countrie, as
Deere . . . do answere in multitude (people for people considered) to
our proportion of Oxen." This was in contrast to the lack of any
"Cattell" in Mexico when the Spanish had invaded it, and promised a
favorable harmony among land, people, and livestock in the English
colony.[64]

English colonists' importation of livestock and other technology
pointed to their assumption that Indian transformation of nature was
incomplete. Rosier concluded that Norumbega had a "pleasant fertility" not fully utilized by natives. Their "understanding" of the world
around them "it hath pleased God so to darken, as they can neither
discerne, use, or rightly esteeme the unvaluable riches in middest
whereof they live sensually content with the barke and outward
rinds." In the meantime, Indians would be adept at hunting and other
forest activities, perhaps more adept than most colonists. English

coastal settlements and native interior habitations would have a kind of synchrony. Natives could do crude preparation of raw commodities, and serve their own needs as they did so. As an early assessment of the beaver pelt trade in Virginia put it, "the more worne, the better" the skins.[65]

That the English were mostly interested in Indians as indicators of America's usefulness to them was especially apparent when they assumed they needed no advice. The fishing villages in northern New England were established on European techniques. Because fishermen did not want native help, they were quick to assert that, if anything, Indians got in their way. One assessment of Newfoundland reassured those who had heard that there were "no Natives in Newfoundland" that this would be a blessing, for the "poore Fishermen" had "found too many badd neighbours of the Natives almost every fishing season." The report went on to list the incidents of violence between fishermen and Indians.[66]

English attitudes toward Indians remained mixed. Colonists still expected Indians to have considerable aptitude in their use of nature, but were also beginning to list natives' technical deficiencies in systematic ways that had been absent from earlier accounts. Further, English willingness to read Indians' bodies for clues about American nature rather than understand natives' statements about it supported a tendency to regard the new world's inhabitants as incapable of interpreting their surroundings. Above all, even if Indians gave clues about the prospects for English settlement, this did not guarantee that colonists' adapting to the new world was harmless. One 1637 account of New England explained that Indians differed from English people because "soyle, aire, diet, & custome make ofttimes a memorable different in mens natures." The addition of "custome" to this list of Hippocratic variables nudged colonists to consider that they had some control over what would happen to them. Settlers had to discover which behaviors could modify America's effects on English bodies and to imitate Indians carefully and selectively.[67]

The best-known example of this apprehension was over tobacco, King James I's abhorred weed. Some used tobacco's alien status to link it to other forbidden practices, such as atheism and sodomy, as when one of Ralegh's associates was said to dry tobacco on pages torn from a Bible. Gossip about Christopher Marlowe suggested that he thought "all those that love not Tobacco & Boies were fooles." Tobacco was also suspect because it came from a non-European place, and so had physical properties unlikely to suit Europeans. Heylyn concluded that the bodies of English people who indulged in too much tobacco would seem to have degenerated into the "natures of the Barbarians," or Indians ("Anglorum corpora qui huic plantae tantopere indulgent, in Barbarorum naturam degene[r]asse videntur"). The satirist Samuel Rowlands praised English beer at tobacco's expense: "Let the *Indians* pledge you till they sweate, / Giue me the element that drowneth heat." Rowlands's lines assumed that tobacco (ignited with fire) was best suited to people from a hot climate such as much of America was supposed to have.[68]

The English were also uneasy that tobacco induced pagan trances. John Gerard reported that "the priests and inchaunters of the hot countries do take the fume thereof untill they be drunken" and had "visions or illusions." When John Underhill was accused of heresy and adultery in Massachusetts, he unwisely claimed that tobacco gave him mystical visions. While "he was taking a pipe of tobacco," Underhill testified, "the Spirit set home an absolute promise of free grace"; just as the Lord had appeared to Paul, "so he might manifest himself to him [Underhill] as he was taking the moderate use of the creature called tobacco." Visions and visionaries were not welcome in puritan New England, and inducing trances with a heathenish weed was especially appalling. Edward Hoby addressed such critics when he termed "lewd lies" the reports that *there is no story, nor miracle in the holy Bible, which some will not deride, when they bibble, and take Tabacco.* Hoby scoffed at this, saying that smoking was "no mortal sin," though perhaps money spent on tobacco should be given to the poor. From Newfoundland, Robert Hayman protested that "since most *Preachers* of our *Nation,* / *Tobacco* drink with moderation, / Why should I feare of prophanation"? To guarantee moderation, Massachusetts authorities regulated tobacco consumption in a spate of sumptuary laws.[69]

The debate over tobacco showed that the association between idolatry and Indians was being redefined, with some American phenomena redescribed in physical terms only. Gerard's 1597 *Herbal* had pointed out that it was mostly native American men who smoked, raising the question whether tobacco suited female bodies. In 1643 Swan corrected Gerard. Native women "do not use to take *Tobacco,* because they perswade themselves it is too strong for the constitution of their bodies: and yet some women of England use it often, as well as men." This was because natives "may take more at once then any one of us." Moderation, not gender, was significant. Likewise, Vaughan abhorred "that *Indian*-borne, / Blood-tainting *Fume*," but blamed its ill effects on smoking it in "quantity," not on "the *Physickes* quality." Further, not all tobacco was alike. Josselyn observed that, even though New England Indians' tobacco was native to the same climate as the English who lived there, it was nevertheless "*odious to the* English." Tobacco grown by or for the English was better for them.[70]

But even seemingly inoffensive American products were possible dangers, and some, unlike tobacco, could not be avoided. According to Hippocratic theory, water could impart its region-specific qualities to people, perhaps with disastrous consequences. Nor was water the preferred beverage. Beer and cider were safer since they were "cooked" and thus better suited to humans, whose civility demanded food different from the raw stuff that animals consumed. Thirsty colonists were likely, however, to have to drink water in the absence of cultivated grain or fruit. Bradford feared that the Pilgrims would, from "change of air, diet and drinking of water," fall prey to "sore sicknesses and grievous diseases." He later protested, however, against Plymouth's critics, that local water was "wholesome enough to us that can be content therewith."[71]

Similar debate occurred over food. Peter Martyr had speculated that maize was best digested in hot climates, like those the Spanish first encountered. This might explain why hot-tempered Spaniards thrived in the Caribbean and South America, but held little reassurance for English colonizers of the north. Dionyse Settle wrote of the Inuit whom Frobisher kidnapped in 1577 "that as yet, they could not digest oure meate." In his influential *Herball,* Gerard noted that potatoes could be grown in England for domestic consumption, but worried that maize was hard to digest and best suited to animals, "although the barbarous Indians which know no better, are constrained to make a vertue of necessitie." But colonists (especially in the notoriously famished early settlements) found it necessary to eat the local produce. Hariot cautiously stated in 1588 that crops like maize were "fed upon by the naturall inhabitants [of Virginia]: as also by vs during the time of our aboad" there.[72]

Exchanging foodstuffs became a rite of arrival. Early accounts reported that Englishmen "tasted" American meat and bread while offering natives some ship's provisions. If natives could eat English food, that indicated the two peoples' foodstuffs (like their weapons) might be interchangeable. When Samoset strode into Plymouth in March 1621 and introduced himself to the Pilgrims, he also asked for some beer. The Pilgrims' beer had probably run out just after Christmas (when it was rationed), so Samoset instead got "strong water, and bisket, and butter, and cheese, & pudding, and a peece of a mallerd, all which he liked well, and had bin acquainted with such amongst the English." Still, it was possible that Indian digestion was more forgiving. Some colonists believed that it would take some adjustment to live on corn, or to learn which kinds (and what amounts) suited English people and their animals. Pory believed that "to such as are used to it is more heartie and nourishing then our English wheate," but Winthrop reported in 1630 that "a Cowe dyed at Plimmouthe, & a goate at Bosten with eatinge Indian Corne."[73]

Suspicion lingered. Sixty-five years after Gerard's dismissive statement about Indian corn, John Winthrop, Jr., rebutted it in a long letter to Robert Boyle and London's Royal Society. Winthrop assured Boyle in 1662 that the colonists "found by much Experience, that [maize] is wholesome." His emphasis on "much" experience indicated that the ability of the English to live on corn was counterintuitive and that, by taking up a native diet, settlers had made a significant adaptation in their behavior and to local conditions. Some believed that they had to keep eating native foods to maintain bodily adjustment. Henry Woodward commented after an absence from Carolina's interior that the country diet "before almost naturalized now seemed unpleasant."[74]

Those who had to eat American foods were eager to claim their health benefits. An early belief that corn loosened the constitution (speeding the flow of blood and the function of excretory organs) became proverbial. The grain so eased costive English people that it was "held by some Physitians, to be restorative." Winthrop agreed that corn kept the human body "in a fitt temperature" and pointed out that London physicians imported it to prescribe. Few settlers in America ever had the stone, Winthrop observed, and the same was true for "the Indians." Thomas Ashe reported that "American Physicians observe that it breeds good Blood, removes and opens Oppellations and Obstructions." Some insisted that European prejudice against American foodstuffs resulted from products that had suffered transatlantic shipment. In the 1640s, one promoter of the West Indies wrote that island potatoes were fresh, therefore "more pleasing to the pallate, and wholsome to the stomack," than the tubers that arrived in England somewhat worse for several months in a ship's hold.[75]

Thriving English livestock and garden crops were ultimate proof that the land was suited to English people. Francis Higginson delighted in 1630 that the price of milk in Boston had dropped to a penny a quart; he also related that Governor Winthrop (or Mrs. Winthrop) had a garden crop of green peas. By the end of the seventeenth century, it was clear that many old world plants and animals had gone native. Indeed, settlers noted that, in climates with year-round pasture, American cattle were larger than their English cousins. Edward Waterhouse claimed that cattle in Virginia were bigger than in England, and horses "more beautifull and fuller of courage." These discoveries reassured the English that they, like their horses and peas, could flourish in the new world.[76]

Some suffering and adjustment was nonetheless unavoidable. Any American climate could alter the complexion, and warm climates were dreaded as sinks of fevers. Because America was associated with syphilis, colonists worried whether they were doomed to become syphilitic. Josselyn explained that "there are Diseases that are proper to certain climates," as leprosy to Egypt, the sweating sickness to northern Europe, and the "great pox" or syphilis to America. Smith wrote that Virginia colonists had died from "the Indian disease, we call the French Pox [syphilis], which at first being a strange and an unknowne malady, was deadly upon whomsoever it lighted." Still, colonists insisted that some American climates were healthier than England's, a geographic counterpart to the argument that maize was better for the body than wheat. One description of Virginia argued that "fewer die in a yeer there, according to the proportion [of people], then in any place of *England*." In public gatherings in New England, William Wood claimed, "it is strange to heare a man sneeze or cough."[77]

By the 1550s, adaptation to American air, sustenance, and diseases had gained the evocative name of seasoning, a term originally applied to cut wood. Bodies were natural products: settlers' bodies were like trees felled in the old world, shipped like so much lumber to America, then dried, hardened, and proved durable in a new climate. A seasoned colonist was an altered person, a contrast to untested newcomers. Winthrop reported that, in a hot June of 1637, "divers of those who were new come on shore, died in their travel [of] a few miles" toward Boston. In 1656 John Hammond wrote of the Chesapeake that "change of ayre does much alter the state of our bodies," resulting in "some sickness, yet little danger of mortality." John Lawson later insisted that seasoning must take "its own course" because medical intervention prevented full adaptation. Not all physical adaptation was insidious, though a high mortality rate was associated with seasoning in southern colonies.[78]

To defend against perceptions that seasoning was too severe, colonial propaganda relied on one of two arguments: either the region had the most temperate climate the English could wish, or its heat promised wealth to compensate for physical suffering. The former strategy was useful for nearly every colony from Newfoundland to Virginia and Bermuda; the latter was necessary for the Caribbean. In part, this search for optimal climates referred to the concept of a temperate zone and to the old disappointment at being barred from Central and South America. The English continued to reassure themselves that their colonies did not need the hot climates associated with precious metals. One early seventeenth-century commentator stressed that "the spanyards may serve us for an example not to seeke for mines of gold & silver," because "the Climate for that country where the gold is excessive is an ennemy both to man & good husbandry."[79]

New England took pride of place in discussions of American climates. John Smith had done puritans a singular favor by coining the name for their region. Thereafter, settlers in Plymouth and Massachusetts triumphantly asserted that "New" England was the best place for English plantation. Thomas Morton compared New and old Englands, both of which lay in "a golden meane betwixt two extreames: I meane the temperate Zones." Wood was almost obsessive in maintaining that New England agreed with "our *English* bodies" and that "*English* bodies have borne out [the] cold" there. Reports on Newfoundland tried to associate it with this new Englishness. Thomas Temple claimed that Newfoundland was "the best part of America, for all things the Earth or ayre can produce to mans nature or nourishment especially to Northern Bodies, such as England is."[80]

But other regions could also claim a temperate climate, and sneers at New England's winter supported factions in favor of the Chesapeake and Bermuda, or even the West Indies. Edward Waterhouse said that Virginia lay "betweene the extremities of heate and colde." Pory claimed that Bermuda's air was "healthfull and apt for the generation and nourishing of all things" and that "anie [living] thing transported from hence thither . . . yeelds a far greater encrease" than in England. Another promoter of Virginia wrote in 1648 that the northern part of the colony was a veritable "New Albion" situated between "hot and aguish" tidewater Virginia and "cold *New England.*" Lord Baltimore had to give up his first attempt at a Catholic colony, Ferryland in Newfoundland, and "shift to some other warmer climate of this new world," for Ferryland's ground stayed frozen until early May, and its air was "intolerable colde." Baltimore reported that his "house hath been an hospitall all this wynter, of *100.* persons *50.* sick at a tyme." Winthrop continually battled attempts to lure people from Massachusetts to the West Indies, which, "for all their great wealth," depended on New England for "supply of clothes and other necesssaries." By 1643 Winthrop believed that outmigration was slackening because "our people" were now "wiser" about Caribbean hazards. This opinion notwithstanding, when James, earl of Marlborough, proposed to settle newly conquered Jamaica in 1660, he recommended getting people from New England, "from whence there may reasonably be expected good store of men willing to change their climate."[81]

Colonists assured themselves that, not only would America not kill or mutate them, but also it would become more English as it was settled. As Richard Eburne concluded, "It be the people that makes the land English, not the land the people." John Mason contended that Newfoundland was cold only because it was "slenderly peopled, voide of Townes and Cities, whereof Europe is full; the smoake whereof and heate of fires much qualifieth coldnesse of the Aire." John White believed that mosquitoes were lessening around settlements. "It may be the hollownesse of the ground breeds them," White thought, "which the treading of the earth by men and cattle doth remedy in time," another benefit of the English "standing" on more of America. Christopher Levett agreed that clearing land and putting more humans to live on it would disperse mosquitoes. Hammond maintained that "it was only [for] want of such diet as best agreed with our English natures" that so many early settlers had died; lack of "good drinks and wholesome lodgings were the cause of so much sicknesses." In New England, Francis Higginson pointed out that colonists could make the temperature what they wished: "Here we haue plentie of Fire to warme us" because the land had plenty of wood.[82]

Next, colonists in Virginia, Maryland, and Bermuda asserted that colonial climates were, if anything, healthier than England's. New Englanders were keenest to argue that they lived in—and had created—a new Albion that excelled the corrupt one they had left behind. Higginson claimed that "the Temper of the Aire of *New-England* is one speciall thing that commends this place. Experience doth manifest that there is hardly a more healthfull place to be found in the World that agreeth better with our English Bodyes." Indeed, sickly English people found health there, especially those "of a Cold, Melancholy, Flegmatick, Reumaticke temper." Higginson's son was cured of the King's Evil (scrofula) in New England, a significant challenge to the idolatrous remedy (the royal touch) that alleged the divine nature of English monarchy. Arguments that America was healthier than England tended to see Indians and English as comparable. Henry Whitfeld believed that England's "weak and bed-rid dispositions" could learn much from Indians. Thomas Ashe claimed that Carolina's climate had "so serene and excellent a temper, that the Indian Natives prolong their days to the Extremity of Old Age," as well as the "English" and "English Children born there."[83]

Successful procreation and healthy children were key. By stressing the small size of native populations, colonists had begged the question of whether they would end up in the same condition. Rather than implicate their new climates, colonists focused on Indians' sexual customs as reason for their small population. William Strachey echoed the concerns of population theory when he considered the "Probleme in Philosophy, whether variety of women be a furtheraunce or hinderaunce of many Birthes?" Looking at Virginia's natives, he answered with the Christian opinion that the sexual use of "many women deviding the [man's] body, and the Strength thereof, make yt generally vnfitt to the office of Increase." John Bulwer claimed that sodomy "hath spread both into the East and West-*Indies,* insomuch as some Countries have been almost depopulated thereby." To sustain population required desperate measures. One account of Maryland claimed that Indians made war "partly for to get their Women."[84]

These examples were meant to demonstrate that America could be better populated by a more fertile people; the monogamous English could outstrip the Indians in fecundity and consequently in prosperity.

A comment on early seventeenth-century plantations specified that they would need "whole families" to "increase & multiply people." This commentator also said that "to make a fruitfull plantation both marriagge & labour are of equall necessity"; marriage would fill the "desert" of America and would provoke "a man to be a better husband" to the land. An account of New England emphasized that the place provided good air and diet, but the "honour of marriage" would also promote large families.[85]

Early accounts of the colonies took care, therefore, to establish that colonial children were being born to properly married English parents. The first creole infants were in fact conceived elsewhere (in Europe or at sea), and were more significant as measures of their mothers' forbearance than as signs that America fostered English reproduction. Such births were evidence of heroic childbirth, either on shipboard or by women weakened by that ordeal. The Roanoke passengers carried an unweaned child, possibly born at sea, and were shortly joined by Virginia Dare and an infant known only as "Harvie." Bermuda had "a Sonne and Daughter" born to two pairs of early settlers. One month after the Pilgrims arrived at Plymouth, Peregrine was born to William and Susanna White; Mary Allerton bore a dead child about three weeks later. Winthrop reported two births among the women in his 1630 party, but only one bore a living child. When John Cotton emigrated in 1633, his son was "borne in their passage & therefore named Seaborne." Edward Johnson marveled that Englishwomen had "travailed and brought forth upon this depthlesse Ocean in this long Voyage, lively and strong Children yet living."[86]

Such births reinforced the English settlers' sense that they came from a vigorous stock and an expanding population. Colonists certainly did not want to believe that America inhibited their reproduction. They instead insisted that Englishwomen gave birth easily in America and had strong children. In some cases, births offset deaths. The Bermuda account of two births also listed two deaths; replacement, if not growth, was possible. New Englanders often boasted of their birthrate. One observer wrote in the 1640s that "God hath so prospered the climate to us, that our bodies are hailer, and Children there born stronger, wherby our number is exceedingly increased." Johnson extolled "Mrs. Sarah Simmes," who raised ten children, "a certaine signe of the Lords intent to people this vast Wildernesse." Southerners defended their climates in the same way. Hammond boasted of Virginia that "Children increase and thrive so well there," and Ashe said of Carolina that "English Children there born, are commonly strong and lusty." Virginians modified the association between fecund Englishwomen and English sheep to create a new proverb for their colony: "*That hogs and women thrive well amongst them.*"[87]

Because reproduction was final proof that the English were well suited to America, the scarcity of Englishwomen was a concern in all colonies outside New England. The famous 1621 "wives for Virginia" (a shipload of unmarried Englishwomen) represented the first attempt to stock plantations with women. In such circumstances, the value placed on women of childbearing age conspired with their dependent status to make single women into a species of chattel. The demand for Englishwomen in Virginia evidently turned kidnapping into a paying business. Owen Evans was accused in 1618 of encouraging men in Somersetshire to "presse him some maydens to be sent to ye Barmothes and Virginia," offering about a shilling for each captive. One woman, Dorothy Scargill, faced exile if she did not submit to marriage in England; her suitor threatened that if she rejected him, "he wold make her serve him Seaven yeares in Virginia, Seaven yeares in India, and Seaven yeares amongst the Turckes and Infidells." When the earl of Marlborough planned English settlement of Jamaica, he stressed that "care be taken for ye sending over Women for Planters wives," preferably "poore Mayds" (though not from London's prisons) who would have low expectations. Marlborough also noted that "the custome of those parts is to give for; and not require aught with their wives."[88]

The English carefully determined how to plant themselves in America and maximize natural generation of a colonial people. They sought to refute assertions that an alien place would change settlers, stressing that migration and change were part of the human condition, and that there were reasons to expect synchrony between English bodies and American environments. Colonists continued to reassure themselves that America was not so strange after all, that English bodies were remarkably tough, and that corporeal types were not always prey to environmental change. But they were also coming to a conclusion even more heartening to their prospects if chilling in historical perspective: that they were better suited to America than Indians and could supplant them as natives of the new world.

CHAPTER FIVE

Death and the Birth of Race

Colonists countered apprehension over America's power to change their bodies by asserting corporeal affinity with the new world and by interpreting that affinity as a naturalized manifestation of their power over that world. The English also explained their power in legal terms, but references to nature were always the most powerful arguments for English authority because they asserted a cosmic synchrony between the invaders and their new place of abode. In the wake of the 1622 Indian attack in Virginia, the colony's governors made the Chickahominy change their name and their identification; "they were no longer *Chicohomines*, or *Naturalls*, of that place, but *Tossantessars*, and King IAMES his subiects."[1] Increasingly, the English used conceptions of nature as well as of the state to argue that people like the Chickahominy were not as natural to America as the colonists were. Interpretation of Indian reaction to European diseases grounded this claim, and reluctance to intermarry with natives evidenced fear that the weakness of Indian bodies might be passed on generationally. Contact between English and Indian remained gendered, with sexual relations and assistance during epidemics defined as misuse of, respectively, male and female English roles which might compromise bodily integrity. When the English began to articulate this sense of innate corporeal difference, their earlier stress on climatic difference between hemispheres seemed, in comparison, less ominously judgmental.

Discourse on nature in America thus helped generate ideas that moved toward racial definitions. Disease and mortality among the Indians were key to this shift, first evident in the 1640s. Scholars have examined the historical consequences of post-Columbian epidemiology by tracing the sharp decline of the native population that first encountered old world contagious diseases, but they have not paid much attention to contemporary European comprehension of the demographic catastrophe.[2] Explanations eventually posited that the native peoples were less resistant than the English to disease and that their susceptibility was natural to their bodies; further, by the late seventeenth century, the English emphasized that their own physical type thrived and persisted in its original form, despite exposure to an American milieu for more than a generation. By applying discourse on nature to native American attrition and English vigor, colonists defined a new idiom, one which argued that the significant human variation in North America was not due to external environment but instead lay deeper within the bodies of its European and Indian peoples.

The historiography on post-Columbian epidemic disease in America has taken care to explain that Indian mortality was not a racial characteristic. High mortality was the standard effect of a virgin soil epidemic, which occurs in a population without previous contact with (and therefore resistance to) a particular disease; the population is then virgin soil for the disease's firm root and rapid spread. During such an epidemic, most if not all people are infected by a microbe against which they have no resistance. In contrast, during European episodes of diseases such as smallpox, measles, or influenza, the younger members of the population were most affected, generally leaving adults able to nurse their children, fetch water, wood, and food to keep everyone warm and nourished, and especially to go about their usual work, including cultivating crops. If most of the work force was affected by an epidemic (as had been the case during episodes of the plague, and was the case for native Americans after sustained European contact), such tasks were not fulfilled. Individuals could not help one another while sick, so mortality rates increased as people were further weakened by exposure, malnutrition, or dehydration. Livestock might remain untended and crops unharvested, severely affecting the food supply for survivors.[3]

Historians have assumed that early modern Europeans did not comprehend the epidemics in these terms because they lacked an understanding of the microbial basis of contagion. Colonists' scientific ignorance has been made to parallel their imperial innocence; the greatest cause of native affliction and population decline was beyond the comprehension, let alone manipulation, of European invaders. Disease helped build empires in America, with Europeans the supposedly unwitting beneficiaries of disaster. At least, they seemed unwitting until the latter part of the eighteenth century, when General Jeffrey Amherst's suggestion that smallpox be introduced into trading goods meant for natives of the Ohio Valley showed a new and insidious understanding of disease vectors.[4]

But theories of contagion were available to early modern English people, who also comprehended many characteristics of virgin soil epidemics. The English understood migration and infection in ways that might have increased their sympathy for Indian victims of old world diseases, but they did not make the causal connections necessary to a compassionate viewpoint. Their downplaying theories of contagion and letting epidemic-stricken Indian villages struggle on their own show colonists' ultimate reluctance to see any corporeal similarity between themselves and Indians. Moreover, epidemics are not merely natural phenomena; they affect human beings, and wherever two or three human beings are gathered together, there is culture. Indians did not die from natural causes only; their mortality rates were affected by their societies' breakdown during epidemics and by colonists' willingness to leave them to die. The English were beneficiaries of native epidemics, but neither unwitting nor innocent ones.

Like the contemporary English understanding of disease, colonists' attitudes toward marriage and sexual relations with Indians have also been misinterpreted. The scholarly literature has emphasized English settlers' abhorrence of sexual relations with Indians. But while marriage between the two peoples was indeed exceptional, sexual activity was not. Nevertheless, colonial officials deemed any children from these liaisons illegitimate (legally or conceptually), and most were absorbed into native communities, leaving few traces in English records. Unlike children of English and African parents, Anglo-Indian children were supposed to be invisible, to melt into native villages rather than stay in English settlements. The abhorrence of intermarriage grew along with the conviction of the English that Indians were weaker in body. Further, sexual relations with Indians and amalgamation of the two peoples seemed to represent the ultimate engulfment of

Englishness, with English people losing themselves in desire, and their children losing English bodily distinctiveness.[5]

The English gestured toward racial identifications of the body without providing, yet, a theory that explained generational transmission of bodily variants: this was a racial idiom, not a coherent ideology. Examination of early modern theories of nature and the body reveals that racial thinking in North America has a long past, even if its earliest manifestations were less coherent than its nineteenth-century descendant. As scholars of the construction of "whiteness" have pointed out, the dominance of the white body was not a given but a labored creation of racial ideology. As part of this creation, the English reified their colonial dominance by interpreting nature in the new world as a material substructure for their power.[6]

Examination of the denigration of all colonized peoples is necessary to understand racism fully. The English identified themselves in relation to Africans (who they said had bodies so durable as to be scarcely human) and Indians (whose bodies were too delicate). The English were sturdier than Indians, but not so much so that they resembled insensible slaves. By these criteria, colonists situated their bodies at a golden mean, as with concepts of temperate climate and constitution, and thus strengthened their arguments for new world slavery. Theories that Africans' appearance was inherited had shown clearly racial opinions that never had sustained equivalents for Indians. The early racial idiom that the English applied to Indians was nevertheless distinctive in its terms of dispossession, in that it declared that the natives lacked the physical ability to thrive in their own homeland. English colonists used theories of nature to explain their own physical suitability to America, then used that explanation to usurp the very habitat of America's previous natives. It is also significant that this argument about innate superiority and inferiority gradually emerged (like the Spanish debates on natural slavery and on creole bodies in New Spain) from an existing European discourse, rather than from a paradigm shift like the polygenetic hypothesis that heretically posited separate creations of different humans.[7]

Ideas of corporeal fixity emerged even as colonists continued to admire Indians' technical capabilities, including Indian medicine. Native pharmacology was praised as a bona fide technology, neither idolatrous (like demonic magic) nor useless; the English believed that Indian drugs could cure diseases, even in Europeans. But most native medicine was described as herbal and ventriloquized as a position in the debate between herbal Galenists and chemical Paracelsians. Native medicine was thereby categorized in terms that made it appear to be at a low level of technological development. While perhaps originally intended as a compliment, this categorization became less flattering, and was the springboard for subsequent denigration of other native technologies, especially those related to the body. The English created difference by focusing on the body, then moved out from this site into the rest of culture.

All the allure of colonization had to be set against the danger that America would take over English bodies. This seductive hazard appeared in the frontispiece to Ferdinando Gorges's *America Painted to the Life* (1659), which showed an Amazonian America, complete with bow, who both enticed and repelled her audience:

> T'is I, in tempting diuers, for to try
> By sundry meanes, t'obtaine me, caus'de them dye
> And, last discouer'd, undiscouer'd am:
> For, men, to treade my soyle, as yet, are lame.

This America's physical attributes were tempting but could kill or cripple the men who tried to obtain them. By gendering the conquest of America as a struggle for male pleasure—and by denoting the physical dangers of attempted rape—midcentury colonizers complicated the personification of America as sister, a woman who deserved assistance and protection, and exaggerated the threats posed by martial Indians (now female as well as male). The feminized land as warrior-seductress, and by implication the land's seductive female natives, presented a message of *noli me tangere*. To court death, to resist desire, and to survive unlamed were the related tasks of the colonist. The threat that America, last discovered of the four continents, might remain undiscovered was a salient one for English people who at times felt themselves likely to be annihilated by America, either to vanish or else to lose all cultural and physical distinctiveness.[8]

The first stages of English reconnaissance and settlement had emphasized a topographical understanding of America—its different latitudes, its outstanding geographical features, its population density, its natural products—and had envisioned ways to establish similarities between English and Indians. Next, the English began to explain

America as dangerously seductive Amazon. From Ferdinando Gorges, *America Painted to the Life* (London, 1659), frontispiece. Courtesy of the John Carter Brown Library at Brown University.

the specific effects the new world would have on them and the ways in which they differed from native Americans. Two main schools of medicine interpreted the body. The Hippocratic tradition emphasized the correspondence between the elements and the four bodily humors and instructed doctors (and patients) to observe, describe, and treat the symptoms that a diseased body exhibited. The Hippocratic idea that "airs, waters, and places" affected humans had of course profoundly affected early English understanding of the new world. The Galenic tradition also related the elements to the bodily humors. Both Hippocratic and Galenic traditions informed the bulk of medieval and early modern medicine, but the new world presented new opportunities for interpretation. As Nicolás Monardes put it in his 1573 text on medicines from America, he had "fledde verie muche from the olde order and maner of Phisicke."[9]

Medicine was changing, even without the impetus of American discoveries. The most important innovation came from the fifteenth-century doctor Paracelsus, who rejected Aristotelian physiology and emphasized Neoplatonic imagery along with renewed empiricism. Paracelsus advocated a "chemical" or mineral pharmacology, a significant adjustment of the standard Galenic practice, which recommended herbal and animal substances. Debate raged between advocates of Galenism and of Paracelsianism, a controversy well known to literate colonists. Anne Bradstreet chided both sides by telling them that they relied on nature for their medical powers. In Bradstreet's *Tenth Muse,* the element Fire reminded "Ye *Paracelsians,* too in vaine's your skil / In chymestry, unlesse I help you [di]stil," and Earth told "Ye *Galenists,* my Drugs that come from thence / Doe cure your Patients, fill your purse with pence."[10] Exploration of America supplied ammunition to both sides. The new disease of syphilis, for instance, was eventually treated with mercury rather than any of the herbal remedies that had proved less effective. Further, Paracelsus's advocacy of ordinary and even illiterate people, who might better understand local diseases and their cures than academic practitioners, boosted the medical reputation of country people and even natives of foreign lands, such as Indians. Advocates of herbal remedies also used native practice (or their perceptions of it) as evidence for their views, pointing out that most American cures came from plants. Theories about medical remedies joined the English debate over strategies to counterbalance the effects of American climates on colonists' bodies.

By the mid-1600s, settlers denied that mere American birth produced children different from old world children. William Wood maintained that New Englanders' complexion was unchanged from that of their English forebears, and "as it is for the outward complexion, so it is for the inward constitution." He further argued that Virginia's heat (while not as beneficial as New England's cooler climate) turned the English complexion not swarthy "but into Palenesse." Indeed, all colonists took pains to report that their newborns resembled English infants, and especially that they had pinkish skin. George Gardyner said that in New England, "the English people are well-colour'd, and have many children which thrive well in that Countrey." Samuel Wilson wrote that Carolina's creole children "have fresh Sanguine Complexions." These statements stood in contrast to opinions that Indians were dark because they applied pigments to themselves but resembled assertions that Africans were dark owing to natural or providential reasons. Skin coloring had begun to designate internal bodily differences as well as religious, climatic, and cultural variation.[11]

It would have been a logical step for colonists next to speculate on the mechanism that maintained continuity of Englishness. That they did not is somewhat puzzling. It is possible that theories of generation required too much technical expertise, referring, as they did, to a highly theoretical literature as well as specialized knowledge of fields such as microscopy. Settlers instead referred to the belief that the main differences in human bodies were induced during infancy (either by maternal impressions or by midwives' actions); this, rather than climate, could explain fetal deformity among creole children in America.[12]

Anxiety over creole births explains the puritans' suspicion of female Antinomians' effects on conception and delivery of infants in Massachusetts. Three Antinomian women received most of this criticism: Anne Hutchinson (a midwife who bore a child during the controversy), Jane Hawkins (another midwife), and Mary Dyer (another mother). Dyer's child was so monstrous that the Reverend John Cotton ordered its body exhumed for further examination, and verified that it was indeed both prematurely born and badly deformed. Shortly after, Dyer moved away, "and indeed it was time for her to be gone, for it was known, that she used to give young women oil of mandrakes and other stuff to cause conception; and she grew into great suspicion to be a witch." Edward Johnson concluded that Hawkins also, who "had much converse with the Devill," had given "drinkes to other Women to cause them to conceive . . . but sure there were Monsters borne not long after." When Hutchinson miscarried a monstrous child in 1638, Cotton examined it and declared it "to be twenty-seven several lumps of man's seed, without any alteration, or mixture of any thing from the woman, and thereupon gathered, that it might signify her error in denying inherent righteousness." Cotton here relied on the Galenic idea that both male and female seed were needed for proper conception. Because the mother in this case was riddled with error, her seed was too weak to help engender a human child. Cotton, who had earlier defended Hutchinson, avoided the worse conclusion: that Hutchinson's seed was monstrous rather than deficient. And all discussion of Hutchinson, Hawkins, and Dyer avoided speculation that they evidenced the deficiency of English bodies in a foreign climate. Englishwomen were supposed to be able to produce normal children in America.[13]

At this point, however, colonists seemed reluctant to rely on inheritance to explain continuity of type. Indeed, puritan authorities accused the Antinomians of believing that spiritual condition was engendered at conception. John Winthrop dismissed their contention "that there was a seed (viz., Abraham's carnal seed) went along in this, and there was a spirit and life in it, by virtue whereof a man might attain to any sanctification in gifts and graces . . . and yet be damned." A 1648 description of northern Virginia warned new colonists to settle in healthful areas lest "their people die, and their posterity extinguish, and their children inherit sicknes and weaknesse." This advice hedged by not specifying whether children inherited sickness from their parents or from the diseased environment bequeathed to them.[14]

Colonists were more willing to argue that Indians were defined by their lineage, specifically that natives' susceptibility to disease was an innate weakness, more easily explained by internal factors (that presented themselves externally as symptoms of imbalance) than by the climatic theory of disease. The bodily superiority of the English in this regard was evidence that they could become stronger natives of America than Indians. Here, colonists were observing that the Indians suffered from remarkable epidemics. As early as 1555, the English could read Richard Eden's translation of Peter Martyr's statement that the

Indians were dying "of newe and straunge diseases." When the English went to America, they witnessed still other epidemics. How did they explain these phenomena? Scholars have pointed to English statements that Indians' affliction was providential, a supernatural mandate against the natives and in favor of the invaders. This was not an opinion specific to religious radicals. For instance, John Smith concluded that "God had laid this Country open for us, and slaine the most part of the inhabitants by civill warres and a mortall disease" that spared the settlers.[15]

Medical theory offered non-providential explanations of mortality, however, and the English discussed epidemics as material as well as moral events. At first, their comparison of Indian and European constitutions was equivocal. In the sixteenth century, no European would have argued that Indians suffered differently from diseases because they had fundamentally different bodies; all people were monogenetically descended from God's original creations, Adam and Eve. André Thevet wrote that because Indians were composed, like Europeans, of the "foure elementes," they were subject to the same illnesses—those conveyed by "the aire" in a particular location or from "the maner of mens liuing," that is, climate and custom. At first the English agreed with these assessments. One account of the Pequot War (not otherwise a moment of intercultural sympathy) said of the Pequot, "Their outsides say they are men" and "Their correspondency of disposition with us, argueth all to be of the same constitution, & the sons of *Adam*" and of "the same matter, the same mould." Roger Williams concluded in 1643 that "Nature knowes no difference between *Europe* and *Americans* in blood, birth, bodies." As late as 1773, when master's candidates at Harvard debated the question "Were the aborigines of America descended from Abraham?" they found in the affirmative.[16]

But neither did the English admit that epidemics in which Indians died had resulted from Europeans' arrival, and this position started new thinking about Indian bodies. To sustain their opinion, colonists had to reject contemporary conceptualization of diseases as infectious entities. Ancient corpuscular theory influenced some understanding of disease. Not all of early modern corpuscular theory was congruent with that of the modern era; the "germs" of disease were sometimes represented as an individual's predisposing factors, rather than discrete and infectious entities. Nor was corpuscular theory the norm.

Nevertheless, it was available to educated men who wrote about America, such as Thomas Hariot, George Starkey, and Michael Wigglesworth. Religious criticism had constrained Hariot from writing openly about atomism, but Starkey and Wigglesworth both composed treatises on corpuscular theory. If America offered new intellectual vistas, as with the application of Paracelsian medicine to syphilis, it is worth considering why the epidemics among native Americans did not prompt intellectual innovation. Hariot had not only hinted at a corpuscular theory, but also asserted that the epidemic among the Roanok was "so strange, that they neither knew what it was, nor how to cure it . . . A thing specially obserued by vs as also by the naturall inhabitants themselues." More elliptically, when Hariot considered whether an eclipse or comet might have caused the illness, he wrote, "To conclude them from being the speciall causes of so speciall an accident, there are farther reasons then I thinke fit at this present to bee alleadged." Both statements insisted that a new disease had somehow appeared in America, though Hariot's reluctance to support an astral explanation left the question open as to how a "special" illness might appear.[17]

Subsequent colonists' denials that they had conveyed new contagious diseases to America were at odds with the recognition that travelers often carried maladies. Everyone knew that foreigners and returning sailors brought infections into port cities. This was how plague had entered England in 1348; Henry Knighton's account from the 1390s related that the disease had begun (he thought) in India, then traveled to the Near East and Mediterranean, then outward through Europe. Migration across the Atlantic might complete a disease's circumnavigation, as Bacon depicted in *New Atlantis*. The Atlanteans allowed a ship's crew from England to land despite their illness; the people hoped that the English were not "infectious," but the Atlantis messenger who met the English carried a fruit "like an orange" against possible infection.[18]

It was not always clear, however, whether travelers had taken diseases from one place to another or had generated them under the rigors of travel itself. Because ships were so unhealthy, it was hard for the English to believe that travelers' diseases had come from their countries of origin. Richard Ligon concluded that rough ocean travel was itself "killing to some Constitutions." The emergence of typhus in the sixteenth century presented a disease that seemed spontaneously generated by foul conditions. Like prisoners in jail, ships' passengers were closely packed together, enduring filth and an unhealthy diet. When Lady Margaret Wyatt, wife of Governor Sir Francis Wyatt of Virginia, came to that colony in 1623, she reported her ship "so pesterd wth people & goods that we were so full of infection that after a while we saw little but throwing [dead] folkes ouer boord." A Captain Warner who sailed to St. Christopher reported much "sicknesse and Mortallity" which "not above 20 of 200 escaped"; forty of his passengers died. After they disembarked, weakened travelers could infect people in colonial ports. Nathaniel Butler, governor of Bermuda, reported in 1620 of the Newgate convicts who had just arrived that it was "verely thought they infected the shyp, and so have bin the occasion of the losse of many an honest mans life." William Wood asserted that Plymouth's first settlers had a high death rate "not because the Country was unhealthfull, but because their bodies were corrupted with sea-diet."[19]

Careful shipboard regulation and quarantine addressed these problems. The English navy tried to prevent high mortality by making sure that ships were cleaned and had fresh and ample provisions. The council of the Virginia Company likewise attempted to regulate provisions for emigrant ships, which "hath bin the death of a great number of the passingers." Ships' cleanliness was also enforced. On the way to Massachusetts in 1630, the captain of the *Arbella* complained to John Winthrop that the main passenger area was "beastly & noysome," so Winthrop "appointed 4: men" every three days to clean it. Pesthouses at colonial ports prevented sick passengers from infecting others upon landing. Virginia had its first pesthouse at Henrico. After news of "the plague, or pestilent feaver" in the West Indies reached Massachusetts in 1648, ships arriving in Boston were required first to put in at Castle Island for medical inspection.[20]

Travel was bad enough, but its risks intensified in warm zones or places associated with particular diseases. Simply being in an adverse climate was thought to make a traveler ill; he or she did not need to encounter the natives of such a place to contract illness. According to Gabriel Archer, the Virginia fleet, which in summer 1609 took a route through the Tropic of Cancer, was especially unhealthy; "by the fervent heat and loomes [sea?] breezes, many of our men fell sicke of the Calenture," or heat-induced fever. Governor John Harvey reported in 1630 that because one ship to Virginia had been delayed in Cape

Verde, "the heate of this climate brought a generall sickness, amonge our people, through our Shipp." A New England ship forced to put in at the Azores found that "the extremity of the heate there, & the continuall rayne, brought sicknesse vpon them." Reports like these could discourage investment in colonial ventures. The Virginia Company was quick to refute Archer's claim that his southern route had induced ship fevers. Ligon also stressed uncertainty about patterns of transmission. A recent epidemic in Barbados might have occurred because "diseases grow at sea . . . and those diseases prove contagious." It was equally likely, however, that the malady was caused "by the distempers of the people of the Iland," especially men who took improper diet and strong drink. That ten men died for every woman supported the second theory, as men were "the greater deboystes [debauched]."[21]

In other instances, people involved in colonization insisted that settlers' epidemics were introduced from outside. Harvey's assessment had hinted at this; John West's was explicit. West worried in 1636 that "much imputation undeservedly lyeth upon the Countrye by the Merchants crime," meaning merchants "whoe soe pester theire ships with passengers, that through throng and noysomenes they bring noe lesse then an infection among us wch is soe easily to be distinguished from any cause in the malignitye of the clymate." In the same year, Edward, Viscount Wimbledon, worried that England's points of embarkation might become infected with the ultimate epidemic, plague. Wimbledon feared that people who had traveled from London to join Governor Harvey's ship to Virginia would "bring that ill" to Portsmouth, "which thanks bee to god as yet wee are cleare of." It is possible that association between congested populations and infection made it difficult for the English to believe that some diseases might thrive in North America and the Caribbean, which lacked dense urban centers, as William Vaughan had pointed out. Colonies were supposed to cure these ills by spreading people out and offering them better material conditions, such as abundant food. One discussion of how colonies might ease the plight of the urban poor conceded that the poor "in their misery are subject to divers diseases & often spread them from among themselves into better Famylies & houses & so are the cause of great mortalityes."[22]

Syphilis remained one of the most puzzling diseases and one that revealed important English attitudes toward America and native Americans. Syphilis was explained in two competing ways: as being indigenous to certain environments or acquired by certain illicit behaviors. It was associated with America, and sometimes explained as a product of its environment. Monardes had called it as "familiare" to Indians as "Measelles" was to Europeans. Indeed, many accounts made it seem as if the disease pooled and festered in every Indian body there. Ligon, describing how old Indian women on Barbados made beer from poisonous cassava (which they chewed, spat out, then fermented), concluded that they could do so because they were syphilitic. The women killed the poison of the raw cassava because their mouths contained homeopathic poisons from "severall poxes, (a disease common amongst them, though they have many and the best cures for it)." Robert Child believed that syphilis was not confined to America's people; "other creatures are infected with it, so that even *Dogs* dye of that disease in our *Northerne Plantations*, perhaps catching this infection, by mingling with *Indian dogs*."[23]

But syphilis was also explained in moral terms, as a disease one caught from particular practices, not a particular climate. (The English tended to associate immorality with a hot climate anyway, thereby combining several forms of xenophobia.) Cannibalism was often believed to be a way to get the disease. Edward Daunce observed that the new world "*Canibals*" had the disease, but knew how to cure it with native guaiacum, a wood that was "a most present remedie for the disease." Syphilis was also thought to thrive among southern Europeans, whose Catholicism and proximity to Islam made them nearly as suspect as America's pagans. Daunce agreed with the commonplace that the French who invaded Italy in the late 1500s got syphilis by eating corpses. Some observers who tried to explain syphilis crammed together their fears of everything and everyone foreign rather than specifying paths of infection, and threw in references to other diseases for good measure. Richard Hakluyt related that American sassafras cured diseased "frenchemen" in Florida. Martin Pring reported that Norumbega had much sassafras for the "French Poxe" as well as for plague. George Gardyner sarcastically noted that some settlers in Virginia had contracted "Country Duties, which they originally caught of the *Indians,* and the cure is the same they use in *England* for the French Pox." Gardyner's observation, which jumbled together English and Indians, England and France, showed that place-specificity could become too broad to retain meaning.[24]

Gardyner's remark reveals the emerging belief in medical specifics—remedies specific to certain diseases, wherever and however contracted. At first, Europeans trained in medicine had preferred a climatic theory of diseases and remedies. But a burgeoning market in foreign *materia medica* complicated the picture, and chemical remedies introduced items that were less tied to specific locations than were herbs. Furthermore, doctors believed that some drugs might be stronger if they came from hot climates. One authority warned that guaiacum from South America might "in hote and dry complexions" be "very hurtfull, because of the heate and dryth of the Country where it groweth." Conversely, a late sixteenth-century prescription for headache recommended "zedoria" (zedoary, a spicy East Indian root), although not that from "our gardens but beyond the seas." Moreover, English people who went abroad might develop tastes or tolerances for foreign materials. Such was the case with Hariot, who, like several Englishmen of his time, quickly took to tobacco. Hariot also dosed himself with South American sarsaparilla, and was finicky, making a note to himself in the early 1600s to "ask my Apothecary whether there be any good sarsaperilla yet." European bodies were now connected to American and Asian plants, which weakened place-specific thinking about disease and the body.[25]

The new universalized conception of diseases gave America increased significance as a source of medicaments, and not just for new world maladies. (Assertions that maize "loosened" Europeans' bodies was part of this tendency.) The Paracelsian Hermanus, who thought the guaiacum of hot climates would be a "hurtfull" cure for syphilitic Europeans, wanted to promote the use of mercury instead, thus replacing a remedy specific to a disease's native climate with one that was universal in its occurrence. Hermanus nevertheless recommended guaiacum for many maladies associated with internal cooling of the body, such as melancholy, migraine, epilepsy, and female infertility. The connection between malaria and cinchona was the best example of a specific, one often repeated in the medical literature and almost universally accepted by the eighteenth century. Some doctors touted other American products as specifics. This was how one doctor justified the use of "Bermudas Berries" for the green sickness, a pining disorder among girls and young women, probably caused by anemia. "The greatest Cures wrought in the World," the Bermuda berry advocate claimed, "are by the use of Specifical Medicines." The American berries could cure other conditions, but their main therapeutic function was to treat young women in Europe for a malady completely unrelated to an American environment. The idea of a specific was not always this precise, however. Robert Child wrote that "where any *Endemicall* or *National disease* reigneth, there God hath also planted a *specifique* for it." This statement combined the idea of the geographic specificity of diseases with the idea of having specific cures for them. One physician's late seventeenth-century commonplace book stated that while cinchona was the "only specifick I know in nature," its existence was enough to confound those who "thinke that every Countrey produced sufficient for the diseases of its own growth."[26]

Shift toward medical specifics represented the adjustment of ideas about place-specific diseases. Commentators had two new options: either to emphasize that diseases were entities (or at least conditions) not tied to certain regions, or to insist that diseases could spontaneously emerge wherever certain conditions permitted. Neither option solved the question of where the diseases in post-Columbian America came from. What is significant, however, is that the English eschewed the explanation that they might themselves have introduced these diseases. Not only did they ignore theories of contagion when they puzzled over epidemics in the colonies, but also they ignored natives' statements that the arrival of the English brought illness and death— the absurd transcription that appeared in Hariot's and John Lawson's writings. Their statements were not unique. Roger Williams wrote that the Narragansett sachem Canonicus had reproached the English "for sending the plague amongst them." Williams replied that only God could send disease, as to "the English for lying, stealing, idleness and uncleanness, (the natives' epidemical sins)." This exchange indicated that both Indians and English had recently suffered from the same disease (thus Canonicus's suspicions). Although Williams emphasized bodily suffering as punishment of sin, he made the more prejudicial point that the sins that sometimes characterized the English were "epidemical" to the natives. In this way, a fallen condition was represented as natural to Indians, comparable to the illnesses that then followed.[27]

Colonists took an interest in native belief about illness when it flattered them, that is, as a supernatural manifestation of their power. But here colonists had to balance carefully their belief in God's favor with their reluctance to accept native idolatry. Ralph Lane recounted that one Roanok allied with the English had told the others that the English "being dead men were able to doe them more hurt, then now we coulde do being alive." This opinion seemed believable because some Indians were stricken by illness without contact with a living, breathing English person. Lane then concluded that "many of them holde opinion, that wee be dead men returned into the worlde againe, and that we doe not remayne dead but for a certaine time, and that then we returne againe." Given colonists' perpetually shaky grasp of native languages, it is unlikely that Lane knew what "many" Indians thought. He had instead solicited information about their supposed supernatural capabilities from a Roanok influenced by the English. Further, Lane's story echoed English insistence that Indians believed in metempsychosis, pagan error about the soul's relation to the body. That the English dwelled on this point rather than on the possibility of their introducing infection should warn us of their propensity to ventriloquize natives.[28]

The English were indeed uncertain how diseases were transmitted. Uncertainty marked Gabriel Archer's 1607 relation of the Indians in Virginia's interior. He began somewhat elliptically by noting native attitudes about property, stating first that "the people steale any thing comes neare them," but also that "they abide not [their wives] to be toucht before their face"; bodies were private but things were not. Archer then concluded that "the great diseaze," syphilis, "reignes in the men generally, full fraught with noodes b[l]otches and pulpable apparances in their forheades." But the order in which Archer had presented these observations of Indians, and his combining views of property with manifestation of disease, showed that he could not determine how the natives got—or passed on—syphilis. His assertion that only native men had external symptoms of the disease pointed to his uncertainty whether it was unique to one sex, and therefore not transmitted through sexual contact. If the Indians were willing to share everything but their wives, how did most of the men end up with syphilis? Their one adherence to European standards of morality and the law of property seemed inappropriately at odds with the pattern of syphilis among them.[29]

Epidemics in colonial settlements, and the persistent problem of seasoning, reinforced a sense that mortality was a constant hazard in America and could decimate the more fragile settlements. Winthrop related that an English enclave on Delaware Bay was afflicted by

"such sickness and mortality among them as dissolved the plantation." Scotsman William Powrey reported in 1648 "very badd news
from the Barbados" that "about 6000 Christians dyed [of illness]
since I cam from thence." Arguments that the new and old worlds
shared the same diseases were another way to reject the idea of America's golden age. Instead, as William Vaughan maintained, universal
incidence of disease confirmed the fallen nature of the "latter age."
Colonists thus saw epidemics as expected features of American nature, not as recent alterations. This view was consistent with a place-
specific theory of disease (if not with a strict environmentalism, which
might have objected that new diseases could not take root in climates
foreign to them). Environmentalism would in fact influence later interpretations. As John Graunt explained in 1662, an "*Epidemical*"
disease resulted from "alterations" in the climate, while a "*Chron-
ical*" disease came from the climate's underlying nature. But earlier,
the English had contrasted their seasoning against natives' morbidity
in a way sharply at variance with the modern understanding of epidemiology and eventually conducive to a racial construction of bodily
difference.[30]

The extent to which the English maintained an environmental view
of disease seemed sometimes a denial of the demographic disaster taking place in the native populations. When Squanto, ally of the Pilgrims at Plymouth, died from what seems to have been a European
malady, William Bradford categorized it as "an Indian fever" in the
same way that John Smith had assumed the "syphilis" at Jamestown
had to be an Indian disease. Likewise, Samuel Argall, governor of Virginia, wrote in the summer of 1617 of "a great mortality among
us, [though] far greater among the Indians and a morrain [murrain]
amongst the deer." His statement not only compared Indian and English illness (emphasizing a higher native death rate) but also associated it with Virginia's environment in his reference to the deer. Winthrop reported in 1634 that smallpox had "gone as farr as any Indian
plantation was knowne to the west" of Boston and, in 1638, that
"much sickness of pox and fevers spread through the country," which
might have indicated that infection was moving outward from the
English settlements. But Winthrop added that the 1638 disease "was
to the east and south also," to emphasize that the settlements were affected at the same time. He also wrote in 1647 of an "Epidemicall
sicknesse" that ran through "Indians & Englishe, Frenche &

Dutche," as if the epidemic were a local pest that did not differentiate among the bodies it found in New England.[31]

From this assumption—that diseases in America were indigenous to America, part of the new world's atmosphere of contagion—settlers drew the conclusion that Indians' suffering resulted from some constitutional failing: either inadequate seasoning to their climate or a fateful propensity within their bodies. It took some time for the latter view to prevail; climatic reasoning remained the norm, possibly because it required less technical expertise to articulate.

It was perhaps because settlers feared that America was diseased and Indians prone to illness that they were reluctant to call themselves "Indians" or even "natives" of America. Colonists would use the first designation to describe whites' cultural rather than physical adaptations, and all settlers were remarkably chary of the second term. Even creoles were instead called "English" or "inhabitants." When John Josselyn explained that respiratory disorders were "maladies that the Natives are often troubled with," his next phrase specified that by "Natives" he meant "*Indians.*" John Hammond likewise referred to Virginia's "Inhabitants," distinguishing them from newly arrived or visiting "strangers." Another commentator stated his intention to describe Virginia's "inhabitants, both Planters and Natives." The Reverend John Clayton worried in 1687 over the "gross mistakes" that arose from referring to "the English or Whites born" in Virginia as "*Natives.*" "Take notice," he instructed his readers, "that when I speak of the natives in general that I mean only the Indians."[32]

Reluctance to describe settlers as natives was perhaps due to the fact that the English word "native" had originally meant a person born into bondage, a legal meaning it carried into the eighteenth century and perhaps beyond. Legal distinctions between conquered and conqueror that had begun in 1066 might have initiated this equation of aboriginal status and subjugated condition. Also, "native" implied misuse of nature rather than refinement of it, as John Bulwer emphasized when he said that the corporeal monstrosities he discussed he would "rather call Native then Naturall." It is also likely that, within Britain's imperial context, the word "native" was acquiring new and denigrating resonance. Further, colonists' continued suspicions about the American climate doubtless provided them with a reason not to want to be native to their adopted place; rather than genuine native affinity to a degenerate physical world, superficial adaptation or seasoning seemed safer. An English identity extended across colonies and was rooted in the body.[33]

To distance themselves from the natives, the English argued that America's main effects on them were cultural, not physical. Such contentions allowed them to deny that the climate would make them inferior to people in Europe. Robert Hayman published his *Quodlibets* in 1628 to prove that living in Newfoundland had not altered his mental capabilities or physical health. The very title of the book, meaning "wherever," indicated that human artifice was not seriously affected by place. Hayman's work included translations of Rabelais's poetry and John Owen's epigrams, as well as verses he had composed. Observing that Newfoundland had the same "foure Elements" as anywhere else, Hayman asked, "What man made of these foure would not liue there"? The region had no plague, smallpox, or ague, was "cleane, and warme"; even its winter was "short, wholesome, constant, cleare." And Hayman wrote especially to "testifie that the Aire there is not so dull, or maleuolent, but that if better wits were transplanted thither, neither the summers heat would dilate them, nor the Winters cold benumme them." Later generations of creoles were less confident and more careful to qualify America's effects on them. Cotton Mather deplored how the climate could culturally "Indianize" the English by making them lazy and disrespectful of authority, though presumably not changed in body. In 1728 William Byrd complained that Virginia's back-country "Lubbers" were sallow and diseased—all owing to sloth, a *behavior* that made them resemble Indians. As Mather's and Byrd's distaste over "Indianized" settlers showed, colonists would not explain any permanent adaptation as their becoming Indians, which would make them, paradoxically, not proper inhabitants of America but inferior ones.[34]

Colonists were reaching two conclusions. First, the English body not only did well in America but also was not essentially changed by its seasoning. Creoles retained the old world stamp despite having been born in places such as Jamestown or Boston. Second, a contrast between the vigor of the English and the mortality among the natives revealed the physical inferiority of the latter group in the place of their nativity. This point would not itself prove racial inferiority; Indians might have been suited to some hypothetical non-American climate. But the English contended that Indians were ill adapted to any region. This subsequent argument relied in part on reports that Indians did not thrive in Europe, as was true of many American creatures. José de Acosta wrote that European plants grew better in America than Indian plants did in the old world; John Parkinson agreed that delicate specimens such as the Virginia "daffodil" did not transfer well to England. It seemed to Europeans that living things from the new world did less well in the old world as the specimens moved up the chain of being. Plants were relatively successful, animals much less so, and humans even less.[35] Spanish accounts of Indians who perished once they crossed the Atlantic had initiated suspicion about native ability to survive the strains of migration. Shakespeare's comment that Londoners were quick to "lay out ten [doits] to see a dead Indian" coldly identified a lasting English fascination with Indianness and mortality. Accounts of the brief life in England of Indians (including Frobisher's kidnapped Inuit and the Christianized Pocahontas) seemed to conclude the matter, though morbid fascination with the Indian body in Europe continued. When four supposed Iroquois envoys visited London in 1710 and one of the four fell ill, the news made the *Tatler*.[36]

Nor was Europe the only non-American climate deemed unsuited to Indians. Speculation that Indians had originated outside America suggested that they had earlier proved unfit in other places. Scholarship on the debate over Indian origins has focused on the meanings of the differing origins; as significant is the simple, overarching assumption that Indians had to come from somewhere else. Reports that native Americans were not just recently arrived but continually wandering supplied more evidence of their unsettled nature. Dionyse Settle reported in 1577 that Inuit houses had "no signe of footway, or any thing else troden, whiche is one of the chiefest tokens of habitation." An early seventeenth-century letter on the conversion of Indians noted that they must have inhabited America "since our Saviour and his Apostles times, and not before . . . there being no seignes or footsteps found amonst them or any monuments of older habitation as there is with us." (The terms "footway" and "footsteps" reiterated opinion that to stand on land was to claim it.) In the early 1700s, John Lawson echoed the by then received opinion that Indians were "a shifting, wandring People" and not the "Ancient Dwellers of the New-World."[37]

These conjectures implied that Indian cultures lacked the dignity of an ancient history and the right to be considered truly indigenous. Like American trees and plants, Indians had shallow roots. At its most cynical, the view of migration could posit a long sequence of new world invasions, one that awarded definitive settlement to the final arrivals: European colonists.

The English thus used the hypothesis that Indians' ancestors were migrants to reinforce their suspicions of native corporeal intransigence. Indians had had to move at least once before they came to the new world, were still unable to thrive in the Americas, and did not do well if transplanted to places such as Europe. In contrast, most English bodies transplanted well to America, and all that survived remained true to type. These beliefs were not universal, but a good measure of their persuasiveness was the fact that they appeared even in the writings of colonists who were sympathetic to Indians and who otherwise argued for native hardiness. Roger Williams admitted that Indians had a "terrible" fear of "infectious disease"; yet his insistence that the natives could "perfectly and speedily cure" syphilis, and that they had their own words for "Pox" and "plague" showed his assumption that Indians had known these diseases before English arrival. Later, Robert Beverley claimed sympathy with Virginia Indians—he stated, "I am an *Indian*" because of his plain style of writing—but downplayed the impact of disease on the natives. Beverley wrote that the Indians were "not subject to many Diseases," though he later admitted that they were somehow "almost wasted" away.[38]

The conclusion, well developed by the late seventeenth century, was that creoles were at least as natural to America as the Indians. Hence Beverley's narcissistic assumption of native identity. Indeed, colonists seemed to believe themselves more natural than the aborigines, as if English bodies had always been meant to be planted in Virginia and Plymouth. To colonists, the fact that another group had arrived first meant little if the earlier people had bodies that never truly acclimatized.

The English were, in part, cushioning themselves against accusations that they were even more effective than Spaniards in killing off Indians. The worst instances of Anglo-Indian warfare in fact showed that the English had much in common with Spaniards. In New England alone, warfare probably accounted for the deaths of one quarter of the native population. Virginia's governor John Harvey was careful to phrase his intention to make war against Indians as an effort "to remove them farr from us," if not far below their original numbers. The Pequot War was an occasion for open gloating about the precipitous drop in native population. One account said that the Pequot were "now seeming nothing but a name, for not lesse than 700. are slaine or taken prisoners." This was preferable to the situation in Virginia, where in the 1622 Indian attack settlers had been killed by "Barbarians" rather than the reverse. Peter Heylyn recounted that, because the English and French had fought so long and hard over St. Christopher, "the *Natives* were destroyed." Josselyn admitted relish over native annihilation when he wrote that "the *Pequots* were destroyed by the *English*," an overstatement, but one the English believed at the time, and a sign that settlers knew they had played an active part in reducing the native population.[39]

Despite this, colonists preferred to emphasize forms of attrition that did not result from English warfare. This was true even of Josselyn, who remarked that first "plague" and then "small pox" had created "great Mortality" among New England's Indians, but this was before "the *English* came into the Countrey." After these epidemics, the Massachusett were reduced to one hundredth of their original number. To sharpen the contrast between themselves and the Spanish, the English continued to examine the West Indies, where variables that affected the native population could be isolated and causes of extirpation determined. Gorges cited Las Casas' diatribe against Spanish cruelty at several points in his 1659 work on America. Gorges's grandson concluded that the death of natives in the English colonies was due more to disease, famine, and Indian-versus-Indian wars than to any English actions; "that is best done," Gorges concluded, "that GOD doth himselfe."[40]

By this point the English were observing not just that some native populations had been decimated by disease, but that many of them continued to be. Settlers began to predict a pattern of demise among the natives that paralleled their replacement by creoles. Edward Johnson, for instance, specified that the epidemic that had beset New England's natives before the settlement at Plymouth had swept away "whole Families, but chiefly yong Men and Children, the very seeds of increase." Johnson observed that the Massachusett had once been a "populous Nation, consisting of 30000 able men," but were "now brought to lesse then 300. and in their roome and place of abode" the English had increased from seven individuals to forty-three "churches" of settlers. Edward Winslow reported to Winthrop that the Pequot had sent their "weomen of esteeme and children" to Long

Island (in present-day New York), where they enacted what he thought a macabre show of physical persistence. The Pequot women and children went to Long Island because "as they were there borne and bred[,] there their bones shall be buried and rott in despight of the English." Hammond said of Virginia's high creole birthrate that it would mean the children born there would "in small time become a Nation of themselves sufficient to people the Country." Johnson's, Winslow's, and Hammond's comments fulfilled the logic of Hariot's calculations that the English would spread over and make the best use of American land, while Indians would soon lie under the land, a grisly foundation for the English plantations.[41]

The aversion of the English to physical intimacy with Indians reinforced their emerging desire to differentiate themselves from natives and to situate this difference within the body. Two measures of difference were notable: colonists were reluctant to endorse sexual relations with Indians, and they shunned Indians during epidemics, even though they knew their neglect would increase the natives' mortality rate. Gender distinctions paralleled these different responses, as male pleasure associated with intercultural sex and female charity with service to the sick.

Though scholars have dwelled on settlers' reluctance to marry Indians, sexual contact was not the only possible form of intimacy between English and Indian. The English did indeed have sex, and children, with Indians, but, in contrast, they were almost never willing to nurse Indians who were ill—despite their assertions that they were tougher than natives, less likely to catch illnesses, and presumably better able to care for the sick. John White remarked, for instance, that the plague could clear the land of natives, and no "other but the Natives," for he had seen "the *English* in the heate of the Sicknesse commercing with them without hurt or danger." This observation did not presage the English colonists' definition of themselves as real neighbors—and therefore charitable helpers—of the Indians. English and Indian communities might exist alongside each other but remained separate. White had claimed, after all, that the Indians "invite us to sit downe by them," but not, he seemed to suggest, *with* them.[42]

To a certain extent, the English were consistent in their desire to avoid domestic contact with Indians, in that they were not certain how some diseases were transmitted and so erred on the side of caution. For instance, sexual contact was supposed to be one of the ways to transmit syphilis, yet some infected people—such as children—did not contract the disease through sexual intercourse. Congenital transmission probably infected children, but contemporary observers could not always fix on this specific point of entry and instead worried about all forms of domestic intimacy. William Clowes related in 1579 that in Europe the disease had afflicted "those good poore people that be infected by unwary eating, or drinking, or keeping company." Several decades later in Massachusetts, John Winthrop reported cases of syphilis that resulted from one woman's infection, and impregnation, by her husband. After childbirth, the woman had considerable pain in one breast, which she treated by breast-feeding as many infants as her neighbors could provide. She also suckled her own child, who was nursed by other women as well, who then had sexual relations with their husbands. And so the disease spread to "16: persons men, women & children." Winthrop declared that "none tooke it of them, but by Copulation or sucking"; even those who "did eate & drinke & lodge in bedd with those who were infected, & had sores" did not come down with the disease. Still, Winthrop admitted that colonists had different ideas about the disease, and that the man who had started the trouble was found free of the disease and innocent of adultery, which kept open the questions of how the infection might spread and whether daily contact with a diseased person might communicate it.[43]

Suspicion over the "infectiousness" of sin or heresy made colonists doubly uneasy about domestic intimacy with outsiders. Perhaps for these reasons, there are only two reported instances of colonists giving assistance to Indian communities in the midst of epidemics. The first occurred near Plymouth in the 1620s and the second a decade later in Massachusetts; both involved smallpox, which caused the worst epidemics among North American Indians.

This paucity of assistance is significant because nursing—as well as quarantines, which the English also neglected—might have lowered death rates in virgin soil epidemics. The English were well aware that absence of nursing increased mortality; fear of abandonment, even by family and clergy, had been a grim theme during the Black Death in England. Thomas Niccolls recognized this problem in early Virginia when he declared, "Women are necessary members for the Colonye." Niccolls remarked that, when ill, the "poore Tenants that have nothing dye miserablie through nastines & many dep[ar]te the World in their owne dung for want of help in their sicknes[;] Wherefore for prevention I could wish women might be sent over to serve the Company for that purpose for certayne yeares whether they marry or no." Commenting on Bermuda circa 1622, John Pory noted that one illness had created "the highest degree of weaknes" in colonists. Unable to do anything for themselves, victims depended for their lives on human assistance: "If there were any in company that could minister any releife, they would strayght-wayes recouer, other-ways they died."[44]

Even well-settled areas experienced crises in nursing care. Virginia specified in 1646 that physicians and surgeons could not legally refuse "helpe and assistance to any person or persons in sicknes or extremity." In 1656 Hammond recognized that the Chesapeake's prospective settlers might fear dying alone if they emigrated without any family. He thus recommended that a servant try to find work in a household "where the Mistresse is noted for a good Housewife" so he would "be carefully looked to in his sicknesse (if he chance to fall sick)." In 1667 the town of Providence complained of the burden of care for an elderly resident who could do nothing for herself: "We have bene forced all of us . . . to take our Turns and to Watch with her, day and night least . . . she should perish amongst us." These were all examples in which obligation to the sick stretched beyond the biological family and the household, and showed awareness that denial of charity would mean death for others. In fact, New Englanders' famous good health and long life (compared to the condition of southern colonists), which has been interpreted as the cause of family increase, was just as likely to have been the result of it: having family nearby increased one's prospects for longevity.[45]

Some colonists realized that similar neglect could afflict Indians. Bradford wrote that when the Indians around Windsor (Plymouth's trading house) fell ill of smallpox, they were on the verge of annihilation. Those with the disease had it "in abundance, and for want of bedding and linen and other helps they fall into a lamentable condition as they lie on their hard mats," which adhered to their sores and tore off sections of the skin, leaving them "all of a gore blood, most fearful to behold." Further, "they fell down so generally of this disease as they were in the end not able to help one another, no not to make a fire nor to fetch a little water to drink, nor any to bury the dead." Thus, "though at first [the English] were afraid of the infection," they nevertheless "had compassion of [the Indians], and daily fetched them wood and water and made them fires, got them victuals whilst they lived." None of the English became ill. The same was true in Massachusetts during the winter of 1633, when Winthrop recorded that smallpox brought "great mortalitye" to the Indians. He noted that "it wrought muche with them, that when their owne people forsooke them, yet the Englishe came dayly & ministered to them." Their assistance may have had limited impact. Winthrop had originally written that "many" of the Indians "were cured by suche meanes as they had from vs" but then thought better of the claim and substituted "some" for "many." In fact, nursing would probably not have helped most adults with smallpox, but it might have saved children and those with less virulent infections.[46]

Nursing was a real test of Christian charity. The Pilgrims said as much in their relations of sickness on the voyage to America and in America. Bradford remarked that the first party was much troubled by one sailor "of a lusty, able body" who "would alway be contemning the poor people in their sickness." The man himself later fell ill and died, and was the first person on the *Mayflower* to be buried at sea, the fate he had promised to others. "Thus his curses light on his own head," Bradford concluded, punishment for lack of charity and humility. Bradford later related that pestilence in 1633 killed over twenty people in Plymouth, a toll that included, "after he had much helped others, Samuel Fuller who was their surgeon and physician and had been a great help and comfort unto them." Fuller's ability to comfort was due not only to his medical training but also to his status as a deacon of the church, a man "godly and forward to do good" even when it put him in mortal danger.[47]

To nurse strangers was an even greater demonstration of Christian resolve, especially to minister to pagans, such as Indians. Nursing involved intimate bodily contact that, unlike sex, brought no immediate gratification. As Niccolls's and Hammond's comments on the Chesapeake had indicated, these were tasks usually assigned to women, specifically matrons. Married women's experience with sexual intercourse, childbirth, and child rearing gave them expertise with the human body, and their subordinate role in society made them proper servants of the sick. (When a soldier was "left sick" at Roger Williams's house in 1637, Williams reported, "My wife hath gott him upon his legs.") A nurse had to face tedious and revolting tasks: to stay awake with a patient night and day; to wipe away blood, excrement, vomit, pus. Except in European hospitals in major cities, there were no professionals to undertake such work. Outside a hospital, people had to hope that their relatives, household members, or neighbors would nurse them. Only in rare instances would a doctor extensively touch a patient's body; sustained bodily contact was left to surgeons, midwives, and nurses, who ranked below physicians, in part because of their contact with bodies and their effluvia. Few men would welcome the task of nursing strangers. To nurse Indians would have required either that Englishmen stoop to women's work, or that they allow their womenfolk to enter Indian houses. So it was with a Massachusetts settler aptly named Maverick, who "himselfe his wife & servantes went dayly to them [Indians with smallpox], ministerd to their necessityes, & buried their dead." Winthrop thought Maverick exceptional and said that he (though not his wife and servants) was "worthy of a perpetuall remembrance."[48]

It is possible that many Indians did not trust the English, and would not have wished colonists to enter their villages and dwellings when they were weakened by illness. Why hand the enemy such an opportunity? (After all, the English tried to conceal their own illness—and the reasons for it—from Indians, as when the sick men at Jamestown "hidd this our weakenes carefully.") It is revealing that both the Inuit whom Frobisher kidnapped in 1577 refused English medical treatment. The woman's infant had been injured by an English arrow, and when the crew put a salve and plaster on the wound, the woman licked them away; later, the man, Calichough, refused to be bled. The Inuit might have suspected such attentions as ways to poison a child or bleed dry a captive, but the English resented rejection of their therapies. George Best compared the Inuit woman's licking her child's wound to a dog's behavior; Dr. Edward Dodding called Calichough's attitude toward phlebotomy "uncivilised." Natives near the Jamestown settlement would have had their own reasons to fear English medical practitioners after a surgeon and physician poisoned Indians with doctored sack in 1623, at a meeting that was supposed to negotiate a peace treaty. In 1658 the Narragansett expected the worst of English physic after some settlers requested that colonial leaders "furnish them with poyson to dispatch Onkas" (the Mohegan sachem Uncas).[49]

But Indians did not always fear English medical attention, or at least the English asserted that they did not. Smith said of the Powhatan that "of our Chirurgians they were so conceited, that they beleeved any Plaister would heale any hurt." Roger Williams reported that Indians begged colonists for physic and plasters. Often the English assumed that the natives' desire for such assistance meant that they recognized the superiority of English medical technology. They did not consider that such requests for medicine and bandages were reaffirmations of the native suspicion that the English had brought foreign maladies with them, and might therefore know more about curing them. It is interesting, however, that some colonists believed medications and therapies had to be tailored to Indian bodies. When Roger Williams solicited medical advice from John Winthrop, Jr., he requested something "suitable to these Indian Bodies in way of Purge or Vomit: as allso some drawing plaister."[50]

The English saw shared medicine as a token of alliance, something that could make natives grateful and loyal. When a Pilgrim military band wounded several Narragansett, they apologized and promised that "if they would returne home with vs, our Surgeon should heale them." A man and woman then "went home" with the Englishmen. When Massasoit fell ill, he "sent to Patuxet for some physic," which the Pilgrims dispatched along with a surgeon. After the native leader recovered, he revealed the "plot of the Indians of Massachusetts against us," demonstrating the blessings that charity would bring to the English. In 1634, during the smallpox epidemic at Windsor, Pilgrims' nursing efforts were likewise "kindly taken and thankfully acknowledged of all the Indians that knew or heard of the same."[51]

While it is possible that New Englanders overpraised themselves, exaggerating their willingness to nurse their Indian neighbors, it is nevertheless significant that no other English settlement in the seventeenth century, outside the praying towns that missionaries organized for Christian Indians, praised itself in this way. Indeed, Pilgrims' willingness to be physically close to natives was unusual. When Bradford first met Massasoit, he kissed the sachem's hand and "the King kissed him," gestures not found in Smith's accounts of meeting Powhatan, for instance. Still, even the Pilgrims did not want Indians to live among them for very long. When Samoset "eyther was sicke, or fayned himselfe so," he remained at Plymouth Plantation, though his companions had to leave since the English "dismissed them so soone as we could."[52]

If nursing was a form of intimacy that did not give physical pleasure to the English, sexual contact did. Sexual desire for Indians' bodies thus warred with apprehension over Indians who were or might easily become sick. These contrasting responses were connected, as both addressed the question of whether reactions to disease were sexually reproduced. That is, when colonists defined a contrast between their own and Indians' bodies, they did not explain how such differences might be transmitted generationally. Though they began to consider this question during the seventeenth century (as with their emphasis on the paleness of creole children), the English were not consistently interested in such issues at the start of colonization, when they instead focused on how individual bodies might or might not be altered in new climates. They avoided defining any possibility that alteration could be passed on to their children, perhaps because they wanted to see bodily change as reversible. Again, English speculation about disease defined a racial idiom within discourse on nature and bodies, not a fully developed form of racism.

Reluctance to consider the mechanics of physical inheritance was related to the troubling question of whether Indians and English could—let alone should—breed with each other. The English understood that intermarriage was a common consequence of invasion; soldiers seized native women, and commanders compelled marriages with women of the conquered elite in order to consolidate their power. Indeed, the English were well aware of their historical status as both conquerors and conquered, and as descendants of mixed marriages or concubinage between British peoples and their unwelcome visitors from Rome, Scandinavia, and France. In Shakespeare's *Henry V* (1590), the Duke of Bourbon points out that the English elite were descended from Anglo-French sexual alliances. Since the English had been conquered by the French in 1066, they were in fact "Normans, but bastard Normans, Norman bastards!" Fear that native women would infect conquerors with an inferior culture and language had inspired the 1366 Statutes of Kilkenny in Ireland, which prohibited any sexual union between Irish and English. Elizabethan and Jacobean policies on Ireland tried to uphold this ideal during the era of western colonization, providing a clear precedent for English antipathy to intermarriage with Indians. The earliest laws against sexual contact between Englishmen and Indian women were designed to maintain discipline among English soldiers and avoid giving offense to Indians.

The laws for Roanoke and Jamestown therefore stipulated that rape of Indian women was punishable by death. Sexual alliance with natives continued to be associated with military force. Balthazar Gerbier related a mutiny in one Caribbean expedition in which the ringleader swore that he would "copulate with one off the cheef Indian his Daughter," seizure of a female body completing conquest.[53]

Furthermore, rape and concubinage were part of the Black Legend, evidence of Spanish refusal to recognize the Indians' humanity. Edward Daunce asked, "What greater beastines can there be in man who hath reason . . . to make his issue captiue, whom nature made free? as the *Spaniards* by selling the *Indian* women conceiued with child by them, haue done to their great obliquie." One commentator in the 1640s, protesting that Caribbean heat and plenty were not always *"Enemies to Procreation,"* pointed out that the Spanish had plenty of children in the West Indies, both in "Wedlocke" and "beget on *Negroes* and *Indian* Women." But this author was not recommending concubinage. His examples from the English Caribbean merely stressed that "many *English* Women have two Children at a birth," the point being that virtuous behavior and intracultural marriage would produce and sustain an English colonial population.[54]

In many instances, the English were determining whether any kind of interchange with Indians would compromise Englishness. Even as colonists envisioned their descendants spreading over the new world, they did not imagine that they would blend into Indian communities. Colonists tended instead to believe that they were planting themselves alongside natives, not within their lands and villages. Trade and evangelization might require some amicable contact, but never enough to threaten English civility and Christianity. One pamphlet recommended that settlement "harbour our people so neere to them [the Indians] in the places where they inhabitt that they may teach them by thir christian & civill conuersation how to live." This did not mean setting up house with Indians. John Smith had housed some of the Jamestown settlers temporarily in an unoccupied Indian village, and Governor Francis Wyatt reported in 1621 that planters' homes were "generally open to the Salvages, who wer alwaies friendly fed at their tables, and lodged in their bed-chambers." But this was an exceptional pattern and, after relations deteriorated (leading to the native attack of 1622), was rarely followed except by a very few people in emergency situations. Indeed, other governors of Virginia criticized domestic proximity, even when Indians lived as a minority among the English. Thomas Argall had disapproved of the situation he witnessed among settlers in 1617, when "the Salvages [were] as frequent in their houses as themselves, whereby they were become expert in our armes." Later, Anglo-Virginians would be more willing to be Indians' neighbors, but never housemates. One commentator noted in 1657 that, once the English had settlements, the natives could "live with them and amongst them," though presumably without acquiring the expertise in English military technology that Argall had feared.[55]

New Englanders were also careful not to have too much contact with natives unless they controlled the situation. Winslow claimed that "we entertaine them familiarly in our houses, and they as friendly bestowing their Venison on vs." But the Pilgrims admitted that when "the Inhabitants flocked so thicke vpon every slight occasion amonst vs," they felt "pestered" by and "wearie of" them. Puritans debated whether to "hold some kind of communion with idolaters." Some of their concern was over contact with non-puritans (such as Catholics who passed through Boston), and over the duration of emergency hospitality for people preparing for exile, such as Anne Hutchinson. But these debates indicated a larger concern over contact with alien people, including Indians. Massachusetts authorities thus stated that "strangers" could not be entertained for more than three weeks, and that contact with "idolaters" was limited to four purposes: maintaining peace, trading, "eating and drinking," and giving "succour in distress." Indeed, it is unlikely that a puritan could have lived with Indians except under these conditions.[56]

Reluctance to live in close proximity with Indians, and fear of providing them with firearms meant that many forms of contact—sharing goods and bodies—might raise suspicion. One recalcitrant trader near Plymouth was therefore put under an extremely prohibitive bond of £500 "not to trade any munition with the Indians." Bradford was concerned, however, that the man had already "committed uncleanness with Indian women." The Pilgrim elders suspected the same of Thomas Morton and his Ma–Re men: lewdness with and selling firearms to Indians. Likewise, when eight or nine people accidentally drowned at Long Island in 1642, Winthrop dismissed them as "loose people, who lived by trucking with the Indians." Roger Williams denounced the town of Warwick, where the Indians "keepe and mingle fields with the English," as a "very den of wickednes" that practiced "all kind of whoredoms, idolatries and conjurations." The old fears of idolatry and diabolical magic were brought up to date with the general apprehension of physical proximity and the specific horror of sexual contact. Further, these cases reveal that some Englishmen defied conventions about cultural separation, though at a cost.[57]

English-recognized marriage was the least likely form of intercultural contact. After the celebration of the Pocahontas–John Rolfe marriage, commentary on—let alone encouragement of—intermarriage between Indians and English died out. One of Pocahontas's female attendants (possibly a half-sister) who had gone to England later married an Englishman in Bermuda, at a wedding attended by more than one hundred colonists. Because Bermuda had no native population, the English there were able to regard Anglo-Indian marriage as less threatening than such an event would have been in North America. One of Virginia's governors, Sir Thomas Dale, did indicate that he was willing to marry another of Powhatan's daughters. But Dale did not tell Powhatan that he already had a wife at home; what he proposed was colonial concubinage, not lawful English marriage. In 1634 the Massachusetts government "referd" the matter of "marriage betwixte Englishe & Indeans," their refusal to make any statement on the matter making it impossible for settlers and natives to marry legally. Many English people probably took Indian partners anyway, outside colonial law. But not until the early eighteenth century did some colonists, such as Robert Beverley, recommend intermarriage in order to amalgamate and preserve both peoples.[58]

From an early date, therefore colonial authorities were busy policing the kinds of intercultural contact men and women could have with each other. Officials lightened their burden somewhat by insisting that native women were chaste, not actively soliciting Englishmen's attentions. This challenged earlier statements, especially from Spanish accounts of America, that the natives were polygamous and lascivious. It also ran counter to early modern assumptions that women were more lustful than men. Reversal of these opinions put the blame on Englishmen who had sexual contact with Indian women and reminded Englishwomen that even savages could display virtue. Somewhat like warnings about idolatry, parables of Indian resistance to lust would shame the less resolute English. Thus, reports existed of several native women who had "sold their [animal skin] coats from their backes" to Pilgrim traders then "tyed boughes about them, but with great shamefastnesse (for indeed they are more modest then some of our English women are)." Winthrop related that John Dawe was whipped in 1631 "for solicitinge an indian Sqa to incontinencye, her husband & she complayned of the wronge, & were present at the execution, & very well satisfied." This case pitted Indian chastity against English lust and rebuked colonists. Josselyn found Indian women comely enough to elicit any man's desire, but he emphasized that they were modest in their behavior. He also stressed that Indians suffered from "Misoxenie or hatred to strangers" and that this was true for both sexes, a finer point that again underscored the English need to believe that Indian women did not solicit sexual attention from colonists.[59]

Sexual contact continued, but was usually designated as extra-marital, instances in which one party exploited the vulnerability of another. A number of cases indicate that Englishmen raped Indian women or contemplated rape. Certainly the English assessed Indian women and their bodies in ways that revealed familiarity with them. After the Pequot War, one English officer specified a female captive he "desireth," a "tall one that hath 3 stroakes vpon her stummach thus − ||| +," which hinted that he had already had a good look at her. Another enslaved Pequot who had been beaten with a piece of burning wood complained in late 1637 that she "of all the natives in Boston is used worst." Roger Williams believed her and when he asked "who burnt her and why, she told me, Mr Pen [Boston's beadle, James Penn?] because a fellow lay with her, but she saith, for her part she refused" the sexual overture. In short, she may have been raped and then punished for it.[60]

Eroticization of Indian women was pornographic, describing sex with women who were not wives but tempted men beyond measure— like Gorges's naked Amazon. Thomas Gray's commonplace book of the 1620s and 1630s related that "An Indian Nimphe invited had of yore / Our Puny trauells to a westerne Shore / to view thos naked beauties which one world / by fames great racket to another Hurld." Josselyn appended to his *New Englands Rarities Discovered* an erotic poem on Gypsy women, "not improperly transferred upon the *Indian SQUA.*" He meant this for "Divertisement, or Recreation" and stressed the exotic charms that dark women had for European men: "Whether White or Black [skin] be best . . . The Black in softness doth excel." If Englishmen were not to marry Indian women, they were expected to marry themselves to the American land. One assessment of new world plantations argued that good land deserved more than "an Idle & naughty husband," and that "our people [were] fitt & able to husband it." Nature might help amalgamate English bodies and American land, but colonists had to resist mixing their bloodlines with those of Indians.[61]

Cross-cultural sexual contact was therefore illicit, rarely resulting in marriage and legitimate children. One William Baker of Plymouth reportedly fled to the Mohegan, where he was "turned Indian in nakednes and cutting of haire, and after many whoredomes, is there maried." Baker was said to have had at least one child with an Indian woman before his marriage to another. In Newport, William Coddington recorded that a Thomas Savory had had a son with an Indian woman, a child who "is not black-haired lick the Indean children, but yelow haired as the English." The mother furthered the case of bastardy against Savory by saying of her child, "English man got it." William Wood wrote that the Indians "call him an *English* mans bastard that hath but the appearance of a beard." Thomas Morton recounted that an Indian whose child's eyes were gray "shewed him to us and said they were English mens eies." Morton was less tactful: "I tould the Father, that his sonne was *nan weeteo*, which is a bastard."[62]

Coddington's and Morton's descriptions of Anglo-Indian children recognized an amalgamation of physical characteristics, a blend of English and Indian. If colonists thought their bodies peculiarly superior to disease, they feared that mestizo children might lose this quality. Belief in their physical superiority and concern to transmit their corporeal type to their creole children help make sense of the reluctance of the English to marry Indians. Conversely, as James Axtell has suggested, Indians too may have thought that the English had superior resistance to disease and hence sought to capture and intermarry with settlers. For whites, positive regard for mestizos would enter public discourse only in the era of the American Revolution, following Enlightenment construction of noble savagery and romanticization of the frontier, and taking form when some colonists wished to portray themselves in contrast to old world culture and needed to attract more supporters of the Revolution, both of which desires played to mestizo populations. In the early nineteenth century, prejudice against mestizos reemerged, supported by modern theories of race and racial degeneration.[63]

Early English sexual attitudes toward Africans were, in contrast, more open—meaning more openly exploitative. European assessments of Africans had already emphasized that they were capable of hard labor, nearly immune to pain and physical want, and could be transplanted into any hot climate. Both their supposed physical strength and the fact that they, unlike most Indians, were isolated from their cultures and subordinate to the English made them less threatening as sexual partners. They were slaves, in part, because they were supposed to be transplantable and durable; their slave status and the English assumption that Africans were less prone to diseases than Indians made enslaved black women targets for sexual exploitation.

Englishmen therefore admitted desire for African women and discussed the possibility of Anglo-African children. This tendency was most common in the Caribbean, and more likely to build on Spanish experiences there, rather than to emphasize (as did the Black Legend) disdain of Spanish practices. Richard Ligon candidly admired African women. He praised the beauty of the mistress of a priest on St. Jago, who lived with the woman and their mulatto child. Ligon said the "black mistresse" was "of the greatest beautie and majestie together: that ever I saw in one woman." Ligon also rhapsodized about twin sisters he saw on Barbados, two "Negro Virgins" who would have been fit subjects for Titian. Their presumed virginity notwithstanding, Ligon said they were as "wanton as the soyle that bred them, sweet as the fruites they fed on." They could be both virginal and wanton, to his mind, because in such cases of youthful beauty, "they force, and so commit rapes upon our affections."[64]

Ligon projected on African women, as he might have done with white women, his era's assumptions about aggressive female desire for men, assumptions that in turn masked male sexual aggression. Ligon's emphasis on the exotic nature of the soil and Caribbean produce that nourished slaves underscored colonists' sense that African slaves were products of places that were distinctly un-English, and their resignation to the prospect that most of the islands' adopted natives were African. In any case, the willingness to write pornographically about African women delineated a differently prejudiced conceptualization of their bodies. Any mestizo children they might have were likely to remain under English control, in contrast to Anglo-Indian children, who tended to remain with Indians. Eroticization of African women was like eroticization of American land: both were proto-Lockean fantasies about how male English bodies might create property.

Furthermore, if the English believed Africans to be inhumanly hardy, they would not have to face the task of nursing African invalids. High rates of mortality among slaves in the Caribbean indicated that physical care for these workers was not a priority until the eighteenth century. This meant that intercultural physical intimacy, dominated by sexual activity between Englishmen and women of other cultures, always carried the selfish connotation of masculine pleasure rather than the selfless connotation of nursing, with its implication of charitable, maternal care for others. By gendering intercultural relations, the English naturalized them, presented them as immutable aspects of the power that supported colonialism.[65]

Henry Neville's fictional account of Terra Australis in *The Isle of Pines* (1668) recapitulated the elements of Englishmen's fantasization about their bodies: their mastery over Africans, their tremendous breeding power, and their consequent ability to fill places that suffered population deficit. Neville recounted how one Englishman, George Pine, had, with four women (three English and one African), engendered a population of ten to twelve thousand on a desert island. The five Elizabethan castaways proved to be much like the unmythical rabbits that overran Australia several centuries later, as if Pine, an Adam with multiple Eves, had taken all too seriously the scriptural urging to be fruitful and multiply. (Some readers thought the narrative was true. Henri Justel insisted to a fellow of the Royal Society that such a story might be possible, for "no one doubts that this number of people could be conceived" from one man and four women.) Neville reflected English beliefs about African bodies as durable and African women as lascivious. His narrator, Pine, claims that he slept with the African woman, Philippa, only because she "longed" for him and approached him "with the consent of [the] others." Neville perpetuated as well the idea that Africans suffered less from physical hardship, explaining that while he and his Englishwomen slept, the African woman sat as sentry, she "being less sensible [of fatigue] then the rest." The unstated, colonial foundation of Neville's fantasy was Pine's desert island, clear of the natives that elsewhere were increasingly unwelcome to English colonists.[66]

Even within the static, non-generational terms of bodily comparison that the English laid out before the eighteenth century, the colonial propensity to move toward racial distinctions was striking. The desire to strip Indian bodies of any natural affinity for America was especially foreboding: they were somehow unnatural natives. Observing that Indians suffered from disease and declined in numbers while the English survived and grew in population, settlers congratulated themselves that they seemed to have been the foreordained inhabitants of America all along. Bodily infirmity provided an opening for the English to question earlier positive assessments of Indians according to their ability to manipulate nature. Descriptions of Indian medicine, especially herbs, began to reinforce the conceptualization of natives' propensity to disease while emphasizing the limitations of their technology.

When colonists insisted that Indians had local remedies for many diseases, they elaborated their belief that such maladies had to be native to America and that Indians could, if they wanted, combat them. This contention drew on the argument that each climate contained complexes of natural phenomena (both diseases *and* plants) peculiar to it. If a region had an herbal cure for a disease, this proved that the disease itself was native. The association between syphilis and guaiacum, for example, indicated that the new world was home to many a virulent malady as well as many an exotic cure. Some early commentaries on the epidemics in New Spain were, however, uncertain about the efficacy of native medicine. George Wateson said that natives in Mexico cured erysipelas (an inflammation of the skin) with tobacco juice, but elsewhere described how "whole Kingdomes in both the *Indias* haue been depopulated: which seemeth to insue of the ignorance of the Sauage people, to minister redresse to themselues."[67]

Even as the English recounted that Indians had redress against illness, they framed this information in a way that ultimately stigmatized Indian medical treatments as primitive. Whatever their admiration for native medical understanding, colonists translated it into terms that made sense within Eurocentric debates. Natives were ventriloquized in the controversy over the Paracelsian chemical pharmacology that challenged the Galenic tradition of herbal and animal medicines; most serious discussions of Indian medicine persisted in dragging it into the fray. One text set this pattern. When John Frampton translated Nicolás Monardes's *Dos libros* (1574), the first treatise to describe the use of American herbs and stones as medicines, Frampton choose a new title rather than render the Spanish into English. His *Joyfull Newes out of the Newe Founde World* (1577) paraphrased the "first translation of a definitive work by Paracelsus," *Joyfull News out of Helvetia,* which the Reverend Stephen Bateman (or Batman) published in 1577. Frampton picked a title that would capitalize on readers' interest in Paracelsus, and made new information from America parallel the continental philosopher's tone of prophecy about the old world. That Bateman's title was Frampton's model is reinforced by the prepositions that followed the main title. Though the *English Short Title Catalog* lists several works that begin with the words "joyful news" (with variant spellings), none of them then employ the phrase "out of"; other prepositions—"to," "from," "about," "for"—are used instead. The shared year of publication, the parallel titles, and the suggestion of new information all showed Frampton's wish to use a text on America to support Paracelsian medicine, news of which had just been translated into English.[68]

American phenomena continued to fuel the debate. William Strachey maintained that the Southern Algonquian could cure the pox with a "sedativa medicamenta," so termed by Paracelsus. When he discussed Newfoundland, Vaughan first stated that minerals were the best medicines (such as mercury for syphilis) in his 1600 *Naturall and Artificial Directions for health,* but then chastised the Paracelsians thirty years later in his *Newlanders Cure,* in which he cited Galenic principles to recommend colonists' moderate diet. Over time, interest in American herbs and ascription of Galenic medicine to Indians outweighed Paracelsian interpretations. This increasingly distinguished English narratives from Spanish commentaries, which tended to discuss Indians' use of minerals to maintain health. Europeans who went to the Amazon often remarked on a pale green stone that the natives used for personal ornaments. Accounts by or linked to the Spanish stated that the natives recognized the stones as having medical application. One Irish Catholic who gave information to the Spanish said that the Amazon had "stones which the Indians value greatly as good for treatment of melancholy and troubles of the spleen." In contrast, English accounts described Indians' stones as mere ornaments which, unbeknownst to them, cured diseases related to the spleen, such as melancholy. One account specified that the people along the eastern Amazon "have great store of greene stones, which we call spleene stones," but which the natives used to weigh down their lower lip until it touched the chin. This description pointed to the Indians' custom as deforming the body and denied that it had, for them, any medical intention. Only Hariot disagreed. He described the Roanok as using "*wapeih,* a kinde of earth," for "the cure of sores and woundes." This earth "hath beene found by some of our Phisitions and Chirurgeons" to be "of vertue."[69]

Native herbal pharmacology received more English praise. Hariot believed that, because native Virginians used tobacco, they were "preserued in health, & know not many greeuous diseases where-withall wee in England are oftentimes afflicted." Robert Burton con-curred, praising tobacco as "divine, rare, superexcellent," though as likely to be "hellish, divelish and damned" if taken as an intoxicant rather than "medicinally used." Josselyn rejected the idea that non-English drugs might have no effect on, or would do harm to, Eng-lish bodies. "Custom" explained why the English who lived abroad would be able to benefit from foreign remedies: they became seasoned to them. "The *English* in *New-England,*" Josselyn explained, "take white *Hellebore,* which operates as fairly with them, as with the *Indi-ans*" there. Robert Child noted that America's "*Salvages* do easily cure" syphilis with either guaiacum, sarsaparilla, or sassafras. Thomas Ashe said that Carolina's peoples had "exquisite Knowl-edge" of "Scorbutick, Venereal, and Malignant Distempers," which included syphilis and fevers, the diseases most associated with Amer-ica and supposed to have local cures.[70]

The Indians' knowledge of herbs was the only example by which their views of nature made their way into English learning. John Gerard's *Herball,* for instance, deferentially referred to the "instruc-tions from the people" of America about their plants, and expected Indians to have technical and sophisticated opinions. As one salvo in the ongoing debate over plants' elemental properties (hot or cold, dry or moist), Gerard reported that "the Indian Physitians which for the most part are Emperickes, hold that Pepper is colde" rather than hot in nature. Gerard was influential and widely consulted well into the 1600s; the Society of Apothecaries in London, for example, received a copy of his *Herball* in February 1652/53, which they placed in the "upper window on the East side of the hall," so all members could consult the opinions of the "Indian Physitians" in America.[71]

The apothecaries' interest in Indian medicine was not merely theo-retical; they and others wanted to know what might actually cure the English, whether in London or on the other side of the Atlantic. John Parkinson worried that, although European gardeners grew Virginia's spiderwort, they did not know "whether the Indians have any use thereof." A 1635 relation of Maryland claimed that the colony would provide "many excellent things for Physicke and Surgery, the perfect use of which the *English* cannot yet learne from the Natives," but would do so as settlement progressed. When William Petty composed a late seventeenth-century questionnaire on Indians in Pennsylvania, he wanted to know "how many Simples do they use in Medicine? and how do they apply them?" as well as "what cures can they certainly do?" a question whose phrasing indicated Petty may have wanted medicines for the good of the English. Still, the focus was on herbs, the Paracelsian context for Indian medicine having fallen by the way-side. George Alsop rejoiced that trade from America would keep England healthy by bringing it "Medicinal Drugs." This should encourage "*Paracelsus*" to "knock down his Forge"; "our Physical Collegians of *London* would have no cause then to thunder Fire balls at *Nich. Culpeppers* Dispensatory," which replaced Gerard as the standard herbal.[72]

The English expected that Indians *should* be similar to them in the mastery of new diseases and medicines, and subsequent accounts insisted that native remedies existed and worked. Instead of being unfamiliar with Europeans' diseases, Indians were familiar with some, if not most. Indians' greater mortality was a sign, therefore, of their physical weakness within a climate now common to both groups. Further, any English praise of natives' ingenuity in medicine could also function as a backhanded notation of their bodily inferiority.

But the English allowed Indians to treat their wounds and prescribe for them, a striking indication of their selective trust in the people they had invaded. Morton recounted that an Indian cured an Englishman of a swelling in his hand, but had probably done so "with the helpe of the devill," a rare statement that Indian magic could work on the English, perhaps because its intention was good. Ligon related that Indian women on Barbados were adept at removing the chiggers that burrowed into his feet: "I have had tenne taken out of my feet in a morning." The women performed this task handily, though the insects were so tiny that Ligon could "hardly discern" one placed on a sheet of paper, even if he wore his "spectacles." The contrast first seen in accounts of the Inuit was still in place: America's natives had remarkable skills, so much so that they seemed the work of the devil.[73]

It is suggestive that respect for Indian pharmacology persisted despite English distrust of shamanic magic. That the English could simultaneously hold both beliefs showed their continuing uneasiness over the natives' ability to control natural processes; they wanted them to be able to do this, and to tell colonists how they did so, but settlers still feared that such cleverness could in the end threaten Christians. The English were to some extent adjusting their opinion on some native technology. Rather than assuming, as they tended to do with Indian magic, that pagan medicine could not affect Christians, colonists did believe in its power. In this way, colonists put different kinds of technology into different categories: that which was of no use to civilized Christians (like demonic magic), that which was useful (herbal medicine), and that which was perhaps beyond the capacity of savage peoples (chemical medicine). Wood revealed this thinking when he said that the Indians in New England were adept at using "vegetatives or diabolical charms" to cure wounds. Ventriloquized Galenism or magic: this summed up the choices the English gave to Indian medicine; they had remedies the Europeans categorized as traditional, even ancient, one of them outdated and the other sinful in its devotion to Satan.[74]

Two ideas therefore reinforced each other: that Indians were weak and sickly, and that they sought ways to strengthen themselves, though these strategies were simple rather than learned remedies. As the English planted more people over more territory, they continued to look to Indians for knowledge about living in the new world. But the wary open-mindedness that had characterized military encounter and early settlement would give way increasingly to assumptions that the Indians' numbers would shrink and that their capacity to care for themselves and to learn new skills was limited.

PART THREE

Conquering America, 1640–1676

CHAPTER SIX

How Improvement
Trumped Hybridity

By the middle of the seventeenth century, colonists were beginning to resent any comparison of themselves to Indians and to stress differences more than similarities. One Indian man who pressed "an honest plain Englishe man" to explain the first principles of a commonwealth had the colonist stumped. The settler was "far shorte in the knowledge of suche matters, yet ashamed that an Indian should finde an Englishe man Ignorant of any thinge." So the colonist improvised, stating that a commonwealth was founded on three principles: salt, which preserved meat and fish, "wheras you [Indians] lose muche for want of it, & are sometymes readye to starve"; iron, to "fell Trees, build howses, till our lande &c"; and ships, to "fetche in suche as we need, as Clothe, wine." "Alas (sayth the Indian) then I feare, we shall never be a Common wealth for we can neither make Salt, nor Iron, nor Shippes." This was a barbed interchange, to say the least. The Indian had asked a complex question about politics of someone he might have known was of low status and limited education. The Englishman responded in a way calculated to insult Indians, but which was far from reassuring to his fellow settlers, who were dependent on English ships that carried salt and iron. Settlers might claim the technological achievements of their mother country, but they had not yet replicated all of them in America, where they lived more like Indians than they wanted to admit. If early colonizers had exaggerated their similarity to natives in order to shame the English for their failings, later settlers overemphasized the differences in order to trumpet their civility.[1]

The colonists' struggle to differentiate themselves from Indians helps adjust our view of cultural development in early America. To explicate cultural connections or distinctions between colonists and Indians, scholars have posited four possible early American worlds, two that were hybrid and two characterized by cultural continuity. The two forms of cultural continuity are the European-derived society dominated by English settlers and the "Indian country" that was not in frequent (or any) contact with Europeans. Settlement culture required significant changes in the landscape: land divided into units of property and cleared for long-term use, fences and European-style buildings, domestic livestock, and water-powered mills. Indian country lay outside this Europeanized landscape and represented many natives' desire to retain indigenous methods of hunting, agriculture, and settlement. The hybrid worlds are the Indians' "new world" and the "middle ground." The first is James Merrell's description of the selective adaptations natives made to the pressures on land, exchange networks, and worldviews that European colonization created; the latter is Richard White's reconstruction of the cultural syncretism that characterized native, French, and British interaction in the Ohio Valley.[2] What these four views have failed to explain is that settlement society was itself hybrid, a mixture of material cultures. It is important to understand that this was so and that colonists became eager to cover up the fact. Their coverup was successful; hence the current typology that makes the settlements "English," Indian country "Indian," and the middle ground and the Indians' new world fundamentally non-European.

Hybridity in the settlements needs another look. In the mid-seventeenth century the English were still borrowing from Indians and admired their technical ingenuity. But colonists also stressed differentiation and for the first time began to emphasize abstract sciences such as chemistry to distinguish themselves from Indians. Further, they labeled their efforts to create a new landscape in America as "improvement," thus linking their handiwork to the ideal of improvement in England. In this way, settlers asserted that European-style improvement trumped hybridity, that is, it was a more sophisticated and important activity than their earlier imitation of America's natives.

It is significant that the English were reinterpreting their hybridity as evidence of their peculiar strength within America. Any admission that they were like Indians implied the ultimate goal of supplanting the Indians. This new confidence meant that the reaction to some forms of hybridity was much more relaxed than it had been when the English were a smaller population that feared cultural engulfment and degeneration. For example, Indian "idolatry" now seemed a situational rather than a pervasive threat; the English accepted more native customs as trivial. When Francis Higginson remarked on the hairstyles of native men in Massachusetts, for example, he said they kept "one locke longer then the rest, much like to our Gentlemen, which fashion I thinke came from hence into *England*." Higginson's commentary was a world away from the disgust over paganism that had characterized Samuel Purchas's earlier observation of hybrid coiffures.[3]

Instead, colonists drew attention to their imitation of Indians and were even more eager to describe Indians' imitation of them. Their response resembled the earlier assessments of military technology, an assumption that humans could easily share any technology, now including the peaceful arts. The development of the colonies at mid-century depended on the passage of European tools across frontiers, and of the cultivation of the landscape along European lines, as colonists grew maize and Indians planted apple trees. Tobacco and maize were the first American products to connect the two peoples; these crops were the counterparts of the metal projectiles and firearms that had earlier flowed across frontiers. If the Indians survived invasion by fighting with English weapons, the English stayed alive by living like Indians. Trade in tools and negotiation of a hybrid agriculture were not always peaceful processes, but in both the English granted that they resembled their wary neighbors. They recognized, for instance, that European metal tools entered the existing trade in metal to which the English had first added weapons. By the mid-1600s, everyone along the frontier used metal axes to clear land and get wood for fireplaces and lumber, and nearly everyone used metal hoes to grow maize.

English views of hybridity were always instrumental, motivated to define benefits for the colonizing project. However much they were willing to share their technology with Indians, colonists wanted to control native adaptation. Specifically, they wanted to monitor the entryways of English skills and tools into native societies, and demanded loyalty of the natives who entered English society or created what appeared to be versions of it. Furthermore, the English never exchanged their own people for Indian goods but eagerly did the opposite, which Indians began to resent. The English nearly always saw such trade as a form of slavery or apprenticeship, in which natives were under their control. In contrast, Indians often saw exchanges of goods for people as less coercive, as rituals for proffering gifts for spouses, adopting honorary kin, or receiving ceremonial hostages. The English accepted such terms only if they denoted temporary arrangements, something less than Christian marriage or godparenthood. Once natives discerned colonists' reluctance to keep the flow of people and goods equal on both sides, they began to ask for gifts without assuming that this would cement personal alliances, and they resisted losing people to English slavery. In a related struggle, the English wanted Indian adoption of English materials to lead to full acculturation. That is, each material change had to be a step in the eradication of native cultures rather than adoption of the tools and practices the Indians preferred, according to their own cultural needs.

By the mid-1600s, the continental colonies were taking a path distinct from that of the colonies in the West Indies. To a large extent, the divergence has been attributed to the spread of plantation agriculture in the Caribbean, especially the cultivation of sugar grown by enslaved Africans. But it is equally significant that the islands lacked the native populations that had been crucial to the experience of English people in North America—indeed, necessary to their survival. Island colonists recognized this fact and complained about it. They knew that in the absence of indigenous peoples to instruct them about life in a West Indian climate, they would need, however reluctantly, to look to the Iberians for models of colonization. This emulation led to the eventual reliance on an imported people (Africans) and product (sugar). The importation of an African population therefore concluded the English movement toward Iberian models of colonization, a situation the English believed was necessitated by the absence of native populations in the first place. Together, the continental and island colonies exhibited the tension between English desires: lamenting the lack of Indians whose knowledge could be appropriated, yet denying Anglo-Indian hybridity by labeling it "improvement."

English views of America had shifted in two important ways. Colonists now realized they would have to work in the new world, and they did not expect Indians to help them much. Even warm regions of America were no longer seen as golden lands that guaranteed leisure. Regarding Bermuda, John Pory, like many observers, considered its climate a "continuall spring," but acknowledged that because it lacked the frost that temperate climate crops needed, there were a "few things" that did not reach "maturitie and perfection" there. One commentator found Virginia "healthy and fruitfull" but "not such a Lubberland as the Fiction of the land of Ease, is reported to be, nor such a *Vtopian* as Sr. *Thomas Moore* hath related to be found out." Christopher Levett agreed: "Neither must men thinke that corne doth growe naturally (or on trees,) nor will the *Deare* come when they are called," nor could one "dipp [fish] up in baskets" out of rivers. Survival, let alone profit, required effort.[4]

Colonial survival was now easier because so many more European people were in the western Atlantic and so much of their equipment littered the landscape. Both factors lessened dependence on natives. One dramatic example of these trends came from Greenland, where eight Englishmen employed by the Muscovy Company and led by Edward Pellham were cast away in 1630. They survived nine winter months—in sharp contrast to the Elizabethan castaways on Kodlunarn Island—because a regular European traffic now guaranteed rescue, and in the meantime they had access to materials from a nearby whaling station to build adequate shelter. Pellham insisted that he and his men had recognized their salvaged materials as *property,* things with a European value. He and his men, though desperate for wood to build shelter and to burn for heat, did not touch the whaling "*Shallops* and *Coolers* that were there, which might easily have overthrowne the next yeares voyage, to the great hinderance of the worshipfull Companie, whose servants we being, were every way carefull of their profite." This was an amazing act of self-discipline, one that the men probably hoped would bring them a reward or pension from their employers, to whom Pellham pointedly dedicated his account. In every way, his account reinforced the awareness that the English had to make their way in America without native assistance, using European materials and relying on a European audience for funds and applause. One of John Winthrop, Jr.'s, correspondents used Pellham's case to prophesy the success of English colonies, for it was "possible to liue without bread by gods blessinge vpon the fleshe of beares and foxes etc." Like Henry Neville with his story of the Isle of Pines, Pellham presented a fantasy of colonization, a scenario cleared of actual natives in order to focus on English accomplishments: pro-creation (for Neville's protagonist) and material ingenuity (for Pell-ham).[5]

What Pellham and his companions did not admit was that their scavenging resembled nothing so much as the way America's natives combed through abandoned English settlements and stripped English shipwrecks of usable materials. Colonists had to consider whether such actions might be criminal. In fact, authorities of the companies that invested in America feared that scavengers would damage their property. Regulations for Newfoundland in 1633 specified that when fishing stages needed repair, the men were to "fetch Tymber out of the woods, and not to do it with the ruining or tearing down of other Stages." Wreckage from ships was more difficult to govern, but the English believed that, when property could be proved for a wreck, Europeans should respect it. In 1636, after the ship *Warwick* was "cast away" near Dorchester, Massachusetts, Governor Winthrop ordered that Dorchester's constable "inventory and appraise the rigging" until "some came to demand them, or till further order."[6]

Some of the English were conscious that their actions resembled Indians' strategies of using European products in non-European ways or in combination with Indian goods. John Nicholl's party, castaway on St. Lucia, had to sail a native periagua to the South American mainland, using their garters as rigging and a lance as the yardarm. When Christopher Levett was set ashore by a storm in New England in 1623, he and his men quickly built a shelter using poles "couered with our boates sailes." Their sailcloth dwelling resembled those Bartholomew Gosnold had seen in native villages, a similarity Levett himself recognized when he termed his shelter a "wigwam." Sometimes the English even competed with Indians as scavengers. In 1636 two Englishmen tried to take European "goods that was cast away" on Long Island, but were chased off by Indians who were already busy salvaging the wreck.[7]

In contrast to their perception of the "criminal" act of taking goods from Europeans, the English felt free to take European goods from Indians. Even the most honest of settlers assumed that such manufactured items were not really the property of Indians. When John Guy's men found such things in one native village, they catalogued the European objects and "brought with us" a brass kettle. When the Pilgrims' exploring party found a ship's kettle near a cache of Indian corn, "after much consultation, we concluded to take the Ketle" along with some corn, but promised themselves they would return the kettle and pay for the corn once the owners were discovered. In a more dubious action, they also took away "sundry of the pretiest things" they found in the grave of a European man, perhaps because they assumed that a fellow Christian should not have burial goods. In contrast, they admired a bow from a native man's grave, but "put in the Bow againe and made it vp as it was, and left the rest vntouched, because we thought it would be odious vnto them to ransacke their Sepulchers," just as Ralegh had warned in Guiana several decades earlier. Still, when the men rifled through two Indian houses, they admired their inhabitants' dishes, baskets, and mats, and "some of the best things we tooke away with vs."[8]

Settlers' acquisition of Indian goods reflected power relations. When the English assaulted one Indian village during the Pequot War, their men "gat some booty of kettles, trays, wampom, etc." (The "et cetera" included women and children sold as slaves.) John Underhill likewise commented, after his troops burned abandoned native wigwams and corn, that "many well-wrought mats our soldiers brought from thence, and several delightful baskets." New England Indians used European goods as tribute to the English, perhaps playing to English assumptions that manufactured goods were of more value. When the Narragansett owed tribute to the Bay Company in 1646, they brought "olde kettles" and wampum, and when the colony's authorities refused the payment, they sold the kettles to a Boston brazier, with the money held in escrow should the government relent. Indians in settlements subordinate to the English crafted items for colonists. Thomas Shepard reported that Indians in praying towns made and sold brooms, staves, eel pots, and baskets. Shepard remarked that the natives needed only metal tools and spinning wheels to be fully equipped for English crafts. John Josselyn commented that the New England Indians who lived near English towns sold "delicate sweet dishes" made of birchbark, as well as baskets, mats, and stone tobacco pipes "with Imagerie upon them." This was a considerable change from an earlier era, when fear of native idolatry had rendered such images suspect rather than decorative.[9]

In other ways the English modified a material culture familiar to them by melding it with native technology. By 1610 the houses at Jamestown were described as having "wide and large Country Chimnies in the which it is to be supposed (in such plenty of wood) what fires are maintained," and the exteriors were covered "now (as [with] the Indians) with barkes of Trees, as durable, and as good proofe against stormes and winter weather, as the best Tyle." In Massachusetts, almost all the first colonial houses were described as "wigwams." Colonists depended on native examples and help in building these houses. Some Englishmen who lost their way outside Boston during December 1630 were "entertayned" in the "wigwam" of some natives, one of whom "builte them a wigwam" to shelter them from the cold. Colonists used canoes as well as wigwams. John Smith described how the English seized two canoes (along with bows and arrows) from Indians they suspected might attack, then received another canoe as a gift from the Patuxent. When Winthrop made notes on how to "make a stronge boate good chepe," he recommended using whole logs, "then hollowe them, & fashion them to the forme of the he[ad] of an Indian Canowe." Later in New England it was thought necessary to state that "no *Indian* shall take an English mans *Canooe* without leave" because it was no longer clear that a canoe was an object uniquely of native manufacture and use.[10]

Tobacco also proved a remarkable bridge across the cultures, both as a shared cultivar and as a sign of friendly relations. The highly critical and satirical literature on tobacco during the first two decades of the seventeenth century makes it look, in retrospect, as if the English protested too much. By the first decade of the seventeenth century, pipes were produced and tobacco was smoked on both sides of the Atlantic. On his 1605 voyage to New England, James Rosier's men smoked Abenaki tobacco in pipes they had brought from England. Other Abenaki sent a gift of tobacco to Captain George Waymouth. Conversely, the English began to give tobacco to Indians, imitating native rituals of hospitality and alliance, perhaps before they understood them. Thus Levett gave some sachems *"Tobacco* and *Aqua vitae"* in 1623. This did not mean that settlers always followed native customs. For one thing, Englishwomen smoked what many Indians regarded as a masculine product. Further, the English still did not seem to realize the deeper significance to natives of smoking tobacco as a ritual indicating amity, recognizing only that natives welcomed English gifts of tobacco and would smoke it with the English themselves. When some colonists invited the Nipmuck Penowanyanquis to share tobacco and then murdered him, an English report of their deed expressed no sense of the depth of foul play, which proffered friendship in order to take a life.[11]

Settlers accepted tobacco even if they were hostile toward Indians. When Nicholl's party washed up on St. Lucia, he and his men had to fight natives as well as a host of hardships, but took some comfort in tobacco. After one loud and drenching storm, the men first prayed, then sat all night "by greate fiers, drinking of Tobacco." (Nicholl's statement about *drinking* tobacco reflected how Indians let the smoke wash over them and inhaled it with open mouths, as if imbibing a liquid.) When the Englishmen finally escaped and sailed to the mainland, they ran short of food. At that point, Nicholl wrote, "Tobacco was the chiefe food I found to do me good, and did preserve my lyfe, and those which could take it downe, did keepe strongest, but those which could not take it at all, died first." Tobacco had become food and medicine for English bodies, as well as a solace when they were under attack by the crop's original cultivators.[12]

Nor did religious objections to tobacco prevent its use among puritan migrants. Some Pilgrim men reported that, at their first meeting with Massasoit, the sachem was wearing "a little bagg of Tobacco" on a chain around his neck, "which he dranke and gaue vs to drinke." Later, when a Pilgrim party trekked inland to contact Massasoit, they discovered that the sachem had not expected them and could give them so little to eat that they feared they "should not be able to recover home for want of strength." They made hasty good-byes and staggered back to Plymouth, subsisting on Indian nocake (corn roasted and ground for travel); "when we dranke [water] we eate each a spoonefull of it with a Pipe of Tobacco, in stead of other victuals." When some Massachusett visited Governor Winthrop in early 1631, he gave them some sack to drink "& the men tabacko"; he gave the leaders of some visiting Narragansett "coats and tobacco" in 1642. Apprehension that tobacco might induce pagan trances therefore did not consistently affect puritan response. Indeed, Roger Williams used tobacco to cure his son of "an Epilepsie" in 1660, with no apprehension that it might cause rather than cure fits. And missionaries used tobacco to bribe prospective congregants. When Edward Winslow reported a meeting with some praying Indians in 1647, he said that the English gave the children apples and the men tobacco.[13]

If tobacco provided recreation, amity, and emergency sustenance, maize was the everyday foundation of English colonization. Jamestown's protracted struggle to extract corn from the local Powhatan was only the most violent demonstration that the grain was essential to settlement. If the English in Virginia had dragged their heels at growing their own corn, those in Plymouth were eager to get at the task. The Pilgrims searched for seeds of native crops and for the best place to grow them: they dug up Wampanoag stores of corn and beans, and scouted out a place to live "where there is a great deale of Land cleared, and hath beene planted with Corne three or four yeares agoe." Looking back at the settlement of Plymouth and Massachusetts, William Wood remarked that Indians were "our first instructers for the planting of their Indian corn."[14]

Even in subsequent settlements, colonists referred to natives for methods of raising corn, though they could have learned these techniques from people in the first colonies. An account of early Maryland said that although the colonists had brought corn from the English in Barbados, they relied on the native women to teach them how to make the grain into bread. And even settlers who knew how to grow corn cited native practice. In 1637 Massachusetts Bay bought near the town of Concord "all the planting ground w[hi]ch hath bene formerly planted by the Indians." Edward Williams explained to would-be settlers of southern Virginia that they could plant maize using the "Indian mode," which meant girdling trees to kill them, thereby removing the foliage that occluded sunlight, then planting corn among the defoliated trunks. As Williams indicated, Indian techniques were increasingly transmitted via colonists. Settlers at Saybrook in New England had struggled to grow potatoes (from Bermuda) until "some virginians" who were passing through "taught vs to plant them after another way."[15]

The English and Indians shared methods to catch fish in weirs and use them to fertilize corn crops, the latter a practice that New England Indians had learned from other Europeans, then taught to the English. The English had their own fish weirs, though not all the Englishmen who went to America knew how to make them. Ralph Lane complained that the Roanoke settlers had "no weares for fishe" nor the "skill of the making of them." Instead, the Roanok leader Ensenore had his men set weirs for the English. When the Massachusetts government bought Indian cornfields near Concord, they also purchased the "weire" to catch fish. Other colonists were better equipped. Just south of Plymouth, the Pilgrims built a fish trap. They had the river "shut in with planks, and in the middle with a little door, which slides up and down, and at the sides with trellice work . . . which they can also close with slides." The trapped fish were collected with baskets to fertilize cornfields. In similar fashion, men near Watertown, Massachusetts, built a "weere" across the Charles River in 1632 to catch shad.[16]

In other ways the English were more thoroughly transforming or hybridizing the landscape. As in the early ventures to the Arctic and Newfoundland, it was important to put new areas on "trial" by planting English crops; if the seeds took, the area was suitable for English settlement, even if the settlers had to cultivate indigenous crops as well. The men on a 1603 voyage to Norumbega, for instance, had planted wheat, barley, oats, peas, and other garden seeds. By the end of 1621, the first full year of settlement, Pilgrims listed local commodities as those things they "could experimentally take knowledge of," meaning those known from colonial experience, not just Indian report. Some of the colonial plans to mix American and European plants did not bear fruit. William Strachey maintained that Virginia's native crab apples should take grafts of "our owne appells, of any kynd, Peares and what ells," though no such hybrids emerged until considerably later. At St. Mary's City, however, where the English had settled in half of an Indian town, they planted English seeds in Indian fields which soon produced a mixture of crops: Indian corn, beans, and tobacco, English garden crops and wheat, plus fruit trees and melons.[17]

Colonists were keen to emphasize the mixture of old and new world foods: hybridity prevented degeneration into pure savagery. It was perhaps important that they believed their bodies to be at least partly sustained by European foods, a corporeal link back to England. John Winthrop, Jr., who defended the edibility of corn to Robert Boyle and the Royal Society, also stressed that English people did not, in any case, cultivate or eat corn in the native manner. Winthrop explained that corn crops were hoed by "the Natives, and English also," but English plows increased the yield per worker. Though the English continued to use what they (wrongly) believed to be the "good husbandry of the Indians" in fertilizing corn crops with fish, they also used cattle dung (and fed cornstalks to the cattle after harvest). While beans and squash were planted between rows of corn, again following aboriginal patterns, the English added turnips. Moreover, Williams wrote, they grew small grains after husbandmen had "scrapt or leveld" the "Indian hills" meant for corn. Hybridity continued from the fields into the kitchen, where Englishwomen made corn into bread in ovens, combined with rye or wheat, and with "Leaven or yeast." Like the famished scouting party from Plymouth, colonists also ate nocake, the parched cornmeal that Indians used for travel or war rations. Such a dish was as wild as it could be without being completely raw—by no means a preferred meal for English people. Winthrop therefore emphasized that the English "for Novelty will procure some of this to be made by the Indian Women, and adding Milke, or Sugar, and Water, will make it much more pleasant to be taken." Throughout his essay on "Maiz," Winthrop suggested that colonists used native produce while improving on its methods of production and consumption. Similarly, Williams reported that the English ate samp (cracked corn) either "hot or cold with milke or butter, which are mercies beyond the *Natives* plaine water, and which is a dish exceeding wholesome for the *English* bodies."[18]

English bodies were less likely to benefit from other kinds of hybridity. As with archery, military technology was an uneasy interface between English and Indians. Fortifications, for instance, gave protection from Indians, borrowed from Indian forms, and influenced Indian constructions. Some early forts were not too different from Indian models, constructed, like the Jamestown fort, of logs and situated in places that were elevated or faced a shoreline. Other models were constructed along European lines. Winthrop reported that a house near Providence in thinly settled Rhode Island had been made "musket-proof with two flankers" or fortified projections from the corners of the structure, such as European forts had. John Winthrop, Jr., who had studied fortifications and ordnance in order to help defend his family's colony, drew plans for forts that could be constructed in North America. In the mid-1640s, Boston-area inhabitants resolved to build a new fort on Castle Island in the bay, one of logs rather than earth, and which included four bulwarks. Even as they preferred European fortifications, colonists admired native forts. At the Fort Mystic massacre during the Pequot War, the English marveled that the tough Indian fort they stormed had been built "without mathematicall skill, or use of yron toole."[19]

Oceangoing vessels likewise measured hybridity. Pride in mastery of the sea was part of English identity, and colonists initially made much of the fact that natives lacked comparable ships. The English began to craft seaworthy ships almost as soon as they arrived in America, starting with emergency constructions based on materials from wrecks. This had been true of the five men Frobisher abandoned in 1578, who had used English materials cached on Kodlunarn. Most likely their ship was a pinnace, a small vessel with sails that was a common secondary or emergency vessel. The crew from the Virginia fleet that was shipwrecked in Bermuda built two pinnaces, the tellingly named seventy-ton *Deliverance* and thirty-ton *Patience*. When the *Sea-Nymph* was castaway at the Amazon River in 1630, the crew built a pinnace called the *Guiana*. Winthrop reported that the captain of an English ship "caste ashore" in Newfoundland in 1633 built "a small pinace of the wrecke of his shippe" and tried to sail out before being taken by the French. Another pinnace, the *Make Shift* (made from a wreck at Sable Island), saved its crew but was itself wrecked in 1640.[20]

Other ships built in the colonies were constructed from scratch and made early and eager use of the forests in eastern North America, harbingers of the colonial shipbuilding industry. The first colonial ship was the *Virginia*, made in the northern Popham colony. Winthrop later noted the construction of the *Desire*, a ship of 120 tons, the first to be built in Massachusetts; he recorded that in a transatlantic run of 1640, the *Desire* took only twenty-three days to cross, whereas a ship made in Bristol took twenty-four. Five more ships were completed in 1642, at Boston, Dorchester, and Salem; two more were built in 1647, one for the growing New England trade with the Canaries. These ships gave English people in America increased confidence that they could get around the scattered colonies in a way native peoples could not and were thus relieved of some of their dependence on English ships.[21]

Sailing technology could take hybrid forms in either English or native hands. Native canoes or periaguas could be seaworthy enough for short coastal runs, or even farther in cases of emergency. Nicholl and his party watched the natives on St. Lucia fit sails to their periaguas, using materials salvaged from some Spanish wrecks; they themselves used a periagua to get back and forth to their damaged ship and then sailed it to South America. Indians who lived near Newfoundland had acquired shallops from the Basque and French, and had for decades observed the performance of different kinds of European ships. Pory reported seeing natives in Damaris Cove with French shallops, "which they can manage as well as anie Christian." Natives told the Pilgrims that a full-sized ship could go "many Myles" up Titicut River, which ran into Narraganset Bay, and that a shallop could make the journey to the head of the river, observations that revealed considerable familiarity with different European vessels. Some Englishmen who lost their ship to the French in Newfoundland luckily "fonde some Indians who gave them a Shallop & victualls, & an Indian pilate" and so "arrived safe at Boston." Captain Venner Dobson "bought a Shallop of the Indians" at Cape Sable in Newfoundland in 1647, a boat the Indians had either made or acquired from other Europeans. Like Indians, colonists fitted sails to canoes in order to speed their travels. Roger Williams offered to send for John Winthrop, Jr., in 1649, promising "My Canow with a wind faire would quickly set you here with ease."[22]

But Indians who could sail watercraft undermined colonists' sense of security and technical superiority. After the Powhatan attack on the Virginia settlers in 1622, one man recommended that ten shallops patrol the waters around Chesapeake settlements to "scoure" the area of lurking Indians. Sometimes, as during the buildup to the Pequot War, the English were wise to suspect that Indians in sailing vessels were dangerous. Jonathan Brewster reported a Pequot plot to board and take "our Plymouth Barke." Winthrop recounted a more serious incident when an English crew saw a pinnace which had belonged to John Oldham yet "was full of Indians." The Indians "let slippe & sett vp sayle"; the English pursued, took the pinnace, and "lookinge about they fonde Io: Oldham vnder an old seyne starke naked his head clefte to the braynes, & his handes & leggs cutt as if they had been cuttinge them off." While the murder of Oldham and theft of his pinnace were discrete acts that the English could punish, the alarming native ability to seize and sail an English vessel indicated a challenge to English control of waterways. A Massachusetts law of 1656 therefore forbade sale of any "boat, skiff, or any greater vessell" to an Indian. But Indians could already make their own sailing vessels; Josselyn later reported seeing one "*Indian*-pinnace" that was made like an aboriginal canoe, of sewn birchbark, but with a deck and sails.[23]

The English tended to accept—and praise—Indians' hybridity when they could interpret it as native service or even subservience to colonists. Gender was particularly important to this perception. Indian women's acquisition of European technology and exchanges between Indian and English women were easy to represent positively, perhaps because for the English these actions seemed the antithesis of the military interface between native and colonial men and safer than sexual relations across cultural lines. Thus Roger Williams emphasized that when the Narragansett gave wampum to Governor Winthrop in May 1639, the sachem Miantonomi's wife also provided a "Basket a present" to Winthrop's wife, Margaret. Likewise, "all the women" of the Pequot town of Pawcatuck promised to send "a present of Corne" to Mrs. Winthrop in late 1648. Josselyn commented that some Indian women were "excellent needle" workers and "will milk a cow neatly," both signs of English housewifery that, for colonists, indicated that Indians accepted a civil way of life. The provision of corn and milk, and the painstaking labor of basketry and needlework, emphasized the correct domestic role to which Indian women submitted. Further, such efforts could be seen as forms of colonizing, rendering more of the American landscape increasingly European: milk cows grazing, handy workers bustling, and Indian mothers anglicizing their children.[24]

If Indian women were to be the shock troops of domestication within native villages, Indian men served a parallel function in relation to the land the colonists deemed wilderness. This expectation elaborated the earlier idea that Indians—by clearing land and indicating places fit for human habitation—had provided the foundation for English settlement. John Winthrop, Jr., stated that in Massachusetts, Indians continued to burn land to plant or to attract deer to graze; little by little, Winthrop reported, natives were clearing underbrush from New England. Winthrop also thought that Indians would excel in forest industries such as lumbering and producing pitch and tar. For colonists, "the labour of felling the trees, and cutting out those [pitchy] knots would far exceed the value of the Tarr," but it would be "a good imployment for the Indians," who could do this work for less pay and while unsupervised. Both Massachusetts and Virginia paid Indians who killed wolves. Josselyn described New England's Indians performing other forest tasks, such as gathering chestnuts and bilberries to sell. These plans proposed that Indians stay close to English settlements, in contrast to the fur trade. Before midcentury, therefore, hybridity represented English interests without entirely dismissing the natives' own abilities or demanding that they shun English settlements.[25]

If settlers and natives on the North American continent created hybrid ways to live in the new world, the West Indian colonies followed another model. By the era of English settlement, the native Caribbean population was quite small; on some islands, such as Bermuda and Barbados, it was nonexistent. English colonists learned much less about the Caribbean environment from natives. Furthermore, settlers had to import much more to the West Indies in order to start their economies and keep them going. Plantations, first growing tobacco and then sugar, required investment in imported labor and manufactures that only commercial agriculture could sustain. Only the Caribbean mainland escaped this lack of natives and dependence on non-American resources. Settlers in Guiana and in the later Scottish colony on the Isthmus of Panama had natives to consult, but these continental examples were exceptional. Elsewhere, Caribbean colonists turned back to their earliest rivals, the Iberians, to glean information about tropical environments.

In a sense, the emergence of plantation agriculture was a final renunciation of English faith in the mining ventures that had enriched Spain. English colonial promoters had once hoped that they would not have to create extensive settlements in America, but could plant enclaves of specialized workers, thus rendering quick wealth for investors. When this strategy failed, the English turned to another Iberian model—plantation agriculture—to gain wealth and looked to the tropics they had initially shunned as unsuited to their temperate English bodies. They also had to look to the Spanish, and to their African slaves, as guides to the Caribbean. Spanish and African bodies were by no means supposed to be like those of the English; but, in the absence of West Indian native populations dense enough to provide test cases, the English had no choice but to accept Spaniards and Africans as their guides.

Richard Ligon fretted over the lack of native assistance. He thought that houses on Barbados should be made of brick, which would survive heat and damp better than the wood everyone was desultorily using. Ligon was encouraged when some finely turned clay pots were discovered on the island, but no one could tell whether they had been made by Indians or by the more recently arrived African slaves. Ligon hoped it was the former, because then the natives could teach the English how to find and use local clay to make bricks. Ligon also believed that each colonist would have to bring "from *England*, better remedies for his health": "though some Simples grow there, that are more proper for the bodies of the Natives, than any we can bring from forraigne parts, and no doubt would be so for our bodies too, if wee knew the true use of them; yet wanting that knowledge, we are faine to make use of our own." Ligon also recommended that English physicans come to Barbados to learn the "Simples more proper to cure the diseases that are bred there." The English had received only haphazard assistance from Indians. Ligon wrote that Barbadian settlers ate cassava bread made by "*Indians, whom we trust to make it, because they are best acquainted with it*"; one Indian woman even taught Ligon "the secret" of making cassava pie crust. Such was Ligon's admiration for Indians and their elusive arts that, although he was a rare defender of Africans' intelligence and ingenuity, he maintained the Indians were "apt to learne any thing, sooner then the *Negroes.*"[26]

William Hughes also stressed the lack of native information when he surveyed the expanded West Indian settlements in 1672. He said that "yams" and "guava" were so called by "*Spaniards, Blacks,* or *English.*" Hughes further specified that plantain trees had been thus called by "the *Negroes,* which were heretofore the *Spaniards* slaves." His references to Indians were, in comparison curt and disdainful, in no way allowing that they were reliable guides to the islands. According to Hughes, manioc was used for "Indian Bread," but it was already "familiarly known to most Planters." Although the "Indians" drank the juice of calabashes, Hughes said, "I like it not." Last, "Indian Pock-wood" (guaiacum) was "often used for that Distemper [syphilis]," possibly the least flattering way to associate Indians with medical wisdom. Hughes's account left the distinct impression that the English had learned how to live in the islands because of the advice of the Spanish and their slaves; the Indians, in contrast, had little to recommend but nasty beverages and remedies for syphilis.[27]

The West Indian heat was at least expected to produce rich harvests, but of what? Except for Bermuda, the islands would not offer foodstuffs and other products familiar to English migrants. Unlike on the continent, introduction of European flora and fauna held significant perils—and resulted in some resounding failures even in the temperate Bermudas. There, rats made themselves at home at least as quickly as English people did. Lewis Hughes wrote of the "rattes" that it was "incredible how they did swimme from Iland to Iland and soddainly like an army of men did invade the Ilands from one end to an other." The islands would not produce wheat and, for a time, did not maintain livestock. Ligon reported that cattle bred quickly on Barbados, but then died of mysterious diseases. Horses suffered the same fate, while sheep could not find good pasture. Only goats did well, which proved little about the Caribbean environment, as goats (like rats) seemed to survive anywhere, even on shipboard. Nor were Mediterranean products suited to the tropics; the Caribbean was too hot even for them. As Ligon concluded by the 1650s, wine could not be produced in climates that had no winter, that is, within twenty degrees of the equator.[28]

As compensation, the tropics produced marvelous exotics, tastes of paradise that simultaneously evoked wonder over novelty and longing for the familiar. Ligon's account of Barbados described the island according to the impressions it made on the different senses and the exchange of "pleasures" one experienced in migration to a "Torrid" from a "Temperate" zone. An unabashed epicure, Ligon claimed that wine made from pineapples was "the Nectar which the Gods drunke." Indeed, his description of pineapple was based on almost Sadean sensations, in that the fruit elicited simultaneous pain and pleasure: "Between these two extreams, of sharp and sweet, lies the relish and flaver of all fruits that are excellent." And since the fruit could not be transported to England (and was not yet grown in hothouses there), English people had to ship themselves to the Caribbean to enjoy it—a divine reward for those who felt keenly the lack of wheat bread and beer.[29]

The ultimate symbol of Caribbean exoticism was, of course, sugarcane, neither a traditional English crop nor one known to the natives of America. Instead, the English followed an Iberian model to use African slaves to plant sugar. Ligon called the cane "a stranger," which the English had learned to plant from "strangers."[30] Indeed, because the islands had been thinly populated or even depopulated by the time the English colonized them, a rather high proportion of the people there were strangers. As Chapter 4 indicated, early descriptions of Indian attrition and of African resettlement of the islands had made it seem that enslaved Africans were the closest thing to natives in the

Caribbean. Populating the islands made them less rather than more English. The demography of the islands therefore contrasted to that of the continent: unlike goats and rats, but like horses and cattle, the English languished in the West Indies. The English continued to compare the fates of the different populations moving into and around the islands, thereby distinguishing themselves from Spaniards, Indians, and Africans.

Accounts from the 1655 Cromwellian invasion of the Spanish islands carried forward these comparisons and proposed a model for successful English settlement. Hybrid settlement seemed the best option, a mixture either of Europeans and Indians or Europeans and Africans. According to Henry Whistler, Martinique was successfully "inhabited with Ingons and french: thay liue very comfortably together, and doue mary the one the other very often." And on Jamaica it was the nearly wild Spanish herdsmen and Africans who had held down the colony: "If it were not for theas Cowkillers and the Negors the Spaniyard ware not abell to hould vp his hand against any ennemie." Europeans and Indians tended to be the weak links in these chains, however, despite Cromwell's own assumption (perhaps based on reports of English North America or of New Spain) that "most of the people" of the islands would be Indians. Whistler and General Robert Venables agreed that Indians and Spaniards were sickly, Jamaica's damp climate was "destroying the Natives," and the Spanish were "soe roten with the pox and soe lothegic that they cannot goe 2 mile but they are redie to die." Only Africans seemed to take to the climate, and the English continued to represent them as truly natural to the Caribbean. When some English troops lagged behind the main train in order to carouse, they were alarmed when "there came downe to them 2 of our owne negroes to drink likewise, which some of them spying cried 'the enemy,'" convinced that Africans must be part of the settled population of the troubled Spanish Antilles. If Indians and Spaniards were dying, that left Africans and English to construct a new colonial foundation.[31]

Comparisons between English and African capacities for work were of particular interest. As Balthazar Gerbier put it, English servants could only "doe as much worke (according unto the constitution off theire boddies) as anny off the *Blacks*, called Slaves." Gerbier seemed to be calculating a proportion between constitution and amount of labor, an estimate that shrank the difference between English and Africans. But others assumed that Africans could be subjected to labor that would kill English bodies. In part this contention supported investment in slaves rather than English servants; the former required more capital but were in some ways cheaper, since English servants required more clothing and food. During the 1655 invasion of Jamaica, Whistler claimed that slave children "cost them noething the bringing vp, they goe all ways naked" and were presumably fed by their mothers rather than their masters. Gerbier noted some benefits of hot climates when he argued that slaves "neede no cloathis against the could, nor bedding, nor anny other such chargeable accomodations as a could Clyme doth require." If allowed one day free from plantation work, slaves could grow all their food. Again, the English were defining slaves as settled natives of the islands, able to look out for themselves.[32]

In every way, the English West Indies were hybrids of different material cultures and did not receive a dominant impression of English culture itself. In the absence of strong native populations, people and crops had to be imported. Food was a good measure of this unsettling hybridity. In Barbados, James Parker wrote, the poorer whites had little meat to eat and "noe bread but casader [cassava], a bread I approve not off." When Ligon described the ordinary diet of servants and slaves on Barbados, he made it clear that no one relished what he or she got. Neither the English nor Africans would have eaten much if any maize in their own countries, yet corn was their dietary mainstay in America. The Africans preferred their corn toasted on the cob, while the English servants boiled cornmeal into a pudding wistfully named after the English sailor's dish, lob-lollie. This the slaves hated, greeting the mere sight of it with "*O! O! no more Lob-lob.*"[33] In the Caribbean, coercive adaptation of material cultures increased settlers' unhappiness and reflected little cleverness on the part of planters. This situation contrasted with that on the continent, where competitive jostling of Indian and English technologies elicited greater inventiveness from the English.

Continental settlers were, however, beginning to distance themselves from Indians and their expertise. This effort took two forms: emphasizing technical improvements unique to Europeans and removing natives from the landscape. English colonists' praise of their own technology stressed, for example, that Indians had learned from it to improve their material life. One description of native Virginians said that they had "howses built with stone walls, and one story aboue another, so taught them by those English who escaped the slaughter at *Roanoak*." This group also domesticated their turkeys, in contrast to natives who typically "neither doe empale for deare, nor breed Cattell nor bring vp tame poultry." Bradford maintained that the Wampanoag could plant more corn once "the English have stored them with their [metal] hoes." Morton said of the Wampanoag that "if any thinge bring them to civility, it will be the use of Salte, to have foode in store." But the English preferred absent natives to improved ones. John Winthrop explained that some lost settlers were saved when "God brought them to an empty wigwam, where they founde 2 fires burninge, and wood ready for vse." The English in Winthrop's story used Indian accomplishments without acknowledging the natives' presence: someone had built the wigwam and stacked the firewood, leaving fires burning before they fled the English party's approach.[34]

In part, this new dismissal of Indians reinforced the old association of native acquisition of English technology with chicanery, theft, and violence. This was nearly always the case with firearms. The authorities at Jamestown and Plymouth had first deplored native handiness with gunpowder technology, even fearing that Indians could repair their own firearms and make their own gunpowder. Hence the restrictions on native acquisition of skills related to guns and the tendency to dismiss native creativity as mere aping of English technology. Roger Williams thus reported an Indian term, "Shóttash," meaning shot or ammunition, "a made word from us." One Massachusett man, Anthony, who had gone to Roxbury in order to apprentice himself to a smith, was refused. The smith replied, "I may not teach him my Trade, lest *Indians* learn to make Locks and Guns," meaning the flintlocks and barrels of firearms. As if warning of this prospect, George Alsop's 1666 map of Maryland portrayed a native man shooting with a firearm, a rare exception to the usual figures of native archers that decorated maps. Josselyn agreed that "of late he is a poor *Indian* that is not master of two Guns, which they purchase of the *French*." Indian use of guns seemed always imbued with chicanery. An Indian accused of trying to assassinate the Mohegan leader Uncas later claimed that Uncas had not been shot but simply "cut his arm on the top and underneath with the flint of his Gun, to make men think he had beene shot through with an arrow."[35]

To guard against independent Indian use of their technology, the English insisted that the trade in tools and skills should be part of a civilizing process under their own control. Acculturation was what colonists wanted, not reciprocal or voluntary exchanges. Inserting native acquisition of English technology within this narrative would lessen fears that Indians were appropriating aspects of Englishness by kidnapping English people and stealing English tools. This explanation was especially powerful in—though not unique to—New England, where attempts to Christianize the natives assumed that they must first be brought to civility. As the missionary John Eliot noted in 1649, his native charges needed to overcome their being "uncivilized and unsubdued to labor and order." Henry Whitfeld agreed that Indians must change, "first, unto Civil Society, then to Ecclesiastical." Eliot told some natives who sought baptism that they had first to live in a town and under its government before being admitted to a church. John Hammond asserted that in Virginia, "Indians are in absolute subjection to the English"; they paid tribute to the English and had their kings appointed by them. In Massachusetts, "divers of the *Indians* Children, Boyes and Girles we have received into our houses, who are long since civilized, and in subjection to us, painfull and handy in their businesse." Thomas Shepard made this point before an Indian audience in the 1640s when he told them that there were but two things they lacked: to "know, serve, and pray unto God," and to "labour and work in building, planting, clothing" themselves in a civilized manner.[36]

As William Strachey had done earlier, missionaries distinguished between the Indians who were in contact with English settlers and had adopted some of their technology, and the more remote Indians whose technology seemed alien. Eliot disparaged the natives who had neither "tooles, nor skill, nor heart to fence their grounds," so their corn was spoiled by roaming English cattle. This meant that the natives sought to avoid the English; Eliot believed that they wished to move away from English cattle, not realizing that the natives might also dislike officious advice about fences. He reiterated natives' lack of proper clothing and tools to plant fields in English fashion. But he also revealed that they were beginning to saw planks in order to make fences for their cornfields and orchards. In a similarly backhanded way, Whitfeld noted the progress of English skills among Indians. He said that one sachem had become dissatisfied with the work his people had performed for him; they had given him the traditional gifts of corn, venison, and beaver skins, and made for him twenty rod (about 110 yards) of fence. But this was not as much as they had once done, and the sachem was irritated that they had had their energies drawn toward the English and their missionary efforts.[37]

Missionaries who helped create praying towns wanted to give their potential converts the benefit of the doubt, noting their intelligence and willingness to learn but emphasizing their own guiding role within these hybrid communities. When some natives at Natick made a fort and houses, the missionary accounts both praised them and took some of the credit. Eliot said that an Indian carpenter had worked on his house "with a little direction of some *English.*" The fort had been made "of Whole trees," resembling both aboriginal and colonial methods of fortification. But the houses within were done in "*English* manner," though with very little English help; John Endecott said that an English carpenter had spent only two days with them, but the houses were nonetheless built properly with chimneys (rather than firepits in the center), sawn boards that were mortised, and studs as fasteners which the Indian men had put in very "artificially." When they built a "Meeting-House," it was "a specimen, not only of their singular ingenuity, and dexterity, but also of some industry." The natives also constructed a bridge over the Charles River and intended to build a watermill. Some were also learning to mow grass and survey town lots, and had planted orchards and fenced land "broken up" for cultivation. Yet when the English praised natives for making a fish weir, they seemed unaware that Indians could have done this on their own—quite a contrast with English dependence on Indian fish weirs at Roanoke.[38]

The English criticized Indians not only for the technologies they lacked but also for the nature of the ones they had. Thomas Morton was careful to differentiate between colonists' and Indians' reasons for burning forests. Native fire assisted the wild pursuit of hunting, while English fire protected settlement by clearing ground to prevent Indian fires from spreading. Josselyn allowed that Indians had made some advance by adopting English dogs instead of breeding their own from foxes or wolves, but he claimed that they kept their new animals "in as much subjection as they do their webbs [wives]." This barbarous domestication kept animals and women under brutal rule rather than softening their nature through gentle treatment. In contrast, a "tame" beaver in Boston, which Josselyn had mentioned a page earlier in his account, would roam the streets at will and return home without being called. The domesticated American rodent was a contrast to Indians dogs: the English ruled the beaver by habit and words, not by "subjection."[39]

Nevertheless, even English criticisms of native accomplishments were important registers of Indians' technical ability. Roger Williams noted that natives in New England made houses of squared boards held together with nails. The Indians were not yet comfortable with their new material life, however. After latching the door in an English-style house, the last person then climbed out the chimney. Williams thus remarked on short-term hitches in Indians' new modes of living, though he did not insist on their permanent backwardness. Similarly, Daniel Gookin complained about the drunkenness of some Indians, but to do so he first had to explain that the natives cultivated fruit trees and made their crop into cider, a product that showed a civilized person's ability to transform raw nature. English colonists' perception of natives as similar to themselves (in accomplishments and mistakes) was strengthened by knowledge that colonists were dependent on overseas trade; no one in the seventeenth-century colonies forged their own axes, saws, hoes, and pruning hooks.[40]

The English even quoted Indians in ways that seemed to recognize native criticism of an English way of life. Underhill related that, during the Pequot War, a group of Pequot men insulted his native interpreter. "Being in English clothes, and a gun in his hand," the interpreter "was spied by the islanders, which called out to him, What are you, an Indian or an Englishman?" Winthrop claimed in 1638 that "the Indians, which were in our families, were much frightened with Hobbamock (as they call the devil) appearing to them in divers shapes, and persuading them to forsake the English, and not to come at the [religious] assemblies, nor to learn to read." Whitfeld reported that some natives blamed all their sufferings (especially illness) on departures from their "old heathenish ways"; he said that the Christianized Towanquitick had been shot while sleeping with a "broad headed arrow" to reproach him for "walking with the English." Josselyn noted that three Indians who had seen "Abbamocho" (Winthrop's "Hobbamock") described him as "all wone *Englishman*, clothed with hat and coat, shooes and stockings." Other Indians reviled those in praying towns "for cutting their Haire in a modest manner as the New-English generally doe." The Mohegan sachem Uncas attacked Indians who lived near New London and took away their English clothing and tools; English New Londoners pointed out that such treatment was wrong when it affected "a people whose tents are yet amonst vs." Gookin reported that Mohawks threatened to kill any anglicized Indians, who were easy to pick out "by their short hair, and wearing English fashioned apparel." On the opposite side, some Indians who allied with colonists identified themselves against those who protested assimilation. This was sometimes done, however, in a way critical of the English. Some praying Indians testified in 1651 that they saw "no difference between the worst *Indians,* and such [pro-fane] *English,* saying, *they are all one Indians.*" In this way, Indian adoption of nonmilitary English goods was construed not neutrally as a testing of different kinds of technology, but as cultural loyalty, either to the English or to indigenous cultures.[41]

Colonial officials were, conversely, critical of English people who lived like Indians. The opinion in Maryland was that "he that is lazy and will not work, needs not fear starving, but may live as an Indian" by hunting and gathering seasonal produce. Few English people within sight of the settlements would have been able to live in true native fashion without interference. Wigwams may have been handy for the earliest settlers, but the English by no means considered them real houses. John Winthrop, Jr., made sketches of English-style houses appropriate to large and small households in New England, in expectation that people would eventually move to proper abodes. At a new plantation in Connecticut in 1646, some English "famylyes" lived in "the Indians wigwams there," but only "while their owne houses were buildinge." When Richard Vines tried to establish a trading post in Maine, he built "a small wigwam" defended with two cannon. Vines denied, however, that he had attempted "to build or fortify at Machias, but only set up a shelter for his men and goods," which their living in a mere wigwam helped prove.[42]

As the English differentiated their skills from those of Indians, they widened the distance by equating Indians' bodies with objects. That is, the English presented themselves as people who controlled valuable trade goods for which Indians had no equivalents except their bodies. Even if colonists were somewhat willing to share tools and technology with Indians, they wanted no parallel exchange of people. The English continued to be reluctant to establish legal family relationships with Indians even if this might have achieved certain colonizing goals such as Christianization of Indians or acquisition of military allies. Colonists understood that many natives considered intermarriage a form of alliance. When the governor of Massachusetts asked Miantonomi to ally his Narragansett with the English against the Niantic, the sachem objected that the Niantic were "as his own flesh, being allied by continual intermarriages." Christopher Levett related natives' offers to accept him as a relative. One group of Abenaki told him that he was their "cozen," and one man, Somerset (or Samoset), with a new son said that his and Levett's sons "should be Brothers" until "*Tanto* carried them to his *Wigwam*." Levett seems not to have rejected these overtures, but he did not say that he reciprocated in any way.[43]

Although Levett did not indicate that his trading partners felt rebuffed, other English accounts record natives' annoyance over rejection of Anglo-Indian family alliances. Further, the English persisted in taking natives away from their villages without leaving any of their own people behind. The English instead preferred to give trade goods for Indians, thereby setting up an early pattern of exchange which, though not always a trade in slaves, consistently proffered English manufactures for Indian people. When Massasoit received a "hat, coat, band and feather" at William Bradford's wedding in 1623, Emmanuel Altham told him he "craved a boy of him" for Sir Edward Altham. Massasoit "would not part with him; but I will bring you one hereafter," Emmanuel assured Sir Edward. The casual equation of objects and Indians was bound to increase natives' resentment.[44]

Powhatan felt that he had been repeatedly insulted in this way, starting with John Smith's reluctance to become his adopted son or son-in-law. Powhatan requested particular goods from the English to demonstrate the friendship they professed but refused to prove with marriage or ritual adoption. Ralph Hamor and Powhatan renegotiated their agreement in 1614 when Hamor discovered among the Powhatan a William Parker, reputed to be dead but clearly alive, though he had "grown so like both in complexion and habite to the *Indians*" as to be unrecognizable. Parker begged Hamor to take him back to Jamestown, but Powhatan resented Hamor's promise to attempt the removal: Why not have an Englishman in exchange for Pocahontas, who had remained with the English? Hamor transcribed Powhatan's angry objection that "you can no sooner see or know of any English mans being with me, but you must haue him away." If Parker left, Powhatan wanted goods in exchange: copper, a shaving razor, an iron froe to cleave timber into boards, a grindstone, two bone combs, one hundred fishhooks or a good seine, a cat, and a dog. He offered a "table book" (notebook) to Hamor "and bade me write them [the goods] down" to record the demand. Hamor asked to keep the table book, but claimed Powhatan said "it did him much good to shew it to strangers."[45]

Like Powhatan, many Indians increasingly emphasized that, if the English did not exchange people, they needed to give or restore materials for displaced persons. After the 1622 attack in Virginia, some Powhatan offered to return hostages if they were allowed to plant their corn at a traditional ground. They sent back one Englishwoman, a Mrs. Boys, "apparrelled like one of their Queenes, w.ch they desired wee should take notice of," again suggesting that the English regarded material exchanges involving women as signs of good intent (and perhaps indicating that Indians realized and played to this expectation). To avoid further conflict, Virginia stated conditions under which Indian children could be taken into English households as servants or for education; such children were not to be used "as slaves," could not be transferred to another party (a pretext for sale), could not be given away by anyone other than their parents, and could not be removed from the colony without their family's agreement.[46]

Eventually, the exchange of people for things settled into a system of enslavement and ransom. If the English complained about being reduced to objects, they nevertheless expected to treat Indians this way. As in Virginia earlier, their practice met with resistance in New England in the 1640s. Colonists made the Narragansett and Niantic agree to pay an indemnity of two thousand fathoms of wampum, leaving four sachems' sons as hostages until final payment. The sachems tried to send four other children until the Commissioners of the United Colonies discovered this and demanded the real hostages, who remained with the English over a year. Richard Morris complained in 1647 that his Indian servant, a "Chilld of deth" whose person had become forfeit in war, wanted to leave his employ, rejecting the English insistence that slavery was a just condition for conquered people. Morris wanted payment to purchase an African slave, "wich is Just for they [the Indians] them selleses mak vs pay ransomes for ours [w]hom they tak captiues."[47] Morris's plea revealed the conviction among colonists that African bodies were clearly marked for slavery, but also that English and Indian bodies were, in this regard, dangerously undifferentiated: either could be enslaved, depending on who had the upper hand.

Despite colonists' desire to differentiate themselves from Indians as a people whose bodies made property but were not themselves property, their dependence on trade goods made them more like natives than they liked to admit. Scholars have not examined this similarity with any thoroughness. While the literature has discussed the extent to which natives became "dependent" on manufactured goods, it does not point out that the same was true of seventeenth-century colonists. Colonists depended on the overseas trade for much of their material culture, from flintlocks to cloth to iron goods. Nor could they always choose what they bought and from whom. However much the authorities in New England may have disliked the Dutch sale of manufactured items, including firearms, to Indians, the English colonies themselves benefited from Dutch traders. Winthrop recorded in 1634 that Massachusetts had bought Dutch sheep, sugar, cloth, and "brasse pannes" to replace worn-out musket pans. The plantations were captive markets.[48]

Colonial dependence was painfully apparent when the English Civil War and then Cromwell's military actions in Ireland and the Caribbean disrupted trade. A 1657 petition from two merchants argued against English prohibitions on exporting leather goods (such as shoes), "Virginia & other the English plantations being not able to subsist" on their own. In 1641 the General Court of Massachusetts decided to "seek out some way, by procuring cotton from the West Indies . . . for our present supply of clothing." By 1643 Winthrop reported "a manufacture of cotton" from Barbados owing to "supplies from England failing much." Pride in this accomplishment revealed settlers' desire to be independent from England and to be different from Indians. Thus the claim that Rowley (center of import substitution) had "the first people that set upon making of Cloth in this Western World." Not only did this claim ignore local Indian textiles (because they were not loomed), but it also overlooked Indian and Spanish production of textiles in Central and South America. The statement indicates how colonists narrowed their focus to themselves and nearby Indians, removed from the larger history of the Americas, in order to emphasize differences between English and native technologies.[49]

Paper was another commodity whose scarcity discomfited colonists. In fact, papermaking was not even well established in England. From the fourteenth through the sixteenth centuries, most "English" paper came from Italy and France; during the seventeenth century, much of it came from Holland. Several Tudor paper mills had popped up but then collapsed. (The first somewhat successful one was on the same river Darent site where Frobisher's ore had been processed.) Not until the early eighteenth century would most English paper be of domestic manufacture. Most of the English books and manuscripts cited in this study were written on foreign paper. And most paper in the colonies was imported from the European continent via England. While Massachusetts established printing (a relatively simple and inexpensive manufacture) in 1639, only in 1690 would colonial paper first be made, in Pennsylvania. The inability to make paper served as another reminder that, despite England's growing colonizing prowess, its people were still not as accomplished as other Europeans.[50]

Access to writing materials therefore concerned colonists. Ink could be made locally; the two John Winthrops shared a recipe for it. Paper was harder to come by. It was probably for this reason that Hamor coveted Powhatan's blank tablebook, incredulous that an item essential to literate English people might see use in an Indian village. In 1632 Francis Kirby shipped to the younger John Winthrop four hundred pairs of shoes as well as nails, cloth, and "paper bookes." John Sandbrooke, isolated in northerly Sable Island, begged Winthrop to send him a Bible, a quire of paper, and sealing wax. Nathaniel Sparhawk's accounts for 1638–39 made explicit the similarity between precious military supplies and paper when he listed together "1/2 li. shott 1 1/4*d*. 3 quire of paper 18*d*."[51]

Military supplies were almost as difficult to produce in America as paper. Neither firearms nor ordnance was made in the colonies before the eighteenth century. Settlers could, in a pinch, melt down other metal items to make shot or to repair their muskets; in 1643 Virginia stipulated that "all lead" be "melted and imployed for the making of shott." But gunpowder was trickier. Shortages of powder were exacerbated by colonists' ability (indeed talent) to destroy it accidentally. Winthrop related in 1640 that the *Mary Rose* "was blown in pieces with her own powder" while in Boston harbor. In Roxbury in 1645, seventeen barrels of powder ignited and exploded (along with other arms) to the loss of £400–500. The explosion "shooke the howses in Boston & Cambridge, so as men thought it had been an earthquake." Bits of burnt rag floated through the air as far as the Boston meeting-house. Winthrop commented that this disaster was particularly embarrassing given that the colony's General Court had refused pleas from Virginia and Plymouth for some gunpowder to defend against Indians. The powder might have been better used elsewhere than wasted in the explosion.[52]

If gunpowder supplies failed, older forms of military defense might be needed. In 1645 Massachusetts ordered that young men should train in archery because "the use of bowes and arrowes may be of good concernment, in defect of powder, upon any occasion." Two years later, Rhode Island required that all men—masters and servants, adults and boys—train as archers, "forasmuch, as we are cast among the Archers, and know not how soone we may be deprived of Powder and Shott, without which our guns will advantage us nothing." This record is intriguing because it expressed the hope that the colonists would "come to outshoot these natives in their owne bow," suggesting apprehension that archery was, by this date, more closely associated with Indians than with the English, but was useful if it prevented Indian conquest. Henry Whitfeld, who lived in a New England praying town, had more reason to see archery as a plausible emergency measure, because his Indian neighbors would know how to use bows more readily than would most mid-seventeenth-century Englishmen. In 1650 Whitfeld predicted that "if we cannot get any Guns, Powder, Shot, Swords, &c. we will make us Slings, Bowes, and other Engines." The inclusiveness of his "we" and "us" elided the difference between English and Indian, at least in an emergency.[53]

Reversion to archery looked increasingly desperate and perpetuated a similarity to Indians that colonists were newly keen to reduce, but settlers could at least distinguish themselves from natives in the manufacture of gunpowder. In fact, gunpowder represented part of the final stage of the mineral obsession, in which colonists emphasized that arts such as chemistry and mining proved their learning and material resourcefulness—a trump card to play against Indians. Two of the ingredients of gunpowder—charcoal and sulfur—were easy to procure, but the third and trickiest component, potassium nitrate or saltpeter, usually had to be made and added last so the mixture would not deteriorate or ignite. During his 1655 invasion of Jamaica, Venables noted that the Caribbean climate rotted gunpowder; the English forces needed supplies of the powder's individual ingredients and men with the skill to combine them as necessary. Saltpeter could be made from urine and either ashes or soil. Virginia in 1630 had passed a law to encourage every "master of a family" to save and deliver wood ashes and urine "to those that require the same to make experiment thereof." Those who successfully made saltpeter would receive a reward.[54]

Not everyone thought that gunpowder was so straightforward. When Edward Howes wrote to the younger John Winthrop about making saltpeter, he used code (in which every other letter was read) to explain how to create "shanlota presthier waidtoh Vortimnoe agnud cloimnoan Ebafretah" ("salt peter with Vrine and comon Earth"). From whom did Howes think he was keeping this information? Many other Europeans knew how to make saltpeter for gunpowder and fertilizer. And the English still insisted (probably wrongly) that adult Indians could not read. The use of code for this military information is a clue to the pretensions of some of the English to use chemistry, and the learned sciences generally, to prove their civility compared to Indians. In this pursuit they received support from and participated in a program to improve material life that preoccupied more people in the old world.[55]

Colonists assured themselves that they were not going native by focusing on the hybridity they created between creole and metropolitan cultures: convergence between settlers and stay-at-homes superseded that between Indians and settlers. To question the significance of Anglo-Indian hybridity required, first, that Indians' tools and artifacts be represented as curiosities rather than as useful items, and second, that colonial material culture be connected to the new "improvement" being undertaken in England. This was the settlers' initial attempt to link themselves to old world learned culture by capitalizing on their colonial setting, on its intrinsic rarities and the fact that it was (from the European perspective) entirely an example of improvement. That is, plantations constituted, within the terms soon to be identified with John Locke, a landscape remarkably transformed by English hands and a demonstration that a civil people could create property out of nature.

Colonists' renewed efforts to present their material culture to men of learning in the old world made a bit of noise after a long silence. Earlier colonial contribution to learned culture had been haphazard. Since Hariot's sojourn at Roanoke, only two Englishmen had traveled to the new world with the intention of contributing to natural philosophy. The first was Roger Fry, a ship's captain who may have received some training from John Bainbridge, professor of astronomy at Oxford. Fry led the final English settlement of the Amazon, 1631–1633, and hoped to observe a 1633 eclipse from a point beneath the equator as well as to make other astronomical sightings in the Southern Hemisphere. As Bainbridge explained astronomy to a potential patron, observations from strategic points on the globe were "the only certain and undoubted principalls and complements of that excellent Science." Fry did observe the 1633 eclipse on the upper Amazon shortly before the Portuguese captured him. He managed to get his notes back to Bainbridge, who had observed the eclipse from Cambridge. The next naturalist who went to America specifically to deploy his skill was the younger John Tradescant (1608–1662). Charles I sent him in 1637 to gather plants and shells in Virginia. After these episodes, however, nothing in the nature of a scientific expedition would go to the Americas until the founding of the Royal Society.[56]

In the meantime, travelers and colonists supplied men of learning (and patrons) with new world curiosities. Though this was a scattershot effort, subordinate to the other needs of colonization, collection of artifacts and souvenirs accelerated from the second half of the seventeenth century onward. At first, collection of rarities gave information to colonial projectors: Indians' weapons provided intelligence about their military capabilities, samples of soil and rock yielded clues about mineral wealth, and botanical specimens indicated potential food supplies and staples. Subsequently, Indian products took the form of booty or tribute, either the foodstuffs and tools that colonists seized in war, or items that colonial governments received or demanded from allied Indians; some of these things then made their way to Europe. This later phase of collection was meant to provide intellectual stimulation and amusement to friends and family, but also, and more important, to patrons and learned individuals who might wish to know about America.

Colonists were well aware that they lived among things that would astonish people in Europe. In the 1620s Emmanuel Altham sent tobacco pipes to his relatives in England, writing that one was "the first and rarest that ever I saw . . . it being a great king's pipe in this country." In early 1640 John Winthrop tried to send an otter to the king, though the poor creature slipped overboard on the way (or so its keeper said). At the same time, Margaret Winthrop sent an "Indian baskett" to Deane Tyndal. This was probably the Narragansett basket she had received from Canonicus's wife the year before, a diplomatic gift between well-placed women in America that Mrs. Winthrop then gave to a friend as a container of information about America. Some gifts were solicited, as when Emanuel Downing asked the younger John Winthrop for a hummingbird "perfect in his fethers in a little box." The traffic in rarities gathered volume and generated collections, museums, and *Wunderkammern* that displayed American items to a larger audience.[57]

John Tradescant organized the first English collection that contained a range of American material. Tradescant and his father incorporated their Virginia specimens in a London museum, "Tradescant's Ark," which they opened in the early 1630s. Tradescant willed the museum to his friend Elias Ashmole, who later established the Ashmolean Museum in Oxford, which retains several of Tradescant's Virginia items, including the deerskin "mantle" embroidered with white shell and reputed to have belonged to Powhatan. Colonists used Tradescant's collections as a reference point in their observations about nature in the new world. Robert Child, who had lived in Massachusetts and knew its flora and fauna, asked the younger Winthrop to supply him "some Simples, or such like to begin a firme society with John Tredislin." When he saw insects in Barbados, Ligon recalled that Tradescant had shown horned Caribbean flies "amongst his rarities."[58]

Tradescant's Ark was intriguing as an accumulation of objects from very different peoples exhibited alongside one another rather than organized in some hierarchical fashion that separated European from non-European items. The Ark's inventory, *Musaeum Tradescantianum* (1656), listed objects from England and from America as if they were similar if not interchangeable. Each page of the catalog contains intriguing assortments: porcupine quill hatbands on the same page as Anne Boleyn's gloves and veil; six kinds of tomahawks and the knife used in Henry Hudson's murder on another page; "a Trunion [pivot for a cannon] of Capt: *Drake's* Ship" and "*Cassava*

Bread 2 sorts" on yet another. The tone here was not judgmental; all curiosities were wonderful. Tradescant's collection also signaled that native artifice was admirable, as when he said his "Black Indian girdles made of Wampam peek [wampumpeag]" were made of "the best sort" of shell bead. And a list of weapons included European devices as well as bows, arrows, and quivers from Asia, Africa, and America ("Canada" and "Virginia"). That no European bows and arrows (ex-

44 Musæum Tradescantianum.

lem made of a branch of one of the 70 Palme-Trees of Elam, which he gave to Sir *Tho: Roe.*

A glaffe-horne for annointing Kings.

2 Roman Urnes.

A Roman facrificing-earthen-Cup, with the word *CAMPANION* printed in the bottome.

Tarriers of Wood made like our Tyring-Irons.

Tarriers of Wood like Rolles to fet Table-difhes on.

Indian Trefles to hang a payr of Skales on, of black varnifht wood.

The plyable Mazer wood, being warmed in water will work to any form.

Blood that rained in the *Ifle of Wight,* attefted by Sir *Jo:Oglander.*

A Hand of Jet ufually given to Children, in *Turky,* to preferve them from Witchcraft.

IX.
Warlike Inftruments.

POleaxe with a Piftoll.
Poleaxe and Piftoll with a Mill and Croffe-bow in it for either Arrow or Bullet.

German Poleaxes.

Count

Musæum Tradescantianum. 45

Count *Mansfield's* Poleaxe, called *Puffacon.*

Indian fquare-pointed Dagger, broad and flat.

Japan Sword and Dagger.
Moores Daggers, 2 forts.

Severall forts of Daggers.

Javelin- $\begin{cases} Japan. \\ Turkifh. \end{cases}$

Indian Lance.

Molocco Sword.

Targets from the $\left\{\begin{array}{l} \text{Reeds.} \\ \text{Leather.} \end{array}\right.$
Eaft India of— $\left\{\begin{array}{l} \text{Skins, and} \\ \text{Crocodill-skin.} \end{array}\right.$

Bowes 12. $\left.\begin{array}{l} \text{From } India, China, Ca- \\ \text{nada, } Virginia, Ginny, \\ Turkey, Perfia. \end{array}\right.$
Arrowes 20.
Quivers 12.
Darts 60.

Drums two forts; 1. from *Ginny* of a whole piece of wood; 2d. from *India* of copper.

Targets feverall forts, viz: $\left\{\begin{array}{l} \text{Knights Templers.} \\ \text{Britaine, } Ifidore \text{ the} \\ \text{Roman.} \quad (Monk. \\ \text{Japan.} \\ \text{Græcian.} \\ Roguza. \end{array}\right.$

Indian drumming Target.

Ginny Drum made of one piece.

China

List of weapons in Tradescant's Ark. From John Tradescant, *Musaeum Tradescantianum* (London, 1656), 44–45. Courtesy of the Folger Shakespeare Library.

cept crossbows) were on this list nevertheless indicated a new distance between English and Indian, a hint at distinctions colonists wanted to emphasize.[59]

After midcentury the English reduced the Indian bow to cold, dead ethnographic artifact: a clue to another culture, divorced from its context because resident in a culture that had no use for it. This more than anything else revealed the rejection of Anglo-Indian hybridity. When Wait Winthrop sent an "Indian bow and quiver of arrowes" to the Royal Society in 1671, he interpreted the arrowheads as made "according to the Indian manner some with horsfoot [horseshoe crab] tayles some with stones and others with deere horn and sharks teeth." This implied that Indians lacked metal arrowheads, a mistake that an earlier generation of settlers could never have made. Winthrop's observations were designed to emphasize cultural distance; he made no comparison between European and American technologies, unlike observers only fifty years earlier, and he had no need to portray any potential damage an Indian bow and arrow could wreak. For his generation, the native bow was a backward tool, not a reminder of traditional British valor.[60]

When they supplied rarities such as Indian arrows to English people, colonists were not explaining themselves as versions of Indians but participating in the construction of an imperial landscape that extended over the Atlantic. This was at first an imaginary set of connections, bounded by comparisons between the hybridization taking place between the colonies and an improved English economy and material life. The series of proposals and promises presaged the actual construction of such a landscape in the next century.

A revival of interest in Baconian science initially defined this imperial landscape. Ideas about material improvement and empirical study of nature quickened toward the middle and end of the seventeenth century. Many of the key figures in this revival were puritans whose vision of improvement was part of their millenarianism: the faithful would perfect the earth as a final stage in its providential history. The Czech philosopher and millenarian Jan Comenius was the main figure in this revival. Comenius's visit to England on the eve of the Civil War galvanized English puritans interested in natural philosophy to organize their efforts in ways that were not possible at the court and in the universities. Samuel Hartlib, a Polish Protestant and natural philosopher who had moved to England, was the central figure in the English redefinition of learning, particularly in the new attention that was being paid to the practical application of sciences (as chemistry to agriculture and mechanics to manufactures) and the desire to create a center for inquiry into nature. London's Gresham College was a plausible center, though its mathematical focus precluded wider influence. More ambitious was the idea of an "Invisible College" (which echoed Comenius's plan for a Universal College), not an institution with a physical location but a network of learned Protestants who communicated knowledge to one another. Hartlib's proposal for an English Office of Address, a government bureau for experiments and practical improvements, was not taken up but provided an idea that the next generation of natural philosophers, including Robert Boyle and Isaac Newton, would try to establish in the Royal Society. That society carried forward the program to blend the experimental philosophy with material improvement, though it would not acknowledge the millenarian impulse that had guided midcentury puritan improvers.[61]

For Hartlib and his circle, the western Atlantic featured as a site of investigation into nature, much as Bacon's *New Atlantis* had defined it. Gabriel Plattes's *Description of the Famous Kingdom of Macaria* (1641) posited a utopia of learning that resembled Bacon's Island of Bensalem. Hartlib had a similar plan for "Antilia," and his associates discussed locating it in Bermuda. More concretely, puritans took an interest in the curricula at Trinity College in Protestant Dublin and at Harvard College. These colonial sites of learning had the advantage over utopias because they already existed and had personnel interested in the sciences, improvement, and true religion. Through puritan lines of communication, learning would span the Atlantic. This newfound confidence was in contrast to the earliest colonial ventures, which had struggled with English technical backwardness and with settlers' failure to exploit American resources effectively.[62]

Robert Child's 1651 treatise *Samuel Hartlib His Legacie* was a germinal work for this new conception of kingdom and colonies. Child (M.D. Padua) had visited Massachusetts from 1638 to 1641, then from 1645 to 1647, until exiled because of his presbyterianism. At Hartlib's request, Child undertook a work on husbandry, though the resulting pamphlet touched on broader issues as well. Child in fact stressed, as his title made clear, that he was reanimating a neglected program, one that united discovery of the new world with discovery of the natural world. He chided English people for their uninventive farming: they had let down their less xenophobic ancestors. There had been more "things from beyond Seas" in Elizabethan gardens than there were in the gardens of his era. Child therefore urged farmers and gardeners to try a few more exotics, including the silk grass, strawberries, squash, beans, melons, pumpkins, and cedar and pine trees of *"our Northerne* [non-Caribbean] *Plantations."* He anticipated the doubters who would say "your forefathers never used them" as proof that new plants would fail in English soil. To which Child replied, "How [do] they know? have they tryed?" Child listed many things not known to English forefathers, including the modern triumvirate at the head of the list: gunpowder, printing, and America—in that order. Discovery of new things accompanied discovery (and control) of new places.[63]

Child's main intention was to elide the difference between the continental colonies and England by comparing their climates and their natural histories, and by being sympathetic to the skills and knowledge of ordinary English people on either side of the Atlantic. Intimate knowledge of local conditions was essential. He specified, for instance, that the "Canada-grape" from the colder part of America would do well in England. Child also believed that the New England practice of planting corn with fish would improve crops in England. Concomitant with his vision of rural economies that were slipping away, Child worried that local wisdom might also be dying out. "All Countrey-people" in England needed to collect knowledge of local medicines from *"Grandame."*[64]

Most interestingly, Child compared the condition of English woods with those in North America, establishing a history of woodlands which posited America's present as England's past. The English had done this in cultural terms when they compared Indians to ancient Britons; Child's generation began to think the same way about the history of nature. Child believed that England had once been much more wooded, Kent with chestnut trees and the north with pines, as proved by many old buildings in Kent made from chestnut wood and many "moore-logs" from long-lost pine trees in northern bogs. This showed that "a *species* of wood, may be destroyed, even totally[,] in a place." Virginia and New England, in contrast, still had abundance of wood in *"commons,"* but this was the problem. Wood available to anyone might soon be "consumed . . . every one making what havock he pleaseth." This analysis prefigured England's later effort to conserve its tiny forests by exporting its wood-consuming industries (such as shipbuilding and iron forging) to the colonies. The first text to focus on this problem was John Evelyn's *Silva: or, A Discourse of Forest-Trees* (1664), though Child's earlier formulation of the problem exemplified the Hartlib circle's vision of an imperial landscape in which the forests of the western Atlantic might help England preserve its trees without compromising its economy.[65]

In this way, Child beseeched English people on both sides of the Atlantic to reject slapdash attitudes toward natural resources. As he did of people in England, so he wished colonists to experiments with new crops. Child thought that because in "*Virginia* also the *Silke-wormes* are found wild amongst the *Mulberry-woods*" they "perhaps might be managed with great profit in those plantations." This was an old pet project of colonial promoters, and Child revealed his ignorance of the Chesapeake's economy when he ventured that silk might replace tobacco as the region's staple. He also fretted that, while the Muscovites were busily pickling sturgeon for the market, "we *English* in *New-England* cannot as yet do [so] handsomely." Child did not, however, think the colonial project on a par with the improvement of English husbandry. He stated outright that "the improving of a kingdome is better than the conquering a new one," showing indifference to the expansion of colonial territory; his vision of empire was static and pacific.[66]

Child's vision was mirrored, on the opposite side of the Atlantic, by colonists who wanted projects that would improve human understanding and material life. It is not surprising that New Englanders, the best educated among the colonists, first articulated their support of this program, formed connections to English improvers, and demonstrated their improvement of America. Puritan sympathies likewise tied New and old Englands together in the Baconian project. But would Indians fit into these plans? Colonists' determination to exclude them from their new efforts to use chemistry and discover mines hinted that the native role as improver would be limited. The millenarian version of natural philosophy was nevertheless interested in education and missionary activity, both of which focused on native Americans. In short, Indians were not yet excluded from the project of improvement, but were increasingly likely to be categorized as objects of it rather than participants in it.

This differentiation between improvers and those to be improved may help explain Howes's encrypted message on saltpeter. He as well as other men interested in alchemy believed that they knew important secrets which they transmitted only to one another, and that saltpeter particularly had mystic connections with heat and life-giving properties; chemistry was also of interest because it revealed the material construction of nature and had practical application for military arts and agriculture. In New England a learned circle of men read and practiced chemistry. Child and the younger Winthrop were at the center of these activities, though others such as George Starkey and Jonathan Brewster had chemical aspirations. Brewster kept a small laboratory on the Connecticut frontier; Starkey began his studies in New England but then moved to London and established himself as a chemical doctor while writing influential alchemical tracts under the pseudonym Eirenaeus Philalethes. Winthrop too acquired a reputation for chemical medicine and applied his skills to practical problems. He had recipes for saltpeter and for gunpowder itself, and was also interested in mining.[67]

The mineral obsession in its chemical form was therefore part of a claim that some men in New England had on European learned culture. Starkey and to an extent Child enjoyed the most success with chemistry because they returned to London. Winthrop struggled on in America, making occasional efforts to lure colleagues (including Comenius) to his adopted homeland and trying to find outlets for his interests. Given New England's accumulation of chemical men, and the greater investment in the landscape that New Englanders made compared to other mainland colonists, it makes sense that the only successful attempts at mining in the seventeenth century occurred in this region and were fostered by the individuals interested in chemistry. Winthrop and Child were principal actors, for instance, in the establishment of salt and iron works and of lead mining in New England.[68]

These activities were, like weaving cloth, some of the first colonial ventures in which the English saw themselves developing resources rather than building on what Indians had established. This contrasted, as well, with the much envied Iberian mines, which had themselves depended on Indian accomplishments; the English created rather than appropriated. Such was the desire to discover mines that in 1641 Massachusetts lifted prohibitions against individual land sales from Indians for "such lands where such mines shalbee found";

a twenty-one-year term of free enjoyment of any mine was in 1648 increased to enjoyment "forever." As with Paracelsian medicine, therefore, mining was supposed to be a culturally specific activity, something that separated English from Indians. Howes's pretension to encrypt saltpeter manufacture makes sense within this context of English suspicion about natives' ability to locate mines. Indian treachery was blamed for the colonists' lack of progress in mining, first as obstructing the hopes of the English to dig wealth out of the American soil, then as destroying mines and their fruits. Edward Williams claimed that Virginia's iron ore was quite promising and that colonists might already have begun to make iron "if the treachery of the Indians had not crushed it in the beginning." This was in contrast to Williams' hope that natives could tell the English about local drugs, and to his belief that they truthfully described deposits of copper, crystal, and silver to the west.[69]

Perhaps because the English feared the Indians' knowledge of mining, they tried to mislead them about their activities. William Pynchon admitted telling one Indian man that an agent had gone to a remote spot in Connecticut "to serch for something in the ground, not for Black lead as they suppose but for some other mettell." In fact black lead (graphite) was precisely what the English were after, and it had been described to them by Indians. The lie was a bit baffling. After Winthrop bought the land for the graphite mine from three Indian men in late 1644, he told the colonist who operated the mine to put the lead "into an house safe from the Indians." Winthrop also bought "all the Lands in the Wilderness . . . Round the said Black Lead Hills" in January 1645 so that Indians (and nosy colonists) would stay at a distance. Further, after work at the mine commenced in spring 1658, the proprietors never considered using Indians as laborers, even though they resented the difficulty of getting colonists to the remote site—this after over a century of English complaints that they, unlike the Spanish, had not been lucky enough to find mineral deposits near usable sources of native labor.[70]

Despite their attempts to separate Indians from mining and from the learned sciences, colonists sometimes blurred the lines. Certainly, the English depended on Indians for information about mines. Settlers had long realized that Virginia's natives got copper from somewhere, and they continued to take seriously Indians' advice about potential mines. One report said that a Chesapeake copper mine would require only "easie labor as the Indian[s] relate." And New Englanders learned about their graphite mine only because some Indians had told John Oldham of this deposit; when Winthrop traveled to the mine he had bought sight unseen, he required native guidance to do so. When Jonathan Brewster sent what he thought was silver ore to Winthrop, he asked him to send "word" by "an Indian" as to the results. Further, Indians helped circulate English chemical equipment. William Berkeley told the younger Winthrop, "I haue hired an Indian to bring the Glasses by whome I would request you to send them." When Williams wrote Winthrop in 1664, he explained that he had opportunity to do so because he had met "an Indian running back for a Glasse bound for Your parts" who could carry a letter. These glasses were probably chemistry equipment, retorts or vials; a ground lens, as for a telescope, would probably have been too expensive to be lent around the countryside. The attempt of the English to distance their mining and chemical activities from the Indians was just that—an attempt. Statements that Indians knew where mineral deposits were and use of natives to circulate information about mines and equipment for chemistry showed the permeability of the barrier between colonists and natives, one that settlers would increasingly try to seal off.[71]

In this manner, the English were making Indians into what Steven Shapin has called "invisible technicians," referring to the men who assisted late seventeenth-century natural philosophers. Some of these individuals were highly trained but none were highborn. Their social status led to their intellectual invisibility; no matter how critical their roles in investigating the natural world, their efforts became part of the visible accomplishment of their elite employers. Likewise, the English in America were usurping Indians' handiwork, appropriating their technologies, reinterpreting a hybrid landscape as improved, and claiming privileged access to the arts that would probe American nature deeper than Indians had been able to do. Colonists continued to use Indians' expertise—as with cartographic information—but they were less inclined to give them credit for it. At best, the English thought that the Indians had laid a crude foundation for their more definitive efforts. But the ambivalent assessment of Indian comprehension of minerals and mining—did they know as much as the English?—indicated a lack of conviction that colonists were the real technicians who had transformed wilderness into landscape.[72]

Indians' technical proficiency remained visible in at least one area, herbal pharmacology. Some improvers discussed how to integrate native knowledge of herbs with European medicine. Thomas Shepard wanted to establish an educational foundation for Indians in New England, not only to teach them but also to solicit information from them. "By this means we should soon have all these things which they know, and others of our Countreymen that are skilfull that way." Here Shepard considered Indians the equivalent of the country folk who Child assumed knew herbs and cures. Shepard concluded that native medicines would be to the "benefit of the people of this Countrey, and it may bee of our native Countrey also." But Shepard made a larger point about acquisition of medical knowledge, saying that his scheme to educate Indians while soliciting information from them would improve the training of Harvard students in physic; they otherwise would have only "theoreticall knowledge" but no opportunity for "making Experiments" or studying anatomy.[73]

The subject of the human body was, however, the basis of the most prejudiced comparison the English made between themselves and natives. Both the growing criticism of Indian technology and the effort to distance colonists from Indians by referring to learned traditions such as chemistry hinted at decreased sympathy with Indians. Though respect for the natives' herbal pharmacopoeia survived, other descriptions of their therapies would stigmatize them as desperate measures, bizarre forms of technology that failed, in the end, to protect Indians from illness and death. War, the context that had paradoxically teased out an initial English sense of resemblance to Indians, would by the late 1600s confirm the denigrating opinions about Indian bodies that had been generated in response to epidemics. That is, though the English thought that natives spent extraordinary amounts of technical energy on the warrior bodies that attacked colonial settlements, this technology only temporarily masked Indians' corporeal inferiority.

Gender and the Artificial Indian Body

Admiration of native warfare, agriculture, and crafts had always competed with assertions that Indians were impractical and idolatrous, less able, for instance, to master minerals than herbs. But when and why did the negative view drown out other, more flattering opinions? Negative opinions on native manipulation of nature did not predominate until the latter half of the seventeenth century, when colonists began to stress their hybridization of old and new world improvements, to dismiss their own Anglo-Indian hybridity, and to face Indians in new and terrible wars. At this time, two earlier ideas about Indians fused, to the increasing detriment of the natives. Belief in native cleverness at manipulating nature and belief that Indians had weak bodies merged into an opinion that they needed to spend an inordinate amount of their technical energy to maintain their bodies. No wonder, settlers concluded, that native arts had been retarded when the English first began to settle among them, and that Indians still depended on colonists for tools and instruction in how to use them. Natives' bodies did not permit sufficient leisure to develop better technology other than that devoted to physic and bodily therapy. This assessment still functioned as a backhanded compliment to Indian medicine, though the flattery was wearing thin.

It was within the context of war that the English especially reexamined their ideas about Indian bodies and further developed their criticisms of native technologies. From the early conflicts in Virginia

244 · *Conquering America, 1640–1676*

(1622) and Massachusetts (1637), war had been an especially powerful reminder that too much contact and combination with natives might endanger the English. Edward Waterhouse had stressed this in his description of the 1622 Powhatan attack in Virginia, warning that the natives had known exactly where different English people would be at particular times of day because of "daily familiarity" with them.[1] The dangers of becoming like Indians were compounded by the danger of coming too near them. By the era of Bacon's Rebellion in Virginia and King Philip's War in New England (1675–76), the English found comfort in arguments that the Indians' strength was illusory, their technology and bodies no match for colonists.

Warfare had long encouraged the English to believe that the male Indian body was powerful and dangerous. Yet the English quickly asserted that this bodily strength was not natural but a product of custom. This emphasis differentiated Indians from Africans (whose bodily strength was natural to them) and from Europeans, who lacked or shunned customs that could give them comparable protection from hardship. To protect themselves from physical suffering, Indians had to develop bodily rigor from infancy through adulthood. The English focused on the role of women in shaping and hardening the bodies of Indian infants, a process later reflected in native women's supposed ease in childbirth and native men's resistance to the fatigue of battle and pain of torture. In the context of English colonization, therefore, Indian bodily strength was the product of artifice, a sign of the natives' misplaced creative energies, which prevented their developing better technologies.[2]

The idea of the artificial Indian body makes sense of a seeming discrepancy in English opinion: that natives were very susceptible to disease, yet were otherwise physically tough, able to resist extremes of temperature, lack of food or water, and the rigors of war and torture. Repeated statements that natives were shaped from birth to be physically straight and strong and that they continually applied ointments to themselves made it seem that they worked hard to form their bones and to manufacture a kind of carapace over their skin. But artificial bone and skin failed to protect the flesh between, which crumpled in the face of smallpox or measles, as it would not have done in freezing weather or pitched battle. As the English began to discuss the movement of disease around the globe, modifying their earlier and place-specific comprehension of epidemics in America, they interpreted Indians' bodies as weak in even more judgmental ways. That is, Indians compared poorly to other peoples who had encountered new diseases when such maladies followed invading or migrating populations.

The native body that the English were constructing from arguments about disease, war, and artifice was also a point of reference in emerging colonial opinion about the technical inferiority of the natives. Just as colonists had earlier cast doubt on the ability of Indian medicine to protect Indian bodies against all forms of disease, so they portrayed Indians' attempts to mold their bodies by artifice as a time-consuming and negligible strategy. By the late 1600s, colonists suggested that much native technology was fruitless, a cultural manifestation of the bodily weakness that it failed to mask. At the same time, colonists were arguing that Indians had gained their most useful tools from their invaders, and were permanently dependent on European technology. These comments were the origins of the commonplace shorthand differentiation between Indians and colonizers that eventually focused on technology, but had begun with observations about the human body. The male body had been the first focus, as the English formed opinions about Indians in the context of recurring military encounter; later, female and male Indian bodies were of equal interest, each gender judged as to its specialized capacity to produce warriors or to produce war.

Commentary on war therefore traced a rejection of the initial parity the English had perceived between themselves and natives and argued that natives' delicacy foretold their physical disappearance. Such views accompanied settlers' growing conviction that they could themselves populate America, and their greater confidence that they no longer needed to rely on Indian labor within the settlements. Explanations of bodily difference were accordingly changing. At first, colonists had remarked on Indians' external appearance, tending to explain it as a product of custom rather than inheritance. The English continued to refer to custom but reemphasized its potential to create a second nature. In this way, narratives about Indians continued to talk around the possibility that bodily differences might be innate and heritable. But settlers remarked on Indian women and their role in childbirth and child rearing in ways that revealed the English fascination with the transmission of corporeal forms, even if their narratives stressed culture as second nature rather than physical inheritance. Discourse on race presented powerful possibilities yet remained idiomatic.

To emphasize these points about reproduction, the English focused on what they assumed were natural differences between the sexes and the ways in which Indian bodies failed to reflect these distinctions. Narratives on Indians were thus returning to the discussion of gender that had begun when the English considered what might happen to their own bodies in America. As Chapters 4 and 5 have pointed out, scholarship on gender in early America has not taken seriously the positioning of sex difference within arguments about the natural world. Conversely, most discussions of gender that do take European theories of nature seriously have not paid attention to colonization and the new questions it raised about non-European men and women. In the English colonies, early modern definitions of gender involved not just Englishmen's and Englishwomen's roles but also those of their gendered Indian counterparts. If men and women were supposed to be differentiated by their humoral composition (men were hot, strong, fit for hard work and battle; women were cold, weak, fit for domestic work and childbearing), Indians' bodies did not make sense (to the English) according to these distinctions, and hence might be artificial rather than natural.[3]

Childbirth and Indian women's child rearing were of particular interest to colonists. Many of their assessments of Indians and gender indeed referred to reproduction, but did so in order to argue that Indian customs surrounding this "natural" process were in fact unnatural. Indian women gave birth outside, alone, and with little or no pain. Their experience defied assumptions that the daughters of Eve bore children in sorrow—with so much blood and pain that they needed assistance and benefited from the advantages of civility, especially giving birth indoors, unlike animals. Indian customs thus defied nature. In this manner, settlers explained why Indian gender roles, by assigning hard agricultural labor to women, were at variance with English distribution of work. Many scholars have interpreted this criticism as the way colonists differentiated their culture from that of natives. But colonists' abhorrence of hardworking Indian women showed a deeper revulsion over the seemingly bizarre Indian resistance to fatigue and pain. Bodily as well as cultural difference mattered. In fact, body and culture were almost impossible to differentiate. It was their hard labor that made Indian women nearly as hardy as Indian men; the former were repeatedly tested in order to prepare them for childbirth, the latter for battle.

In the end, native adults were seen as remarkably resistant to all manner of pain, examples of which supported an emerging argument that Indians were stolid, passionless, contemptuous of hardship. William Wood claimed that Indians' "hardiness" would "procure admiration, no ordinary pains making them so much as alter their countenance." With unseemly relish, Wood elaborated that one could "beat them, whip them, pinch them, punch them, [but] if they resolve not to winch [wince] for it, they will not." Roger Williams concluded that toothache was "the onely paine [that] will force their stout hearts to cry." Indians were unnatural beings, bodies for which artifice had created a kind of unfeeling inhumanity. What could cause their extraordinary fortitude? And how was it that their marvelous bodies were nevertheless so susceptible to disease?[4]

If colonists first identified characteristics of Indian men's bodies when they saw them fight, they first explicated Indian women's bodies when they saw them work. Indian modes of distributing labor between men and women perplexed colonists. At issue especially was the fact that Indian women nearly always performed the bulk of agricultural work, taking up strenuous outdoor tasks that in England were the occupations of lower-class men. It is not the case that the English never gave such work to women. In the early Chesapeake, for instance (and despite promotional pamphlets' claims to the contrary), female indentured servants did work in the tobacco and corn fields. But to have women perform most agricultural production was alien, and the English wondered at Indian women's fortitude and Indian men's good fortune at being spared such labor. Thus Wood's claim that the native women in New England would come to settler women to lament their lot and receive sympathy. Wood's motive was clear: "Let [Englishwomen] peruse these few lines, wherein they may see their owne happinesse, if weighed in the womans ballance of these ruder *Indians*." In short, gender roles revealed the presence or absence of civility.[5]

Perhaps as significant as this argument over gender and work was a parallel one over gender and war. As had been the case with archery, the English used war to explore cultural comparisons, but, unlike in their attitudes toward bows and arrows, they were not eager to share Indians' ideas about gender and battle. The military interface nonetheless led colonists to believe that they shared at least one important feature with natives: the masculine cult of the warrior, in which Indian and English men agreed to agree that the worst insult they could fling at each other was the epithet "woman." In English accounts, both sides seemed to be converging on similar attitudes about gender and war, making it impossible to determine whether their shared method of denigration was anything but an artifact of the frontier experience rather than an important part of anyone's precontact culture.

Certainly, throughout the era of early colonization, Europeans had had strongly mixed opinions on women and war. Like other Europeans, the English had thought that warrior women were not natural beings. It was in the nature of a man (whose element was fire) to be prone to rage and violence, but women could not engage in such activities unless they were viragoes, females whose temper was hotter and more masculine than normal. Nevertheless, some women played a role in European warfare, particularly those who came from the extremes of the social spectrum. Highborn women participated in the aristocratic culture of war, while women in the lower classes took up arms in desperate circumstances. Christine de Pisan, who wrote *Le Livre des Fais d'Armes et de Chevalerie* (1488), was one elite woman who had studied the art of war and described it to male and female readers. During the late sixteenth century, when Spain threatened the Low Countries and England, Queen Elizabeth likewise garnered a reputation as a virago-like defender of Protestants, a veritable Amazon who would defeat Spain and Rome. Mythology about Elizabeth's rallying her troops against the Armada at Tilbury (where she supposedly claimed to have the heart and stomach of a man) grew apace in the early seventeenth century, when in fact England's monarchs and Protector were male. Anne Bradstreet repeated the myth in her 1650 *Tenth Muse,* which praised Elizabeth as "Our *Amazon* i' th' Camp at Tilberry" who would have awed even the fierce "*Sythians* Queen."[6]

Women even undertook the highly masculine practice of archery. In fact, the first use of the English term "long bowe" comes from a letter that Margaret Paston wrote to her husband, John, in 1448 during the Wars of the Roses. From the late Middle Ages into the seventeenth century, women used the bow to hunt, though this was mostly true of noblewomen. Hunting, unlike war, would not require continual shooting, so a woman—who would have less upper-body strength than a man—could kill an animal during a hunt, if not many humans in battle. Women of the yeoman class, whose menfolk were archers, did not hunt. But lower-class Englishwomen made bows and arrows. London's Company of Fletchers allowed widows of members to continue as members and remain in the trade, and the company also accepted women as apprentices. The same was true for the Company of Bowstringmakers, which had female apprentices into the 1600s; these women could take apprentices of their own once they had "mastered" the craft. Still, there was reluctance to consider women, even viragoes, as the military equivalent of men. While Tudor literature on archery had praised Prince Arthur, King Henry VIII, and King Edward VI as defenders of England, Elizabeth was not celebrated in the same terms used for her uncle, father, and brother, except during the extraordinary circumstances of the Armada, when Protestant propaganda acclaimed all of Spain's enemies.[7]

That Elizabeth was sometimes called an Amazon indicates the uneasiness that surrounded martial females. Early modern Europeans used the image of the Amazon to express the sense that a woman warrior was something unnatural. She was a being who had altered her upper body in order to bear arms: she removed one breast, the more easily to draw a bow, throw a spear, or hold a shield without impediment. An Amazon was therefore something like an Algonquian warrior, who likewise made himself (or at least his hair) asymmetrical through an artifice designed to facilitate archery. An Amazon's missing breast was a synecdoche; the bodily deformation was a reminder of "natural" female weakness and signified the unnatural characteristics of women strong enough to draw the bow and fight wars on their own. Discussion of Amazons was therefore an elliptical debate about upper-body strength and gender difference which admitted that a body might be carved into something contrary to its original nature. John Bulwer quoted della Porta, for instance, saying that an Amazon would sear off her right breast in order to strengthen her right hand, "which was but weake by Nature." Others stated the more common opinion that Amazons removed the breast that might, like hair on the side of the head, impede the bow.[8] The idea of the Amazon, like the idea of a virago, stressed that her body was contrary to nature.

Perhaps because the English wanted to see archery as a masculine strength peculiar to their nation, they were not eager to find Amazons in America. Some early Spanish reports had claimed their existence, but Ralegh's history of Guiana was the only sustained English discussion of American Amazons. Because Ralegh was describing the area near the Amazon River, and because he wrote his work mainly for Queen Elizabeth, he had reason to emphasize the possible existence of women warriors who "shall heereby heare the name of a virgin, which is not onely able to defend her owne territories and her neighbors, but also to inuade and conquere so great Empyres and so farre remoued." No one else was willing to go this far. Ralegh's contemporary John Ley in 1598 hazarded that the women on the lower Amazon lived apart from men but had both breasts; they would "draw their bowes" while holding the bow "far from the bodie, soe that their brest is no impeachment to their shooteing." Some non-English discussions of the Amazon region continued to describe native women who were physically adapted to make war. In the early 1620s, for instance, an Irish settler who defected to the Spanish wrote that the Amazon's native women "have very small right breasts like men, [treated] by arts so that they do not grow, in order to shoot arrows, and the left breasts are as large as other women's." John Smith's assessment of Powhatan women who performed an "anticke" dance denied them any such military role. Although the women carried weapons and gave "hellish cries," Smith did not consider that they might have been enacting a ritual related to war. For him, the dancers were not Amazons but "Nimphes" whose attentions to him were highly gendered; they later "tormented" him by "most tediously crying, love you not mee?"[9]

Separation of women and war required new efforts once firearms were the standard weapon for soldiers. In some ways, gunpowder made female participation more likely, since many hands might be needed for the emergency work of fortification that ordnance required. Sir Roger Williams accordingly reported considerable female action in the Low Countries. In the siege of Haarlem, three hundred women of the town acted as pioneers, the workers who dug entrenchments and reinforced bulwarks. The female pioneers were, Williams reported, "all vnder one Ensigne . . . a most stout dame, named Captaine *Margaret Kenalt.*" It was at this moment that popular ballads about female soldiers appeared. The first version of the Ur-ballad about the modern woman soldier, "Mary Ambree" (ca. 1600), clearly refers to the 1584 siege of Ghent. The women celebrated in this and later songs did not need to unsex their bodies to fight; they were neither viragoes nor Amazons, but genuine females who could pass as men if they wore the right clothing and functioned well in battle. The ballads stressed gunpowder technology as key to the masquerade; the soldier lasses of the earliest ballads fought in sieges, and by the 1640s they shouldered muskets.[10]

But Englishmen were uneasy over the prospect that they might lose pride of place in battle. Firearms did not need the extensive training and upper-body strength that bows (or pikes) required. Assertions that gunpowder was a masculine material, associated with fire and destruction, were therefore used to shore up the man's position in battle. The larger context for debate over women and war continued to trouble some colonists. Seventeenth-century Anglo-America's notorious cross-dresser T. Hall certainly brought the problem home to Virginians in 1629. That Hall did both men's and women's work, dressed alternately in men's and women's clothing, and had hermaphroditic genitals vexed Virginia authorities. Hall's earlier career had evidently included a stint of military service in the Low Countries. As the Virginia court records noted, Hall, who had been christened with the female name Thomasine, "changed his apparell into the fashion of man and went over as a souldier in the *Isle of Ree* being in the habit of a man." The repeated reference to costume—putting on male clothing in order to go to war—emphasized a category error that particularly troubled the English and stressed the ease with which it could be performed: merely by slipping into different clothes, women could seize the ultimate male role. It is of course possible that Hall never actually went to war but lied to the nosy Virginians in a way calculated to challenge their gendered notions about bodily capacities and social roles.[11]

In the colonies, therefore, and even in moments of military extremity, Englishmen were unwilling to admit that women could or should fight. Arguments for women's contribution to war were few, strained, apologetic—and tremendously revealing of the anxieties over involving women in warfare against non-Europeans. Captain John Underhill made one such comment during the Pequot War, when he reported that in battle he had "received an arrow . . . against my helmet on the forehead." Underhill reflected that had he not allowed his "wife to persuade me to carry [the helmet] along with me . . . I had been slain." "Let no man despise advice and counsel of his wife," he cautioned, "though she be a woman." While it is impossible to believe that all women remained as far from the fray as the thoughtful Mrs. Underhill, there are in fact very few descriptions of colonial women handling firearms until the eighteenth century. One rare example appeared in an account of King Philip's War, which related that a female servant defended her master's house and children against one Indian man. The man shot at her twice but missed, while she "charged" a musket and then shot him in the shoulder. (Just how she had become such a good shot is tellingly unexplained.) The wounded man stormed up to the house, and the woman resorted to a shovel filled with coals from the hearth as her last and most effective weapon against him.[12]

As this example shows, King Philip's War elicited some of the most desperate responses to Indian attack, even to the point of bringing women into the fray. Laurel Thatcher Ulrich has pointed out that, in this context, puritans even celebrated as viragoes some Englishwomen who resisted Indians. But this resistance was carefully coded, especially in relation to firearms. In contrast to the servant who shot an Indian, Mary Rowlandson emphasized in her famous captivity narrative from the same war that she never used a weapon against her Wampanoag captors, though her account acquired illustrations after her death that portrayed her bearing a musket. Both the account of the desperate servant and Rowlandson's care to establish her distance from firearms indicated that the prospect of arming Englishwomen on the American frontier was a distasteful one. As will be shown later in this chapter, explanations of Englishwomen's violence against Indians tended to follow arguments about how the female body could undertake military actions that did not involve firearms.[13]

While Algonquian societies had their own prohibitions on women's participation in war, Indians' actions indicate that they did not always assume Englishwomen to be excluded from the European art of war. In contrast to the English, for example, native cultures reserved the making of bows and arrows to men. Often, too, native women were prohibited from handling weapons. The same was not true of the English, though natives might not have known this at the start. The earliest English expeditions, which had relied in part on bows, had also included few women. Inuit and Indian observers of the Frobisher and Roanoke expeditions may accordingly have assumed that English bows and Englishmen went together as a gendered unit for hunting, war, and invasion. Later, the numbers of guns and Englishwomen both increased in the settlements. After this point, natives could observe Englishwomen in contact with firearms, shot, and powder. This may have led to some misunderstanding about the extent of female participation in the new art of war. During the Pequot War, Edward Johnson recounted, a party of natives captured two young Englishwomen and "questioned them with such broken English, as some of them could speak, to know whether they could make Gunpowder." Because the women could (or would) not, the Indians' "prize proved nothing so pretious a Pearle in their eyes as before."[14]

It seems that Indians quickly perceived and learned to exploit English reluctance to consider females as combatants. William Strachey reported that Opossunoquonuske tricked and killed a party from Jamestown when he asked them "to leave their Armes in their boat, because they said how their women would be afrayd ells of their pieces." When Pilgrim soldiers raided a Narragansett village, they observed that "those boyes that were in the house seeing our care of women, often cried *Neensquaes,* that is to say, I am a Woman," or, more precisely, not an adult man, not a combatant. Rituals and actions that surrounded war were careful to identify emergency female roles that would not threaten the other side. When Miantonomi, a Narragansett sachem allied with the English against the Pequot, wanted to recover some firearms, "he sent the women for the guns." Perhaps this was because Indian women could carry weapons without causing any English observers alarm that they might start shooting. This followed the pattern by which both sides used women to indicate amity: thus the gift of a Narragansett woman's basket to Margaret Winthrop, and thus the Powhatan's return of the kidnapped Mrs. Boys in the apparel of an Indian "queen." Likewise, the Wampanoag and their allies used Englishwomen as diplomats and scribes in King Philip's War.[15]

The intercultural struggle over gender and battle meant that the categorizing of women (and children) as noncombatants had repeatedly to be negotiated and reinterpreted. The 1622 Powhatan attack in Virginia had not spared women, though among the English captives taken, only the women survived, "for the men that they tooke they putt them to death." During the planning for the final English assault on the Pequot, Roger Williams warned that the Indians allied with the English did not want a total war: "It would be pleasing to all natives, that women and children be spared." English promises on this score evidently did not convince the Pequot. One sachem's wife who was taken with her children begged "that the English would not abuse her body and that her children might not be taken from her." When the Mohegan threatened the English in the 1640s, John Winthrop chided their sachem, Uncas, for "puttinge [English] women in feare" even after Uncas had "inuited our people to come and sitt downe by you." The English even used the expectation that women were not combatants to criticize one another. One denunciation of Nathaniel Bacon stressed that his forces had killed Indian women. The Royal Commissioners who sought to restore order after Bacon's death noted that the Pamunkey's weroansqua or female chief leader, Cockacoeske, was horrifed to find the corpse of another Pamunkey woman and fled from all the English, "fearing their cruelty by that gastly example." [16]

As we have seen, in terms of gender, the one thing Indians and English agreed on was that they could insult each other's soldiers most woundingly by calling them women. Underhill's party was taunted by Indians who had killed some Englishmen, taken their arms, and put on their clothing. "Come and fetch your Englishmen's clothes again," the Indians yelled. "Come out and fight, if you dare; you dare not fight; you are all one like women." The English, not willing for their manhood to be thus held in contempt, increasingly responded with similar jeers about Indian men. Even after the English had adopted tactics they associated with Indians (particularly using sneak attacks and firing weapons while concealed), they continued to claim that when the Indians did such things, their fighting was cowardly. And colonists began to equate vanquished Indian men with women, either following or inventing a native custom. Richard Davenport wrote in a letter to John Winthrop that the natives allied with the English in the Pequot War "would bee glad to make women of all the Pecotts now"; Davenport specified in the margin of his letter that by "women" he meant "slaves," though it was in his main text that he deployed the gendered insult. [17]

Still, Englishmen had reasons to concede that Indian men were masculine in a way that no women were, even (or especially) Englishwomen. Exclusion of colonial women from warfare functioned in part as a defense against accusation that anyone could learn to fire a musket—even savages or women. The English could not keep firearms out of the hands of natives, but they could keep them away from their womenfolk. The English thus granted manhood, however grudgingly, to male Indians, first when they had admired them as archers, then when they conceded that Indian men could use guns. The English continued to poke fun at Indians who failed to recognize that women were not warriors. Edward Waterhouse said that the natives in contact with new settlements in Virginia were cowards who would flee even at "the presentment of a staffe in manner of a Peece" and at "an vncharged Peece in the hands of a woman." That Indians would flee from a woman who bore a firearm showed their fear of English weaponry, even when handled by mere females; that Waterhouse was careful to employ an instance in which a women bore an unloaded rather than a charged musket may have indicated English apprehension over the mixing of women and war. In this way, the masculine cult of the warrior, from ancient Briton to modern colonizer, persisted in its nostalgic rendering of an English society that in some ways stayed the same, however much it moved forward in time and westward across the Atlantic. Englishmen faced worthy opponents in the person of male Indian warriors, while Englishwomen, for the most part, kept out of the fight. Neither gunpowder nor the colonial setting was presumed to threaten this gendered order.[18]

If Englishmen were supposed to be the manliest of all, this raised the question why Indians sometimes beat them in battle. The answer was, increasingly, that Indian men had been subjected, since their infancy, to a regimen that artificially strengthened their bodies. This discipline indeed made them admirable soldiers, but at the cost of undermining their humanity, though with negligible effect on their resistance to disease. Colonists therefore registered yet more ambivalence over Indian technology. Technologies unfamiliar to the English had long been associated with trickery or shamanism; colonists now suspected that native *techne* rendered the human body artificial, a piece of machinery designed to subsist despite violence and scarcity. English arguments about Indians' physical regimen accordingly carried an undercurrent of suspicion about the innate weaknesses that their transformations of the body concealed, and about the peculiar therapies their bodies had had to undergo to acquire their artificial strength.

The conviction of the English that Indians manipulated and altered their bodies paralleled their fascination with native pharmacology, especially because both topics generated narratives about Indians that were simultaneously flattering and patronizing. Representations of practices that transformed the body had taken shape, initially, in the discussions of corporeal types as products of custom, climate, or inheritance. Like all northern peoples, North America's natives were believed to be somewhat phlegmatic, that is, taciturn and physically stoical. This humoral opinion had probably informed Peter Heylyn's description of native Virginians as "accustomed to the cold, which they patiently endure, or feel not." But climate did not explain everything. The contrast between Indians and Africans had underscored the belief that custom explained the former's skin color but not the latter's. In part, this assertion had reassured colonists that their skins would not darken if they moved to America, nor would their creole children lose the English complexion—so long as none of them adopted the Indian practice of applying colored ointments to their skin. Climate thus remained an unsatisfying explanation of bodily variations in America and the mechanisms of inheritance too arcane.[19]

In relation to Indians, therefore, the English gradually dismissed climatological explanations, avoided arguments overtly based on reproduction and claimed that it was custom that visibly altered the Indian body. Culture provided a second nature. Custom especially helped explain why children came to resemble the adults within the same region or culture. English commentators did not say that these customs could also confer resistance to disease; nor did they argue that inherited factors caused any difference not apparent to the eye, such as skin coloring and form of the body. These arguments that focused on Indian custom therefore talked around the problem of inheritance, but raised the question why, if custom made such a difference in the body, it could not protect Indians from epidemics.

Analyses of Indian customs continued the ethnographic observation that colonists had constructed in their first encounters with Indians. It perpetuated the focus on behaviors that manipulated the body. At first, colonists had been quick to condemn Indian adornment as a species of idolatry, a self-love that turned the human body, the image of God, into an object to be sinfully adorned. Christian prejudice had informed most descriptions of Indian practices such as body painting, tattooing, decorating hair, and wearing talismans. Yet even John Bulwer's *Anthropometamorphosis* had given a significant exception in the case of native Americans, who might paint themselves as protection from climate rather than for idolatrous reasons. The gathering of military intelligence had, in parallel, characterized Indian warriors as strong and dextrous, even taller than the English. These two forms of description would continue, with English observers eager to identify which features made Indians into admirable enemies and which into detestable savages.

Gradually, however, the English began to focus a more secular criticism on a few native customs related to the body, especially practices meant to make the body stronger. Such accounts focused on the maternal role in hardening children. This was in accordance with the English belief that mothers, midwives, and nurses could easily alter the body of an infant, whose bones were still plastic. Commentators such as Bulwer had deplored as vanity female meddling with infants, unless it had direct medical benefit for a child. Increasingly, descriptions of Indians were more likely to assess such practices without referring to sin, as Bulwer had done when he excused Indians' artificial pigmentation as protection against cold. Such statements began to stress that Indian mothers manipulated their children's bodies to inure them against hardship.

English descriptions of Indian women's child rearing emphasized that native adaptation of the body was a long-term process that transformed nature through artifice; it was an elaborate if subtle species of technology. William Strachey explained that native women would wash their young children outdoors even when it was cold and would "tanne their skynns" with ointments so "no weather will hurt them." Thomas Morton agreed, noting that Indian mothers bathed their infants with a walnut dye that would "staine their skinne for ever." Even in the eighteenth century, this interpretation of Indians' coloring persisted. According to John Lawson, the Carolina Algonquians' tawny color came from an ointment made of bear oil and "a Colour like burnt Cork." Because the Indians' use of the dye began in infancy and continued throughout life, the unguent gradually "fills the Pores, and enables them better to endure the Extremity of the Weather," while also making the dye adhere to the skin. This was indeed making custom into nature, a sooty grease gradually changing the skin.[20]

The skin was only the surface; Indian children's very bones were transformed. Strachey stated that Indian mothers in Virginia bound the limbs of infants straight on cradle boards. Thomas Morton argued that this practice guaranteed that Indians were "well proportioned" and never "crooked backed or wry legged" like Europeans, whose swaddling was less efficacious. Strachey also explained that natives used walnut oil "to drappe their ioynts and smeere their bodies with, which doe make them supple and nymble." Roger Williams likewise observed that native men were agile and fleet of foot because "their legs being also from the wombe stretcht and bound up in a strange way on their Cradle backward, as also annointed."[21]

It was critical that augmentation of bodily strength begin just after birth, when children's bodies were still pliable. If plunging an infant into cold water or strapping it to a rigid surface seemed cruel, such practices were necessary to begin the gradual process of making weak children into strong adults. Wood asserted that a newborn was "greased and sooted" for protection; John Josselyn added that she or he was immediately bound to a cradleboard. Lawson refined this idea further when he described how Indian women would "lay the Back-part of their Children's Heads on a Bag of Sand, (such as Engravers use to rest their Plates upon.)" They then placed the child on a flat board and swaddled it "hard down" from the "one End of this En-gine, to the other. This Method makes the Child's Body and Limbs as straight as an Arrow." The cradles were "apt to make the Body flat" but otherwise made the child grow straight and tall, and the head-binding made her or his eyesight better. Lawson's terminology was re-markable: a cradleboard was an "engine" or piece of machinery; an infant's pillow was like the equipment an engraver used to preserve a carved image. Native American artifice produced an admirable physi-cal specimen, the straight-backed, clean-limbed, sharp-eyed Indian. Rather than make Indian technology seem backward, Lawson's ac-count made it seem a development that Europeans might want to em-ulate. Robert Beverley probably drew on Lawson when he described Indian mothers who washed newborns in cold water then bound them on boards "till the Bones begin to harden, the Joynts to knit, and the Limbs to grow strong."[22]

Still, some descriptions of Indian child rearing were far-fetched, al-most designed to shock English readers. In part, this propensity to think the worst of Indian parents probably resulted because English-men (who authored most narratives on America) did not have a good idea of how Indian mothers raised their children. When Edward Maria Wingfield described Powhatan customs in 1607, he reported that although the natives were not cannibals, they spent "most part of the night in singing, or howling, and that every morning the Women Carryed all the litle Childrenn to the Rivers sides, but what they did there he did not knowe." Despite Wingfield's dark intimations of some barbaric rite, it is likely that the singing did not presage infant sacrifice. Instead, women were cleaning away the vegetable fiber that they used to diaper their infants overnight, and then washing and re-swaddling the children. (An English*woman* might have guessed this.) Inclining to the same exaggeration in the 1620s, Christopher Levett claimed that New England's natives would bury their children in snow to inure them to cold and fling them into the sea to teach them to swim.[23]

Colonial observers emphasized that, in contrast to this harsh treatment of children's bodies, Indian parents were for the most part indulgent of their behavior. The desire to harden their children physically therefore revealed Indian parents' particular anxiety over their bodily endurance, which canceled out their usual affection for their children. According to Wood, Indian mothers took care to sing "lullabies to quiet their children, who generally are as quiet as if they had neither spleen or lungs." Such cosseting contrasted with children's treatment of their parents. Josselyn claimed that natives sometimes killed their elderly parents, either by starvation or by burying them alive; he cited an instance of live interment "as it was supposed an *Indian* did his Mother at *Casco* in 1669." In short, indulgence was restricted to certain actions toward one's children; adults, even one's parents, did not merit such treatment.[24]

The revocation of parental indulgence seemed particularly striking when Indian boys came of age. At this point, the native regimen took able-bodied youths and made them into inured warriors. John Smith's early depiction of Powhatan initiation rites for adolescent males had defined colonial suspicions about how Indians raised their children. He claimed to have witnessed a ceremony of the "Black-boyes" in which about fifteen adolescents, between ten and fifteen years of age, were painted white and made to run the gauntlet while the adult men struck them with "Bastinadoes." Their mothers protested this treatment, or at least did so ritually; the "women weepe and cry out very passionately." After the beating, the boys were "cast on a heape, in a valley as [if] dead." Indeed, some were killed by the devil or *"Okee"* who sucked blood from the "left breast" of his victims. The survivors were accepted back into village life, though a few remained isolated from the village for nine months, a ritual rebirth that signified their new role as shamans. Smith's account therefore brought together English fears: of paganism, human sacrifice, abnormally cruel parenting, and powerful warriors like the archers who besieged Jamestown, turning English men and dogs into bloody pincushions.[25]

Just as early military intelligence had shaped initial English ethnography, the threat of war continued to influence accounts of natives. This was so much the case that natives' child rearing was sometimes thought to have peculiar emphasis for male Indians, as Smith's description indicated. During a visit to Plymouth, Isaack de Rasieres described how Wampanoag rituals for male adolescents prepared adult men to endure "privation in the field." When he came of age, a boy was banished to the wilderness with a bow, arrows, knife, and hatchet, and had to survive a New England winter armed with only these tools. At the end of this exile, wrote Rasieres, the youth next took doses of poison (immediately followed, at first, by antidotes) until he could retain the poison without vomiting—or dying. By this point, his body could withstand harsh weather, lack of food and water, contact with toxins, and the injuries of war or accident. This was a critical goal within cultures that, from the European perspective, lacked extensive material resources, the plentiful supplies or the monetary incentive to wage war. Wood marveled, for instance, that Indian men had "such lustie bodies" despite their "slender" means of support. This was because natives were neither "brought downe with suppressing labour" nor "drowned in the excessive abuse of overflowing plenty." If civility bestowed an unhealthy luxury on the rich and ground the faces of the poor in the dust, Indians' lack of civility was a relative advantage because it gave strong constitutions to all natives.[26]

Though early accounts had stressed the similarity between English and Indians, the later focus on bodies began to differentiate the peoples, even as it carried forward the tendency to admire native warriors. William Strachey remarked that in Virginia, native "men are very strong of able bodies, and full of agility, accustoming themselues to endure hardnes." Wood noted that the Indians north of Massachusetts Bay were "between five or six foot high, straight bodied . . . broad shouldered, brawny armed"—the perfect physique for a soldier. A 1635 account of Maryland reported that the natives had "able bodies, and [were] generally, taller, and bigger limbed then the *English,* and want not courage." John Winthrop noted that when one English war party was drawn into an ambush during the Pequot War in 1637, "the Indians were so hardy, as they came close up to them, notwithstanding their pieces." Josselyn, who discussed at length Indian acquisition of strong bodies, from childbirth through child rearing, also concluded that the men "are lusty Souldiers to see to and very strong."[27]

Perhaps because strong native soldiers were the last people colonists wanted to face, native men's remarkable bodies elicited some of the suspicions of sorcery that had appeared in early narratives of exploration, especially accounts of the Arctic. Virginia's tormented "black boys" were the best example of continued English association of pagan practice with savage child rearing. The Council of the Virginia Company claimed to have extracted a confession from Opechancanough in 1622 that God was angry with his people because of "theire Coustome of making their Children black boyes" (though Opechancanough was poised to orchestrate his attack on the Virginia settlements that year and was unlikely to abjure methods of strengthening his male population). Edward Johnson reported an uncanny episode in the Pequot War when some native warriors could not be pierced by swords or rapiers for "a long time, which made some of the Souldiers think the Devil was in them, for there were some Powwowes among them, which work strange things with the help of Satan." For example, one man whose neck was thrust through with a halberd simply "caught the halberts speare in his hand, and wound it quite round" as if the perverse action caused no sensation in his body yet was sensational to his English audience.[28]

If resistance to pain seemed bizarre, the English nonetheless admired native men's rejection of rape during war, an additional proof of their almost inhuman resolve but one that at least promised mercy toward some English people. (Algonquian and Iroquoian men shunned sexual relations before and during war and would not rape female captives, lest the captives be adopted and intercourse with them prove retroactively incestuous.) At first, the English assumed that Indian soldiers would rape women on the other side; this was common behavior in European wars. Perhaps for this reason, Wood claimed that the Mohawk attacked their neighbors by "slaying men, ravishing women." But Wood admitted that the English were not yet familiar with the Mohawk and that he knew them only secondhand. One of the earliest remarks on natives' avoidance of rape occurred during the Pequot War, when the Pequot abducted the two "maids" who they hoped knew how to make gunpowder. The emphasis on the women's status as maids, or virgins, emphasized their vulnerability and the possibility that the enemy could offer particular insult to women. The English were therefore surprised when the women were "well used by the Pequods, and no violence offered them."[29]

Only in some accounts of King Philip's War would colonists claim that Indian men "defiled" Englishwomen. To a certain extent, these assertions reflected English fears that the Wampanoag and their allies might push colonists off the land and take over their settlements. The conviction that population demonstrated a claim to territory made the English anxious that their women not become captive breeders of a new people who, though partly descended from the English, would gain an Indian identity and restock the dwindling native population. A colonist who "knew" her attackers claimed that she also knew that they planned to kill all Englishmen "but to save as many Women and Houses" as possible for themselves. Rumors that Mary Rowlandson had been pressured to marry one of her captors further increased the anxiety that settler women, the primal source of English power over America, would be abducted and their fertility exploited by the enemy.[30]

Whatever they thought about Indians and rape, it was not the case that the English believed that Indians spared women from all physical hardship. Instead, the English thought that an Indian woman's ability to withstand the pains of childbirth paralleled the Indian man's endurance in battle; both resulted from the training of the body that occurred during infancy. Comments on this subject reflected a long-running argument over the characteristics of foreign peoples. Remarkable ease in childbirth was a feature the English ascribed to many foreigners. This was perhaps the case because male visitors to other cultures were unlikely to learn much about the midwifery of their hostesses, and because men of high status were unlikely to witness childbirth among peasants, servants, and slaves; if such men did not see suffering, they did not suppose it to exist. These factors united to create a picture of female endurance across many and surprising cultural lines. Peter Heylyn said of the Spanish that their women were "wondrous strong and beyond beliefe, patient in the throwes of childbed." Richard Ligon reported that the African women on Barbados gave birth with little or no assistance, and returned to work within a fortnight. Such was not usually the case with people closer to the home of the male observer, and with people who were not, like slaves, forced back to work.[31]

Scripture had specified, however, that postlapsarian women would bring forth children in sorrow; if any women were exempt from this curse, they and their people might be free from original sin—or else were more animal than human. When the English described easy childbirth among Catholic Spaniards or pagan Africans, they begged the question of the spiritual status of these peoples. Some commentators were suspicious of the contention that certain women were free of the curse of Eve and referred again to the competing theories of custom and inheritance. In the case of the Irish, Bulwer claimed, women probably broke the pubic bone of female newborns, which would allow them to "have very quick and easie deliverance in Childbirth" as adults. In the case of Africans, as Jennifer Morgan has pointed out, English observers linked their argument for all sub-Saharan Africans' inhuman bodily endurance with specific observations on childbirth, representing African women as conveniently unfeeling and durable, subhuman units for production of plantation wealth and reproduction of a slave population. Over time, English commentators on America would tend to argue that custom changed the Indian woman's body (as with the Irish), and to avoid contending that female natives were, like African women, insensible and tough by nature.[32]

In the early years of Anglo-Indian contact, observers had not always assumed that childbearing Indian women had an easy delivery. The authors of the 1590s "Drake Manuscript" or "Histoire naturelle des Indes" had executed and annotated one watercolor of native men from the Caribbean who were engaged in driving away the pain from a woman in childbirth. The men passed around the house where the woman was in labor, dancing, playing music, and singing loudly. By the early seventeenth century, however, English accounts stressed that Indian women gave birth with little effort or pain. At first, the reasons for this were not clearly focused on transformation of the female body. Thomas Morton explained that native women had "a faire delivery, and a quick" because "their women are very good midwifes," though he marveled that pregnant women worked hard at their usual tasks even "when they are as great as they can be" and would within a day or two of delivery return to work.[33]

But the problem of Eve's curse was compounded in America, where the new world's natives had only recently learned of the gospel. Subsequent commentary would push further Morton's connection between female Indians' hard work and their durable bodies rather than suggest Indians' freedom from sin. Roger Williams allowed that "it hath pleased God in wonderfull manner to moderate that curse of the sorrowes of Child-bearing to these poore Indian Women: So that ordinarily they have a wonderfull more speedy and easie Travell [travail], and delivery then the Women of *Europe.*" But this was due to "the hardnesse of their constitution," not evidence that "God is more gracious to them above other Women." Williams linked performance in childbirth to the fact that women performed unnaturally demanding physical labor, especially out in the fields, where they grew corn: "They plant it, dresse it, gather it, barne it, beat it . . . which labour is questionlesse one cause of their extraordinary ease of childbirth." Josselyn agreed that native women were accustomed to working abroad and easily delivered; pregnant women needed no human assistance, instead going individually to the woods to bear a child, then "home they trudge."[34]

If ease in childbirth evidenced Indian women's remarkable physiology, torture was final proof of native men's hardiness, sign of their gender-specific adaptation to war. At first, English accounts stressed that torture was something that native groups did to one another's men, a wartime practice that identified the enemy yet was shared with the enemy. Strachey observed that when native warriors were tortured, they "never cryed, complayned, nor seemed to aske pardon." But the natives also tortured the English, and gradually the English learned that their own manhood was in question. Strachey recorded a Powhatan song (the first English rendition of spoken Algonquian) about capturing and killing Englishmen, a song with the onomatopoeic refrain of "whe whe," representing how the English screamed shamefully when they were tortured. Native men seemed stronger. George Alsop commented of Susquehannock men that no torment "makes them lower the Top-gallant sail of their Heroick courage, to beg [mercy] with a submissive Repentance."[35]

English descriptions of native torture grew more elaborate and more wary of the possibility that the practice could be used against settlers. William Wood described the torture and cannibalistic ritual attributed to the Mohawk, who gradually excised living human flesh and ate it raw and bloody before the eyes of the person who was reduced to butcher's meat. Wood also described the Indian "custom to cut off their [enemies'] heads, hands, and feet to bear home" as trophies. When a colonist lost his way between Dorchester and Watertown in the fall of 1642 and heard some wolves howling, he "cried out help, help." A man who lived near Cambridge heard the cries and, when the lost man did not respond to his calls, feared "that the Indians had gotten some English man and were torturing him." All this shrieking was embarrassing to English masculinity. Colonists were therefore careful to note instances when their fellows did not cry out under Indian torture but (despite their lack of Indian-style training) met the test with dignity. When John Tilley was captured by Pequot in 1636, the warriors "cut off his hands, and sent them before, and after cut off his feet. He lived three days after his hands were cut off; and [the Indians] themselves confessed, that he was a stout man, because he cried not in his torture."[36] Thus did torture test male bodily endurance and, in the case of Indians, gradually dismantle the corporeal strength and integrity that had been constructed with such care.

If torture was something that the English described as appalling, it was not as unfamiliar as they claimed. Further, torture still posited similarities among men (English or Indian) that were not available to the different women who lived on the frontier. Wartime atrocities were hardly unknown to Europeans, and judicial torture and dismemberment were likewise familiar. But as had been the case with archery, the military interface between English and Indian focused on gender-specific similarities. The English were, after all, just as incredulous that Indian women could give birth alone and with little pain as they were that Indian men could be cut apart and burned without crying out. This portrayal of savage life might *exaggerate* a male role recognizable to Europeans—the unflinching warrior—but it did not reinforce a proper female role. The perception of Indian women instead *inverted* the European woman's role as a frail domestic creature by enduring hardship out of doors. Further, this was a cultural inversion, not a manifestation of an intrinsic nature; custom created the woman's toughened body that bore children, and custom dictated that she in turn manipulate their infant bodies in order to make them as tough.[37]

The focus on Indian childbirth and maternal care of a malleable infant analyzed sexual reproduction in its final stages: the actual delivery of a child and subsequent forming of its body. English commentary thus drew a veil over (or ignored) the material events that preceded childbirth, particularly the production of seed that formed the Indian infants in the first place. In this way, discourse on bodily differences continued the idiomatic definition of racial differences—continuity of corporeal forms that did not specify bodily functions to guarantee it—which had characterized English discussions of Indian susceptibility to disease. George Alsop, for example, said of the Susquehannock that they were tall, straight, and "stately," and that they withstood heat and cold though "cloth'd with no other Armour to defend them" than "What nature gave them when they parted with the dark receptacle of their mothers womb." English analysis never penetrated the darkness of the Indian womb, though the obsession with the body that surrounded that organ of generation showed colonists' anxiety over its function in the production of Indian bodies. The female Indian body especially elicited fear that the bloody businesses of childbirth and of warfare might get mixed together.[38]

In the case of Indian women, settlers believed that the physical trials of their childhood and their hard labor as adults created unfeeling creatures whose attitudes toward the human body were monstrous. Colonists' accounts, accordingly, expressed horror that Indian women might participate in ritual torture and that Englishwomen might be tortured. Both experiences underlined English fears that Indians thought of women in ways that were contrary to nature and that repellently mingled women and warfare. One account of King Philip's War insisted that Indian women delighted as much in cruelty toward wartime captives as did their menfolk. They had not "the two proper Virtues of Womankinde, Pity and Modesty," both of which would have distanced them from judicial torture and the bloody humiliations of war.[39]

Two reports of violence against and by Englishwomen during King Philip's War carefully demarcated the circumstances under which women could forsake pity and modesty. Childbirth, giving life, was the inversion of war, the female counterpart to the male function of taking life; each role was specific to one gender. If childbirth were disrupted by war, the rupture released a woman from the expectation that she would abstain from warlike activities. Indians' interruption of English childbirth was in this sense the ultimate violation and a threat to the English procreation that predicted colonial hegemony. These fears were apparent in a story of a pregnant Englishwoman who tried to escape her Indian captors by acting like an Indian woman but who was then forced into a bloody parody of English customs regarding childbirth. The woman was captured by Narragansett and their Wampanoag and Nipmuck allies at Lancaster during the same 1675 raid that took Mary Rowlandson. As she began labor, she tried to creep into "the Woods to be privately delivered." But "the Indians followed and in a jeering Manner, they [said they] would help her, and be her Midwives." What this meant was that the Indians ripped the child out of the woman and burned it before her eyes, then clubbed her to death. This tableau mimicked an English childbirth but exaggerated the pain and danger of childbed, as if the Indians mocked the physical weakness of Englishwomen and denied that they could deliver children in the manner of native women.[40]

Two other Englishwomen revenged this kind of assault. Hannah Dustin and Mary Neff, who had just assisted Dustin in childbirth, were taken captive from Haverhill, Massachusetts, in a raid during King William's War (1689–1697). Dustin reported that the Indians killed her newborn, rounded up some survivors, and began to march north, dispatching the weaker captives on the way. A month and a half later (still 150 miles from their destination), Dustin convinced Neff and another captive, a young Englishman, that they must kill their captors while they slept. This was imperative because if the three reached the village of their captors they would face torture, in the form of running the gauntlet, and humiliation when Indians "derided some of the Fainthearted English, which they said, fainted and swoon'd away under the Torments of this Discipline." Dustin's plan of attack succeeded; only one Indian woman and one boy managed to escape. The English trio then scalped their dead captors, returned home, and received a bounty for the scalps. It was unprecedented for female violence to be so celebrated and rewarded. The narrative stresses why this should be so: the inhumane attack on a woman not yet out of childbed, the murder of her child, the fact that she faced shameful torture. Having used her body and risked her life to produce a child, then been forced out into the wilderness, Dustin had reason to accept the inversion of her role: from female producer of life to masculinized taker of life. Further, the nurse who assisted Dustin in her normal role assisted her in her exceptional one. The gender inversion worked only because, as the account explained events, Indians had created the inversion and should suffer thereby. Otherwise, Englishwomen were not to fall into such savage behavior, lest they pervert their colonial role as reproducers of English bodies.[41]

If the female role was nonnegotiable, a "natural" state that the

English believed native custom perverted, the masculine role in war continued to compare and connect English and Indian men. Just as colonists and Indians shared military tactics and weapons, so they began to share assumptions about what could be done to a combatant's body, either living or dead. The English had, after all, taken an early interest in what native warriors' bodies looked like. Increasingly, they connected their older ideas about customs that shaped an Indian man's appearance with their new sense that such a man's body could and should be subjected to extraordinary violence. During the skirmish that led to Bacon's Rebellion and Anglo-Indian warfare in Virginia, one of the English captains, George Brent, seized the Doeg "King" by "catching hold of his twisted Lock (which was all the Hair he wore)" and killed him. The scalp lock, which had earlier drawn ethnographic commentary from the English about how natives prepared themselves to hunt and wage war, was, at this point, a useful handle by which to seize and defeat an Indian.[42]

Though the English were also willing to torture Indians, they tried to distinguish between their own and native ways. Colonists represented native torture in terms the English would understand but recognize as negatively coded. Wood described how one Indian man whose skin was flayed became a "walking maypole" for the "bare skinned morris dancers" who attacked him until he was executed by a "satyre." Indian torture of captives was thus a pagan ritual like those that needed to be rooted out of Protestant practice. This did not mean that Englishmen were above torturing Indians. During the Pequot War, when the English killed five Indian men at Saybrook, they also took one man alive, "whom the English put to torture; and set all their heads upon the fort. The reason was, because they had tortured such of our men as they took alive." In the same war, one captured Pequot man was torn to death by English soldiers. He was acknowledged to have had "courage" even "when all is desperate. But it availed this Savage nothing; they tied one of his legs to a post, and 20 men with a rope tied to the other, pulled him in pieces, Captain *Vnderhill* shooting a pistol through him to dispatch him." In 1644, during Keift's War, an Indian man accused of attacking an Englishwoman in Stamford with a lathing hammer was put to death in a way that tested his resistance to pain. The man was beheaded with a falchion, but the executioner "had eight blows at it before he could effect it, and the Indian sat upright and stirred not all the time." The crime and the punishment mirrored each other, representing both an Indian and an Englishman hacking at human bodies with imported tools.[43]

Further, the English used dismemberment to demonstrate that Indians could be reduced to mere matter, and they displayed enemies' body parts to signal their own martial prowess. The Pilgrims had of course used a "standard" dyed with native blood and a native man's head to show their increasing power over the Indians and their land around Plymouth. Reducing Indians to pieces would continue. Roger Williams disliked the practice but argued that it was necessary. In 1637 Williams acknowledged to Governor Winthrop that the hands of three Pequots (sent by the Narragansett) were "no pleasing Sight," but he sent them on to Winthrop because "if I had buried the present my selfe I should have incurd suspicion of pride and wronged my betters, in the natives and others eyes." William Coddington feared that he had made the mistake Williams had avoided, reporting to Winthrop that the Narragansett sachems "haue not sent vnto me sence I reiected a present of 30 fingers and thumes."[44]

Wartime torture further manifested the hybrid material culture in and around the English colonies. George Alsop's account of Maryland explained that when the Susquehannock tortured their Indian captives (who defiantly sang throughout their ordeal), they would sear the victims' flesh with "pieces of Iron, and barrels of old Guns." The English also used their products in new ways to differentiate between allies and enemies, and between free Indians and those who had been conquered. During the Pequot War, Roger Williams advised the English to give "signes or marcks" to their Narragansett allies. "You may please therefore to prouide some yellow or red for their heads," he wrote, probably meaning yellow or red headcloths. John Winthrop later noted that forty-eight women and children taken during the war were "disposed" as slaves to "particular persons." Some ran away, and, when recovered, "those we branded on the shoulder" to facilitate future detection.[45]

By 1675, when both the Chesapeake and New England experienced climactic Anglo-Indian conflicts, the conceptualization of Indian bodies as suited to war, hardship, and pain was little questioned. Indian torture was a familiar part of frontier warfare, a stated reason for the English to hate and fight against the natives. Frontier planters in Virginia presented as one reason why they needed to attack neighboring Indians the information that "the Indians hath allready most barberously and Inhumanly taken and Murdered severall of our bretheren and put them to most cruell torture by burning of them alive and by cruell torturing of them." Likewise, New Englanders reported that five or six colonists taken by the Wampanoag had been killed "in such a manner as none but *Salvages* would have done," including cutting out sections of flesh and searing the wounds with fire.[46]

Increasingly, the accounts of the English colonists emphasized that they participated in actions that did not simply kill Indians but destroyed their bodies. Dismemberment and burning of the bodies of vanquished Indians reversed the slow processes that had created strong native constitutions. When Nathaniel Bacon's forces attacked the Susquehannock at their fort, they "destroid" the "men, woemen and children . . . all burnt." Bacon repeated that he and his forces had abjured taking prisoners, and instead "burn't and destroid all." He emphasized, for good measure, that his attacks had aggravated conflicts between different Indian groups, whose "civill warre" the English could play to their "advantage to [the Indians'] utter Ruine and destruction." During and after King Philip's War in New England, the English delighted in dismembering Indians and displaying their body parts as trophies, evidence that their threatening bodies had lost all life and integration. An account from New England emphasized that the Wampanoag leader Philip or Metacom had been shot and decapitated, and his body cut into quarters and burnt. Philip was, and by implication his people were, annihilated. Their cultivation of tough warriors and matrons had gained them nothing. Their population was defeated, both as individuals and as a tenable group.[47]

The body remained the ultimate site of cultural identity and intercultural contention, colonial proof that English and Indian peoples were fundamentally different. Warfare, and its female counterpart, childbirth, were tests of the body, and the English were increasingly suspicious that natives devoted themselves to customs that gave them unnatural corporeal advantages. These ideas about Indian bodies joined the existing discourses on native weakness during epidemics and on antipathy to Anglo-Indian intermarriage. Instead of cooperation during hardships such as epidemics, and instead of marriage between English and Indians, warfare remained the identifying form of contact between invaders and invaded: it reified the stated desire of the English not to merge peacefully with Indian populations. As Roger Williams put it in 1658, "It is the wonderfull mercy of God that the English and pagan bloud hath not bene Yearely mixt togeather" in war. Williams's unstated assumption was that the two peoples' blood could be mixed in no other way.[48]

It is significant that, in the last decades of the seventeenth century, colonists perfected their conceptualization of an inferior Indian body just before they would have to admit that they enjoyed some material advantages in the initial encounter with Indians. European recognition and public discussion of global migration of diseases would finally occur by the early 1700s, and the English to a certain extent reconsidered whether Indians really had been prepared for the epidemics that devastated some communities. But most of the work of deriding Indian bodies as deficient had by this point already been done. The English put two final nails in the coffin right at the end of the seventeenth century: an argument that Indians' humoral construction disposed them to choler and war, and a contention that they were prone to drunkenness and ill health related to drink.

It was important for the English to reiterate that nature itself excused their bloodiest attempts to dominate and dismiss Indians. Despite their participation in the practices of torture and dismemberment, and notwithstanding the hybrid material culture that reinforced these customs, colonists emphasized that Indians' bodies were the basis for their cruelty. The native endurance of pain and propensity toward violence were rooted in an unnatural bodily construction; if the natives were contrary to nature, so English actions toward them must be. It is significant, for example, that mid- and late seventeenth-century descriptions of Indians tended to emphasize their choleric dispositions rather than the melancholy character once ascribed to them. At first, the English had agreed with Spanish accounts that Indians were melancholy. A description of Frobisher's third voyage had called the Inuit both "sullen and desperate," the latter meaning they were quick to commit suicide rather than face captivity. As late as the 1620s, descriptions of "spleen" stones among the natives along the Amazon reinforced the idea that Indians suffered from spleen-related diseases such as melancholy. Twenty years later, Roger Williams similarly described the North American natives' "naturall Temper, which inclines to sadnesse." But the English simultaneously emphasized the natives' choleric temper, part of the ethnography that identified the military strengths of a potential enemy. For example, Dr. Dodding's postmortem report on Calichough, Frobisher's second male captive, concluded that the man had been inclined to choler.[49]

A more definitive shift in humoral emphasis appeared in English reactions to the early seventeenth-century conflicts in Virginia and New England. According to one account of the Pequot War, the "Inhabitants" of New England, and especially the Pequots, had fire or choler predominant in their physical constitutions, and their choleric temperament made them "terrible to their neighbours, and troublesome to the *English*." William Pynchon concluded that diplomatic delays could modify Indians' tendency toward vengefulness; "their reuengefull desyer will soone be cooled," he suggested, if they were forced to wait before taking up arms. Josselyn concluded that Indians were by nature hot, therefore prone to choler, lust, and violence. Melancholy (created by too much phlegm) was in their nature, too, but the dry heat of their nature overrode the clammy sadness that was only an occasional characteristic. The humoral interpretation of Indians' militarism made it possible for colonists to see this as a medical condition, even a form of illness. The English even interpreted Indian discontent as madness, a violent insanity that overtook them. The younger John Winthrop wrote of Connecticut in 1649–50 that the Indians "all over the country [were] taken with a suddaine madnesse" the likes of which "they doe not remember." Henry Whitfeld also remarked on the "strange disease" among the Indians. They were wont to run up and down, blackened their faces, "snatched up any weapon, spake great words, but did no hurt."[50] (These incidents may have been phases of mourning war, in which Indians sought war captives either to mollify the spirits of the recently deceased or to supplement population, or expressed forms of spiritual revitalization during moments of cultural stress.)

Just as Indians' humoral composition now was said to make them warlike, so their artificially hardened bodies, which made them frighteningly immune to pain, were becoming less admirable. Roger Williams had grown more and more critical of Indians over the course of his life, and his views on native women's ease in childbirth likewise grew more negative. Williams had first modified his impression that Indians might not suffer the curse of Eve to an opinion that they were not supernaturally blessed but altered in body because of their agricultural work. Still later he found their bodily endurance too unnatural to be admired. In 1669 Williams wrote disgustedly of "Barbarians and Indian Women [who] (ordinarily) when being in Pains and Sorowes they cry not out." "Experienced Women," meaning presumably English matrons and midwives, "will bid such travelling [travailing] women to cry and spare not, for by their Cries their Griefes are much allayed." If men should not scream under torture, women should do so in labor.[51]

But the representation of the Indian body as durable and pain-resistant was suspiciously at odds with simultaneous English assertions that Indians had little resistance to diseases, even common diseases that barely affected English children. All the English observations on epidemics in and near the early settlements stressed that Indian populations were more affected than the English; colonists had repeated and elaborated this claim in order to argue their power over American territory. Yet these same Indian bodies were the ones that were so powerful and terrifying in war. It is not the case that these two contrasting opinions on the Indian body emerged from different sets of writers; the same people stated both ideas. Wood, for instance, who had admired Indian men's straight, broad-shouldered bodies, also repeated the information that a large sector of the native population had been decimated by "the sweeping plague." He nevertheless insisted that the survivors had "healthful bodies" and were unfamiliar with "those health-wasting diseases" of other countries, such as fevers and consumptions. Robert Beverley likewise claimed that Virginia's Indians were "straight and well proportion'd" and "not subject to many diseases" but were nevertheless "almost wasted." These seemed ill-sorted opinions, but their authors evidently saw no contradiction; the ability to fight in combat and the inability to combat diseases could exist within the same body.[52]

By the end of the seventeenth century, colonists began to cite liquor as another reason for Indians' unhealthiness, though they insisted that Europeans did not need to take full blame for introducing this commodity's ill effects. Earlier, the English had used gifts of tobacco and liquor to open and perpetuate friendly relations with chosen groups of natives. Later on, encouraging Indians to drink in tense diplomatic situations seemed a bad idea. Further, colonists began to describe Indians' use of liquor as if their inebriation proved something about their physiology. The propensity to drink and become drunk was, like the propensity toward morbidity and mortality in general, deep-seated within some quality of Indians' bodies. Massachusetts therefore in 1657 forbade sale of any liquor—even the milder drinks such as beer, cider, and perry—to Indians: "No moderation can be attayned to p[re]vent drunkenes amongst them." Williams also ridiculed the "distinction of Druncken and Sober honest Sachims" because "all the pagans are so given to Drunckennes."[53]

In this way, like Indians' supposed humoral propensity to war, native response to liquor was naturalized, presented as an inevitable consequence of infirm bodies. Josselyn related that rum has "killed many of them, especially old women who have dyed when dead drunk." Josselyn and others duly chided Europeans for helping natives to a fatal poison: rather than teach the gospel, the English had taught vice "for a little profit." As was the case with earlier fears over native idolatry, alcohol was a sign of universal human sin. Unlike in the earlier case, however, the sinfulness of Indians was only a tepid reminder of English vice rather than a vigorous alarm. Further, Josselyn's emphasis on the "old women" who were prone to drunkenness made it seem as if alcohol picked off natives who were about to die anyway. This could lessen English guilt over introducing liquor to the inhabitants of America. Similarly, Williams gave medical reasons for the Indian propensity to drink, comparing the deadly effects of liquor to the "sudden deaths" Indians suffered from *"Consumptions* and *Dropsies."* In this way, discussions of Indians and liquor provided a way for the English to believe that America's natives had not been significantly weakened as a result of contact with European culture; instead, their weakness preceded any such contact and was intrinsic to their corporeal nature, like lack of resistance to diseases that the English had assumed to be native to America.[54]

This assumption was not unchallenged, but it was hard for many colonists to resist. In the 1670s, Daniel Gookin wrote that several young Indian men who went to English schools had died of fever and consumption; he admitted that some colonists "attributed it unto the great change upon their bodies, in respect of their diet, lodging, apparel, studies." In other words, some settlers believed that Indians were undergoing a kind of seasoning or adaptation to new physical conditions that resembled colonists' seasoning. But Gookin flatly denied such speculation: "The truth is, this disease is frequent among the Indians; and sundry die of it, that live not with the English." Set-

tlers were also slow to realize that proximity to Indian populations
that were more susceptible to diseases such as smallpox increased the
likelihood that contagion would continue to pass back and forth between themselves and Indians.[55]

Only in the early 1700s would colonists openly admit that some
diseases were foreign entities introduced to America. Smallpox
seemed the best example of a disease new to the new world, though it
took some time for English accounts to acknowledge this. Winthrop
had reported a "great mortalitye" among the smallpox-stricken natives around Boston in 1633, and specified that some were "cured by
suche meanes as they had from vs," though he did not reason from
this latter point that the disease also came from the English. But by
1700, John Lawson believed that because smallpox was foreign to
America, the Indians were dying from it. One 1710 account specified
that the Iroquois had no remedy against smallpox, though they used a
local bark to cure malaria. Still, other English compared native and
settler mortality rates as if both peoples were equally familiar with all
recurring diseases and displayed mere variation on the theme of common struggle with America's climate. In 1672 Josselyn wrote that
New England's cold northwest wind brought illness that struck "the
Inhabitants both *English* and *Indian.*" Cotton Mather revealingly
wrote in 1716 that smallpox "has usually proven a great plague to us
poor Americans, and getting among our Indians hath swept away
whole nations of them." Both peoples were plagued by smallpox;
only the latter, however, were "swept away" on a national scale.[56]

Negative opinion of native resistance to disease was therefore resurrected in English speculation about global migration of disease.
That is, when colonists finally complicated their Hippocratic ideas of
place-specific disease to portray diseases as entities that could change
locations, they nevertheless continued to think of themselves as particularly hardy human specimens. Again, their image was of a *shared*
atmosphere of disease (global rather than local) in which the English
survived better than Indians. In this way, too, colonists drew together
their opinions about invasion, population dynamics, and disease in
order to place their experience in America in a larger historical context. Mather speculated in the 1720s that smallpox was for Europeans a *"New Distemper,"* unknown to the ancients and *"spread over
the Face of the Earth"* during the *"Saracen* Conquests" of the early
Middle Ages. Mather also stated the by then axiomatic assumption

that "*America* first convey'd this Great Pox [syphilis] to *Europe,* in re-
quital whereof, *Europe* has transmitted the *Small Pox* to *America.*"
Mather's imagery dismissed any possibility that Indians' assault by
new diseases was historically unique—though their delicate nature
might be.[57]

Again, the implication was that epidemic disease existed within a
complex of fatal occurrences that tested the different peoples of the
world, a contention that deflected criticism away from what the English actively did to diminish the native population. English military attacks on Indian populations, in other words, were the least significant
of the varied factors that reduced natives' numbers. Josselyn emphasized that Indians could live long if "not cut off by their Children,
war, and the plague . . . [along] with the small pox." By war, Josselyn
meant warfare among natives themselves, and his understanding of
plague and smallpox did not admit that they could not have been endemic to the new world. None of his causes of Indian decline were
problems that the English themselves had introduced to America, and
all were more virulent than Anglo-Indian warfare.[58]

In this way, the English continued to talk about Indians within a racial
idiom, a form of discourse that did not yet identify mechanisms of inheritance, though some of the reasons for Indians' mortality (susceptibility to liquor and to epidemics) were constructed as features unique
to their lineage. Further, these signs of weakness could not be miti-
gated by the therapies that transformed Indian infants into tough men
and women. Instead, lack of resistance to disease and to alcohol lay
deeper within the body, in some physiological function or corporeal
part less affected by application of unguents, exposure to cold, or
binding to a cradleboard. These technologies, like the native herbal
pharmacopoeia, did not effectively preserve health or delay death.
Again, the English laid out but then carefully stepped around definitions that marked out racial distinctions: they fixated on sexual reproduction but provided no theory of inheritance, focusing instead on
custom in the form of artifice and its effects on Indian bodies. The
English settlers' dismissal of Indians' technological aptitude, which
accelerated once they relabeled the colonies' hybrid landscape as primarily their own accomplishment, would gain power from descriptions of the natives' obsession with preserving their children, a fruitless pursuit. If the earliest English descriptions of American nature

had been careful to place Indians within it, by the end of the 1600s such descriptions tended to remove them, to deny their precolonial handiwork, and to question their place within the geographic and cultural spaces the English had settled.

As they grew more inclined to describe America without referring to Indians, the English took greater delight in the wild and alien features of the land. This appreciation of wilderness and of creole landscapes was in part due to the emergence of a literary genre that celebrated rustic life and countryside. Revival of the georgic enabled colonists to see another positive connection between their new abode and old world discussions of agriculture and rural economy. The seventeenth-century georgic (modeled on ancient georgic poetry) was related to the earlier admiration of primitive society that had lamented the loss of ancient virtues along the lines Tacitus had defined. But romanticization of the primitive this time focused on the natural rather than civil world. In relation to America, it was as if English people were now interacting only with the landscape there rather than with the people who had once been settled on the landscape. The land was cleansed of its original inhabitants and reattached to the English, physically and culturally.[59]

One manifestation of this new view of English America appeared in Edward Waterhouse's description of Virginia. Waterhouse wrote that Indians had a "barbarous sauagenesse [that] needs more cultiuation then the ground." This was a considerable modification of earlier assumptions that the natives would give settlers clues as to how to cultivate the ground. Indeed, the redefined natives did not just exhibit wildness but, because of their indiscriminate patterns of hunting, actually impeded English efforts to tame the wilderness. If the natives proved their ultimate barbarity by revolting against the English project of domesticating America, they could be swept off the land, thus simplifying the imperial project. "Now their cleared grounds . . . shall be inhabited by vs," Waterhouse exulted; even the game would thereby flourish, no longer overhunted, as he supposed the Indians had done.[60]

The English also had an aesthetic appreciation of the unexpected or un-English features of American landscapes. Even in this pre-Burkean era, wilderness had its charms. In 1650 Edward Williams said of the unsettled parts of southern Virginia that its "present Wildnesse" had a "particular beauty." This attitude had been almost unthinkable among earlier colonists. Similarly, settlers of the West Indies began to insist on the exotic allure of their tropical islands. Charles de Rochefort observed of Anglo-French St. Christopher that the fields of strange crops were visually diverting. "The delightful bright-green of the Tobacco, planted exactly by the line, the pale-yellow of the Sugar-Canes . . . and the dark-green of Ginger and Potatoes" all together made "so delightful a Landskip, as must cause an extraordinary recreation to the unwearied eye." Richard Ligon admired tropical fruit on Barbados, which looked "beautifully on the tree, and to me the more beautifull, by how much they were the more strange." Like Rochefort, Ligon also used the variety of color to describe the beauty of the Caribbean, but he incorporated Africans into the colored landscape, underscoring the way the English forced Africans into the Caribbean and then insisted they were natural to the place. Watching slaves return from harvesting plantains, Ligon remarked, "'Tis a lovely sight to see a hundred handsome *Negroes,* men and women, with everyone a grasse-green bunch of these fruits on their heads . . . the black and green so well becomming one another." The visual contrasts functioned to describe the colonized Caribbean as if it were a world destined to come together in this way for the pleasure and profit of the English.[61]

In addition, colonists elaborated their view that America might have medical benefit for English bodies by referring to the land's wildness. Physical hardship and primitive conditions, they argued, could be good for humans. This had been presaged in earlier fulminations against vanity and luxury, which debilitated the body with surfeit of food, harmful cosmetics, and unwise manipulation of the head and limbs. America's settlers, deprived of costly foods and fashionable clothing, were stronger. John Graunt asserted that Englishwomen's "affected straightning of their Bodies" with stays would "hinder the facility of the *Child-bearing*" and increase the number of deaths in childbed. Rates of mortality for childbearing women were lower, Graunt claimed, on England's frontiers. "Certainly in *America,* where the same [use of corsets] is not practised, Nature is little more to be taxed as to women, then in *Brutes,* among whom not one in some thousands do die of their Deliveries: What I have heard of the *Irish-women* confirms me herein."[62]

Thus were the healthy English busy breeding in their transatlantic colonies: they and their children creolized the population, improved the landscape, replaced Indians as the true denizens of America, and grew to admire the alien features of the natural world in which they had planted themselves. Warfare would sporadically reiterate the English sense of distance and difference from Indians, and epidemics and alcohol were wearing down the natives who managed to survive despite their proximity to English settlements. Over time, colonists implied, the only land left for Indians who lived near the English would be that in which they were buried. The macabre prophecy of the Pequot women and children who had fled to Long Island, to possess in death the land they were denied in life, would indeed be fulfilled, if the English had their way.

It is in this context of increased colonial antagonism to Indians that we discover the first piece of writing in English done by Indians. After they had raided and burned Medfield, Massachusetts, during King Philip's War, some of Philip's Nipmuck allies left a taunting note for the English:

> Know by this paper, that the Indians that thou has provoked to wrath and anger, will war this twenty one years if you will; there are many Indians yet, we come three hundred at this time. You must consider the Indians lost nothing but their life; you must lose your fair houses and cattle.

This is our first indication that Indians were directly engaged in argument with the English over the material conditions that the colonists considered vital to their success: increased population and an improved landscape. These non-ventriloquized Indians retorted that the improvement simply put the English at risk of greater loss and that, in any case, "many" Indians still had their lives, had living bodies with which to attack colonists and their improvements. This was what the English had to keep explaining away. Further, they would need to refine their contention that Indians could not aspire to European learning, given that natives could get or make ink, commandeer precious paper, and write denunciations—in English—of colonists and colonization.[63]

CHAPTER EIGHT

Matter and Manitou

Recent excavation of an Indian child's grave at Long Pond, Rhode Island, yielded surprising contents. The grave dates from the late seventeenth century. The child, who was about eleven years old, did not go unarmed into the hereafter, but carried a medicine bundle, a piece of fine woollen material wrapped around a bear claw and a folded page from an English Bible. The page of Scripture, though deteriorated, still has the first six lines of Psalm 98 from the 1611 edition of the King James version. The psalm promises that God will be equitable in the way He judges all nations: "The LORD hath made known his salvation: his righteousness hath he openly shewed in the sight of the heathen . . . for he cometh to judge the earth: with righteousness shall he judge the world, and the people with equity."

What might the medicine bundle have represented? Provision of grave goods was a long-standing tradition in most Indian groups, and many incorporated European materials into the custom. Protestants disapproved of grave goods, however, and an English person would probably not have torn a page from a Bible to bury it. If the medicine bundle represented religious syncretism, it both employed and violated Protestantism's stress on Scripture. It hints at several ways in which Indians might have connected matter to spirit and indigenous concepts to Christian beliefs. The medicine bundle might have represented a creative merging of religious traditions or talismans. Or the sheet of paper might have been used in a legalistic way, to call God's attention to a written covenant of mercy to someone like the child who might carry the document into the afterlife, even if he or she had not converted to Christianity, or came from a family of unbelievers. The bundle might indicate faith in a universal destiny for humanity: this Indian person would live again, despite an early death on this earth. Life, death, and afterlife might be connected, coterminous, or simultaneous; material objects and spiritual power likewise might exist together. Or the bundle might have had a practical function and been meant for a living rather than an otherworldly audience. Indians had long been aware that the English ransacked their graves. Perhaps this child's family supplied a written rebuke to anyone who would deface the resting place, a reminder of what an English grave robber's God might believe about Indians, whether the Indians themselves agreed. The grave was, in any case, a grim reminder that communication between colonizers and colonized increasingly focused on death. Words and things, texts and objects, would be juxtaposed in this debate, as in the medicine bundle at Long Pond.[1]

"Nullius in verba," warns the motto of the Royal Society: the truth is not to be found in words. This epigram from Horace urged natural philosophers to turn from texts to experience. The founders of the society rejected disputatious verbiage, which they associated with the medieval schoolmen and their slavish dependence on Aristotle. To idolize the pagan authors of classical antiquity, as the scholastics had done, would no longer provide the basis of learning. The Bible had a divine author and revealed truth, but no other text had such status, not even the Aristotelian corpus that had been the foundation of natural philosophy. Further, God's creation, like God's word, contained truth; experimentation on and observation of matter revealed knowledge. As the Royal Society helped define an official way to regard nature, theology and natural philosophy were carefully distinguished from each other even as religion continued to imbue learned views of nature. Colonists therefore proposed for Indians a dual conversion to worldviews they were coming to regard as parallel: rational comprehension of the material world and apprehension of God's miraculous power over and above that world. In neither process of conversion did the English elicit full understanding of natives' previous forms of faith; they instead represented those beliefs as errors that had been eradicated among reasonable Christians and that needed to be extirpated among the world's remaining pagans.[2]

As this chapter will therefore indicate, there is a frustrating lack of commentary on native religious beliefs, aboriginal or syncretic, which could help us understand the grave at Long Pond. English explanations of natives and the cosmos were dependent on contemporary debates over natural philosophy and too eager to ventriloquize native opinions within the forms of that debate. What we can tell from the burial at Long Pond is that attitudes about the human body as a form of matter and words as a system of truth were important and contested issues along the frontier at the end of the seventeenth century.

The body, center of so many arguments for the imperial destiny of the English, was once more the focus of controversy when the colonists tried to convince the Indians of the truth of Christian doctrine about the body and soul while simultaneously maintaining the truth of natural philosophy's distinctions between matter and spirit. Indians who were the targets of this dual conversion were perhaps understandably puzzled by assertions that matter was dead, devoid of spirit, but that human bodies that had died could be resurrected, brought back to life by the creator of the cosmos. The death of the body and the role of language in distinguishing between inanimate things and animate beings were aspects of a concluding debate over the different capacities of colonizers and colonized to make sense of the world around them. The English were at this point arguing that natives failed to make "manitou" and matter into separate categories. This was tendentious. Both cultures recognized difference between spirit and matter yet proposed connections between them. Furthermore, the English understanding of manitou distilled several northern Algonquian cultures' beliefs into an improbable pan-Indian concept, the belief that spiritual power always pervaded material entities. The distinctions the English made between spirit and matter were different from native beliefs, and the English were therefore quick to claim that the Indian ideas were simply mistaken. By the 1660s, learned definitions of nature were, for the first time, a method of identifying and stigmatizing certain peoples as benighted, and puritan missionaries in particular forced Indians into a highly prejudicial role as a people whose ideas about nature were counterexamples to natural philosophy. This categorization may indeed have been unique within contemporary European colonization experiences, and therefore a harbinger of what was to come during the eighteenth and nineteenth centuries, when Europeans would regard science and technology as points of superiority over non-Europeans.[3]

Much of the important intellectual work of the late seventeenth century redefined the material creation, and particularly defined matter as an inanimate object of inquiry. Within this new context, native beliefs were more commonly used to represent intellectual failure than to point critiques at the equally sinful English; the idea of the human propensity toward idolatry was succeeded by that of the propensity of some toward superstition. It is therefore significant that the project of converting Indians to Protestantism was, at several points in its late seventeenth-century history, linked to definitions of the sciences. Much has been written about English missionaries, but nothing about their revealing connections to patrons who were natural philosophers. Efforts to educate Indians and to study their languages were especially interesting to English naturalists, particularly Robert Boyle (a founder of the Royal Society). As scholars of the early modern sciences have argued, the desire to disenchant the world was intended to discredit religious enthusiasts and Catholics, and to reduce the capacity of religious sectarianism to influence other realms of experience, such as examination of nature.

What has not been noted is that American Indians increasingly became prototypical figures of the backward opinions about the material creation originally associated with certain European sects. The defeat of natives' supposed worldview represented a final stage of English conquest—over nature, and over those who had improper views of nature. In this stage, colonists in Massachusetts saw an opening to defend themselves and the religious foundation of their colony against the suspicion that they were pernicious dissenters and against concomitant threats to their colony's charter. Drawing attention to Indians' pagan status and comparing their intellectual deficiencies to those of scholastics and religious radicals would thus defend the English in New England, and their mission to convert Indians, by allying them with the stable, reforming elements in late seventeenth-century England, including reform of natural philosophy.

Differentiation of Indians and English according to different intellectual capacities therefore generated the idea of the savage mind. Further, this point illuminates a deficiency in scholarship on early America which has stressed the growing colonial antipathy to Indians' adoption of some elements of European culture. Resentment over Indians' literacy in New England, for instance, has been interpreted as a cause of King Philip's War. But some of the English were crafting a far more reassuring argument against the native ability to achieve cultural parity. Violence and war might keep Indians away from English culture, but it was more effective to conceive of them as incapable of easily realizing any intellectual advance. This was precisely the point of arguments about northern Algonquians' inability to describe correctly the material world. The transatlantic debates over religion and nature were the context for these arguments.[4]

Condemnation of vitalism (the belief that spirit existed in all matter) gave English colonists a new way to criticize native beliefs. The English had long since made native assessment of spiritual power within material things into a species of religious error. Such ideas were still classified as errors, but no longer in the older sense of universal idolatry; now they were superstitions specific to deficient peoples. Missionaries based in New England were the first to assert this belief and also insisted that this new method of denigrating northern Algonquians could be applied to all natives of North America. If this one region's missionary zeal and its propensity to analyze Indians were not fully representative of all the colonies, New England nevertheless made itself into the representative of the colonies on these matters. The close connection between New England's missionary work and definitions of natural philosophy (mostly within the Royal Society) is noteworthy in this regard.

One feature of this redefinition was especially troubling: the association between Indian conversion and death. This had a predictive function of interest to the colonists, who had found another way to foretell the gradual waning of the native population. It also brought English discourse on America to a critical moment: discourse on nature was being brought into a technical orthodoxy concerning the deadness of matter, just as Indian bodies were conceived as tending toward death—even while the English believed that they were finally bringing the truth of eternal life to America's natives. Even if natives were the objects of conversion, they were excluded from the realm of learning that identified their bodies as weak and their ideas as superstitious. In contrast to earlier perspectives that compared the cultural and technical abilities of English and Indian peoples, there was a new emphasis on contrast; the English had the learning that mattered.

The separation of animate and inanimate realms concerned both late seventeenth-century natural philosophy and the revived Protestant missionary effort in North America. Various forms of vitalism had characterized earlier interpretations of nature. To some extent, the concept had been a way to identify how the natural world had life, grew, and made itself orderly without being guided by the souls that existed within humans or by the constantly overseeing will of God. The mid-seventeenth-century Cambridge Platonists, for instance, concluded that God could not be responsible for the everyday ordering of matter, even living matter. Instead, subsidiary spirits executed divine law, together constituting a spiritual force the Platonists labeled "plastic nature" or a "subordinate ministry."[5]

Anglicans and moderate dissenters believed, however, that religious radicals saw no intermediate stage or agency between God and nature. For members of these "sects," vitalism unified God, spirit, and matter; it could even mean pantheism, the creation at one with its creator. If human souls were aspects of divine energy, then humans could claim direct revelation, their minds being forms of godly wisdom; this was an illuminist view of the material world as a source of inspiration that rivaled Scripture. In addition, vitalism united matter and spirit, so that the earth was like God's clothing or body, which shimmered and heaved and even cogitated with the power of its divine wearer. Such beliefs had been characteristic of the most challenging of the religious radicals during the Civil War and interregnum, and vitalism and illuminism were associated with lack of order in church or civil governments. That is, belief in the earth's spontaneous life and order, and in the unity of God and human spirit, encouraged antinomianism, distrust of humanly imposed order. Suspicion of antinomianism had been characteristic of authorities in the colonies, especially but not exclusively New England, and it was therefore unlikely that vitalism would have had many powerful supporters on the western side of the Atlantic, even though forms of pantheism survived in American folk religion into the nineteenth century.[6]

Yet few people interested in natural philosophy wanted, by rejecting vitalism, to throw open a welcoming door to materialists. If vitalism tended toward antinomianism, materialism tended toward atheism, denial of any divine energy in the cosmos. As had been the case with Thomas Hariot, many atomists were still regarded as mere atheists because their explanations of matter focused on the orderly behavior of these blind units of stuff, as if no creator needed to have been present even at their birth. This prejudice against atomism, and desire to avoid materialist explanations of the world, had permanently tarred the reputation of Thomas Hobbes—a God-fearing man, as he frequently protested to his detractors, but fatally marked by his commentary on atomism. Puritans especially had feared the reduction of the creation to an endless, random bombardment of atoms against one another, as Epicurus would have had it. Reformers preferred safer visions of nature, such as Pierre Gassendi's, which took the spirits out of things without erasing all traces of the divine hand.[7]

Religious moderates therefore argued that the creator, not the creation, was to be worshipped; further, Scripture was the only way in which God had directly spoken to humans. True Christians were latitudinarian, avoiding narrowly sectarian battles over Scripture, and they marveled at the divine power that had established nature even if that power did not reside in it. Maintaining providential power, without giving way to vitalism, required careful distinction between physics and metaphysics. This was, at the moment, an unachieved task, partly because the sciences had not yet defined a concept of organic nature, and therefore did not explain why some forms of devitalized matter seemed quite lively indeed. In addition, for all the insistence that matter was dead, English Protestants still maintained the orthodox Christian opinion that a human body whose spirit had departed (even a body that had long since decayed) could be resurrected at the Last Judgment. Faith in this tenet, in the teeth of attacks on vitalism, represented the final boundary that no opinions on physical nature could cross. If compromise over Reformation challenges to the use of objects in religious services had defined indifferent things (*adiaphora*) as those objects and practices irrelevant to salvation, compromise over the scientific reformation defined *all* things as indifferent to spiritual matters, with the one important exception of the human body.[8]

It was not the case that "science" was designed to dispute with "religion"; the intention instead was to prevent any such dispute, and especially to prevent religious radicals from posing questions that had no empirical answer but would raise troubling questions about earthly authority. English reformers sought both to protect religion and to create a dispassionate realm of inquiry into the material world. The latter would increase worship of God, first, because it intensified appreciation for the miraculous moments when the creator reintervened in the creation; second, because it urged proper respect for the everyday wonders of nature. These positions allowed the Royal Society and its network to participate in a non-atheistical and non-doctrinal sphere, one calculated to attract a designated spectrum of Christian believers, running from moderate dissenters (such as New England puritans), through Anglicans, and even to some crypto-Catholics (such as the post-Restoration Stuarts).[9]

The Royal Society's statutes stated that it had no interest in adjudicating questions of "Divinity, Metaphysics, Moralls, Politicks, Grammar, Rhetorick or Logick." As Thomas Sprat put it in his *History of the Royal Society of London* (1667), members of the society "have attempted, to free it from the Artifice, and Humors, and Passions of [radical] Sects; to render it an Instrument, whereby Mankind may obtain a Dominion over *Things*, and not onely over one anothers *Judgements*." To a large extent, the society's self-definition as neutral ground was remarkably successful. Could Charles I and John Winthrop have imagined that their sons would belong to the same London club? Their heirs did just that; Charles II was patron of the learned society in which John Winthrop, Jr., was the first colonial fellow. Religion could not divide men who agreed not to talk about its doctrinal niceties and who shared faith that the universe had a divine creator and providential meaning.[10]

The trick was how to draw the line between physics and metaphysics, and between the now separate activities that examined each realm of being. Boyle's activities were exemplary in this regard. He was able even to transform the corpuscular philosophy, long associated with materialism and atheism, into a respected theory of matter because it was now propounded by someone who proclaimed his faith in the power that lay above material things: corpuscles did not have souls within them, nor did their lack of internal animation mean that there was no animating principle in the cosmos. This middle way did not reassure everyone. As Steven Shapin and Simon Schaffer have noted, Hobbes feared that Boyle and his supporters had left far too much leeway for enthusiasts. Hence Hobbes's distress about the thing Boyle claimed he had created with his air pump, a *vacuum*, a space where nothing existed. If Boyle's experiment showed religious radicals that there was no body in that space, they could then populate it with the vital spirits that would challenge civil authority.[11]

These concerns were not unknown in the colonies. By the 1660s and 1670s, colonists were newly interested in defining their control over the new world as part of an intellectual project that tied them back to the mother country. They presented their creole landscape as their own handiwork, the product of interaction between the English and nature, not between English and Indians. This required that settlers present Indians as unable to achieve certain technical skills. Written language and formal education had long separated Europeans from North America's natives, but these were discrete skills which Indians might eventually learn. Some colonists, such as John Winthrop, Jr., had begun to define skills they believed Indians could not attain. The mineral obsession, especially expressed in the form of chemistry, had begun to do this. This difficult, arcane subject—key to cultural superiority but difficult even for many English to attain—raised the bar, and made more than mere familiarity with letters a prerequisite to cultural advance. More of Winthrop's fellows were accordingly concerned to demonstrate that men of learning thrived in the colonies. Any form of education was a measure of this, but much more definitive was the establishment of a reputation in the sciences.

It was therefore important for colonists with intellectual ambitions to demonstrate that they had followed the recent shift in natural philosophy, especially the separation of physics and metaphysics. At Harvard College, the subjects debated by candidates for master's degrees were a good index of this intellectual transformation, even as the college simultaneously maintained orthodoxy in religious training. The designated subjects for debate showed an insistence that everything but the soul (and its creator) was composed of matter, but that matter had no power to order itself. The question "Are intelligences composed of matter?" was found in the affirmative in 1655; the question "Is form derived from the power of matter?" was, in 1659, found in the negative. Later concessions meant drawing a more careful distinction between theological and physical matters. Thus the question "Is Pneumatics a science distinct from Metaphysics and Theology?" was answered in the affirmative first in 1688, then again in 1709 and 1715. Harvard's students were not the only colonists to cudgel their brains over these distinctions. William Hughes's 1672 treatise on the medicinal plants "Growing in the English Plantations in America" wondered at nature's "varieties of objects, whether of animated or inanimated Bodies." This concern to distinguish between forms of matter and the principles of animation would strongly influence the missionary efforts in America that took shape during the same years when natural philosophy was being redefined.[12]

Though the stereotype of English colonists as uninterested in evangelization is not quite accurate, it is true that the mission to convert Indians to Protestantism was slow to develop and stumbled easily. Conceptions of America as a field for evangelization had nevertheless always characterized English overseas expansion, beginning with Richard Hakluyt's *Discourse on Western Planting* and the baptism of Manteo at Roanoke. Except for sporadic successes, as with Manteo and Pocahontas, subsequent attempts to convert and baptize Indians languished. A 1619 plan for an Indian school in Virginia, Henrico College, came to nothing after some ill-advised methods of investment wasted the endowment, and after the Powhatan uprising of 1622 caused settlers to lose interest in the salvation of their Indian neighbors. Colonial schools and churches served only the English populations. Education and attempted conversion of Indians mostly occurred in cases of captives taken to Europe.[13]

But missionary activity remained part of the stated goal of colonization, even when it was little more than a strategic gloss on more materialistic motivation. In part, Protestant evangelization proceeded slowly because it demanded thorough understanding of religious tenets. It was necessary for converts to have some comprehension of Scripture, which required actual literacy or considerable acquaintance with literate culture, especially the ability to memorize scriptural lessons, either word for word or by paraphrasing their main points. Some individuals in the Bay Colony stated sincere support of these goals, which expanded within the wider Atlantic (and European) contexts of millenarianism that informed the activities of reformers such as Samuel Hartlib. Education and conversion, especially, were the twin goals necessary to perfect humanity in the final days.[14]

During the 1640s and 1650s, religious authorities rededicated themselves to the task of evangelization in Massachusetts and Plymouth. An institution and personnel for a more aggressive missionary effort took shape in the weeks after King Charles's execution in 1649, when Parliament passed Edward Winslow's "Act for the promoting and Propagating the Gospel of Jesus Christ in New England." This act chartered the Corporation for the Propagation of the Gospel in New England (reorganized and rechartered in 1662, after the Restoration rendered null and void all Commonwealth legislation), which is known as the New England Company to distinguish it from the later Society for the Propagation of the Gospel in Foreign Parts (1701), or S.P.G. Before the eighteenth century, therefore, efforts to convert Indians focused on the New England Company. Its main personnel in New England would be Winslow, Jonathan Mayhew (and other Mayhews), Daniel Gookin, and above all John Eliot, "apostle to the Indians." Eliot's efforts, especially, would reflect the millenarian connections among education, improvement of the material world, and Christian conversion that Hartlib and Comenius had defined.[15]

Though the company focused its efforts on a small part of America, it enjoyed considerable support. Its missionaries produced a steady stream of pamphlets that reported on their progress. Some of these were taken up and reprinted in other sources. Benefactors were generous to the organization. Between 1649 and 1660, the company received an astounding £15,910. Initially, the largest unit of monetary support came from the New Model Army, which gave over £3,000. Parishes and towns in England also gave large gifts, as did some individuals, mostly in the form of property from which the company would receive annual income. The company's effort's were known abroad. A mysterious "Monsieur Mowsche" of Paris gave £360 in 1668.[16]

The company took as its task the education and conversion of New England's Indians. If the ability to read Scripture was essential to conversion, education was the first step to bring the gospel to Indians. The first schools to include Indians were planned in 1645 for Roxbury and Boston, Massachusetts. These were meant primarily for colonists' children, but provision was made for "Indians children . . . to be taught freely." Even before the New England Company's founding, John Eliot had pioneered a more plausible educational effort in his religious instruction of Indians by himself learning the Natick dialect of Massachusett. By 1646 Eliot had taken "great paynes to gett their language, & in a fewe monthes could speake of the thinges of God, to their vnderstandinge." Eliot then preached alternate weeks at the homes of Waban, a Massachusett convert who lived near Watertown, and of Cutshamekin, near Dorchester. His instruction involved the reading of a text first in Massachusett, then in English, then an hour-long sermon on the text in Massachusett, followed by questions from the "cheife" people in the audience. Eliot catechized children separately, without the questioning he tolerated from adults who already believed in another religion.[17]

Eliot and others then organized mobile missions that went out into native villages and designated "praying towns" organized around communities of converts. Such towns had rudimentary facilities for schools and churches. The largest praying town was Natick, organized in 1651 between the Charles and Concord rivers in Massachusetts. Praying towns like Natick demonstrated to the English the growing success of evangelization, though they were sites of extreme cultural contestation. Praying Indians were frequently annoyed by English micromanagement of their lives, and they suffered the criticism and assault as well of Indians who resisted conversion and anglicization. Nevertheless, conversions occurred. In 1670 the first Indian church in the English-speaking colonies was finally covenanted, at Maktepog within the Plymouth patent. There, congregational services were held in English and Massachusett, an important event in the history of the English-Indian encounter, though one that would be challenged by King Philip's War. Outside Plymouth and Massachusetts, efforts to organize Indian missions languished until the early eighteenth century.[18]

Because this kind of missionary effort required money to pay ministers and schoolteachers and to buy materials for praying towns, missionaries were always looking for patrons. Patronage could provide funds, ensure access to power, and heighten the prestige of colonial activities. The search for patrons took an interesting turn after the Restoration, when radical supporters of the New England Company were discredited. This was especially the case with the New Model Army, long suspected as a hotbed of sectarianism. Further, puritans in New England feared that the crown might not grant a new charter for Connecticut or might even revoke that of Massachusetts. Religious and civil authorities in New England had to renew support for their colonies and for their evangelization of Indians. Establishing affinity with latitudinarian religion and with naturalists who emphasized the divinity of the creator, not the creation, were ways to prove that New Englanders were avoiding rather than stirring up doctrinal conflict. John Winthrop, Jr., first colonial fellow of the Royal Society and governor over the successfully chartered colony of Connecticut, was an important contact for intersecting networks of dissenters and natural philosophers. Thus John Endecott thanked Robert Boyle in 1664 for the information Boyle had sent Winthrop that "the king intends not any injury to our [Massachusetts] charter, or the dissolution of our civil government, or the infringement of our liberty of conscience."[19]

Boyle and the Royal Society were obvious sources of patronage for any mission to spread Christian knowledge broadly over the English-speaking dominion. Boyle was a stalwart supporter of missionary efforts. He funded translation of the Bible into Irish Gaelic, Scots Gaelic, and Welsh; the New Testament into Turkic; the Gospels and Acts into Malay, and (as will be discussed later in this chapter) into Massachusett. Henry Oldenburg (who emigrated from Bremen in 1653 and joined the Hartlib circle in England) became Boyle's protégé and acted as the society's first secretary, for which he deployed his acquaintance with European natural philosophers. Oldenburg combined an interest in the mechanical sciences and experiments (which in fact set him apart from Hartlib) with continued devotion to Hartlib's wider definition of improvements as ultimately beneficial to humanity; Oldenburg's interest in experimentation and in the spread of knowledge resembled Boyle's pursuits. Oldenburg had a regular correspondence with advocates of Indian education in the colonies. The Royal Society itself, however, was unwilling to promote evangelization directly, lest its support of one branch of Protestantism annoy the others as well as crypto-Catholics.[20]

Caution was therefore necessary before Oldenburg or the Royal Society could fund missionary efforts. In 1668, for instance, Richard Norwood wrote Oldenburg for support to reopen a free school in Bermuda for "children of this place as for some Indian children," presumably the children of enslaved Indians from the mainland. Norwood's former school had lasted about three years before the sectarian battles of the Civil War made it impossible to run. Oldenburg wrote back to Norwood to promise the society's help in reestablishing the school without making any potentially divisive statement about its specific religious goals. If men in the Royal Society wanted to support missions' religious goals more directly, they worked through other channels. This was especially the case with the New England Company, of which Boyle was governor from 1662 to 1689, from the time the company was rechartered until two years before his death.[21]

Boyle, who never went to America, was nevertheless a logical choice to govern the New England Company. His family's estate in Ireland gave him experience in colonial affairs; his piety was famous. Further, Boyle was highly placed and respected, able to get attention and money from donors. He also subscribed his own money. Although Boyle was an Anglican, he, like Oldenburg, had sympathetic associations with dissenters, and therefore did not shy away from New England's congregationalists, as some Anglicans might have done. Because of his high position and his Anglican status, Boyle was also in a good position to mediate between royal officials and the company, which after all had been chartered just after the present king's father had been executed. From 1660 to 1662 (when it was rechartered), the company was uncertain it would regain a charter and financial backing, and it was at this moment that members approached Boyle for help.[22]

Support for the education of Indians and study of their languages were strategically neutral ways to designate interest in evangelization. Eliot and John Winthrop, Jr., played to these goals by supplying samples of their success to the Royal Society. Winthrop, for instance, sent the society two Latin orations composed by two Indian men at Harvard College. The essay by Caleb Cheeshateaumauk, "Honoratissimi Benefactores," was clearly designed as an appeal to patrons; education of Indians was valorized by the oration's comparison between "the transformation of the nature of barbarians" (Indians) and the enchantment that Orpheus effected with his music on rocks, trees, and "brute beasts." Boyle delivered Eliot's presentation copy of the Massachusett Bible to the king and also showed the student orations to certain men at court. In October 1669, when Winthrop sent four boxes of materials to the Royal Society, he included "Two Bibles in the Indian tongue; Three books of the Practice of Piety, translated into the Indian tongue . . . One book of Mr. Baxters Call of the Converted, turn'd into the Indian Language. One Indian Grammar." Winthrop also sent a copy of Eliot's "Indian Dialogue" to Oldenburg in 1671, but it never arrived, evidently because transport was "so hazardous this warr tyme."[23]

John Eliot's *Indian Grammar Begun* (1666) was the study of Indian language most calculated to appeal to benefactors in the Royal Society. This work was the first English treatise since Roger Williams's *Key into the Language of America* (1643) to examine a native language systematically. But the differences between the two works are striking: Williams exhibited the old tendencies to compare Indians to the English and use them to criticize universal sin; Eliot instead maintained that Indians' differences from Europeans were paramount and their errors peculiar. The Key into the Language of America took the form of a dialogue in which Williams arranged phrases of Narragansett as responses to English questions or statements. As such, the dialogues guided English speakers through Narragansett in situations ranging from war to trade; the "key" was just that, a primer that opened a way to further comprehension and use of an Indian language through conversation with actual Indians. As Williams put it, his text would help English people "converse with *thousands* of *Natives* all over the *Countrey*." Williams took care to point out the deficiencies in native belief, particularly the belief in manitou, the spiritual force that dwelled in things, rather than faith in God and transcendent providence. Thus, Williams said, natives erred fundamentally when they split the "God-head into many Gods" and tried to "attribute it to Creatures." They also called manitou "every thing which they cannot comprehend," including, supposedly, "a stranger that can relate newes in their owne language, they will stile him *Manittóo*, a God." But Williams also ventriloquized Indians as critics of English sins. If this generation of Indians, utterly damned though they were, had inklings of virtue and providence, this was a telling reproach to nominal Christians. "He that questions whether God made the World," Williams lectured, "the *Indians* will teach him."[24]

In contrast, Eliot did not use the Massachusett and their language to criticize Christian Europeans. He instead presented the grammatical structure of Massachusett as evidence of Indians' conceptualization of the world, especially concepts that stood outside the realm of knowledge promoted by European philosophy. His work made a key decision about grammatical categorization in Massachusett. He explained that the native speakers did not distinguish among nouns according to gender or by the use of cases, the main forms of grammatical organization in European languages. Instead, the main distinction was between animate and inanimate. The former category included people, gods, devils, and animals, all of them beings that Europeans would also recognize as animate in the sense of living, though not in the sense of having souls, which this clustering implied. But the native category also included stars, which educated Europeans would no longer consider living entities. The native category of inanimate encompassed stones, plants, the parts of the body, virtues and vices, and all tools or practical creations of humans (such as *"Apparel, Housing"*), plus *"Fruits, Rivers, Waters."* Again, the schema was unfamiliar to educated Europeans, particularly the classification of body parts, plants, and fruit as "inanimate" rather than living.[25]

Eliot chose a schema that accentuated the English tendency to see Indian cosmology as an inaccurate representation of the world. Rather than seek a logical reason why the natives might group together people and stars, or stones and fruit, which might have required use of categories other than "animate" and "inanimate," Eliot used categories that pointed up the bizarre conglomerations of things and hinted at Indian mystification of natural things. In doing so, Eliot did not draw a comparison between Indian error and comparable European forms of ignorance. He did not represent in any way, for instance, the long-standing English perception that Indians thought some artificial objects had manitou, which had contributed to earlier anxieties that Indians might idolize their invaders as possessors of marvels such as guns. It is puzzling that Eliot omitted this possible category, thing-as-manitou. Perhaps his silence on this issue obviated the problem—and the concomitant anxiety—that Europeans tended to be idolatrous of their own handiwork. Eliot simply elided it, sweeping away nearly a century of worrying about whether the English were different from Indians, or as prone to sinful vanity about their status as makers of tools.[26]

Eliot's connection to Boyle helps explain his emphases in the *Indian Grammar*. Eliot thought that Boyle, as governor of the Company for the Propagation of the Gospel in New England, had solicited the book: "I doubt not but [the request] springeth from yourself." Eliot then dedicated the grammar to Boyle. The opposition between animate and inanimate used categories congruent with the contemporary concern to distinguish physics from metaphysics. Eliot's knowledge of debates over natural philosophy, and his connections with relevant figures in that concern (such as Boyle), indicate that his choice of categories was as much related to English as to native conceptions of order. In this manner, it was easy to stress Indians' difference from educated and Christian people, which makes it difficult to determine what Eliot's converts (or any other Indians) truly did believe. Consider again the Indian burial at Long Pond. The medicine bundle in the grave might reveal Indian belief that some objects did have supernatural power, which they radiated even in a person's afterlife. But the bundle might reveal the poverty of the opposition between animate and inanimate, or life and death, or matter and manitou; the juxtaposition of the different items and their placement in a grave prevents easy separation of any qualities the different elements were supposed to have, let alone easy identification of the function they together might have had. And our inability to know what these things meant is a consequence of English ventriloquism of Indians in the seventeenth century.[27]

The Long Pond grave itself had a clearer meaning, one at the heart of the Anglo-Indian struggle to control American territory. Indian bodies had increasingly been associated with death, and their heightened mortality underlined the spiritual concern some English had for them. Missionary compassion might, however, have rendered suspect the individuals who took such a strong interest in natives. The men involved in New England's missionary effort were eager to make clear that, by living with Indians and learning their languages, they were not themselves going native. It was perhaps for this reason that Eliot chose the eighth verse of the eighth book of the Song of Solomon to explain his mission to the Indians. Why select the scripture most imbued with sexuality to define the true Christian's duty to Indians, particularly if the English were determined not to acknowledge sexual relations between Indians and colonists? Eliot's interpretation of this text squarely faced the most contentious scenario in English-Indian interaction, sexual contact, and ingeniously interpreted such contact as incest, abuse of the intimate sympathies that should connect members of a family. The verse from the Song of Solomon states, "We have a little sister, and she hath no breasts: what shall we do for our sister in the day when she shall be spoken for?" The sister stood here for the natives, gendered as weak and undefended, but who could be nurtured to maturity, and then married and brought to fruition. Further, because the breast could signify either the gospel or philosophy, that an Indian lacked breasts indicated isolation from knowledge and the word of God.[28]

Also, by choosing this image Eliot opted for the sororal imagery that had characterized many geographical representations of North America at the start of English colonization. That Indians might be sisters to the English postulated an intimate relationship but one that precluded sexual meddling. A sister would always be subordinate to a male relative, so Indians would always be subordinate to the English, even when grown and married. And they had to be married off outside the "family" of Christian English. Eliot's choice of the Song of Solomon thus raised and dismissed the troubling possibility of interracial sex while insisting on familiarity with Indians and intimacy between them and the English. The English would share the gospel with the Indians, but the two peoples should not share their bodies with each other.

Despite the sympathy with Indians that missionaries expressed, therefore, their tracts on evangelization propound the difficulty of recovering native beliefs. Ventriloquism continued. Edward Winslow echoed the appeal of the seal of the Massachussetts Bay Colony when he asked readers of a 1649 tract to "perceive how these poor Creatures cry out for help; Oh come unto us, teach us the knowledge of God." The English also recorded, without really perceiving the significance of, native criticisms of the effort to improve them. One older Indian man had said to Thomas Mayhew that "he wondered the English should be almost thirty years in the Country, and the Indians fools still." If Mayhew wrote down this statement because he thought it an admission of Indian foolishness (or a critique of English sloth), he was unaware that the man might have meant a criticism of the English, whose desire to improve the natives had possibly borne so little fruit because it was not in earnest. Further, missionaries quickly discovered that Indians found some key Christian doctrines foolish. Even more troubling, they found it difficult to respond satisfactorily to these criticisms.[29]

Definitions of soul and body, and especially the issue of bodily resurrection, were particularly difficult. The English represented themselves as disagreeing with natives over three points: that the soul was immortal, that all human bodies would be resurrected, and that it was unlikely anyone (let alone pagans) would be resurrected before the Day of Judgment. As suspicion of Hariot's atheism had shown, debates over the proper understanding of the distinct characteristics of human body and soul had long been on the minds of migrants who went to the new world to protect the true faith and project it over the western Atlantic world. In his 1582 "Thanksgiving Hymn," meant to celebrate expeditions to Newfoundland, Stephen Parmenius had praised God's ultimate power to revive dead bones and flesh: "But if you should restore those elements [of the soul], / The living body will emerge again / From animated dust." These were words to inspire the Protestants who went west in the hope that they were protected by such miraculous power. Less than a century later, however, it would be harder to defend the idea that dust could be "animated." This was precisely the notion Eliot presented unsympathetically in his *Indian*

Grammar Begun. And Boyle in his 1675 treatise on resurrection explained that it exemplified the "supernatural" power God could manifest outside "the common course of Nature." Christians had to understand the differently wonderful qualities of nature and of miracles.[30]

In the earlier period of colonization, English willingness to believe that many forms of matter contained vital properties had yielded some mixed assessments of what natives might believe about resurrection. This was evident in Hariot's cryptic discussion of statements by Roanok that some of their people had regained life after death. Slightly later, William Strachey wrote that the Powhatan believed "that the Comon people shall not live after death." The souls of the elite only would go to a place beyond the mountains; each soul would "waxe ould there as the body did on earth, and then yt shall dissolue and dye, and come into a womans womb againe, and so be a new borne vnto the world not vnlike the heathen Pythagoras his opinion and fable of Metempsychosis." Strachey also likened the natives to "the Epicures," who believed that the soul was a "vitall power" that "dyed and extinguished togither with the body." Nor was such a belief "more Hethenous then our Athists." This was a clear case of ventriloquism, perhaps intended to be helpful (to counter horror over natives' being at odds with Christian definitions of the body and soul), but no less willing to represent natives' beliefs in terms they had never themselves used, and which were meaningful only within contemporary debates in Europe. Further, the comparisons emphasized that paganism, whether ancient or contemporary, was inexcusable. Strachey's representation was therefore most likely an argument over what Christian Europeans should extract from or shun in ancient philosophy, using a narrative on Virginia's Indians as evidence for his case.[31]

After the English colonies took stronger root, willingness to consider natives' opinions with sympathy lessened, though colonists thereafter tried to identify fragments of Indian religion that were similar to Christianity. Thomas Morton remarked that the Wampanoag maintained "some touch of the immortality of the soule" along the hierarchical lines—immortality for nobles but not commoners—which Strachey had established. William Wood reported that the Massachusett believed in the soul's immortality; in the 1660s John Josselyn agreed with Morton that "some small light they have of the Souls immortality." This "small light" was not a great compliment to native belief, but it is significant that this point was not one that authorities granted to religious radicals. One of the accusations against Anne Hutchinson was that she believed "the soul is mortal, till it be united to Christ," and that she "denied the Resurrection from the dead," therefore making a wholesale assault on the orthodox position that God's power had made the soul immortal and could make even long-dead bodies live again.[32]

Notwithstanding the dubious quality of English suppositions about Indian beliefs, natives did seem to question the prospect of universal resurrection. Williams related an instance of Narragansett incredulity when he ran through the basic Christian understanding of the cosmos, divine power, and humanity, broken down into the succeeding topics of the creation, the soul, sin, and salvation. Thus far, his listener "assented; but when I spake of the rising againe of the body, he cryed out, I shall never believe this." In a rare example of public native capitulation to this doctrine, John Speene, in 1652, stated that "when Christ judges the world, our bodies rise again." Another man, when examined by the missionaries at about the same time, stated that "the dead bodies of all men shall rise againe," and more specifically, "this body which rots in the earth, this very body, God maketh it new."[33]

If Josselyn saw only a "small light" in Indians' understanding of Christian religion, this might in part have been because the English had to struggle to explain the fate of body and soul after death. Some questions about religion gave offense, as Morton realized when Indians recoiled from his inquiries about the dead; but the natives grew used to colonists' treatment of death "by our example" in discourse, by their casual treatment of burial (the Pilgrims refused to make any popish "monuments"), and by the willingness of the English to live near cemeteries, which northern Algonquian shunned. Restricted understanding of native languages did not help matters. Eliot, who indeed probably knew more Massachusett than any other Englishman who was not a trader, insisted that he had faithfully translated into English all Indian testimony. "I have not knowingly, or willingly made them better, than the Lord helped themselves to make them, but am verily perswaded on good grounds, that I have rather rendered them weaker." Problems remained. Edward Winslow confessed that he and his fellow evangelists had told some Indians that sinners would after death be "*Chechainuppan*, i.e., tormented alive (for wee know no other word in the tongue to expresse extreame torture by)." The phrase made it seem that the body was alive after death, but unresurrected, which was not the meaning the missionaries wanted the Indians to receive. Further, Christian instruction, which relied on parables and recitation of miracles, conveyed supernatural understanding of nature and garbled lessons about half-living and reanimated bodies.[34]

One prime example of this difficulty was connected with the missionaries' fondness for the Book of Ezekiel, chapter 37, which promised a new life for the children of Israel, who had been lost among the heathen. In this chapter of the Hebrew Bible, God conveys Ezekiel to a valley which is full of bones and tells him to prophesy, "O ye dry bones, hear the word of the LORD." At this, the bones acquire sinew and flesh, rise up in human form, and become an army of the House of Israel. God then promises a covenant with the Israelites, who will multiply and dominate the heathen around them. Invoking Ezekiel in sermons to Indians (and in letters to one another), the missionaries meant to emphasize that Indians, however lost, could be recovered and brought to new life in the service of the Lord. Christians thought the text prefigured the coming of Christ, which brought physical renewal, a new law, and the resurrection and final judgment according to that law. Eliot preached this text to the Indians at least once, without realizing that it might sit uneasily with the other points missionaries wanted to make. The image of revivification, and of rekindling the faith among God's chosen, made sense for an evangelizing effort among those whom the gospel had never reached; its sympathetic representation of Indians as part of God's chosen people, and the imagery that made them into an army and victors over the people around them, would also seem to be flattering to potential Indian converts, particularly men. But it might also make missionaries appear to believe in resurrection achieved not according to Christian eschatology, but from time to time as God saw fit.[35]

The verses from Ezekiel would also make it appear that English religion was complicitous with the Great Dying among the natives; resurrection of Indian bones was meant to promise eternal life, but prophesying about it in this manner made the English seem eager to promote earthly death in order to start the cosmic renewal. Certainly, verses 12 and 13 of Ezekiel 37 graphically dwell on the death that precedes resurrection. In these verses God promises, "I will open your graves, and cause you to come up out of your graves." Given that natives suspected the English arrival had sent many Indians to their graves, missionaries' emphasis on Ezekiel may have seemed a bit tactless. In a 1649 letter to Henry Whitfeld, Eliot rejoiced that "our God[,] who can and will gather the scattered and lost dust of our bodies at the Resurrection, can and will finde out these lost and scattered Israelites." He again referred to Ezekiel, saying that the wind would make the scattered dry bones gain flesh and rise again, and claiming that the name of the native man Waban, who was helping to gather natives into the fold, meant "wind."[36]

Ezekiel's images of death, which the missionaries used to explain their efforts to one another and to their native audience, contrasted with the images of fructification and wealth that they used with their sponsors. The idea of Indian souls as the "first fruits" of New England's plantation was a stock metaphor. Joseph Caryl's introduction to one of Eliot's tracts (of 1655) played on commercial imagery to represent the harvest of souls in "your spirituall *Factory in New England.*" For God, the natives were "a kind of first fruits of his (new) creatures there." Their souls were a *"Merchandize"* that was worth more than "Gold and Silver," objects of the long-standing mineral obsession. In the end, once settlers "have Planted themselves in the *Indian Wildernesses,*" they would be able to "Plant the *Indians as a Spirituall Garden,* into which Christ might come and eat his pleasant fruits." These were images of vigorous life, which also represented eternal life—more cheerful than the images the missionaries used with the Indians themselves, despite the image of Christ as a Cronus who consumed his children's bodies.[37]

It is also clear that missionaries associated Indians' sickness and dying with their acceptance of the gospel. Spiritual conversion prefigured or paralleled corporeal degeneration; Indians' souls were saved just in time. John Winthrop had noted this in the early days of settlement in Massachusetts, when smallpox killed many natives near the English. When John Sagamore fell ill of the disease in 1633, he "promised (if he recovered) to liue with the Englishe, & serve their God. he left one sonne, which he disposed to mr *willson* the paster of *Boston,* to be brought vp by him." Indeed, after Indian parents died, the English "took home many of their Children," whether or not dying Indian parents had requested it. Winthrop also said of the 1633 epidemic among the Indians that "many of their children escaped & were kept by the English." He therefore noted the common epidemiological pattern that spared children while adults died, thus guaranteeing, in the context of colonization, that native orphans would end up in English households, usually as servants. Winthrop believed that "most of" these children "died soone after," perhaps of other infections they caught through prolonged contact with the English.[38]

Debility and death continued to inform conversion. Wequash Cook, who had "attained to good knowlege of the things of God and salvation by Christ, so as he became a preacher to other Indians," met with accident in 1642 when "he fell sick, not without suspicion of poison" from nonconverted Indians. Wequash "died very comfortably," that is, confident of God's mercy, but his demise warned of the connection between Indian conversion and cultural and physical death. Waban himself had moved toward Christianity "after the great sikness"; another Indian, Totherswamp, had gravitated toward the missionaries after some of his friends had died. Similarly, natives testified that they had first promised to pray or to accept some other Christian doctrine during an encounter with death or illness. After he was severely injured, an Indian named Antony promised that he would begin to pray to God if his life was spared. An epidemic during 1652 provided other examples of the bitter role Christianity played in natives' lives. The missionaries recounted that two very small children (about two or three years old) had died while calling upon God and Christ. Robin Speene, the father of one of the children, said that he "could not tell whether the sorrow for the death of his Child, or the joy for its faith were greater." Another spate of sickness during an abnormally rainy season in 1658 and 1659 led to similar responses. Waban exhorted the natives with verses from the Book of Matthew that emphasized Christ's role as a healer. Many were "at this time sick in body," Waban claimed, "but more are sick in their souls." Christ was a "great Physitian," however, who could "heale us both soul and body." John Speene acknowledged that "the burying place of this Town hath many graves, and so it is in all our Towns among the praying *Indians*," then took comfort from the Book of Matthew. Wutasakompauin used the same text to encourage fasting and prayer in the face of the "many sicknesses, and deaths among us," saying, "Christ is the great Physitian."[39]

That the Book of Matthew, with its accounts of miraculous healings, was printed in Massachusett at the conclusion of the collection of these Indian narratives showed how the missionaries emphasized to natives that Christ was the savior of those who suffered disease and infirmity. Sometimes, however, the missionaries were not clear whether they and the natives were talking about the same thing. One of Eliot's tracts described, in 1660, how Ponampam had come to the gospel through fear of sickness. Ponampam said that when he was eight years old, "my father did chide me for playing. I wondered at it, for he said we shall all die. I wondered and sat amazed about half an hour, but I soon forgot it." Ponampam remembered well enough when "that Winter the [small]Pox came, and almost all our kindred dyed." This testimony resembled many other Indian accounts, except for the father's particularly dire prophecy: "We shall all die." The missionaries were intrigued, and "in private we asked him what ground or reason moved his Father so to speak?" If they wanted insight into native infirmity and extinction, Ponampam's answer tended toward a different explanation. He "thinketh that his Father had heard that Mr *Wilson* had spoken of the flood of *Noah.*" In this regard, "all" might have meant English as well as Indians. It is also unclear whether natives thought that Christian ideas of providence explained their illnesses, that is, whether their views matched those of their instructors. According to Eliot, one Indian woman told him "she still loved God, though he made her sick"; another Indian asked, "Why doth God make good men sick?"[40]

If Indians could not control their material circumstances, they could learn about the powerful providence that controlled the world around them. English plans for education and catechism therefore stressed that Indians must not continue in their native beliefs about nature. The main lesson they needed to learn was that the world was God's creation, and He master over it. This point was meant to challenge what missionaries took to be native belief that nature had spontaneously emerged and was not the intended work of any divine being. The native testimony that the missionaries recorded gave examples of this. Ponampam said that although he had heard that "*God made all the World,* yet my heart did not beleeve, because I knew I sprung from my Father and Mother." Magus said, "Heretofore I beleeved not, that God made the world, but I thought the world was of it self, and all people grew up in the world of themselves." The Indian named Peter struck closer to the missionaries' intended point when he said, "Now I konw [*sic*] that God made all the world, and I fear him." Another testifier answered the question "Out of what matter did God make the world?" with the orthodox reply, "Not of any thing at all." Further, Indians were instructed that the world was preserved only through God's power, and not through any naturally generative quality that matter had in and of itself. An Indian named Anthony was reported in 1660 as saying that God made the world, and all in it; Waban also told Monotunkquanit that "God is a great God, and made all the world."[41]

The argument from design also supported the missionaries' contention that the natives had to begin to respect and emulate a civil way of life even before they could become Christians. One tract explained that just as man was above the animals, so God was above man; if animals could not understand man, so man could not fully understand God. Yet human superiority to animals was demonstrated by artifice: man could "become learned" and perform such feats as to "sayl over the seas," and to "plant and govern Common-weales"—the culture- and gender-specific tasks that the English had performed in order to effect proper rule over America. If God was to man as man was to animals, this analogical reasoning emphasized God's extraordinary dominion while also supporting the colonial regime that the godly English had created, and which the natives were supposed to follow.[42]

But lessons about order (cosmic and earthly) followed a cautious schedule, one that prioritized religion over abstract learning. The English plan to educate Indians began with practical adaptation of their way of life, then moved on to the gospel. A significant step was missing: to train Indians in European doctrines about nature. Missionaries did not bother with this task, except as it related to religion. But why not train Indians in European ideas about nature along with practical arts and religion? Any Protestant education required some form of literacy, but narrow training without higher learning guaranteed that most Indians would fall beneath the level of the colonial elite; they would be like women. A few native men were selected for learned study, at grammar school, then later at Harvard College. In 1659 Charles Chauncy, Harvard's president, provided a certificate of proficiency for two grammar school–trained Indians, Caleb Cheeshateaumauk and Joel Hiacoomes, who had together translated a chapter of Isaiah into Latin. When Eliot reported on the success of his mission in 1671 (just after the first Indian church was covenanted at

Maktepog), he also spoke of his next task, "to make it one of my chief cares and labours to teach them [the natives] some of the Liberal Arts and Sciences." Learning was possible only after conversion.[43]

Missionaries were therefore annoyed that natives asked questions about nature along with questions about the gospel. Winslow was pleased with the questions on religion one group had posed at a meeting, "far different from what some other *Indians* under *Kitchomakia* in the like meeting about six weeks before had done," when they had taken up time asking about the causes of thunder, tides, and the wind. Even so, Winslow had already given in to such inquiries, and specified that preachers to the Indians must have "learning," because "these had sundry philosophicall questions, which some knowledge of the arts must helpe to give answer to." Thomas Shepard likewise reported that natives at a later meeting had asked "many Philosophicall [questions] about the Sunne, Moon, Stars, Earth and Seas, Thunder, Lightning, Earthquakes, etc.," but Shepard did not wish to go into the specific questions and answers, "lest I should clog your time with reading." Eliot was careful when he lectured Indians on "the liberal Arts" to stress "Logik," which would presumably help natives unpack the missionaries' theological explanations.[44]

Missionaries believed that religious explanations, where appropriate, were better suited to a people they increasingly regarded as simple. Persistent questions about nature during religious instruction were therefore not evidence of a salutary curiosity, but showed that Indians could not see that these were two separate realms of inquiry. When some natives asked why seawater was salty and land water fresh, the English responded that it was due to God's "wonderful" workings, "yet wee gave them also the reason of it from naturall causes which they lesse understood." Missionaries' preaching therefore separated the English from the Indians, the former as a people who comprehended nature's obscure movings, the latter as a people who "lesse understood" such abstractions. Given that not all missionaries had university training, and that even those (such as Eliot) who did were by no means natural philosophers, these claims were overstated. They were cultural assertions rather than comparisons between individual Indians and colonists.[45]

But this categorization contrasted with assumptions in the earliest phase of colonization. Idolatry had become specific to the ignorant rather than endemic to credulous humans, whatever education they might have. For example, colonists had more confidence that representations of things had no power, as idols, to carry the power of the things themselves. Instead, they stressed that belief in such a thing showed credulous superstition. Winslow wrote that it had been explained to natives that the image of an "*Indian*, Bow and Arrowes on a tree . . . is not an *Indian* but the Picture or Image of an *Indian*, and that Picture man makes, and it can doe no hurt nor good." Similarly, images of God were made by "wicked men," but "can doe no good nor hurt to any man as God can." This would have been at odds with early Reformation opinion on idols but congruent with late seventeenth-century discussions of objects and spirits.[46]

In the manner in which the English always recorded native questions that puzzled over the delineation between spirit and matter, however, they admitted that the boundary was a perplexing one even to them. One Indian pressed for further information about just how incorporeal the soul was by posing a remarkably specific question. If a man "*should be inclosed in Iron a foot thick and thrown into the fire, what would become of his soule, whether could the soule come forth thence or not?*" Not only was this a question about the soul, but it was also an indication of the centrality of death and torment to the interactions between English and Indian. It also used the European material of iron to represent strength, thus revealing the propensity for the material objects of trade to creep into intercultural dialogue. This resembled Mayhew's testimony that a native man said he had been possessed by "*Pawwawnomas*, not only in the shape of living Creatures, as Fowls, Fishes and creeping things, but Brasse, Iron, and stone."[47]

At the same time, settlers and creoles were strengthening their identity as a people whose greater culture included natural philosophy. They had first articulated these claims when they asserted that natives either withheld information about mines in America, or were simply ignorant of minerals and chemistry. Later accusations of Indians' ignorance were broader, and attacks on Indian knowledge of nature reached farther. A few colonists began to turn Indians themselves into things to be studied, analysis of which pointed up the supposed lack of analytic insight Indians had into the world around them.

Science and empire were finally beginning to be defined through each other. While the redefinition eventually involved colonists (and Indians) throughout the anglophone Atlantic, the connection took its initial form in New England. The region's specific experiences would affect general English assessments of the natives of America, even to the point where New Englanders insisted that they could interpret for those at home what Indians and America were like, based on their experience in a small part of the western hemisphere. New Englanders believed that their dual efforts—natural philosophy and evangelism—gave them unusual power to interpret Indians to the English back home. As Stephen Winthrop wrote to John Winthrop, Jr., in 1649, "The conversion of the Indians with yow maks New England very Famous."[48]

The men who were redefining natural philosophy agreed that Indians were intellectually backward, and some even ventured to suggest that the sciences should be deployed to impress the natives as to the superiority of colonists. Thomas Sprat's *History of the Royal Society* compared the scholastics to Indians, both of them people who lacked system or method to develop their skills, the former in philosophy, the latter in ornamental arts. The school men, "like the *Indians,* onely express'd a wonderful Artifice," without making anything worthwhile. Oldenburg wrote to Winthrop, "I doubt not but the Savage Indians themselves when they shall see the Christians addicted as to piety and Virtue, so to all sorts of Ingenuity's pleasing Experiments, usefull Inventions and practices, will thereby insensibly and the more chearfully Subject themselves to them." In this way, the superiority of knowledge among the English would work toward the ends of empire without the use of force.[49]

In his writings, Boyle repeatedly used Indians as an example of inappropriate confusion between material objects and spiritual power. Some of these examples continued the long-standing concern over idolatry; in "Of Piety" (ca. 1650), Boyle derided the people on "an American Iland" who "ador'd a wooden Bell." But some of Boyle's descriptions of Indian responses to European technology exemplified the new assertions of Indians' backwardness. In his "Aretology or Ethicall Elements" (ca. 1645), he referred to the "silly" Indians who gave English sailors "precius wares and substantiall meat" for mere "Beads and Whistles and Gugawes." As an example of the "Ignorance of the Uses of Natural Things," Boyle referred to "some barbarous *American*" who might find from a "Shipwrack" a "key of a Cabinet" which he would know only as "a piece of Iron." This contrasted with earlier representations of Indians as all too canny salvagers of European technology. Even more tellingly, Boyle placed Indians at one extreme as he defined a reasonable way between atheistic materialism and idolatrous vitalism. He rejected the mistake of ancient "Atomists" who had excluded God's power from matter, but equally ridiculed how the mechanical clock at Strasbourg "might, to a rude Indian, seem to be more intelligent then [its maker] *Cunradus Dasypodius* himself."[50]

These views were much like those of the New England Company's missionaries, but the opinions of people in England were distinctive in their willingness to lump all natives together, as if all cultural groups in North America were more or less alike. This thinking was not yet typical of colonists, who thought that Indians had some shared characteristics (though they tended to overstate this point), but recognized other differences based on language, physical location, proximity to settlers, and so on. So Eliot was careful to explain in his *Indian Grammar Begun* that he had analyzed only one Indian dialect. He described variations in pronunciation in northern Algonquian dialects, for example, "We *Massachusets* pronounce the *n*. The *Nipmuk Indians* pronounce *l*." Still, because Eliot's title made a grandiose claim about a purportedly universal Indian grammar, it would not be surprising if readers in England might have missed its regional specificity. (This was even more true of Williams's *Key into the Language of America*.) Unlike Eliot, but like Oldenburg, English contemporaries described Indians as if they all belonged to one language and culture. Sprat hoped, for instance, that "the *Barbarians* of our Times," meaning "the *Turks*, the *Moors*, the *East-Indians*, and even the *Americans*," would be brought into the "*Universal Light*" of improvement. Sprat's statement about Indians was doubly dismissive; he flattened cultural differences among peoples in the East and West Indies, and he implied that it was American Indians who were least likely to be enlightened.[51]

While they may have been more likely to distinguish among different groups of Indians, colonists stereotyped them in other ways. The early colonial correspondents of the Royal Society were eager to state their credentials in terms of understanding matter, and they used Indians as examples of the ignorance they had themselves overcome. The society wanted colonial informants, though usually for concrete tasks such as observing celestial phenomena that could not be seen in Europe, or giving information about local flora and fauna. But men who lived in or were to go to the colonies did not always regard their roles as so lowly. Thus Richard Kemp informed Henry Oldenburg, the society's secretary, that he was an expert in "chymistry," though "not in ye vulgar way, but as a bould aspirer to ye secret of secrets." For Kemp, chemistry had been "a science in ould times" but "now a dayes it is disgraced by trivial cheaters, imposters and ignorant Artists." This was unfortunate, for the science should be preserved as "a secret Providence of God," meaning that not all could know it; the learned inquiry into nature defined it as exclusive to a European minority.[52]

Much correspondence to the Royal Society was, accordingly, a restatement of that long-standing goal of American colonization—the mineral obsession—while updating it with a new appeal to learning. Kemp had resolved to go to the "new world," which he, like many others, still conceived as "that grand Magazin of mineral treasures, and natures chiefe forge." He was at least wise enough to associate heat and mineral wealth with Spanish America, and so went to Puerto Rico, then on to Mexico. Still, Kemp noted that the Spanish had not always made progress in mining, and saw an opening for his own expertise. He made plans to visit a cave said to be covered with gold leaf, "which had deluded many Spaniards . . . they never being able to reduce it into a body, nether by quicksilver nor fusion." If Kemp contrasted himself to Spaniards in terms of skill, he was puzzled outright by Indians' lack of helpfulness in mining. He insisted that "auncient Indians knew how to make use of" the mine, but contemporary natives held it to be "haunted with Malignant Spirits." Kemp's Indian "Guyd" refused to enter the cave for fear of "hobgoblings or Divels," and the Englishman's attempts to reason with the man were upset by their candle's suddenly going out, leading to panic and flight. Kemp was exasperated. "Why yee Indians otherwise valiant and undaunted men are so fearefull to discouer minerals to Europeans and white men is an ould superstition of theires, of too tedious circumstances to be rehearsed here." His statement reflected the overdetermined understanding of native men's military valor and elaborated on the superstitious practices that were a comparably distinguishing characteristic.[53]

In a letter to the Royal Society, John Winthrop, Jr., made connections between natives' valor and their lack of information about the mineral world that were far more critical than Kemp's. Winthrop followed the trend of stigmatizing Indians as fit for war but otherwise ill fitted to their physical surroundings. In 1668 he complained of the "constant Warrs wch. Rage continued amongst the Indians." War had made Indians who had once supplied him with "specimins" afraid to travel to likely sources, or else war had already killed them off. Winthrop did expect information about copper from one Indian, "yf he be not slaine"; he hoped that "better tymes may promote better discoveries." Still, Winthrop predicted that the natives would continue to be of limited help. They found only "small peices" of the minerals Europeans might want, and only "accidentally in their huntings." "Nor can they in likelihood meet with a solid veine of good mettall, which usually lyeth deepe in the earth, never opened by them, nor have they meanes to doe it." As a consequence, "the remote Inland" was "little discovered, [and] matters reported by Indians many tymes uncertaine"; indeed, colonists had "no certainty, of what is underground." This was a considerable remove from the belief, early in the century, that natives knew the land better than any English person could. Further, it built on the emerging opinion that Indians had received their most useful tools from Europeans and, because of their too recent adoption of iron tools, had never dug deep enough in the earth to discover its hidden secrets. Sometimes they discovered minerals "where an earthquake hath shaken down the sides of an hill, or made some rent among the Rocks," but this was serendipitous.[54]

Winthrop was aware that the colonists had themselves made little progress in discovering minerals, and did not wish the English in the mother country (let alone his contacts in the Royal Society) to think that they suffered from the same disadvantages as natives, namely, lack of good tools and learning. He excused colonists' ignorance of mines, writing, "It may be, God reserves such of his bounties to future generations: Plantations in their beginnings have worke ynough." Settlers' early search for "subsystence" had preoccupied them with building, fencing, farming. The early plantations had been "as in ye beginning of ye world," wrote Winthrop, yet another pre-Lockean connection between civility and property. Subsequent colonists continued to blame Indians for lack of help in establishing mines and, like Kemp, associated their behavior with superstition. Robert Beverley claimed that the English in Virginia had learned of a lead mine only because an Indian "under Pretence of Hunting" had signaled its location by "dropping his *Tomahawk* at the place, (he not daring publickly to discover it, for fear of being murder'd)." Even so, the site was never found again. "I know not by what Witchcraft it happens,"

Beverley concluded, that Indians could conceal what they themselves could not use. Each part of this story—the warlike implement as a signal, the fear of native reprisal, the suspicion of witchcraft—reinforced English inclinations to regard Indians as martial, treacherous, superstitious.[55]

Partly to defend their own efforts in America, colonists' accounts of the later 1600s steadily eroded the earlier contentions that Indians had coherent and meaningful ways of seeing the universe, and could see it in both practical and abstract terms. Native astronomy, for instance, took quite a beating. Despite earlier accounts, such as Williams's, that Indians had a remarkable comprehension of the heavens, later narratives argued their ignorance. Josselyn concluded that Indians "have but little knowledge of the Starrs and Planets." He repeated later that they did not know arithmetic or astronomy, but were nevertheless good country guides, evidently knowing the landscape empirically rather than through the abstractions rendered by maps, compasses, and knowledge of navigation. In other ways, colonists reiterated their contention that Indians were useful for the rough frontier work of settlement, but would then have to give way to the English. It was in Winthrop's first formal paper to the Royal Society that he described the forest industries of New England, specifying that Indians burned pines in their annual firing of the woods, and the English then gathered the pine knots to make into pitch.[56]

Even more significant, the English began to discard their earlier opinions that natives had considerable skill in medicine. This was an important transition. Indian herbal pharmacology had been the earliest and strongest example of natives' ability to protect their bodies and manipulate nature. Early seventeenth-century English accounts that had distinguished between chemical medicine and Indians' herbal medicine had set boundaries around the extent to which natives understood nature. But even in the mid-1600s, colonists had compared Indians to England's country "empiricks" who had considerable knowledge of simples. By the later 1600s, two new trends were converging. First, religious criticisms of native shamans derided an essential component of native medicine; and second, colonists had more confidence that they had displaced Indians as America's natural inhabitants, and could therefore themselves interpret American nature, including its herbal remedies.

The English had long conceptualized shamans' power as demonic, derived not from an understanding of nature's properties but from an ability to pervert them with Satan's assistance. Now missionaries emphasized that the devil and his shamanic minions were fighting a battle to survive as masters of the natives. Mayhew reported that since the gospel had been brought among the Indians, the shamans "in stead of curing have rather killed many." He continued by suggesting the Indians admitted that the devil had power over enchantment and death. The devil would, for instance, "abuse the real body of a Serpent" by inhabiting it, and then would "shoot a bone (as they say) into the Indians Body, which sometimes killeth him." Mayhew's "as they say" conveyed a sense that not everything occurred just as the Indians said, but instead that their metaphor was culture-bound and even childish. The description is very unlike Hariot's complex narration of the Roanok's "invisible bullets"; the regression in technology from bullets to bone darts or arrows underlines the English sense that Indian superstition was in every way primitive. Mayhew's remarks about the devil "abusing" the "real" body of a snake indicated the colonists' agreement with Indians that the devil could indeed do such a thing. Mayhew also explained that the Indians' "god of the Dead" was the devil, "for the same word they have for *Devil,* they use also for a *Dead Man,*" who they believed was translated to the devil after death. This should have been a clue to the English that the natives had concepts of bodily death and spiritual reanimation that competed with the Christian conceptualization of these processes.[57]

Criticism of shamans became criticism of all native medical knowledge, as the English (particularly missionaries) increasingly assigned knowledge of American herbs to white creoles. Eliot concluded that Indians "have no meanes of Physick at all, onely make use of Pawwawes when they be sick"; he emphasized the need to convince Indians of the "diabolicall practice" of shamanic medicine and to provide them with proper "Physick and Chyrurgery." Eliot believed that the natives needed to engage in the "full casting off their Pawwaws." He knew "they much idolized them, and albeit they know not as yet, any meanes of help when sick, but them," yet still they needed to demonstrate faith in Christianity by forswearing sorcerers. Even converts, Henry Whitfeld warned, were still spiritually weak enough to "fear the Pawwawes." Thomas Shepard concluded that "though some of them understand the vertues of sundry things, yet the state of man's body, and skill to apply them they have not." His phrasing indicated that he was judging Indians according to western standards of medicine; knowing the virtues of herbal cures would find little purchase if Indians did not comprehend the first principles of anatomy and physiology.[58]

Just as Indian bodies had been stripped of their Americanness when colonists noted native attrition in new world epidemics, so Indians were now stripped of the knowledge of remedies for their repeated illnesses. If earlier defense of natives' herbal pharmacology had strategically marshalled it against the Paracelsians, this ventriloquism had at least admitted the efficacy of Indian medicines. By the late 1600s, however, the medical properties of American plants were supposed to be best known to settlers, not to Indians. Thus Boyle wrote in his corpuscular interpretation of medicines that Virginia snakeroot was used by "the *English* Planters" against the creatures that "the *English* call Rattle-snakes." This statement separated Indians not only from areas of learning such as corpuscular theory, but also from practical understanding of the land of their nativity.[59]

It followed, then, that missionaries believed they would have to take responsibility for the medical care of converts and potential converts. They gave Christian charity to Indians in the manner that had inspired a very few New Englanders earlier to intervene in Indian villages during smallpox epidemics. In later instances of medical care, missionaries intended to render service at all times, rather than only during emergencies. In 1651 and 1652 the New England Company equipped its workers with a "phisicall directorie" and another "booke of phisicall directions." These books might have been meant for the health care of English and Indians in praying towns, but other instructions made clear that the health of Indians was of particular concern. In 1657 provision was made to purchase "physicall Druggs" from an apothecary in Boston "for ye use of ye Indians there."[60]

The provision of medical attention, perceived as part of Christian charity, was also deployed to undermine native confidence in shamans. Medical attention paralleled evangelical attention: the gospel was physic for the soul, European medicine physic for the body. Mayhew reported that he had been approached by three Indians who were so ill that the "Pawwawes" had given up on them. Mayhew evidently gave them medicine as well as prayer, and bled one man. All recovered. Eliot insisted that the smallpox which broke out in 1650 had not much affected the natives, except the "profane Indians that lately are come to a place near *Wamouth*." Eliot also insisted that the praying Indians, "who call upon God in preserving them from the small Pox," were rewarded when "fewer of them have dyed thereof, then of others who call not upon the Lord," including "their prophane Neighbours" who "were cut off by it." The English were also eager to present Indian statements that the Christian way of life might protect them. Thus Whitfield quoted Hiacoomes as wondering whether the English might have a better way of "health and life."[61]

This hope did not preclude the English from stating that some praying Indians endured more physical suffering than unconverted Indians did. While missionaries recounted many instances of illness and death as moments of Christian epiphany, they recorded cases in which the suffering went against the standard image of natives' stoicism and indifference to others. Eliot noted that some converts showed "mercy to them that were sicke," which evidenced their Christian forbearance and charity, even to those who were not themselves convinced of the gospel's truth. Eliot also reported in 1671 that a native man had died of "the Stone," and was "the first *Indian* that ever was known to have that disease; but now another hath the same disease." Shepard agreed with the belief in Indian stoicism. They were "well known not [to] bee much subject to teares," even under extreme torture. It was therefore almost miraculous that the gospel could make them weep. It was as if the Indians gave up their natural durability once they became civilized, especially once Christianity softened their hearts.[62]

Childbirth among converted Indian women also provided an index of bodily change. The English believed that pain in childbirth was atypical for natives. Just as Indian men could endure battle and torture without complaint, so native women barely felt the pain of labor. Would this be true of praying Indians? Converted native men were for the most part stripped of the warrior status that had initially impressed the English, but women in praying towns continued to bear children. As Indians were anglicized, they could no longer (publicly) follow the practices that artificially strengthened their bodies—no plunging infants into snow, no administering poison to adolescent males. From the English point of view, praying Indians were instead dependent on faith and providence for their health and longevity. Daniel Gookin related, for instance, that one converted woman had a difficult childbirth lasting several days, "a thing unusual with the Indian women." William French reported that an Indian man had prayed for his wife, who was three days and nights in childbirth. This was meant to indicate native faith in the power of prayer, but also to note that some native women suffered the pains of childbirth at least as much as Englishwomen. The emphasis underlined English assumptions about native bodies: because they were inherently frail, they required extraordinary (if not supernatural) care to maintain them. In the absence of demonic magic or painstaking techniques, Indians had to trust in God.[63]

It was probably the case, instead, that the English were merely seeing more Indians and learning more about them. Adherence to civil and Christian standards of behavior proscribed Indians' semi-migratory behavior, the labor of women outdoors in the fields, and the separation of women during menstruation and childbirth. It was less likely, therefore, that women would give birth while isolated from their families, or that they would need to bind children to cradleboards in order to transport them easily from home to fields and back. The bloody and painful business of childbirth was therefore more visible to all men, including English missionaries, and was probably exacerbated by the ill health that the Indians suffered as a result of proximity to the English.

Natives' suffering was real, and it is not impossible that Christianity, and the charitable actions of the missionaries, brought genuine comfort to them. A gospel of eternal life and bodily resurrection may well have appealed to Indian communities repeatedly hit by epidemics. As with the Pilgrims who had taken care of smallpox-stricken natives, Eliot and his colleagues were among the few Englishmen who lived intimately with the natives and were willing to offer them physical aid and sympathy, albeit always with the exhortation to accept their beliefs. But it is important to keep in mind how the English reported these events, and that there were other ways they could have made sense of them. It would have been possible for the English to note that such suffering had not actually increased, but rather that their familiarity with Indians was bringing many more such instances to light. The contrast between praying Indians and unconverted natives was overdrawn. Further, if the narrators had wished to, they could have used examples of Indian suffering in praying towns to challenge the prevailing image of Indians as inhumanly passive and patient under physical agony. Instead, the missionaries used these cases to point out instances of faith: Indians did not usually have to endure such pain, but their faith and prayer helped them in the face of this unfamiliar trial for which their traditional lives had not prepared them. Further, missionaries' medical care underscored that praying Indians were dependent on English learning and assistance. Indian bodies and souls were subject to their colonizers.

When Sprat dedicated his *History of the Royal Society* to the king, he remarked that "to increase the Powers of all Mankind, and to free them from the bondage of Errors, is greater Glory than to enlarge *Empire,* or to put Chains on the necks of Conquer'd *Nations.*" Other definitions of natural philosophy and native ignorance or weakness similarly implied that the superiority of knowledge among the English would work toward the ends of empire without the use of force. Sprat's history was firm on this point. Just as the first generation of colonizers had represented geography as evidence that England was destined peacefully to colonize and proselytize in North America (which reached toward Albion for help), so Sprat claimed that geography guaranteed England's preeminence in learning. "*Universal Intelligence,* is befriended by *Nature* itself," Sprat asserted, "in the situation of *England:* For, lying so, as it does, in the passage between the *Northern* parts of the World, and the *Southern;* its *Ports* being open to all Coasts, and its *Ships* spreading their Sailes in all Seas; it is thereby necessarily made, not onely *Mistress* of the *Ocean,* but the most proper *Seat,* for the advancement of *Knowledg.*" London was "the head of a *mighty Empire*" reaching over the seas.[64]

Sprat's phrasing about "the advancement of Knowledg" was intended to echo Bacon's *Advancement of Learning.* It was at this point that the Royal Society, and more European natural philosophers, began to articulate the Enlightenment interpretation of modernity that Francis Bacon had prefigured. That is, the discovery of the new world had been part of a wider discovery of new "arts" like gunpowder and the compass which had guaranteed European supremacy over transmarine territories. The frontispiece of Sprat's history made clear these connections between inventions and empire. The image displays an array of beings, dead and alive, natural and supernatural. A bust of the society's patron, King Charles II (still living, but rendered here as a marble fragment), is being crowned by Fame. William, Viscount Brouncker (also still alive), sits on one side of the bust; his inscription indicates that he was president of the society when this image was

Restoration *nova reperta*. From Thomas Sprat, *The History of the Royal Society of London* (London, 1667), frontispiece. By permission of the Syndics of the Cambridge University Library.

made. Francis Bacon, long dead but here revivified, sits on the other side. Above them hovers the motto "nullius in verba"; behind them stretches a room filled with books and technical instruments (words and things), and beyond is the material world, a cultivated landscape complete with a telescope and busy observer of the heavens. While Brouncker points to his king, Bacon points to what he had prophesied: the implements that constructed European imperium over the globe, including navigational devices and a firearm.[65] The river in the background is probably meant to be the Thames, the great conduit to the ocean that made London, and England, mistress of empires. This was therefore part of the improved landscape that midcentury reformers such as Samuel Hartlib and Robert Child had begun to promote, and whose transatlantic manifestation had by the end of the century some basis in reality. Beyond the river, beyond the ocean, lay America and the Indians Bacon had supposed were conquered by superior technology.

But what place, exactly, did Indians have within this imperial landscape? Natural philosophy now had recognized methods for assessing colonial territories and peoples, including indigenous populations. These formulas often followed the model of political arithmetic, the determination of the size and character of a population along the lines of the analyses that had informed early accounts of America. In 1662 John Graunt pioneered the new population analysis for the metropole, using London's bills of mortality. Graunt summarized the long-standing concerns of population theory: the impact of epidemics, the customs that supported a high birthrate, the availability of people to work and men to fight. To analyze these variables, Graunt supplied data—crude but effective demonstrations that political power (in the form of humans) could be measured. Further, Graunt linked his effort to the sciences by citing Bacon's definition of *"Natural History"* and by praising King Charles as *"Prince of Philosophers."* He also flattered the Royal Society by calling it "the Parliament of *Nature,"* where all questions about the material world were adjudicated. To make even clearer the society's new role in determining facts, Graunt ritually deplored the religious *"Schismaticks"* whose experiments were "Ceremonies," not "useful Arts."[66]

William Petty (who shortly after Graunt's 1662 study coined the term "political arithmetic") was at the same time writing on population theory. Petty had been part of the Hartlib circle and had shared some of that group's interest in colonies as sites where the rise and fall of different peoples, and their differential capacities to develop natural resources, offered instructive examples of improvement. Hartlib had persuaded former New Englander Robert Child to go to Ireland to write a study of its land, people, and products, but Child never completed the task. Petty instead began to define colonial populations by looking at Ireland. He estimated that during the 1640s reconquest of Ireland, 145,000 people had died or were banished. This meant that parts of the country were cleared and ready to be planted with the English. Still later, Petty looked at America, specifically the new colony of Pennsylvania. A list of questions about the colony restated the concerns Hariot had had about population density and carrying capacity, and asked what kinds of bodies and technology the natives of the place had. Petty set out a hypothetical unit of one thousand Indians, then asked about the age and gender distributions within this group, the height and weight of individuals, and their fertility. Petty's interest in Indian mortality was particularly apparent in his inquiry into how many women died during or after childbirth, and how many Indians died of smallpox (and how this compared to rates in England). Petty thus made clear that even though the Irish and the Indians suffered the same fate—attrition—the reasons for their demise were different; the Irish were displaced by war, the Indians by natural causes. Petty's proposal that Ireland and Scotland be further cleared of people through forced emigration in order to facilitate ranching, which would enrich the greater empire, underscored the assumption that England's nearby dependencies did not, unlike America, contain too few people.[67]

Political arithmetic thus reduced the Indians to natural bodies that the English could study and whose numbers they could expect to diminish. Petty's subsequent questions did little to allow Indians any more active role within the colonies. Instead, he followed the established trends of comparing Indians unfavorably to Europeans and insisting that most of the natives' effective technology was gained through their trade with Europeans. For instance, Petty wondered, "Do they understand Gunpowder?" and "Do they think the Condition of the Europeans happyer than their owne?" Petty conceived of two ways only to measure what the Indians of Pennsylvania might have known and could impart to settlers. First, "What works of Ornament have they, not easily imitatable by the English?" and second,

"How many simples do they use in Medicine?" This reduced Indian technology to ornamentation (a nonreligious version of what once had been labeled idolatry) and herbal pharmacology—the lone survivor out of the range of Indian skills and tools that colonists had previously used and acknowledged as important inventions. Petty's penultimate question showed the ultimate thrust of his thinking: How did Indians sell land to the English? The assumption that Indians could be studied as transient natural entities was not unique to Graunt and Petty. It became the common mode in questionnaires about colonial regions, a subject of particular interest to colonial administrators, correspondents of the Royal Society, and doctors interested in the local pharmacopoeia.[68]

Above all, this kind of analysis hinted at Indians' possible weaknesses: lower birthrates and higher death rates than among colonists, limited technology, trading dependency on the English, propensity to exhaust their energies and their people in warfare against one another, and tendency to cede territory to colonists. As the English consolidated their empire, they made it look as if their using violent means to subjugate or disperse native populations was beside the point. Nature demonstrated that Indians were removed from the prospect of life in America. Their bodies were conceived as unsuited to the places the English had settled, their forms of medicine were inadequate to treat their continuing debility, and their conceptions of nature did not promise an easy transition to English learning. Indians did not belong in the plantations the English had made in America. They were uprooted.

Coda

In his history of East and West Florida, the eighteenth-century naturalist and cartographer Bernard Romans carefully examined the different peoples who lived in that part of the British empire and then questioned the Indians' right, as aboriginals, to claim "American" status there. "We might call them Americans," Romans conceded, "as the inhabitants of the old world are each distinguished by a name expressive of, or relative to the quarters, from which they respectively originate, but this would be confounding them with the other natives, as well white as black, which i think by no means reasonable." This is an astonishing statement, though one easy to read too narrowly within the context of its 1775 publication date, when the colonies' maturity and stirrings of independence might have made sense of Romans's words as a hint at the political and cultural primacy of the British migrants who had introduced themselves into the new world. Romans's statement was indeed an early version of an emerging argument for an exceptional American cultural identity. Yet at least as importantly it was also the conclusion of the long argument about the exceptional nature of Anglo-American corporeal identity which this book has traced.[1]

Did the English conquer America? That question began my book and has guided my attempt to chart the relationship between science and empire. It had been an indeterminate relationship, except for the English colonists' claims that Indians' bodies were inferior to their own. The body was the springboard from which the English then launched arguments about Indians' technical inferiority. Englishmen's claims of first their bodily superiority, then their technical superiority, then finally their intellectual superiority were all assertions of mastery over nature, over America, and over Indians. By the 1660s, discourse on America had reached a point of intellectual completion in which imperial and scientific goals were intertwined. The asserted deadness of matter made nature into a passive thing to be studied. That task now resembled colonial rule over dying Indians, whose persons and natural world were now subject to the English. The empire of nature and the emergent Atlantic empire were now subjected to an English state.

By this point, the English had constructed an image of the Indian that fits the modern stereotype: the native as pre-scientific and technologically deficient. Increasingly, English accounts referred not to the earlier concept of idolatry (which at least took Indian religion seriously as spiritual abomination) but to the more dismissive concept of superstition. Superstition designated religious error and deficiency of understanding both of spiritual matters and of the natural world. Thus George Alsop emphasized the Susquehannock's "Customs" and "Manners," but also their "Absurdities, and Religion." This opinion was evident as well in Robert Beverley's history of Virginia of 1705. Beverley's image of an Indian woman and child, taken from Theodor de Bry's version of John White's watercolor, replaced the English objects in the Indians' hands with native things, as if the possibility that Indians would gain understanding of English goods and technology was now at an end. Furthermore, in seventy-four pages of discussion on the natives, Beverley only twice mentioned instances in which they had adopted European technology; he spent most of his energy representing their "simple State of Nature," their "Idolatrous Adorations" and magical "Conjuration." Indians stood as reminders of the ignorance that no longer characterized educated people. Backwardness and lack of learning were personified; Indians were pathetic images of error.[2]

But this image was the product of colonization, not a supposition that had shaped early colonizers' opinions. The English had rethought their imperial ambitions. They approached the next phase of colonization with a new insistence on difference between themselves and those they believed they had conquered. The English had not begun to settle in the new world with the conviction that they had superior scientific and technological abilities, but they would later think this way *because* they colonized America and invaded a people whom they would, in the end, decide that they could not think of as similar to themselves. In the mid-eighteenth century, when the comte de Buffon argued that America's natural products were stunted and degenerate, English-speaking Americans would worry over their asserted physical suitability to the new world. Their worries are the subject of my present research. I hope to examine the elaboration of ideas of race and colonization, trace colonists' insistence that Baconian science and discovery of America were causally connected, and analyze debate over whether organic nature generated universal laws along the lines that physics had suggested or whether the new world somehow had a nature too lawless to be so described. These inquiries had significant consequences for the creoles who lived in British America, who would be forced to rethink the distribution of racial identities and cultural roles within the empire.[3] But settlers had already gained considerable psychological and corporate strength from the belief that, at the deepest physical level, they were the true and *natural* residents of America—the powerful racist fiction that remains the basis of creole identity in North America.

It is important to realize, however, that English imperial ideology had failed on the terms it had laid out for itself. As Alsop's and Beverley's statements demonstrate, arguments for the cultural advantages of Englishness (better tools and better concepts) took on a life of their own and would become orthodoxy in the eighteenth and nineteenth centuries, thus obscuring the original basis for this opinion. That is, the asserted English place in America rested on the foundational claim that English bodies were better suited to the new world than were Indian bodies. English discussion of the fate of the natives had repeatedly proclaimed that they were dying and thereby leaving more room for the invaders. Ever since Thomas Hariot had calculated the number of people who could "stand" within England, and the number who could "stand" on the entire face of the earth, the English had been fantasizing about planting their bodies overseas and dominating more of the globe. As colonizers' bodies pushed into America, the bodies of Indians were sickening and dying. They left behind the skulls and bones that had made New England into the "new found Golgotha" that fortuitously welcomed puritans as migrants.[4]

But the natives did not in the end die off. Some groups indeed became extinct within the earliest period of English colonization, and their loss must never be underestimated or glossed over. The English had expected, however, that natives who came into contact with them would permanently shrink into small, tractable groups, or that they might vanish entirely, consumed by disease and by the wars on which they mistakenly lavished too much of their technical energy. (This fantasy of Indian extinction would in fact inform much of nineteenth-century Indian policy.) What colonists never expected was one of the most significant developments in twentieth-century United States history: the reemergence, after centuries of attrition, of a native American birthrate that exceeds the death rate. The United States Census—descendant of the population analyses of Hariot, Botero, Graunt, and Petty—recorded that between 1890 and 1900, the native American portion of the population reached its nadir. Since then, natives' numbers have been rising. In part, this demographic recovery is due to a reversed relation between death rate and birthrate, but it is also the result of other factors, including willingness on the part of individuals to identify themselves as Indians, immigration of people of native descent, and enumeration of an increasing number of "mixed-blood" children as Indians. In other words, two of the prospects that English colonists wished never to see are now occurring apace: growth rather than decline of the native population, and intermarriage between people of European descent and Indians.[5]

This was not the resurrection Eliot, Boyle, or their fellow missionaries had thought they were preaching to the Indians. Nor was it the afterlife toward which the Indian child's grave at Long Pond might have been gesturing. The demographic recovery is a physical and cultural rebirth that challenges the assumption that people of old world descent were destined to replace the new world's dying inhabitants and that such a succession was part of a plan nature itself had dictated. The English had formed this assumption out of early modern theories of nature. A permanent state of native attrition was the imperial hypothesis that the English put on trial in America. Fortunately, their hypothesis was wrong.

Notes

Index

Notes

Abbreviations

AHR	*American Historical Review*
AS	*Annals of Science*
Bacon, *Works*	James Spedding, Robert L. Ellis, and Douglas D. Heath, eds., *The Works of Francis Bacon,* 15 vols. (Cambridge, Mass., 1863)
BHM	*Bulletin of the History of Medicine*
BL	British Library, London
Bodleian	Bodleian Library, University of Oxford
Boyle, *Works*	Michael Hunter and Edward B. Davis, eds., *The Works of Robert Boyle,* 14 vols. (London, 1999)
Bradford, *Plymouth Plan.*	William Bradford, *Of Plymouth Plantation, 1620–1647,* ed. Samuel Eliot Morison (New York, 1952)
CO	Colonial Office, Public Record Office, London
DTHSOP	*Durham Thomas Harriot Society Occasional Papers*
Eng. Books	Edward Arber, ed., *The First Three English Books on America,* [?1511]–1555 (Birmingham, 1885)
Frobisher Voyages	Richard Collinson, ed., *The Three Voyages of Martin Frobisher* (London, 1867)
HL	Huntington Library, San Marino, California
JAH	*Journal of American History*
JAS	*Journal of American Studies*
JHI	*Journal of the History of Ideas*
Josselyn, *Two Voyages*	*John Josselyn, Colonial Traveler: A Critical Edition of "Two Voyages to New-England,"* ed. Paul J. Lindholdt (Hanover, N.H., 1988)

Nathaniel B. Shurtleff, ed., *Records of the Governor and Company of the Massachusetts Bay in New England, 1628–1686,* 5 vols. (Boston, 1853–54)

MHS Pro.
Proceedings of the Massachusetts Historical Society

Mourt's Relation
[William Bradford and Edward Winslow], *Mourt's Relation or Journal of the Plantation at Plymouth,* ed. Henry Martyn Dexter (New York, 1969)

NAS
National Archives of Scotland, Edinburgh

NAW
David Beers Quinn et al., eds., *New American World: A Documentary History of North America to 1612,* 5 vols. (New York, 1979)

NEQ
New England Quarterly

Oldenburg, *Correspondence*
A. Rupert Hall and Marie Boas Hall, eds., *The Correspondence of Henry Oldenburg,* 13 vols. (Madison, Wisc., 1965–1986)

P & P
Past and Present

PCSM
Publications of the Colonial Society of Massachusetts

PRO
Public Record Office, London

RS
Library of the Royal Society, London

RVCL
Susan Myra Kingsbury, ed., *The Records of the Virginia Company of London,* 5 vols. (Washington, D.C., 1906–1935)

SCJ
Sixteenth Century Journal

Smith, *Works*
Philip L. Barbour, ed., *The Complete Works of Captain John Smith (1580–1631),* 3 vols. (Chapel Hill, 1986)

Va. Statutes
William Waller Hening, ed., *The Statutes at Large . . . of Virginia,* 13 vols. (Richmond, Va., 1809–1823)

VMHB
Virginia Magazine of History and Biography

Williams, *Correspondence*
Glenn W. LaFantasie, ed., *The Correspondence of Roger Williams,* 2 vols. (Providence, R.I., 1988)

Winthrop, *Journal*
Richard S. Dunn, James Savage, and Laetitia Yeandle, eds., *The Journal of John Winthrop, 1630–1649* (Cambridge, Mass., 1996)

Winthrop Papers
Allyn B. Forbes, ed., *The Winthrop Papers, 1498–1654,* 6 vols. (Boston, 1929–)

WMQ
William and Mary Quarterly, 3d series

Prologue

1. *Instauratio Magna* (1620), in Bacon, *Works*, 8:162.
2. John Lawson, *A New Voyage to Carolina* (1709), ed. Hugh Talmage Lefler (Chapel Hill, 1967), 26–27.

1. Transatlantic Background

1. Perry Miller's work set the pattern for twentieth-century scholarship on colonial America that focused on the distinctive culture that settlers created in a "wilderness"; see *The New England Mind: The Seventeenth Century* (Cambridge, Mass., 1954) and *The New England Mind: From Colony to Province* (Cambridge, Mass., 1953). On the "Great Dying," see Alfred W. Crosby, "Virgin Soil Epidemics as a Factor in the Aboriginal Depopulation in America," *WMQ*, 33 (1976), 289–299; Henry F. Dobyns, *Their Number Become Thinned: Native American Population Dynamics in Eastern North America* (Knoxville, Tenn., 1983). For recent interpretations that follow or investigate the idea of a distinctive identity in America, see John Canup, *Out of the Wilderness: The Emergence of an American Identity in Colonial New England* (Middletown, Conn., 1990); Jack P. Greene, *The Intellectual Construction of America: Exceptionalism and Identity from 1492 to 1800* (Chapel Hill, 1993), 54–60, 162–199. For a critical view, see Francis Jennings, *The Invasion of America: Indians, Colonialism, and the Cant of Conquest* (Chapel Hill, 1975), chap. 2. On ethnohistory as recovery of native experience, see James Axtell, "The Ethnohistory of Early America: A Review Essay," *WMQ*, 35 (1978), 110–114. For two more recent examples, see James Hart Merrell, *The Indians' New World: Catawbas and Their Neighbors from European Contact through the Era of Removal* (Chapel Hill, 1989); Richard White, *The Middle Ground: Indians, Empires, and Republics in the Great Lakes Region, 1650–1815* (Cambridge, 1991).
2. I use the term "English" because it was the dominant language of those who went to England's colonies, it was the language they used to define themselves against the native populations, and it was the corporate term they used for themselves, especially to describe their bodies. There is no easily encompassing term, however, for the native peoples of the Western Hemisphere whom the English invaded. "Indian" would not include the Inuit peoples discussed in Chapter 2; "native American" is not the best name for the northern peoples whose descendants live in Canada and prefer the term "First Nations"; "native" is the most encompassing name but had, for the English of the time, a denigrating connotation. I use all these terms carefully, choosing the best for the context under discussion.
3. On the cultural contrast, see Edmund S. Morgan, *American Slavery, American Freedom: The Ordeal of Colonial Virginia* (New York, 1975), chaps. 2–4; Bernard W. Sheehan, *Savagism and Civility: Indians and Englishmen in*

Colonial Virginia (Cambridge, 1980); Alden T. Vaughan, "From White Man to Redskin: Changing Anglo-American Perceptions of the American Indian," *AHR*, 87 (1982), 917–953; Anthony Pagden, *The Fall of Natural Man: The American Indian and the Origins of Comparative Ethnology* (Cambridge, 1986), and *European Encounters with the New World: From Renaissance to Romanticism* (New Haven, 1993). On the modern (rather than early modern) pedigree of racism, see Stephen Jay Gould, *The Mismeasure of Man* (New York, 1981), esp. chap. 2; Pat Shipman, *The Evolution of Racism: Human Differences and the Use and Abuse of Science* (New York, 1994); Ivan Hannaford, *Race: The History of an Idea in the West* (Washington, D.C., and Baltimore, 1996), pt. 2. For a work that emphasizes both lack of racial difference and presence of technological difference, see Jared Diamond, *Guns, Germs, and Steel: The Fates of Human Societies* (New York, 1997).

4. On African bodies, see Philip D. Curtin, "Epidemiology and the Slave Trade," *Political Science Quarterly*, 83 (1968), 198–211; James H. Sweet, "The Iberian Roots of American Racist Thought," *WMQ*, 54 (1997), 143–166.

5. Miller, *New England Mind: The Seventeenth Century*, 207–235 (quotation from 216); idem, *Orthodoxy in Massachusetts, 1630–1650* (Gloucester, Mass., 1965), xi, xii. Miller made a better contribution to the history of modern science in *New England Mind: From Colony to Province*, 345–366, 437–446. Most studies of the English colonies have examined the growth of a European-based empirical science, and most focus on the late seventeenth and eighteenth centuries. Raymond Phineas Stearns, *Science in the British Colonies of America* (Urbana, Ill., 1970), is an excellent and neglected study of the seventeenth and eighteenth centuries, but it slights inquiries that do not conform to Stearns's definition of modern science; Brooke Hindle, *The Pursuit of Science in Revolutionary America, 1735–1789* (Chapel Hill, 1956), covers only the late colonial period, as does (for medical theory) Richard Harrison Shryock, *Medicine and Society in America, 1660–1860* (New York, 1960). On early modern inquiry into nature, see Ronald Sterne Wilkinson, "'Hermes Christianus': John Winthrop, Jr., and Chemical Medicine in Seventeenth-Century New England," in Allen G. Debus, ed., *Science, Medicine, and Society in the Renaissance: Essays to Honor Walter Pagel* (New York, 1972), 1: 221–241; William R. Newman, *Gehennical Fire: The Lives of George Starkey, an American Alchemist in the Scientific Revolution* (Cambridge, Mass., 1994). On the Spanish colonies, see especially Antonello Gerbi, *Nature in the New World: From Christopher Columbus to Gonzalo Fernandez de Oviedo*, trans. Jeremy Moyle (Pittsburgh, 1985).

6. For views of the functional relationship between modern science and imperialism, see Lucile H. Brockway, *Science and Colonial Expansion: The Role of the British Royal Botanic Gardens* (London, 1979); Nathan Reingold and Marc Rothenberg, eds., *Scientific Colonialism: A Cross-Cultural Comparison* (Washington, D.C., 1987); John MacKenzie, ed., *Imperialism and the*

Natural World (Manchester, 1990); Michael Adas, *Machines as the Measure of Men: Science, Technology, and Ideologies of Western Dominance* (Ithaca, N.Y., 1989); James E. McClellan III, *Colonialism and Science: Saint Domingue in the Old Regime* (Baltimore, 1992); Mary Louise Pratt, *Imperial Eyes: Travel Writing and Transculturation* (New York, 1992); David Philip Miller and Peter Hanns Reill, eds., *Visions of Empire: Voyages, Botany, and Representations of Nature* (Cambridge, 1996).

7. For examples of parallels between colonization and environmental degradation, and of contrast between Europeans and Indians, see Alfred W. Crosby, Jr., *The Columbian Exchange: Biological and Cultural Consequences of 1492* (Westport, Conn., 1972); Calvin Martin, *Keepers of the Game: Indian-Animal Relationships and the Fur Trade* (Berkeley, 1978); William Cronon, *Changes in the Land: Indians, Colonists, and the Ecology of New England* (New York, 1983); Carolyn Merchant, *Ecological Revolutions: Nature, Gender, and Science in New England* (Chapel Hill, 1989); Timothy Silver, *A New Face on the Countryside: Indians, Colonists, and Slaves in South Atlantic Forests, 1500–1800* (Cambridge, 1990); Kirkpatrick Sale, *The Conquest of Paradise: Christopher Columbus and the Columbian Legacy* (New York, 1991). Other scholars have, however, questioned this differentiation of Indians and Anglo-American colonists and equation of science with empire. See Lynn Ceci, "Watchers of the Pleiades: Ethnoastronomy among Native Cultivators in Northeastern North America," *Ethnohistory*, 25 (1978), 301–317; Cecelia Tichi, *New World, New Earth: Environmental Reform in American Literature from the Puritans through Whitman* (New Haven, 1979); Karen Ordahl Kupperman, *Settling with the Indians: The Meeting of English and Indian Cultures in America, 1580–1640* (Totowa, N.J., 1980), esp. chap. 5; Shepard Krech III, ed., *Indians, Animals, and the Fur Trade* (Athens, Ga., 1981); idem, *The Ecological Indian: Myth and History* (New York, 1999); Bruce G. Trigger, "Ethnohistory: Problems and Prospects," *Ethnohistory*, 29 (1982), 7–8; Richard H. Grove, *Green Imperialism: Colonial Expansion, Tropical Island Edens, and the Origins of Environmentalism, 1600–1860* (Cambridge, 1995).

8. The literature on these questions is vast. See the introduction given by Sydney Ross, "'Scientist': The Story of a Word," *AS*, 18 (1962), 65–88; and the synthesis in Steven Shapin, *The Scientific Revolution* (Chicago, 1996).

9. Charles B. Schmitt, *Aristotle and the Renaissance* (Cambridge, Mass., 1983); William A. Wallace, "Traditional Natural Philosophy," and Alfonso Ingegno, "The New Philosophy of Nature," both in Charles B. Schmitt and Quentin Skinner, eds., *The Cambridge History of Renaissance Philosophy* (Cambridge, 1988), 201–263. On medical theories, see Lester S. King, *The Growth of Medical Thought* (Chicago, 1963), chaps. 1–4; Allen G. Debus, *The English Paracelsians* (New York, 1965), esp. chap. 1; Nancy Siraisi, *Medieval and Early Renaissance Medicine: An Introduction to Knowledge and Practice* (Chicago, 1990), 1–16.

10. Keith Thomas, *Religion and the Decline of Magic* (London, 1971), chaps. 8, 10, 11; Wayne Shumaker, *The Occult Sciences in the Renaissance: A Study in Intellectual Patterns* (Berkeley, 1972); Frances A. Yates, *The Occult Philosophy in the Elizabethan Age* (London, 1979); Charles Webster, *From Paracelsus to Newton: Magic and the Making of Modern Science* (New York, 1982); William Eamon, "Technology as Magic in the Late Middle Ages and the Renaissance," *Janus*, 70 (1983), 171–212; idem, *Science and the Secrets of Nature: Books of Secrets in Medieval and Early Modern Culture* (Princeton, 1994), 194–233; Ingrid Merkel and Allen G. Debus, eds., *Hermeticism and the Renaissance: Intellectual History and the Occult in Early Modern Europe* (Washington, D.C., 1988); Nicholas H. Clulee, *John Dee's Natural Philosophy: Between Science and Religion* (London, 1988), esp. chaps. 3, 8–9; Brian Copenhaver, "Natural Magic, Hermetism, and Occultism in Early Modern Science," in David C. Lindberg and Robert S. Westman, eds., *Reappraisals of the Scientific Revolution* (Cambridge, 1990), 261–301. On alchemy, see Betty Jo Teeter Dobbs, *The Foundations of Newton's Alchemy: or, "The Hunting of the Greene Lyon"* (Cambridge, 1975); J. Andrew Mendelsohn, "Alchemy and Politics in England, 1649–1655," *P & P*, no. 135 (1992), 30–78; Newman, *Gehennical Fire*.
11. William T. Costello, *The Scholastic Curriculum at Early Seventeenth-Century Cambridge* (Cambridge, Mass., 1958), 70–106; Siraisi, *Medieval and Early Renaissance Medicine*, 48–77.
12. Stillman Drake, "Early Science and the Printed Book: The Spread of Science beyond the Universities," *Renaissance and Reformation*, 6 (1970), 43–52; B. S. Capp, *Astrology and the Popular Press: English Almanacs, 1500–1800* (London, 1979); Eamon, *Science and the Secrets of Nature*, 234–266; David D. Hall, *Worlds of Wonder, Days of Judgment: Popular Religious Belief in Early New England* (New York, 1989), chaps. 1–2; Ann Blair, *The Theater of Nature: Jean Bodin and Renaissance Science* (Princeton, 1997), esp. chap. 5. But cf. Adrian Johns, *The Nature of the Book: Print and Knowledge in the Making* (Chicago, 1998), which questions whether science spread easily in printed sources.
13. George Peckham, *True reporte* (1583), NAW, 3:35 (university), 41–42 (climate, geography), 54–55 (people and products); R. Rich, *Nevves from Virginia* (London, 1610), A3^r. On early descriptions of American nature, see Clarence J. Glacken, *Traces on the Rhodian Shore: Nature and Culture in Western Thought from Ancient Times to the End of the Eighteenth Century* (Berkeley, 1967), 357–374; Stearns, *Science in the British Colonies of America*, 67–80; Anthony Grafton, *New Worlds, Ancient Texts: The Power of Tradition and the Shock of Discovery* (Cambridge, Mass., 1992).
14. On population, see James Bonar, *Theories of Population from Raleigh to Arthur Young* (Bristol, 1931), chap. 3; D. V. Glass and D. E. C. Eversley, eds., *Population in History: Essays in Historical Demography* (London, 1965), intro.; Glacken, *Traces on the Rhodian Shore*, 398–405, 425–426; J.

Overbeek, *History of Population Theories* (Rotterdam, 1974), 28–34; Robert S. Gottfried, *The Black Death: Natural and Human Disaster in Medieval Europe* (New York, 1983); James C. Riley, *Population Thought in the Age of the Demographic Revolution* (Durham, N.C., 1985), intro., chap. 1; Colin Platt, *King Death: The Black Death and Its Aftermath in Late-Medieval England* (London, 1996). On Locke, see James Tully, *A Discourse on Property: John Locke and His Adversaries* (Cambridge, 1980), 104–130. On disenchantment, see Thomas, *Religion and the Decline of Magic,* esp. 767–800.

15. Charles Webster, *The Great Instauration: Science, Medicine, and Reform, 1626–1660* (London, 1975), 44–47; Glacken, *Traces on the Rhodian Shore,* 461–497; Stearns, *Science in the British Colonies of America,* 3–8; Robert A. Williams, Jr., *The American Indian in Western Legal Thought: The Discourses of Conquest* (New York, 1990), 246–251; Wilcomb E. Washburn, "The Moral and Legal Justification for Dispossessing the Indians," in James Morton Smith, ed., *Seventeenth-Century America: Essays in Colonial History* (Chapel Hill, 1959), 15–32; James Tully, *An Approach to Political Philosophy: Locke in Contexts* (Cambridge, 1993), 137–176; Barbara Arneil, *John Locke and America: The Defence of English Colonialism* (Oxford, 1996).

16. John Rastell, *An Interlude of the Four Elements* (n.p., 1519), Ai[r], Avi[v]–Bi[v], Ci[r], (Experience's map).

17. Charles George Herbermann, ed., *Cosmographiae Introductio of Martin Waldseemüller,* trans. Joseph Fischer and Franz von Wieser (New York, 1907); Edmundo O'Gorman, *The Invention of America: An Inquiry into the Historical Nature of the New World and the Meaning of Its History* (Bloomington, Ind., 1961); Eviatar Zerubavel, *Terra Cognita: The Mental Discovery of America* (New Brunswick, N.J., 1992); Valerie I. J. Flint, *The Imaginative Landscape of Christopher Columbus* (Princeton, 1992), chap. 1; Frank Lestringant, *Mapping the Renaissance World: The Geographical Imagination in the Age of Discovery,* trans. David Fausett (Cambridge, 1994). Quotation from Rastell, *Four Elements,* Aii[r]–Aii[v].

18. Stearns, *Science in the British Colonies of America,* 22–42 (Spanish), 44–80 (Europe and England); Gerbi, *Nature in the New World;* "The Life and Labours of Richard Eden, Scholar, and Man of Science," *Eng. Books,* xxxvii–xl, 355; David Gwyn, "Richard Eden: Cosmographer and Alchemist," *SCJ,* 15 (1984), 13–34.

19. *Eng. Books,* xl (Cortes), 207 (Oviedo).

20. John Dee, preface to *The Elements of Geometrie of the most auncient Philosopher Euclide of Megara,* trans. H[ugh] Billingsley (London, 1570), iij[r]; Richard Hakluyt, *Discourse of Western Planting* (1584), *NAW,* 3:99; Richard Hakluyt to Walsingham, April 1, 1584, *NAW,* 3:273 (quotations). See also E. G. R. Taylor, *Tudor Geography, 1485–1583* (New York, 1968).

21. Richard Helgerson, *Forms of Nationhood: The Elizabethan Writing of England* (Chicago, 1992), chaps. 3, 4; Lesley B. Cormack, *Charting an Empire:*

Geography at the English Universities, 1580–1620 (Chicago, 1997). Quotations from Robert Norman, *The nevv Attractiue* (London, 1585), Aiiʳ, Aivʳ.

22. Taylor, *Tudor Geography,* 75–139; Clulee, *John Dee's Natural Philosophy,* 27, 180–189; William H. Sherman, *John Dee: The Politics of Reading and Writing in the English Renaissance* (Amherst, Mass., 1995), chap. 7; Michael Lok's notes, 1576, *NAW,* 4:191 (quotation).

23. D. D. Hogarth, P. W. Boreham, and J. G. Mitchell, *Martin Frobisher's Northwest Venture, 1576–1581: Mines, Minerals, and Metallurgy* (Hull, Quebec, 1994), 38–39; "Introduction" to David B. Quinn and Neil M. Cheshire, eds., *The New Found Land of Stephen Parmenius* (Toronto, 1972), 3–72; Edward Hayes, cited in *NAW,* 4:29 (Gilbert); Richard Hakluyt, *Discourse of Western Planting, NAW,* 3:83; Richard Hakluyt the elder, "Inducements to the Liking of the Voyage intended towards Virginia," ca. 1585, *NAW,* 3:68; notes for Ralegh and Cavendish [1584–1585], *NAW,* 3:275; Gary C. Grassl, "Joachim Gans of Prague, America's First Jewish Visitor," *Review of the Society for the History of Czechoslovak Jews,* 1 (1987), 53–90; Stearns, *Science in the British Colonies,* 67–80; Morgan, *American Slavery, American Freedom,* 84–86.

24. Eden to Cecil, August 1, 1562, *Eng. Books,* xliv; examination of the survivors of the *Discovery* (1611), *NAW,* 4:293.

25. On the connection between natural philosophy and medicine, see Siraisi, *Medieval and Early Renaissance Medicine,* 2–7; C. B. Schmitt, "Aristotle among the Physicians," in A. Wear, R. K. French, and I. M. Lonie, eds., *The Medical Renaissance of the Sixteenth Century* (Cambridge, 1985), 1–15.

26. Studies that address colonists' attitudes toward nature have rather narrowly defined American nature as wilderness. See Henry Nash Smith, *Virgin Land: The American West as Symbol and Myth* (Cambridge, Mass., 1950); Richard Slotkin, *Regeneration through Violence: The Mythology of the American Frontier, 1600–1860* (Middletown, Conn., 1973), esp. 25–222; Canup, *Out of the Wilderness;* Catherine L. Albanese, *Nature Religion in America: From the Algonkian Indians to the New Age* (Chicago, 1990), 47–79. On the transition from non-biological views of race, see John G. Burke, "The Wild Man's Pedigree: Scientific Method and Racial Anthropology," in Edward Dudley and Maximillian E. Novak, eds., *The Wild Man Within: An Image in Western Thought from the Renaissance to Romanticism* (Pittsburgh, 1972), 281–307; Gould, *The Mismeasure of Man,* esp. chap. 2.

27. See especially Leonard Barkan, *Nature's Work of Art: The Human Body as Image of the World* (New Haven, 1975); Michel Foucault, *Discipline and Punish: The Birth of the Prison,* trans. Alan Sheridan (New York, 1979), 3–31, 135–169; Caroline Walker Bynum, *Holy Feast and Holy Fast: The Religious Significance of Food to Medieval Women* (Berkeley, 1987), 48–69, 76–93, 208–218, 260–276; idem, *The Resurrection of the Body in Western Christianity, 200–1336* (New York, 1995); Peter Brown, *The Body and Society: Men, Women, and Sexual Renunciation in Early Christianity* (New York, 1988); Thomas Laqueur, *Making Sex: Body and Gender from the*

Greeks to Freud (Cambridge, Mass., 1990); Lucy Gent and Nigel Llewellyn, eds., *Renaissance Bodies: The Human Figure in English Culture, c. 1540–1660* (London, 1990); Gail Paster, *The Body Embarrassed: Drama and the Disciplines of Shame in Early Modern England* (Ithaca, N.Y., 1993).

28. Stearns, *Science in the British Colonies of America,* chaps. 3–4; [Anne Bradstreet], *The Tenth Muse Lately Sprung up in America* (London, 1650); Samuel Eliot Morison, *The Founding of Harvard College* (Cambridge, Mass., 1935), 435–440; idem, *Harvard College in the Seventeenth Century* (Cambridge, Mass., 1936), vol. 1, chaps. 10, 11, 13; Ronald Sterne Wilkinson, "The Alchemical Library of John Winthrop, Jr. (1606–1676), and His Descendants in Colonial America," *Ambix,* 11 (1963), 33–51; idem, "New England's Last Alchemists," *Ambix,* 10 (1962), 128–138; idem, "'Hermes Christianus,'" 221–241; Stearns, *Science in the British Colonies of America,* 152–153; John L. Brooke, *The Refiner's Fire: The Making of Mormon Cosmology, 1644–1844* (Cambridge, 1994), 5–29, 33–58; Newman, *Gehennical Fire,* chap. 1.

29. Edward Said, *Orientalism* (New York, 1978), and *Culture and Imperialism* (New York, 1994). On the most important postcolonial literature which follows Said, see Gayatri Chakravorty Spivak, "Can the Subaltern Speak?" in Cary Nelson and Lawrence Grossberg, eds., *Marxism and the Interpretation of Culture* (Urbana, Ill., 1988), 271–313; Homi K. Bhabha, *The Location of Culture* (London, 1994). The most influential poststructuralist analysis of imperialism in the Americas is Tzvetan Todorov, *The Conquest of America: The Question of the Other,* trans. Richard Howard (New York, 1984); but see also Stephen Greenblatt, *Marvelous Possessions: The Wonder of the New World* (Oxford, 1991). For critical views of postcolonial theory, see Dennis Porter, "*Orientalism* and Its Problems," in Francis Barker et al., eds., *The Politics of Theory* (Colchester, 1983); Carol A. Breckenridge and Peter van der Veer, eds., *Orientalism and the Postcolonial Predicament: Perspectives on South Asia* (Philadelphia, 1993); Nicholas Thomas, *Colonialism's Culture: Anthropology, Travel, and Government* (Princeton, 1994); and Chapter 3 of this book. For interpretations that are influenced by postcolonial theory but also consider the problems of agency and historical context, see James A. Boon, *Other Tribes, Other Scribes: Symbolic Anthropology in the Comparative Study of Cultures, Histories, Religions, and Texts* (Cambridge, 1982); Javed Majeed, *Ungoverned Imaginings: James Mill's "The History of British India" and Orientalism* (Oxford, 1992); Pratt, *Imperial Eyes;* Stuart B. Schwartz, ed., *Implicit Understanding: Observing, Reporting, and Reflecting on the Encounters between Europeans and Other Peoples in the Early Modern Era* (Cambridge, 1994).

30. Stephen Greenblatt, "Invisible Bullets," in *Shakespearean Negotiations: The Circulation of Social Energy in Renaissance England* (Oxford, 1988), 21–39; idem, "Learning to Curse", in *Learning to Curse: Essays in Early Modern Culture* (London, 1990), 16–39; Myra Jehlen, "The Literature of Colonization," in Sacvan Bercovitch, ed., *The Cambridge History of American Litera-*

ture, 1590–1820 (New York, 1994), 1:13–168; Mary C. Fuller, *Voyages in Print: English Travel to America, 1576–1624* (New York, 1995).

31. See Trigger, "Ethnohistory: Problems and Prospects," 1–19; James Axtell, *The Invasion Within: The Contest of Cultures in Colonial North America* (New York, 1985); and note 1 above. Four recent histories of Indians and on cultural frontiers that have garnered great acclaim are Merrell, *The Indians' New World;* Daniel K. Richter, *The Ordeal of the Longhouse: The Peoples of the Iroquois League in the Era of European Colonization* (Chapel Hill, 1992); White, *Middle Ground;* Jill Lepore, *The Name of War: King Philip's War and the Origins of American Identity* (New York, 1998). Except for Richter, all focus on the late seventeenth or eighteenth century; Richter and White use French sources to examine the earlier period, Richter in more detail.

32. Ives Goddard and Kathleen J. Bragdon, eds., *Native Writings in Massachusett,* 2 vols. (Philadelphia, 1988), 1:238–245 (the last entries in this volume are annotations in religious volumes and cannot be dated with precision); Wolfgang Hochbruck and Beatrix Dudensing-Reichel, "'Honoratissimi Benefactores': Native American Students and Two Seventeenth-Century Texts in the University Tradition," in Helen Jaskoski, ed., *Early Native American Writing: New Critical Essays* (Cambridge, 1996), 1–14; Neal Salisbury, ed., *The Sovereignty and Goodness of God . . . and Related Documents* (Boston, 1997), 131–132 (Nipmuck note).

33. On early communication: Lois M. Feister, "Linguistic Communication between the Dutch and Indians in New Netherland," *Ethnohistory,* 20 (1973), 25–38; James H. Merrell, "'The Customes of Our Countrey': Indians and Colonists in Early America," in Bernard Bailyn and Philip D. Morgan, eds., *Strangers within the Realm: Cultural Margins of the First British Empire* (Chapel Hill, 1991), 126–31; Edward G. Gray, *New World Babel: Languages and Nations in Early America* (Princeton, 1999), chap. 1. On early English study of Algonquian: Frank T. Siebert, Jr., "Resurrecting Virginia Algonquian from the Dead: The Reconstituted and Historical Phonology of Powhatan," in James M. Crawford, ed., *Studies in Southeastern Indian Languages* (Athens, Ga., 1975), 292 (Strachey); John W. Shirley, *Thomas Harriot: A Biography* (Oxford, 1983), 107–112; Vivian Salmon, "Thomas Harriot and the English Origins of Algonkian Linguistics," *DTHSOP,* no. 8 (1993), 1–28. On missionary and education projects: James M. Crawford, "Southeastern Indian Languages," in Crawford, *Studies in Southeastern Indian Languages,* 6–7; Axtell, *Invasion Within,* 131–241 (which discusses Williams and Eliot); Goddard and Bragdon, *Native Writings in Massachusett,* 1:2–13, 18–22; Gray, *New World Babel,* chap. 8. Quotations from Peter Wyn[ne] to John Egerton, 2nd Earl Bridgewater, November 26 [1608], Ellesmere-Bridgewater Ms. 1683, HL; [John White], *The Planters Plea* (London, 1630), 52.

34. Roger Williams, *A Key into the Language of America* (1643), ed. John J. Teunissen and Evelyn J. Hinz (Detroit, 1973), 58, 138 (quotation).

35. On archeology, see Mark P. Leone and Parker B. Potter, Jr., eds., *The Recovery of Meaning: Historical Archaeology in the Eastern United States* (Washington, D.C., 1988); Bruce G. Trigger, "Early Native North American Responses to European Contact: Romantic versus Rationalistic Interpretations," *JAH*, 77 (1991), 1205–6; Laurier Turgeon, "The Tale of the Kettle: Odyssey of an Intercultural Object," *Ethnohistory*, 44 (1997), 1–29. On historical linguistics, see Siebert, "Resurrecting Virginia Algonquian," 285–453; Dell H. Hymes, *Essays in the History of Linguistic Anthropology* (Amsterdam, 1983), 1–57; Goddard and Bragdon, *Native Writings in Massachusett*, vol. 2. On hidden meanings and transcription, cf. James C. Scott, *Domination and the Arts of Resistance: Hidden Transcripts* (New Haven, 1990), chap. 1; David Murray, *Forked Tongues: Speech, Writing, and Representation in North American Native Texts* (Bloomington, Ind., 1991).
36. See, for instance, Michael M. Pomedli, *Ethnophilosophical and Ethnolinguistic Perspectives on the Huron Indian Soul* (Lewiston, N.Y., 1991). On savage minds, see Lucien Levy-Bruhl, *Primitive Mentality*, trans. Lilian A. Clare (New York, 1923); idem, *How Natives Think*, trans. Lilian A. Clare (New York, 1966); Claude Lévi-Strauss, *The Savage Mind* (Chicago, 1966); Gananath Obeyesekere, *The Apotheosis of Captain Cook: European Mythmaking in the Pacific* (Princeton, 1992); Marshall Sahlins, *How "Natives" Think: About Captain Cook, for Example* (Chicago, 1995).
37. Thomas Hariot, *A briefe and true report of the new found land of Virginia* (London, 1588), E4^r, F2^r. See also Stearns, *Science in the British Colonies of America*, 67–71; Shirley, *Harriot: A Biography*, 105–112.
38. Greenblatt, "Invisible Bullets," 21–39.
39. Robert Hugh Kargon, *Atomism in England from Hariot to Newton* (Oxford, 1966), 24–27; Jean Jacquot, "Harriot, Hill, Warner, and the New Philosophy," in John W. Shirley, ed., *Thomas Harriot, Renaissance Scientist* (Oxford, 1974), esp. 107–108, 115 (optics); Christoph Meinel, "Early Seventeenth-Century Atomism: Theory, Epistemology, and the Insufficiency of Experiment," *Isis*, 79 (1988), 68–103; B. J. Sokol, "Invisible Evidence: The Unfounded Attack on Thomas Harriot's Reputation," *DTHSOP*, no. 17 (n.d.), 22–26; idem, "The Problem of Assessing Thomas Hariot's *A briefe and true report* of His Discoveries in North America," *AS*, 51 (1994), 14–15; Amir Alexander, "The Imperialist Space of Elizabethan Mathematics," *Studies in the History and Philosophy of Science*, 26 (1995), 575–579.
40. Edward Rosen, "Harriot's Science, the Intellectual Background," in Shirley, *Harriot, Renaissance Scientist*, 4–6; Alexander, "Imperialist Space of Elizabethan Mathematics," 579–591 (breaks within continuum); Shirley, *Harriot: A Biography*, 242 (cannon shot); Thomas Harriot Mathematical Manuscripts, Add. MS., 6782, 29^v, 46^r, 160^r, 336^v (abstract representations and doodling), 362^r–363 (the continuum and infinite progression), 369^r (atoms' extension and interpenetration); Ms. 6786, 226^r (atoms), 377r–378^v (chemical signs represented by patterns of dots), BL.
41. Quotations from Helkiah Crooke, *Microcosmographia: A Description of the*

Body of Man (London, 1615), 8; John Aubrey, *Brief Lives, Chiefly of Contemporaries* . . . , ed. Andrew Clark (Oxford, 1898), 1:286. On Hariot's atomism and reputation for atheism, see Jean Jacquot, "Thomas Harriot's Reputation for Impiety," *Records of the Royal Society,* 9 (1952), 164–187; Shirley, *Harriot: A Biography,* 179–199, 316. On corpuscles and disease, see Vivian Nutton, "The Seeds of Disease: An Explanation of Contagion and Infection from the Greeks to the Renaissance," *Medical History,* 27 (1983), 1–34.

42. Harriot Mathematical Ms. 6788, 417^v (shot), Ms. 6789, 76^r (bullet), Add. MSS., BL; Balthazar Gerbiers, *The Second Lecture being an Introduction to Cosmographie Read Publiquely* (London, 1649), 18. In experiments on specific gravity, Hariot noted the rates at which different pieces of shot fell; he used both musket and pistol balls but used the word "bullets" to describe all twenty specimens. See Shirley, *Harriot: A Biography,* 263–264.

43. Hariot, *Briefe and true report,* F^v–F2^r; F. Kydds to Sir John Pickering, n.d., Harl. Ms. 6849, 218, BL. On Harriot's supposed disbelief in bodily resurrection, see John W. Shirley, "Sir Walter Ralegh and Thomas Harriot," in Shirley, *Harriot, Renaissance Scientist,* 24; idem, *Harriot: A Biography,* 190–191, 193 (quotation re Allen).

44. Salmon, "Thomas Harriot and the English Origins of Algonkian Linguistics," 4–5; Hariot, *Briefe and true report,* E4^r. Hariot's limited Algonquian makes it hard to *conclude,* as Sokol has done, that the Roanok had a germ theory. (See note 39 above.)

45. Hariot, *Briefe and true report,* F2^r.

2. Technology versus Idolatry?

1. David Gwyn, "Richard Eden: Cosmographer and Alchemist," *SCJ,* 15 (1984), 13–34; John W. Shirley, *Thomas Harriot: A Biography* (Oxford, 1983), 73–75; Nicholas H. Clulee, *John Dee's Natural Philosophy: Between Science and Religion* (London, 1988); D. D. Hogarth, P. W. Boreham, and J. G. Mitchell, *Martin Frobisher's Northwest Venture, 1576–1581: Mines, Minerals, and Metallurgy* (Hull, Quebec, 1994), 10–12. Quotation from Richard Eden, preface to Vannuccio Biringucci, *Pyrotechnia* (1540), *Eng. Books,* 355; see also xxxvii–xl on Eden's natural philosophy.

2. On magical and occult traditions, and their fit within the rest of natural philosophy, see Chapter 1, notes 9 and 10. Quotation from John Dee's preface to *The Elements of Geometrie of the most auncient Philosopher Euclide of Megara,* trans. H[ugh] Billingsley (London, 1570), [1^v].

3. Keith Thomas, *Religion and the Decline of Magic* (London, 1971), 681–698; Dee, preface, *Euclide,* Aiij^r; Richard Barnes, "A note containing the opinion on Christopher Marley," Harl. Ms. 6848, 185^r, BL.

4. *The New Organon,* in Bacon, *Works,* 8:76–78. See also John Phillips, *The Reformation of Images: Destruction of Art in England, 1535–1660* (Berke-

ley, 1973), esp. xi–xii, 206–210; Eamon Duffy, *The Stripping of the Altars: Traditional Religion in England, c. 1400–c. 1580* (New Haven, 1992), esp. 565–593; Kenneth Gross, *Spenserian Poetics: Idolatry, Iconoclasm, and Magic* (Ithaca, N.Y., 1985); Ernest B. Gilman, *Iconoclasm and Poetry in the English Reformation: Down Went Dagon* (Chicago, 1986); Margaret Aston, *England's Iconoclasts* (Oxford, 1988); idem, *The King's Bedpost: Reformation and Iconography in a Tudor Group Portrait* (Cambridge, 1993); Thomas, *Religion and the Decline of Magic;* Brian Vickers, "Analogy versus Identity: The Rejection of Occult Symbolism, 1580–1680," in Vickers, ed., *Occult and Scientific Mentalities in the Renaissance* (Cambridge, 1984), 95–164. Cf. Kenneth Mills, *Idolatry and Its Enemies: Colonial Andean Religion and Extirpation, 1640–1750* (Princeton, 1997).

5. On travelers' testimony, see Mary B. Campbell, *The Witness and the Other World: Exotic European Travel Writing, 400–1600* (Ithaca, N.Y., 1988), 218, 260; Anthony Pagden, *European Encounters with the New World: From Renaissance to Romanticism* (New Haven, 1993), intro., 54–56, 83–87. On experience and science, see Charles B. Schmitt, "Experience and Experiment: A Comparison of Zabarella's View with Galileo's in *De Motu,*" *Studies in the Renaissance,* 16 (1969), 80–138; Timothy J. Reiss, *The Discourse of Modernism* (Ithaca, N.Y., 1982); Peter Dear, *Discipline and Experience: The Mathematical Way in the Scientific Revolution* (Chicago, 1995); Lorraine Daston, "Marvelous Facts and Miraculous Evidence in Early Modern Europe," *Critical Inquiry,* 18 (1991), 93–124. Cf. Jim Egan, *Authorizing Experience: Refigurations of the Body Politic in Seventeenth-Century New England Writing* (Princeton, 1999), chap. 2, for a later period of colonization.

6. On humanity's liminal state, see Clarence J. Glacken, *Traces on the Rhodian Shore: Nature and Culture in Western Thought from Ancient Times to the End of the Eighteenth Century* (Berkeley, 1967), chaps. 3, 4; Jeremy Cohen, *Be Fertile and Increase, Fill the Earth and Master It: The Ancient and Medieval Career of a Biblical Text* (Ithaca, N.Y., 1989).

7. *The New Atlantis* (1627), in Bacon, *Works,* 5:361.

8. Arthur Barlowe, cited in *NAW,* 3:280; Walter Ralegh, *The Discouerie of the Large, Rich, and Bewtiful Empyre of Guiana* (London, 1596), 42, 48.

9. Eden cited in *Eng. Books,* xlvi. See also George Best, *A True Discourse* (1578), *Frobisher Voyages,* 28–30.

10. Andrew [André] Thevet, *The New found Worlde, or Antarctike . . . ,* trans. Thomas Hacket (London, 1568), ij^r; *Advancement of Learning* (1605), in Bacon, *Works,* 6:145 (ancients), and *New Atlantis* (1627), 5:411–412 (moderns). See also Charles Fitz-Geffrey, *Sir Francis Drake* (Oxford, 1596), B3^v; Robert Johnson, *Nova Britannia* (1609), *NAW,* 5:248.

11. John Rastell, *An Interlude of the Four Elements* (n.p., 1519), Ci^r. On wealth, climates, and colonies, see Richard Eden, preface to Sebastian Munster, *A treatyse of the newe India,* in *Eng. Books,* 7–8; Glacken, *Traces on the*

Rhodian Shore, 449; Karen Ordahl Kupperman, "Fear of Hot Climates in the Anglo-American Colonial Experience," *WMQ,* 41 (1984), 213–240.

12. Robert Thorne cited in *NAW,* 1:180, 188; Roger Barlowe, "A briefe summe of geographie" (1541), *NAW,* 1:215.

13. Joseph [José de] Acosta, *The Naturall and Morall Historie of the East and West Indies* (1590), trans. E[dward] G[rimeston] (London, 1604), 35; Olaus Magnus, *Description of the Northern Peoples* (1555), ed. Peter Foote (London, 1996), 3:868–872; Peter Martyr, *Decades of the Newe Worlde,* trans. Richard Eden, *Eng. Books,* 296, 307; William Cuningham, *The Cosmographical Glasse* (London, 1559), 68. On global exploration and its challenges to classical geography, see Glacken, *Traces on the Rhodian Shore,* 357–363, 436–438; on the Norse voyages (and English interest in them), see Anne Stine Ingstad, *The Norse Discovery of America,* 2 vols. (Oslo, 1985), 2:374–397; Kristen A. Seaver, *The Frozen Echo: Greenland and the Exploration of North America, ca. A.D. 1000–1500* (Stanford, 1996), chap. 10; David B. Quinn, "Frobisher in the Context of Early English Northwest Exploration," in Thomas H. B. Symons, ed., *Meta Incognita: A Discourse of Discovery. Martin Frobisher's Arctic Expeditions, 1576–1578,* 2 vols. (Hull, Quebec, 1999), 1:7–18.

14. William C. Sturtevant and David B. Quinn, "This New Prey: Eskimos in Europe in 1567, 1576, and 1577," in Christian F. Feest, ed., *Indians and Europe: An Interdisciplinary Collection of Essays* (Aachen, 1987), 112.

15. E. G. R. Taylor, *Tudor Geography, 1485–1583,* 2d ed. (New York, 1968), 79–109; Harry Kelsey, *Sir Francis Drake: The Queen's Pirate* (New Haven, 1998), 93–204; James McDermott, *The Navigation of the Frobisher Voyages* (London, 1998), 3–4. Quotations from *Frobisher Voyages,* 8; Best, *True Discourse,* 70.

16. "The Life and Labours of Richard Eden," *Eng. Books,* xli; Best, *True Discourse,* 19; Humphrey Gilbert, *A discourse of a discoverie for a new passage to Cataia* (1576), *NAW,* 3:7.

17. *NAW,* 4:xxi–xxii, 179–182.

18. William W. Fitzhugh and Jacqueline S. Olin, eds., *Archeology of the Frobisher Voyages* (Washington, D.C., 1993), 63–80 (Frobisher structures on Kodlunarn), 90–91 (tile), 241–251 (list of personnel); Hogarth, Boreham, and Mitchell, *Mines, Minerals, and Metallurgy,* 27–29, 40–44; Best, *True Discourse,* 118 (felons), 119 (quotation), 226–227 (fort and hundred-man colony), 252 (sermon); Eric Klingelhofer, "Three Lost Ceramic Artifacts from Frobisher's Colony, 1578," *Historical Archaeology,* 10 (1977), 133–134. Subsequent explorers probably knew that 15 ships was an unwieldy unit.

19. M. B. Donald, "Burchard Kranich (c. 1515–1578), Miner and Queen's Physician, Cornish Mining Stamps, Antimony, and Frobisher's Gold," *AS,* 6 (1950), 314–321; Hogarth, Boreham, and Mitchell, *Mines, Minerals, and Metallurgy,* 73–141; James McDermott, "Humphrey Cole and the Frobisher

Voyages," in Silke Ackermann, ed., *Humphrey Cole: Mint, Measurement and Maps in Elizabethan England* (London, 1998).

20. Quotation from Dr. Burcot's "Articles and Conditions," *Frobisher Voyages,* 201. See also Donald D. Hogarth, "Mining and Metallurgy of the Frobisher Ores," and Réginald Auger, "Sixteenth-Century Ceramics from Kodlunarn Island," in Fitzhugh and Olin, *Archeology of the Frobisher Voyages,* 138, 147–150; Hogarth, Boreham, and Mitchell, *Mines, Minerals, and Metallurgy,* 39.

21. Best, *True Discourse,* 129 (cross), 256–258 (orders), 283 (music). On Jamestown, see Edmund S. Morgan, *American Slavery, American Freedom: The Ordeal of Colonial Virginia* (New York, 1975), 79–81.

22. Best, *True Discourse,* 63, 250–251; Parmenius to Richard Hakluyt, 1589, in David B. Quinn and Neil M. Cheshire, eds., *The New Found Land of Stephen Parmenius* (Toronto, 1972), 175; Newfoundland Co. Council to John Guy, May 26, 1610, *NAW,* 4:141; Henry Crout to Sir Percival Willoughby, April 10, 1613, in Gillian T. Cell, ed., *Newfoundland Discovered: English Attempts at Colonisation, 1610–1630* (London, 1982), 80; Richard Whitbourne, *A Discovrse and Discovery of Nevv-Found-land* (London, 1622), 7; Arthur Barlowe, "Briefe summe of geographie," *NAW,* 1:216; "The relation of the Whole Voyage to Virginia," *NAW,* 3:437.

23. [Edward Hayes and Christopher Carleill], "A discourse Concerning a voyage . . . ," *NAW,* 3:163; Maurice Browne to John Thynne, August 20, 1582, in Quinn and Cheshire, *New Found Land of Parmenius,* 193; Agnello's report, *Frobisher Voyages,* 93. See also Donald D. Hogarth, "Mining and Metallurgy," in Fitzhugh and Olin, *Archeology of the Frobisher Voyages,* 138–42; Hogarth, Boreham, and Mitchell, *Mines, Minerals, and Metallurgy,* 46, 47.

24. Accounts of Davis's voyages, *NAW,* 4:239, 248. On the Inuit captives, see Neil Cheshire, Tony Waldron, Alison Quinn, and David Quinn, "Frobisher's Eskimos in England," *Archivaria,* 10 (1980), 23–50 (quotation on 23); Sturtevant and Quinn, "This New Prey," 61–140.

25. On trade circuits that involved metal, see Bruce J. Bourque, "Evidence for Prehistoric Exchange on the Maritime Peninsula," in Timothy G. Baugh and Jonathon E. Ericson, eds., *Prehistoric Exchange Systems in North America* (New York, 1994), 35; J. V. Wright, "The Prehistoric Transportation of Goods in the St. Lawrence River Basin," ibid., 49, 63; R. Michael Stewart, "Late Archaic through Late Woodland Exchange in the Middle Atlantic Region," ibid., 88; Jay K. Johnson, "Prehistoric Exchange in the Southeast," ibid., 102, 112–113. On Norse artifacts in Newfoundland and Greenland, see Ingstad, *Norse Discovery of America,* 1:155, 192 (meteoric iron, which the Inuit might have substituted for Norse wrought iron), 1:221, 248–251; 2:409–411 (carvings of Norse); Seaver, *Frozen Echo,* 36–37, 124 (chain mail).

26. See Winthrop D. Jordan, *White over Black: American Attitudes toward the Negro, 1550–1812* (Chapel Hill, 1968), 40–43; Ivan Hannaford, *Race: The*

History of an Idea in the West (Washington, D.C., and Baltimore, 1996), 166–167.

27. Donald D. Hogarth, "The Ships' Company in the Frobisher Voyages," in Fitzhugh and Olin, *Archeology of the Frobisher Voyages*, 16; Walter A. Kenyon, ed., "The Canadian Arctic Journal of Capt. Edward Fenton," *Archivaria*, 11 (1980–81), 198; Settle cited in *NAW*, 4:214; Best, *True Discourse*, 284; John Janes, "The First Voyage of Master John Davis" (1586), *NAW*, 4:236.

28. Kenyon, "Journal of Capt. Edward Fenton," 186; Best, *True Discourse*, 283, 285 (iron arrowheads and bars); John Ellis, *True Report*, *NAW*, 4:220; Ingstad, *Norse Discovery of America*, 1:192; Seaver, *Frozen Echo*, 29–30; Jacqueline S. Olin, "History of Research on the Smithsonian Bloom"; Garman Harbottle, Richard G. Cresswell, and Raymond W. Stoenner, "Carbon-14 Dating of Iron Blooms from Kodlunarn Island"; and William W. Fitzhugh, "Questions Remain," all in Fitzhugh and Olin, *Archeology of the Frobisher Voyages*, 49–55, 173–180, 232–234.

29. Guy's account in Cell, *Newfoundland Discovered*, 75, 84; Ellis, *True Report*, 224; John Davis, *The Worldes hydrographicall Discription* (1595), *NAW*, 4:231.

30. Dionyse Settle, *A True reporte* (1577), *NAW*, 4:213, 214. On views of polar areas, see Martyr, *Decades*, 294–307; Karen Ordahl Kupperman, "The Puzzle of the American Climate in the Early Colonial Period," *AHR*, 87 (1982), 1262–89.

31. Best, *True Discourse*, 286–287; Settle, *True reporte*, 211 (same episode); report of Dr. Edward Dodding, November 8, 1577, *NAW*, 4:216–218. See also Cheshire et al., "Frobisher's Eskimos in England," 30, 37 (nursing child).

32. Janes, "The First Voyage," 237.

33. Account of the second Davis voyage (1587), *NAW*, 4:240.

34. List of Frobisher's abuses against the company (1578), *Frobisher Voyages*, 360; Hogarth, Boreham, and Mitchell, *Mines, Minerals, and Metallurgy*, 37 (Spain), 52 (investment), 136–138 (tainted assays); McDermott, "Humphrey Cole and the Frobisher Voyages," 17–18; David Beers Quinn, *England and the Discovery of America, 1481–1620* (New York, 1974), 234–235, 282–283, 293–294 (Gilbert); Thomas McDermott, "The Company of Cathay: The Financing and Organization of the Frobisher Voyages" (on the risky financing), and Bernard Allaire and Donald Hogarth, "Martin Frobisher, the Spaniards and a Sixteenth-Century Northern Spy," in Symons, *Meta Incognita*, 1:147–178, 2:575–588.

35. William W. Fitzhugh, "Exploration after Frobisher," and Susan Rowley, "Frobisher Miksanut: Inuit Accounts of the Frobisher Voyages," in Fitzhugh and Olin, *Archeology of the Frobisher Voyages*, 17–21, 27–40.

36. Rowley, "Frobisher Miksanut," 29–32, 36, 38.

37. Ibid., 33, 36–37; William W. Fitzhugh, "Questions Remain," in Fitzhugh and Olin, *Archeology of the Frobisher Voyages*, 234–236.

38. *NAW*, 4:207; John Dee, *To the Kings most excellent Maiestie* (London, 1603), A4^r, B^v.

39. Roy Strong, *The English Icon: Elizabethan and Jacobean Portraiture* (London, 1969); Frances A. Yates, *Astraea: The Imperial Theme in the Sixteenth Century* (London, 1975), 79, 108–109; Sydney Anglo, *Images of Tudor Kingship* (London, 1992), esp. 10–15, but cf. 117–118; Aston, *King's Bedpost*, 97–134. Quotation from accounts for the *Gabriel* and the *Michael* (1576), *NAW*, 4:200.

40. Ivor Noel Hume, *The Virginia Adventure: Roanoke to Jamestowne: An Archaeological and Historical Odyssey* (New York, 1994), 38 (sixpence); E. W. Ives, *Anne Boleyn* (Oxford, 1986), illus. 36, 290–291; Roy Strong, *Gloriana: The Portraits of Queen Elizabeth I* (London, 1987), 134 ("Ditchley" portrait), 138–140 (sphere), 156 ("Rainbow" portrait). Cf. Patricia Seed, "Taking Possession and Reading Texts: Establishing the Authority of Overseas Empires," *WMQ*, 49 (1992), 183–209, which emphasizes words (rather than symbols) as key to English colonization.

41. Francis Fletcher, *The World Encompassed* (1628), *NAW*, 1:476; Maurice Brown to John Thynne, spring 1583, in Quinn and Cheshire, *New Found Land of Parmenius*, 205.

42. Best, *True Discourse*, 138–139.

43. Ralegh, *Discouerie of Guiana*, 7; Quinn and Cheshire, *New Found Land of Parmenius*, 99, 101. See also "A discourse of Sir Fraunces Drakes jorney," *NAW*, 1:467; Edward Daunce, *A Briefe Discovrse of the Spanish State* (London, 1590), 20.

44. Thomas More, *Utopia: Latin Text and English Translation*, ed. George M. Logan, Robert M. Adams, and Clarence H. Miller (Cambridge, 1995), 146–155, 168–171; Rastell, *Four Elements*, Aiii^r and Aiii^v; Eden cited in *Eng. Books*, 355; Quinn and Cheshire, *New Found Land of Parmenius*, 93; Cuningham, *Cosmographical Glasse*, 1. And see G. J. R. Parry, "Some Early Reactions to the Three Voyages of Martin Frobisher: The Conflict between Humanists and Protestants," *Parergon*, 6 (1988), 149–161. The antimaterialist critique was not, however, unique to radical Protestants.

45. Eden cited in *Eng. Books*, 149, 355.

46. Ralegh, *Discouerie of Guiana*, 11, 12, 16, 49.

47. Edward Daunce, *A Briefe Discovrse Dialoguevvise* . . . (London, 1590), 20; Ralegh, *Discouerie of Guiana*, q3^v, 74, 93 (graves), 96.

48. George Percy, "A Discourse of . . . Virginia" (1606–7), *NAW*, 5:267; J[ohn] B[ulwer], *Anthropometamorphosis: Man Transformed, or, the Artificiall Changling* (London, 1653), frontis., A3^r (anachepheloisis), [B4^v] (man), 529.

49. Virginia Co. of London to Sir Thomas Gates [1609], *NAW*, 5:213. See also William Strachey, *The Historie of Travell into Virginia Britania* (1612), ed. Louis B. Wright and Virginia Freund (London, 1953), 18, 24–25.

50. James Rosier, "Extracts of a Virginian Voyage" (1605), *NAW*, 3:385; Janes, "First voyage," 235, 236.

51. Bruce G. Trigger, "Early Native North American Responses to European Contact: Romantic versus Rationalistic Interpretations," *JAH,* 77 (1991), 1200–1206; William M. Hamlin, "Imagined Apotheoses: Drake, Harriot, and Ralegh in the Americas," *JHI,* 57 (1996), 405–428. Quotations from P[eter] H[eylyn], *Microcosmus, or A Little Description of the Great World* (Oxford, 1621), 402; Richard Hakluyt, "The Famous voyage of Sir Francis Drake," *NAW,* 1:465 (self-laceration), 466 (God); Fletcher, *World Encompassed,* 471 (eating and drinking). For Drake's location in California, see Kelsey, *Sir Francis Drake,* 186–188.

52. B[ulwer], *Anthropometamorphosis,* 165; Roger Williams, *A Key into the Language of America* (1643), ed. John J. Teunissen and Evelyn J. Hinz (Detroit, 1973), 64–65, 219.

53. Gabriel Archer, "Discovery of our River," in Edward Arber, ed., *Travels and Works of Captain John Smith* (Edinburgh, 1910), 1:xlvi.

54. For Merrymount, see Bradford, *Plymouth Plantation,* 206; 1 Samuel, 5:1–7 (Dagon); Neal Salisbury, *Manitou and Providence: Indians, Europeans, and the Making of New England, 1500–1643* (New York, 1982), 152–165; Michael Zuckerman, "Pilgrims in the Wilderness: Community, Modernity, and the Maypole at Merry Mount," *NEQ,* 50 (1977), 255–277. For royal ensign, see Winthrop, *Journal,* 131–132, 136, 140, 144–145, 177–178, 747; Francis J. Bremer, "Endecott and the Red Cross: Puritan Iconoclasm in the New World," *Journal of American Studies,* 24 (1990), 5–22. See also Ann Kibbey, *The Interpretation of Material Shapes in Puritanism: A Study of Rhetoric, Prejudice, and Violence* (Cambridge, 1986).

55. Strachey, *Virginia Britania,* 55.

56. Account of second Davis voyage (1587), *NAW,* 4:240; Williams, *Language of America,* 192.

57. Gary C. Grassl, "Joachim Gans of Prague: America's First Jewish Visitor," *Review of the Society for the History of Czechoslovak Jews,* 1 (1987), 53–90; Thomas Hariot, *A briefe and true report of the new found land of Virginia* (London, 1588), B3ʳ (iron), B3ᵛ (copper); Hume, *Virginia Adventure,* 79 (crucible); see also Chapter 1.

58. Hume, *Virginia Adventure,* 215–217.

59. Voyage of the *Marigold* (1593), *NAW,* 4:62; John Nicholl, *An Houre Glasse of Indian Newes* (London, 1607), C2ʳ; *Mourt's Relation,* 25; James Rosier, *True relation* (1605), *NAW,* 3:379; Williams, *Language of America,* 156.

60. On Indian lack of writing and seeming belief that it was a kind of magic, see Stephen J. Greenblatt, "Learning to Curse," in *Learning to Curse: Essays in Early Modern Culture* (London, 1990), 16–39; James Axtell, *The Invasion Within: The Contest of Cultures in Colonial North America* (New York, 1985), 102–104. Examples from Taylor, *Tudor Geography,* 276; Settle, *True Reporte,* 212; Best, *True Discourse,* 146; Gabriel Archer's narrative, *NAW,* 3:353.

61. Richard Hakluyt, *Discourse of Western Planting* (1584), *NAW,* 4:98; Ellis,

True Report, 224; Hariot, *Briefe and True Report*, E2ᵛ; George Peckham, *True reporte* (1583), *NAW*, 3:54.

62. Robert Harcourt, *A Relation of a Voyage to Guiana* (London, 1613), Bᵛ; *A True Relation of . . . Virginia* (1608), in Smith, *Works*, 1:47.

63. Winthrop, *Journal*, 55. On navigation, see Taylor, *Tudor Geography*; John J. Roche, "Harriot's 'Regiment of the Sun' and Its Background in Sixteenth-Century Navigation," *British Journal for the History of Science*, 14 (1981), 245–261; Shirley, *Harriot*, 86–104; McDermott, *Navigation of the Frobisher Voyages*, 3, 17.

64. John Brereton, *A Briefe and true Relation* (1602), *NAW*, 3:348; Gabriel Archer, *The Relation of Captaine Gosnol[d]s Voyage* (1602), *NAW*, 3:353.

65. Account of Davis's second voyage, 240–41; Archer, *Relation*, 353.

66. Arthur Barlowe, first Virginia voyage (1584), *NAW*, 3:279; Nicholl, *Indian Newes*, Cʳ; *Mourt's Relation*, 21 (kettle), 36.

67. Relation of John Stoneman (1606), *NAW*, 3:405. See also Ian K. Steele, "Surrendering Rites: Prisoners on Colonial North American Frontiers," in Stephen Taylor et al., eds., *Hanoverian Britain and Empire: Essays in Memory of Philip Lawson* (Rochester, N.Y., 1998), 137–157.

68. Fitzhugh and Olin, *Archeology of the Frobisher Voyages*, 34–35, 87–88, 119, 147, 214–218; *Mourt's Relation*, 33, 34; Quinn, *England and the Discovery of America*, 392; Hume, *Virginia Adventure*, 191–192.

69. Nicholl, *Indian Newes*, Cᵛ; Virginia Co. of London to Sir Thomas Gates, *NAW*, 5:216; Bradford, *Plymouth Plan.*, 207.

70. Emmanuel Altham to Sir Edward Altham, September 1623, in Sydney V. James, ed., *Three Visitors to Early Plymouth* (Plymouth, Mass., 1963), 31.

3. No Magic Bullets

1. Samuel Purchas, *Purchas His Pilgrimage*, 2d ed. (London, 1617), 954. Christian F. Feest, "Virginia Algonquians," in William C. Sturtevant, ed., *Handbook of North American Indians*, vol. 15, *Northeast*, ed. Bruce G. Trigger (Washington, D.C., 1978), 260, 262 (archery and Oke); Helen C. Rountree, *The Powhatan Indians of Virginia: Their Traditional Culture* (Norman, Okla., 1989), 131. Cf. Margaret Holmes Williamson, "Powhatan Hair," *Man*, new ser., 14 (1979), 392–413.

2. For the traditional view, see Geoffrey Parker, *The Military Revolution: Military Innovation and the Rise of the West, 1500–1800* (Cambridge, 1988), though Parker recognizes that Indians were defeated "not so much through any technical inferiority as because their numbers dwindled throughout the seventeenth century" (119); Geoffrey Parker, ed., *The Cambridge Illustrated History of Warfare: The Triumph of the West* (Cambridge, 1995), chap. 8; Jared Diamond, *Guns, Germs, and Steel: The Fates of Human Societies* (New York, 1997). For the newer intepretation, see Patrick M. Malone, *The Skulking Way of War: Technology and Tactics among the New England Indi-*

ans (Lanham, Md., 1991); Ian K. Steele, *Warpaths: Invasions of North America* (New York, 1994).

3. Bert S. Hall, *Weapons and Warfare in Renaissance Europe: Gunpowder, Technology, and Tactics* (Baltimore, 1997), 18–20 (bow's speed in firing); Frank Tallett, *War and Society in Early Modern Europe, 1495–1715* (London, 1992), 22 (matchlocks vs. snaphaunces); Harold L. Peterson, "The Military Equipment of the Plymouth and Bay Colonies, 1620–1690," *NEQ*, 20 (1947), 202–204; Malone, *Skulking Way of War*, 31–36. On natives' quick acquisition of firearms, see J. Frederick Fausz, "An 'Abundance of Blood Shed on Both Sides': England's First Indian War, 1609–1614," *VMHB*, 98 (1990), 21; Steele, *Warpaths*, 45; J. H. Elliott, *Britain and Spain in America: Colonists and Colonized* (Reading, 1994), 15 (English inability to control trade in firearms).

4. Margaret T. Hodgen, *Early Anthropology in the Sixteenth and Seventeenth Centuries* (Philadelphia, 1964); Anthony Pagden, *The Fall of Natural Man: The American Indian and the Origins of Comparative Ethnology* (Cambridge, 1986), chaps. 6–8; Mary B. Campbell, *The Witness and the Other World: Exotic European Travel Writing, 400–1600* (Ithaca, N.Y., 1988), 2–5, 218; Kenneth R. Andrews, *Trade, Plunder, and Settlement: Maritime Enterprise and the Genesis of the British Empire, 1480–1630* (Cambridge, 1984), which contrasts western expansion—a paradoxical mixture of aggression and economic advantage—to eastern ventures, which were dominated by trade.

5. On warfare within Europe, see Henry J. Webb, *Elizabethan Military Science: The Books and the Practice* (Madison, Wisc., 1965); Lindsay Boynton, *The Elizabethan Militia, 1558–1638* (London, 1967); Geoffrey Parker, *The Army of Flanders and the Spanish Road, 1567–1659* (Cambridge, 1972); idem, *Military Revolution,* which has one chapter on overseas expansion; Colin Martin and Geoffrey Parker, *The Spanish Armada* (London, 1988); Barbara Donagan, "Halcyon Days and the Literature of War: England's Military Education before 1642," *P & P*, no. 147 (1995), 65–100; Hall, *Weapons and Warfare.* See also Michael Murrin, *History and Warfare in Renaissance Epic* (Chicago, 1994), which sees colonies as sites for the most convincing modern epic poetry.

6. See especially Tzvetan Todorov, *The Conquest of America: The Question of the Other,* trans. Richard Howard (New York, 1984); James A. Boon, *Other Tribes, Other Scribes: Symbolic Anthropology in the Comparative Study of Cultures, Histories, Religions, and Texts* (Cambridge, 1982), esp. chap. 5; Stephen Greenblatt, "Learning to Curse," in *Learning to Curse: Essays in Early Modern Culture* (London, 1990), 16–39; Hayden White, "The Forms of Wildness: Archaeology of an Idea," in Edward Dudley and Maximillian E. Novak, eds., *The Wild Man Within: An Image in Western Thought from the Renaissance to Romanticism* (Pittsburgh, 1972), esp. 4–5 on wildness as a symbolic concept that validates civilization. For less theoretical studies that

continue the structuralist opposition, see Francis Jennings, *The Invasion of America: Indians, Colonialism, and the Cant of Conquest* (Chapel Hill, 1975), esp. chap. 1; Bernard W. Sheehan, *Savagism and Civility: Indians and Englishmen in Colonial Virginia* (Cambridge, 1980), esp. 1–3. On binary opposition and inversion within Europe, see Natalie Zemon Davis, *Society and Culture in Early Modern France* (London, 1975), 97–123; Stuart Clark, "Inversion, Misrule and the Meaning of Witchcraft," *P & P*, no. 87 (1980), 98–127.

7. Elliott, *Britain and Spain in America*, 19–20; Richard Slotkin, *Regeneration through Violence: The Mythology of the American Frontier, 1600–1860* (Middletown, Conn., 1973), esp. 3–24; Pagden, *Fall of Natural Man*; Richard White, *The Middle Ground: Indians, Empires, and Republics in the Great Lakes Region, 1650–1815* (New York, 1991), chap. 2.

8. Inga Clendinnen, "The Cost of Courage in Aztec Society," *P & P*, no. 107 (1985), 44–89, and "Cortes, Signs, and the Conquest of Mexico," in Anthony Grafton and Ann Blair, eds., *The Transmission of Culture in Early Modern Europe* (Philadelphia, 1990), 87–130.

9. On views of wild peoples that appropriated them as variations on European identities, see David Quint, "A Reconsideration of Montaigne's *Des cannibales*," in Karen Ordahl Kupperman, ed., *America in European Consciousness, 1493–1750* (Chapel Hill, 1995), 166–191; Roger Bartra, *Wild Men in the Looking Glass: The Mythic Origins of European Otherness*, trans. Carl T. Berrisford (Ann Arbor, 1994), esp. 1–8, 171–202. On "savages" as historically prior to civil peoples, see Hodgen, *Early Anthropology*, chap. 11 (eighteenth and nineteenth centuries); Pagden, *Fall of Natural Man*, 15–26, 146–200; idem, *European Encounters with the New World: From Renaissance to Romanticism* (New Haven, 1993), chap. 4; idem, "History and Anthropology, and the History of Anthropology: Considerations on a Methodological Practice," in Jonathan Hart, ed., *Imagining Culture: Essays in Early Modern History and Culture* (New York, 1996), 33.

10. On the trans-Atlantic hairstyle, see Karen Ordahl Kupperman, "Presentment of Civility: English Reading of American Self-Presentation in the Early Years of Colonization," *WMQ*, 54 (1997), 225–226. On soldiers as magpies, see Tallett, *War and Society*, 120, 143.

11. On bow construction, see Saxton T. Pope, *Bows and Arrows* (Berkeley, 1923), 10, 31–33; Robert Hardy, *Longbow: A Social and Military History* (Cambridge, 1976), 9, 17, 30; C. A. Bergman, E. McEwen, and R. Miller, "Experimental Archery: Projectile Velocities and Comparison of Bow Performances," *Antiquity*, 62 (1988), 659–660. On the archer's posture and deformities, see Jim Bradbury, *The Medieval Archer* (Woodbridge, Suffolk, 1985), 73, 157; Hardy, *Longbow*, 25; Margaret Rule, *The Mary Rose: The Excavation and Raising of Henry VIII's Flagship* (London, 1982), 184–186.

12. James N. Loehlin, *Henry V* (Manchester, 1997), 9; "The Battaile of Agincourt," in J. William Hebel, ed., *The Works of Michael Drayton*, vol. 3 (Ox-

ford, 1932), 40–41, 45–46; Christopher Allmand, *The Hundred Years' War: England and France at War, c. 1300–c. 1450* (Cambridge, 1988), 59–62; Bradbury, *Medieval Archer,* 152–154 (Wars of the Roses), 155–158 (Tudor archery); Hardy, *Longbow,* chap. 6 (Agincourt), 86, 131, 133 (Henry VIII); John Keegan, *A History of Warfare* (New York, 1993), 329; Roger B. Manning, *Hunters and Poachers: A Cultural and Social History of Unlawful Hunting in England, 1485–1640* (Oxford, 1993), 5, 13–27; M[ichael] Oppenheim, *A History of the Administration of the Royal Navy and of Merchant Shipping in Relation to the Navy,* vol. 1, *1509–1660* (London, 1896), 47, 57; Rule, *Mary Rose,* 168–183; Martin and Parker, *Spanish Armada,* 49–50. Quotation from [Giovanni Botero], *An Historicall description of the most famous kingdomes and Common-weales in the World,* trans. R[obert] I[ohnson] (London, 1603), 5.

13. Hugh Kearney, *The British Isles: A History of Four Nations* (Cambridge, 1989), chap. 7; John Gillingham, "The Beginnings of English Imperialism," *Journal of Historical Sociology,* 5 (1992), 392–409; Steven G. Ellis, *Tudor Frontiers and Noble Power: The Making of the British State* (Oxford, 1995), esp. chap. 2.

14. Roger Ascham, *Toxophilus* (1545), facsim. (Menston, 1971), Second Book, quotation from [Uii^v].

15. Ibid., frontis., [Kii^v–Kiii^r].

16. Bradbury, *Medieval Archer,* 155–158; Joyce Youings, "Bowmen, Billmen, and Hackbutters: The Elizabethan Militia in the South West," in Robert Higham, ed., *Security and Defence in South-West England before 1800* (Exeter, 1987), 52–65; Rule, *Mary Rose,* 149–183; Tallett, *War and Society,* 23 (Armada); [R. S.], *A Briefe Treatise . . . of Archerie* (London, 1596), C3^r (Tilbury).

17. Dennis Brailsford, *Sport and Society: Elizabeth to Anne* (London, 1969), 20, 22, 29–31, 42, 48, 60, 71, 77, 101–102, 118; David Underdown, *Revel, Riot, and Rebellion: Popular Politics and Culture in England, 1603–1660* (Oxford, 1985), 47. Quotations from Thomas Elyot, *The boke named the Gouernour* (London, 1531), 98^r; *The Kings Maiesties Declaration to His Subjects, Concerning lawfull Sports to be used* (1618), in James Craigie, ed., *Minor Prose Works of King James VI and I* (Edinburgh, 1982), 107; Ascham, *Toxophilus,* [a^r].

18. For decline of military archery, see N. A. M. Rodger, *The Safeguard of the Sea: A Naval History of Britain,* vol. 1, *660–1649* (London, 1997), 313; Boynton, *Elizabethan Militia,* 46, 65–69, 112–113, 170–171; Thomas Esper, "The Replacement of the Longbow by Firearms in the English Army," *Technology and Culture,* 6 (1965), 382–393; James E. Oxley, *The Fletchers and Longbowstringmakers of London* (London, 1968), 20–21, 138; [Charles Cotton], *The Compleat Gamester* (London, 1674), 203. Quotation from John Winthrop, "Experienca" (1628), *Winthrop Papers,* 1:405.

19. William Wood, *The Bow-mans Glory; or, Archery Revived* (London, 1682),

46, 53; Zachariah G. Whitman, *The History of the Ancient and Honorable Artillery Company,* 2d ed. (Boston, 1842), 9–10; James Balfour Paul, *The History of the Royal Company of Archers: The Queen's Body-Guard for Scotland* (Edinburgh, 1875), 18–20; H. Soar, "Prince Arthur's Knights: Some Notes on a Sixteenth-Century Society of Archers," *Journal of the Society of Archer-Antiquaries,* 31 (1988), 31–39.

20. G. A. Hayes-McCoy, "The Early History of Guns in Ireland," *Galway Archaeological and Historical Society,* 18 (1938–39), 43–65; Parker, *Military Revolution,* 29–33; Rolf Loeber and Geoffrey Parker, "The Military Revolution in Seventeenth-Century Ireland," in Jane H. Ohlmeyer, ed., *Ireland from Independence to Occupation, 1641–1660* (Cambridge, 1995), 66–88; Steven G. Ellis, "The Tudors and the Origins of the Modern Irish States: A Standing Army," in Thomas Bartlett and Keith Jeffery, eds., *A Military History of Ireland* (Cambridge, 1996), 118, 119–120, 126; John McGurk, *The Elizabethan Conquest of Ireland: The 1590s Crisis* (Manchester, 1997), 227, 229 (firearms), 232–233 (gunpowder shortages); Nicholas Canny, "Religion, Politics, and the Irish Rising of 1641," in Judith Devlin and Ronan Fanning, eds., *Religion and Rebellion* (Dublin, 1997), 58 (Waterford); Malone, *Skulking Way of War,* 67–106 (King Philip's War); Steele, *Warpaths,* 51–58 (Bacon's Rebellion).

21. William W. Fitzhugh, "Introduction," in Fitzhugh and Jacqueline S. Olin, eds., *Archeology of the Frobisher Voyages* (Washington, D.C., 1993), 14; David Beers Quinn, *Set Fair for Roanoke: Voyages and Colonies, 1584–1606* (Chapel Hill, 1985), 52 (queen's gunpowder); Tallett, *War and Society,* 169 (Berwick-on-Tweed); report of Luis Aranha de Vasconcelos, in Joyce Lorimer, ed., *English and Irish Settlement on the River Amazon, 1550–1646* (London, 1989), 247.

22. Malone, *Skulking Way of War,* 70–72. See also George Percy, "A Discourse of Virginia" (1606), *NAW,* 5:268 (Virginia's natives "creeping upon all foure, from the Hills like Beares, with their Bowes in their mouthes"); Robert Gordon of Lochinvar, *Encouragements. For . . . the new plantation of* CAPE BRITON (Edinburgh, 1625), Dᵛ (natives had arrows made only of reeds and no "edge tooles"); Francis Fletcher, *The world encompassed by Sir Francis Drake* (1628), *NAW,* 1:475 (west coast Indians' bows and arrows were "their onely weapons, and almost all their wealth"); *The True Travels* (1630), in Smith, *Works,* 3:202, 209, 210 (Transylvanians and most Africans lacked firearms).

23. Eden cited in *Eng. Books,* xlvi–xlvii; *A Counter-Blaste to Tobacco* (1604), in *Minor Prose Works of King James VI and I,* 88, 92; Samuel Rowlands, *The Letting of Humovrs Blood in the Head-Vaine* (London, 1600), A2ʳ; [John Swan], *Speculum Mundi* (Cambridge, 1643), 300–301 (quotation on 300). Roy S. Wolper, "The Rhetoric of Gunpowder and the Idea of Progress," *JHI,* 31 (1970), 589–598; J. R. Hale, "Gunpowder and the Renaissance: An Essay in the History of Ideas," in Charles H. Carter, ed., *From the Renaissance to*

the Counter-Reformation (New York, 1965), 113–144; Murrin, *Renaissance Epic,* pt. 3.

24. Boynton, *Elizabethan Militia,* 6, 68–69; Hall, *Weapons and Warfare,* 19–20; Parker, *Military Revolution,* 17. On the Smythe-Barwick debate, see Webb, *Elizabethan Military Science,* 38–42, 49–50; John Smythe, *Certain Discourses Military,* ed. J. R. Hale (Ithaca, N.Y., 1964), which reprints Smythe's text. Quotations from Roger Williams, *A Briefe Discourse of Warre* (1590), in John X. Evans, ed., *The Works of Sir Roger Williams* (Oxford, 1972), 39; John Smyth[e], "An aunswer to contrarie opynions militarie," 10[r], 76[v], Harl. Ms. 135, BL; Josselyn, *Two Voyages,* 186.

25. Martin and Parker, *Spanish Armada,* 47.

26. Roger Williams, *The Actions of the Lowe Countries* (1618), in *Works,* 90, 109, 111; [Edward Cooke], *The Prospective Glasse of Warre* (London, 1628), 43.

27. [John Tiptoft], *Julius Cesars Commentaryes* (London, 1530), title page; Clarence W. Mendell, *Tacitus: The Man and His Work* (New Haven, 1957), 349–351; Kenneth C. Schellhase, *Tacitus in Renaissance Political Thought* (Chicago, 1976), esp. 3–16, 30–65; Ronald Mellor, *Tacitus* (New York, 1993), 139, 144–149; Simon Schama, *Landscape and Memory* (New York, 1995), 76–78, 81–87. On the classical background to military literature generally, see Webb, *Elizabethan Military Science,* 3–16.

28. Thomas Whitfield Baldwin, *William Shakspere's Small Latine and Lesse Greeke* (Urbana, Ill., 1944), 2:564, 570–572; Quentin Skinner, *Reason and Rhetoric in the Philosophy of Hobbes* (Cambridge, 1996), 22. Quotations from Elyot, *Boke named the Gouernour,* 39[v], 40[r].

29. Tiptoft, *Cesars Commentaryes,* [aiv[v]], [biv[r]], [div[v]]; Clement Edmonds, ed. and trans., *The Commentaries of C. Julius Caesar* (London, 1655), 25, 91; Richard Grenewey, trans., *The Annales of Cornelius Tacitus. The Description of Germanie* ([London], 1598), 269, 270.

30. Grenewey, *Annales of Tacitus,* 262.

31. Richard Bernheimer, *Wild Men in the Middle Ages: A Study in Art, Sentiment, and Demonology* (New York, 1970); Schama, *Landscape and Memory,* 96–98, 139–153; Donald R. Kelley, "*Tacitus Noster:* The *Germania* in the Renaissance and Reformation," in A. J. Woodman and T. J. Luce, eds., *Tacitus and the Tacitean Tradition* (Princeton, 1993), 167. Quotations from Henry Savile, trans., *Life of Iulius Agricola,* 2d ed. (London, 1598), 193; P[eter] H[eylyn], *Microcosmus, or A Little Description of the Great World* (Oxford, 1621), 241.

32. Ascham, *Toxophilus,* [a[v]] (health), [C[r]–Cii[v]] (music), [Diiii[r]–F[v]] ("Sirens, and Circes" on final page); Smythe, *Certain Discourses Military,* 31; J. C. Holt, *Robin Hood* (London, 1989), 142–145.

33. Smythe, "An aunswer," 5[v], 24[v], BL.

34. On rise in vernacular culture and literacy, see Joan Simon, *Education and Society in Tudor England* (Cambridge, 1966), 15, 248–250, 274–280, 369–

403; Michael van Cleave Alexander, *The Growth of English Education, 1348–1648: A Social and Cultural History* (University Park, Pa., 1990), 30–32, 89–91, 171, 185–186, 233–246; Baldwin, *Shakspere's Small Latine,* 577; Jonathan Barry, "Literacy and Literature in Popular Culture: Reading and Writing in Historical Perspective," and Tim Harris, "Problematising Popular Culture," in Tim Harris, ed., *Popular Culture in England, c. 1500–1850* (New York, 1995), 1–27, 75–79.

35. Manning, *Hunters and Poachers,* 21 (Robin Hood); John Rastell, *An Interlude of the Four Elements* (n.p., 1519), Eviii^r–Eviii^v; Benjamin Franklin to Sir Joseph York, March 7, 1781, in Albert Henry Smyth, ed., *The Writings of Benjamin Franklin* (New York, 1907), 8:443.

36. David Beers Quinn, *England and the Discovery of America, 1481–1620* (New York, 1974), 419–431 (canoe); Alain Holt, "The Elizabethan Shooting Grounds," *Journal of the Society of Archer-Antiquaries,* 28 (1985), 4.

37. George Peckham, *True reporte of the late discoveries* (1583), NAW, 3:54; Hakluyt cited in NAW, 3:68; Smythe, *Certain Discourses Military,* 107n.

38. Accounts for the *Gabriel* and the *Michael* (1576), NAW, 4:195; arms for the hundred-man colony, D. D. Hogarth, P. W. Boreham, and J. G. Mitchell, *Martin Frobisher's Northwest Venture, 1576–1581: Mines, Minerals, and Metallurgy* (Hull, Quebec, 1994), 41; George Best, *A True Discourse* (1578), in *Frobisher Voyages* 142; Dionyse Settle, *True reporte of the last voyage* (1577), NAW, 4:210, 211 (first quotation); Hakluyt, cited in NAW, 3:68; "For Master Rauleys Viage," in David B. Quinn, ed., *The Roanoke Voyages, 1584–1590* (London, 1955), 1:130–131; John White's narrative, NAW, 3:318; *A Sea Grammar* (1627), in Smith, *Works,* 3:107.

39. Barlowe cited in Quinn, *Roanoke Voyages,* 1:112–113; *Generall Historie,* in Smith, *Works,* 2:144.

40. Hakluyt cited in NAW, 3:24; anonymous instructions, 1582 or 1583, NAW, 3:244; James Rosier, *A true relation of the most prosperous voyage* (1605), NAW, 3:374; *Mourt's Relation,* 98; Edward Williams, *Virgo Triumphans: or, Virginia richly and truly valued* (London, 1650), I3^r.

41. Stuart Piggott, *Ancient Britons and the Antiquarian Imagination: Ideas from the Renaissance to the Regency* (London, 1989), Chap. 1, Robert Johnson, *Nova Britannia* (1609), NAW, 5:240; Smith, *Generall Historie,* 41; fragment on Caesar, NAW, 3:325–326; [Edward Waterhouse], *A Declaration of the State of the Colony and Affaires in Virginia* (London, 1622), 25 (the text is *Agricola*). See also William Strachey, *The Historie of Travell into Virginia Britania* (1612), ed. Louis B. Wright and Virginia Freund (London, 1953), 24.

42. Piggott, *Ancient Britons,* 73–86, 89–94 (arrowheads); David Armitage, "The New World and British Historical Thought: From Richard Hakluyt to William Robertson," in Kupperman, *America in European Consciousness,* 63–64. Ascham, *Toxophilus,* Iii^v–Iiii^r.

43. John Brereton, *A Briefe and true Relation* (1602), NAW, 3:351; Martin

Pring, "A Voyage . . . for the discouerie of the North part of Virginia, in the yeere 1603," in David B. Quinn and Alison M. Quinn, eds., *The English New England Voyages, 1602–1608* (London, 1983), 220–221; Rosier, *A true relation*, 371; [Philip Vincent], *A True Relation of the Late Battell fought in New England* (London, 1637), 11.

44. George Percy, "Discourse of Virginia," *NAW,* 5:271; *A True Relation of . . . Virginia* (1608), in Smith, *Works,* 1:89 (gloves); Smith, *Generall Historie,* 117 (shape of bow), 148 (vambrance). On gloves and bracers, see Ascham, *Toxophilus,* [Niiii^r]–Oi^r.

45. Best, *A True Discourse,* 131; John Nicholl, *An Houre Glasse of Indian Newes* (London, 1607), [C4^r]; *True Relation,* in Smith, *Works,* 1:45–47; orders for the Council for Virginia, December 10, 1606, in Philip L. Barbour, ed., *The Jamestown Voyages under the First Charter, 1606–1609,* 2 vols. (Cambridge, 1969), 1:52; "A relatyon . . ." (1607), ibid., 96.

46. Robert Bartlett, "Symbolic Meanings of Hair in the Middle Ages," *Transactions of the Royal Historical Society,* 6th ser., 4 (1994), 43–60; Paul Hulton, ed., *America 1585: The Complete Drawings of John White* (Chapel Hill, 1984), 78 (White's watercolor), 109 (de Bry's double image), 129 (tattoos in the form of arrows); "Hinde de Loranbec," in "Histoire naturelle des Indes" (Drake Manuscript), MA 3900, fol. 090, Pierpont Morgan Library, New York City. This man was recorded as being near the latitude of 36.5 degrees, in present-day South Carolina. But the notation may not be by the original artist; the manuscript seems to have been the work of at least two different scribes and two different artists. See Verlyn Klinkenborg, "Introduction," in Patrick O'Brian, Verlyn Klinkenborg, et al., eds., *Histoire naturelle des Indes: The Drake Manuscript in the Pierpont Morgan Library* (New York, 1996), xvi, xix. See also J[ohn] B[ulwer], *Anthropometamorphosis: Man Transformed, or, the Artificiall Changling* (London, 1653), 54–55, which refers to Virginia Indians' hairstyles.

47. Smith cited in Barbour, *Jamestown Voyages,* 1:137–138; Smith, *Generall Historie,* 106–107 (Susquehannock); John Underhill, *Newes from America* (1638), *Massachusetts Historical Society Collections,* 3d ser., 6 (1837), 5. See also *Mourt's Relation,* 53. On English admiration for native technology and hunting, see Karen Ordahl Kupperman, *Settling with the Indians: The Meeting of English and Indian Cultures in America, 1580–1640* (Totowa, N.J., 1980), chap. 5; Matt Cartmill, *A View to a Death in the Morning: Hunting and Nature through History* (Cambridge, Mass., 1993), chap. 4; Manning, *Hunters and Poachers,* 1–31.

48. *Mourt's Relation,* 86, 91 (Hunt), 97 ("peeces"), 103 (courage), 114.

49. Ralph Hamor, *A Trve Discovrse of the Present Estate of Virginia* (London, 1615), 26. English longbows had a "pull" of sixty to seventy-five pounds; eastern woodland bows were usually below fifty pounds; Inuit composite bows were probably more powerful than English longbows. See Pope, *Bows and Arrows,* 10, 31–33; Malone, *Skulking Way of War,* 18 (which uses

Pope); Bergman, McEwen, and Miller, "Experimental Archery," 658–670 (which questions Pope's tests). The replica medieval longbow that Bergman and his co-authors tested was still the best among their group of selfbows, though this excluded northeastern weapons, but did include those of Sioux and Apache.

50. Ivor Noel Hume, *The Virginia Adventure: Roanoke to James Towne: An Archaeological and Historical Odyssey* (New York, 1994), 152 (gunpowder usage); *RVCL*, 3:614, 676; (Tower supplies); 4:507–508 (depletion of gunpowder); William L. Shea, *The Virginia Militia in the Seventeenth Century* (Baton Rouge, La., 1983), 31–32, 42.

51. Hamor, *Trve Discovrse*, 13; [Vincent], *Late Battell*, [6]; Roger Williams to John Winthrop, ca. August 25, 1636, in Williams, *Correspondence*, 1:54; J. Hammond Trumball, ed., *The Public Records of the Colony of Connecticut*, vol. 1, *1636–1665* (Hartford, Conn., 1850), 75.

52. [David Lloyd], *The Legend of Captain Jones* (London, 1659), A4[v], 3 (Crotona), 5–7 (bows and arrows on 5), 37–44 (Irish), 61–63 (African king); Hume, *Virginia Adventure*, 229, 230 (Smith's falchion); *Mourt's Relation*, 55.

53. Bradford, *Plymouth Plan.*, 96; Champlin Burrage, ed., *John Pory's Lost Description of Plymouth Colony in the Earliest Days of the Pilgrim Fathers* (Boston, 1918), 43.

54. Underhill, *Newes from America*, 26, 27; Nicholl, *Indian Newes*, [C4[r]].

55. Lorimer, *English and Irish Settlement on the Amazon*, 42 (steel), 434 (gold and silver); R. Rich, *Nevves from Virginia* (London, 1610), B2[v]; Burrage, *Pory's Lost Description*, 50.

56. Susan Rowley, "Frobisher Miksanut: Inuit Accounts of the Frobisher Voyages," in Fitzhugh and Olin, *Archeology of the Frobisher Voyages*, 38 (Inuit testimony); William W. Fitzhugh, "Archeology of Kodlunarn Island," ibid., 87–88; Michael L. Wayman and Robert M. Ehrenreich, "Metallurgical Study of Small Iron Finds," ibid., 216; Thomas Hariot, *A briefe and true report of the new found land of Virginia* (London, 1588), B3[r]; Ralph Lane's discourse (1589) in Quinn, *Roanoke Voyages*, 1:281; John White's narrative, 1590, 2:614; Strachey, *Virginia Britania*, 107.

57. Nicholl, *Indian Newes*, C[v]; *A Relation of Maryland* (London, 1635), 19–20.

58. John Harvey to Viscount Dorchester, Sec. of State, April 15, 1630, 1/5, CO; petition of "Mr. Yong" [April 1634], f. 23, 1/8, CO; Col. Thos. Temple to Lord Fienes, December 29, 1659, 1/13, CO.

59. Burrage, *Pory's Lost Description*, 49; Smith, *Generall Historie*, 171, 453; *Mourt's Relation*, 92; Roger Williams, *A Key into the Language of America* (1643), ed. John J. Teunissen and Evelyn J. Hinz (Detroit, 1973), 121; Ferdinando Gorges, *A Briefe Narration of the Originall Undertakings . . .* (London, 1658), 28; Winthrop, *Journal*, 759.

60. Barbour, *Jamestown Voyages*, 1:91; *Mourt's Relation*, 102; Emmanuel Altham to Sir Edward Altham, September 1623, in Sydney V. James, Jr., ed., *Three Visitors to Early Plymouth* (Plimoth Plantation, 1963), 29; J. Franklin

Jameson, ed., [*Edward*] *Johnson's Wonder-Working Providence, 1628–1651* (New York, 1910), 263. Indian ability to use firearms probably was superior; see Malone, *Skulking Way of War,* 80–87.

61. Orders for the Council for Virginia, *Jamestown Voyages,* 1:52; Percy, "Discourse of Virginia," *NAW,* 5:271; Smith, *True Relation,* 51 and note 118; [Robert Evelin], *A Description of the Province of New Albion* ([London], 1648), 18.

62. Accounts of the John Guy expedition to Newfoundland, *NAW,* 4:155, 160, 162; Smith, *Generall Historie,* 106, 171.

63. Best, *True Discourse,* 142; William M. Kelso, Nicholas M. Luccketti, and Beverly A. Staube, eds., *Jamestown Rediscovery IV* (Jamestown, Va., 1998), 21–22; *RVCL,* 1:100; 3:676 (supplies from the Tower).

64. Lion Gardiner to John Winthrop, Jr., March 23, 1637, and John Higginson to John Winthrop, ca. May 1637, *Winthrop Papers,* 3:382, 404. Virginia Indians might initially have held the gun barrel with the left hand and pulled the trigger with the right, a posture almost identical to that needed to hold a bow (left hand) and pull its string (right hand); see Feest, "Virginia Algonquians," 259. On the trade in firearms, see Fausz, "England's First Indian War," 21; Steele, *Warpaths,* 45; Martin H. Quitt, "Trade and Acculturation at Jamestown, 1607–1609: The Limits of Understanding," *WMQ,* 52 (1995), 227–258.

65. See de Bry's images in Michael Alexander, ed., *Discovering the New World* (New York, 1976), 24 (bows and arrows for sacrifice), 50 (to declare war), 57 (mourning and burial). See also Colin G. Calloway, *New Worlds for All: Indians, Europeans, and the Remaking of Early America* (Baltimore, 1997), chap. 5. Observation of Inuit composite bows indicates the English respected weapons unfamiliar to them. Composite bows were not made of one piece of wood but were either reinforced with horn and sinew (a modified composite bow) or composed of layers of wood, bone, and sinew (the classic composite bow). Sinew, with or without bone, allowed greater compression of a shorter bow; unreinforced wood would have broken. Because such a weapon was shorter, it could be used from horseback, or in the case of the Inuit, from a kayak. Dionyse Settle, who described Inuit composite bows, noted that they were only a yard long (instead of nearly the height of a man) and were "sinewed on the back with strong veines." Settle, *True reporte,* 214. See also William C. Sturtevant and David B. Quinn, "This New Prey: Eskimos in Europe in 1567, 1576, and 1577," in Christian F. Feest, ed., *Indians and Europe: An Interdisciplinary Collection of Essays* (Aachen, 1987), 77, 93, 112; Hardy, *Longbow,* 14; Bergman, McEwan, and Miller, "Experimental Archery," 660–661.

66. Benjamin Franklin to Charles Lee, February 11, 1776, in William B. Willcox, ed., *Papers of Benjamin Franklin* (New Haven, 1982), 22:343. On the new, creolized frontier primitivism, see Slotkin, *Regeneration through Violence,* esp. 21–24, 146–179; Pagden, *European Encounters,* 168–169. On tall tales,

see George N. Gage et al., *History of Washington, New Hampshire, from 1768 to 1886* [1886], facsim. with foreword by Ronald Jager and Grace Jager (Washington, N.H., 1976), 67; Richard M. Dorson, *Jonathan Draws the Long Bow* (Cambridge, Mass., 1946), 102.

67. James Axtell and William C. Sturtevant, "The Unkindest Cut, or Who Invented Scalping?" *WMQ*, 37 (1980), 451–472; Malone, *Skulking Way of War*, 141, note 11.

68. David D. Smits, "'Abominable Mixture': Toward the Repudiation of Anglo-Indian Intermarriage in Seventeenth-Century Virginia," *VMHB*, 95 (1987), 181–182; and see Chapter 5.

4. Domesticating America

1. Nathaniel Bacon quoted in Stephen Saunders Webb, *1676: The End of American Independence* (New York, 1981), 80; John Bradstreet to [Charles Townshend], December 3, 1766, Charles Townshend Papers, William L. Clements Library, University of Michigan, Ann Arbor.

2. John Canup, *Out of the Wilderness: The Emergence of an American Identity in Colonial New England* (Middletown, Conn., 1990); Jim Egan, *Authorizing Experience: Refigurations of the Body Politic in Seventeenth-Century New England Writing* (Princeton, 1999).

3. Richard Hakluyt, *Discourse of Western Planting* (1584), *NAW*, 3:100; Peter Heylyn, *Cosmographie in Four Books*, 2d ed. (London, 1657), 23.

4. Quotations from William Cuningham, comp., *The Cosmographical Glasse* (London, 1559), aii^r, see also 6–10 (overview of cosmography); Edward Arber, "The Life and Labours of Richard Eden," and Eden, preface to Sebastian Munster, *A Treatyse of the newe India (1533), Eng. Books*, xlii, 5. On cosmography and the human place in it: William T. Costello, *The Scholastic Curriculum at Early Seventeenth-Century Cambridge* (Cambridge, Mass., 1958), 104–106; Clarence J. Glacken, *Traces on the Rhodian Shore: Nature and Culture in Western Thought from Ancient Times to the End of the Eighteenth Century* (Berkeley, 1967), 432–460; Margaret T. Hodgen, *Early Anthropology in the Sixteenth and Seventeenth Centuries* (Philadelphia, 1964), 386–404; Nancy Siraisi, *Medieval and Early Renaissance Medicine: An Introduction to Knowledge and Practice* (Chicago, 1989), 79, 97–104, 120–123, 135–136. On astrology: Don Cameron Allen, *The Star-Crossed Renaissance: The Quarrel about Astrology and Its Influence in England* (New York, 1966); Keith Thomas, *Religion and the Decline of Magic* (London, 1971), 335–458; Brian P. Copenhaver, "Astrology and Magic," in Charles B. Schmitt and Quentin Skinner, eds., *The Cambridge History of Renaissance Philosophy* (Cambridge, 1988), 264–300; Wayne Shumaker, *The Occult Sciences in the Renaissance: A Study in Intellectual Patterns* (Berkeley, 1972), 1–11, 16–27, 42–53; Jon Butler, "Magic, Astrology, and the Early American Religious Heritage, 1600–1760," *AHR*, 84 (1979), 317–346. On America:

Karen Ordahl Kupperman, "The Puzzle of the American Climate in the Early
Colonial Period," *AHR,* 87 (1982), 1262–89; David Gwyn, "Richard Eden,
Cosmographer and Alchemist," *SCJ,* 15 (1984), 13–34.

5. On concern over new or American environments, see Andrew Wear, "Making Sense of Health and the Environment in Early Modern England," in
Wear, ed., *Medicine in Society: Historical Essays* (Cambridge, 1992), 126–
129; Richard S. Dunn, *Sugar and Slaves: The Rise of the Planter Class in the
English West Indies, 1624–1713* (Chapel Hill, 1972), chaps. 8, 9; Karen
Ordahl Kupperman, "Fear of Hot Climates in the Anglo-American Colonial
Experience," *WMQ,* 41 (1984), 215–240; Canup, *Out of the Wilderness,*
chaps. 1, 2, 6; Anthony Grafton, *New Worlds, Ancient Texts: The Power of
Tradition and the Shock of Discovery* (Cambridge, Mass., 1992), 159–194;
Joyce E. Chaplin, "Climate and Southern Pessimism: The Natural History of
an Idea, 1500–1800," in Don Doyle and Larry J. Griffin, eds., *The South as
an American Problem* (Athens, Ga., 1995); Egan, *Authorizing Experience,*
chap. 1.

6. Scholars who proceed from gender to nature have followed the pattern set by
Louis Montrose, "The Work of Gender in the Discourse of Discovery," *Representations,* 33 (1990), 1–41. Two examples of this kind of analysis are
Kathleen M. Brown, *Good Wives, Nasty Wenches, and Anxious Patriarchs:
Gender, Race, and Power in Colonial Virginia* (Chapel Hill, 1996), esp. 17–
19, which discusses nature only to identify it with femaleness, though the
way nature was used to define female and male is the missing prior step; and
Mary Beth Norton, *Founding Mothers and Fathers: Gendered Power and the
Forming of American Society* (New York, 1996), esp. 5–8, which defines gender as social relations without reference to arguments about nature. For analyses that simultaneously define nature and gender, see Ian Maclean, *The Renaissance Notion of Woman: A Study in the Fortunes of Scholasticism and
Medical Science in European Intellectual Life* (Cambridge, 1980), chap. 3;
Thomas Laqueur, *Making Sex: Body and Gender from the Greeks to Freud*
(Cambridge, Mass., 1990); Joan Cadden, *Meanings of Sex Difference in the
Middle Ages: Medicine, Science, and Culture* (Cambridge, 1993); Dror
Wahrman, "Gender in Translation: How the English Wrote Their Juvenal,
1644–1815," *Representations,* 65 (1999), 1–41.

7. John Parkinson, *Paradisi in Sole Paradisus Terrestris, or A Garden* (London,
1629), 11, 13; John Josselyn, *New-Englands Rarities Discovered,* 2nd ed.
(London, 1675), 85; Joseph [José de] Acosta, *The Naturall and Moral
Historie of the East and West Indies* (1590), trans. E[dward] G[rimeston]
(London, 1604), 308. See also Alfred W. Crosby, Jr., *The Columbian Exchange: Biological and Cultural Consequences of 1492* (Westport, Conn.,
1972), 64–121.

8. *Eng. Books,* xlii.

9. Helkiah Crooke, *Microcosmographia: A Description of the Body of Man*
(London, 1615), 2, 5 (body as microcosm and of a middle temperature);
Henry Cuffe, *The Differences of the Ages of Mans Life* (London, 1633), 81,

95–96, 113–135 (heat and life); Shumaker, *Occult Sciences in the Renaissance*, 170–186; Kupperman, "Fear of Hot Climates," 213–240. Quotations from Winthrop, *Journal*, 675; [Anne Bradstreet], *The Tenth Muse Lately Sprung Up in America* (London, 1650), 22–26 (quotation on 26), 41–55.

10. Eden, preface to Munster, *Treatyse of the newe India, Eng. Books*, 11; P[eter] H[eylyn], *Microcosmus, or A Little Description of the Great World* (Oxford, 1621), 6.

11. Crooke, *Microcosmographia*, 88; *The Divine Weeks and Works of Guillaume De Saluste, Sieur du Bartas*, trans. Josuah Sylvester, ed. Susan Snyder, 2 vols. (Oxford, 1979), 1:457 (Africans' melancholy). See also Robert Burton, *The Anatomy of Melancholy* (1632), ed. Thomas C. Faulkner, Nicolas K. Kiessling, and Rhonda L. Blair, 3 vols. (Oxford, 1989), 1:233–237 (extreme cold or heat and melancholy); Heylyn, *Cosmographie*, 242 (Spanish), 931 (Libyans).

12. Dionyse Settle, *True reporte* (1577), *NAW*, 4:215; H[eylyn], *Microcosmus*, 271; Glacken, *Traces on the Rhodian Shore*, 451–456.

13. Cuningham, *Cosmographical Glasse*, 184–185; Burton, *Anatomy of Melancholy*, 1:247; draft of an act for baptizing "Negroes & Infidells," MS. Tanner, 447, f. 53, Bodleian; Jean Bodin, *The Six Bookes of a Commonweale* (1606), ed. Kenneth Douglas McRae (Cambridge, Mass., 1962), 551.

14. Anonymous notebook (ca. 1680s), MS. Rawlinson C.406, 37, Bodleian. On conceptions of disease, see Richard Harrison Shryock, *Medicine and Society in America, 1660–1860* (New York, 1960), 49–53; L. Deer Richardson, "The Generation of Disease: Occult Causes and Diseases of the Total Substance," in A. Wear, R. K. French, and I. M. Lonie, eds., *The Medical Renaissance of the Sixteenth Century* (Cambridge, 1985), 175–196 (for an unorthodox view); Eric H. Christianson, "Medicine in New England," in Ronald L. Numbers, ed., *Medicine in the New World: New Spain, New France, and New England* (Knoxville, Tenn., 1987), 110–111; Siraisi, *Medieval and Early Renaissance Medicine*, 104–106, 117; Wear, "Health and the Environment in Early Modern England," 119–147.

15. See Vivian Nutton, "The Seeds of Disease: An Explanation of Contagion and Infection from the Greeks to the Renaissance," *Medical History*, 27 (1983), 1–34, and Catherine Wilson, *The Invisible World: Early Modern Philosophy and the Invention of the Microscope* (Princeton, 1995), chap. 5, for early germ theories. On syphilis, see Grafton, *New Worlds, Ancient Texts*, 176–193; Winfried Schleiner, "Moral Attitudes toward Syphilis and Its Prevention in the Renaissance," *BHM*, 68 (1994), 389–410. On cannibalism and the pox, see Edward Daunce, *A Briefe Discovrse of the Spanish State* (London, 1590), 28–29; on sodomy and the pox, see William Clowes, *A short and profitable Treatise touching the cure of the disease called (Morbus Gallicus) by Vnctions* (London, 1579), preface (n.p.) Cf. Arthur Williamson, "Scots, Indians, and Empire: The Scottish Politics of Civilization, 1519–1609," *P & P*, no. 150 (1996), 46–83.

16. William Vaughan, *Natvrall and artificiall directions for health* (London,

1600), 54–55, 67; Acosta, *Historie of the Indies,* 62–81, 503–505; [Bradstreet], *Tenth Muse,* 16. See also Burton, *Anatomy of Melancholy,* 1:125–126; Glacken, *Traces on the Rhodian Shore,* 366–368 (Acosta and America), 379–382 (deterioration).

17. J. Overbeek, *History of Population Theories* (Rotterdam, 1974), chaps. 3, 4; John Dee, preface, *The Elements of Geometrie of the Most Auncient Philosopher Euclide of Megara,* trans. H[ugh] Billingsley (London, 1570), aiiij^v.

18. Thomas Harriot Mathematical Papers, Add. MS. 6782, 31^r–31^v; 6788, 507^r–537^r, BL.

19. Harriot Mathematical Papers, 6782, 31^v, BL. See also Barnett J. Sokol, "Thomas Harriot—Sir Walter Ralegh's Tutor—on Population," *AS,* 31 (1974), 205–214.

20. Richard Helgerson, *Forms of Nationhood: The Elizabethan Writing of England* (Chicago, 1992), chap. 3 (114–115 on "Ditchley" portrait).

21. Bodin, *Six Bookes,* 576, 640–641; Giovanni Botero, *The Greatness of Cities,* trans. Robert Peterson (New Haven, 1956), 227, 245, 277–278. See also Glacken, *Traces on the Rhodian Shore,* 368–374 (Botero), 434–447 (Bodin).

22. *Divine Weeks and Works of Du Bartas,* 1:19 (king's copy), 446 (quotation); Walter Ralegh, *The Historie of the World* (London, 1614), 1:77, 157; Heylyn, *Cosmographie,* 5; Glacken, *Traces on the Rhodian Shore,* 448–449; Bradford, *Plymouth Plan.,* 121n; Winthrop, *Journal,* 768n; Eliot's copy of Heylyn, *Cosmographie* (1657), Houghton Library, Harvard University; "Beloved if wee intend to prosper in our plantations . . . ," 97^v, 1/4, CO. See also Louis B. Wright, "The Purposeful Reading of Our Colonial Ancestors," *Journal of English Literary History,* 4 (1937), 92 (Du Bartas and Bradstreet).

23. Overbeek, *History of Population Theories,* 31–32.

24. Botero, *Cities,* 278, 279.

25. William H. McNeill, *Plagues and Peoples* (Garden City, N.Y., 1976), 168; Paul Slack, *The Impact of Plague in Tudor and Stuart England* (London, 1985), 58, Table 3.2; Colin Platt, *King Death: The Black Death and Its Aftermath in Late-Medieval England* (London, 1996), 9, 19–31, 125; David Herlihy, *The Black Death and the Transformation of the West* (Cambridge, Mass., 1997). Quotation from Burton, *Anatomy of Melancholy,* 1:78.

26. John More, *A Table from the Beginning of the World to this Day* (Cambridge, 1593), 209, 213, 215, 220, 225; David B. Quinn and Neil M. Cheshire, eds., *The New Found Land of Stephen Parmenius* (Toronto, 1972), 198n; Platt, *King Death,* 19–20 (Boston); John Graunt, *Natural and Political Observations . . . Made upon the Bills of Mortality* (London, 1662), 4. On "plague" as a label for Indian epidemics, see Smith, *Works,* 3:274; William Wood, *New England's Prospect* (1634), ed. Alden T. Vaughan (Amherst, Mass., 1977), 58; Thomas Morton, *New English Canaan, or New Canaan* (Amsterdam, 1637), 23, and other examples given in this and Chapter 5.

27. Heylyn, *Cosmographie,* 976, 1028; Sokol, "Harriot—on Population," 212.

28. Geffrey Whitney, *A Choice of Emblemes* . . . (Leyden, 1586), 178 ("Coelum, non animum"); Ralegh, *Historie of the World,* 1:15.

29. [Bradstreet], *Tenth Muse,* 181; Roger Williams, *The Bloudy Tenent* (1644), in Samuel L. Caldwell, ed., *The Complete Writings of Roger Williams* (New York, 1963), 3:323; Edward Williams, *Virgo Triumphans: or, Virginia richly and truly valued* (London, 1650), [B4ʳ].

30. Quotation from Josselyn, *Two Voyages,* 88. On migration generally, see Robert Wauchope, *Lost Tribes and Sunken Continents: Myth and Method in the Study of American Indians* (Chicago, 1962); Lee Eldridge Huddleston, *Origins of the American Indians: European Concepts, 1492–1729* (Austin, Tex., 1967). For specifically early modern theories, see Don Cameron Allen, *The Legend of Noah: Renaissance Rationalism in Art, Science, and Letters* (Urbana, Ill., 1963), 113–137; Alfred A. Cave, "Canaanites in a Promised Land: The American Indian and the Providential Theory of Empire," *American Indian Quarterly,* 12 (1988), 277–297; idem, "Thomas More and the New World," *Albion,* 23 (1991), 220–227; Gwyn A. Williams, *Madoc: The Making of a Myth* (Oxford, 1987), chaps. 3, 4.

31. H[eylyn], *Microcosmus,* 405, 416; idem, *Cosmographie,* 1094 (Puerto Rico); George Gardyner, *A Description of the New World* (London, 1651), 54, 69.

32. Stanley Pargellis and Ruth Lampham Butler, eds., "Daniell Ellffryth's Guide to the Caribbean, 1631," *WMQ,* 1 (1944), 281 (Dominica), 302 (Macoris), 315 (Trujillo); Heylyn, *Cosmographie,* 1096, see also 1094–95.

33. C. S. L. Davies, "Slavery and Protector Somerset: The Vagrancy Act of 1547," *Economic History Review,* 2d ser., 19 (1966), 533–549; Mildred Campbell, "English Emigration on the Eve of the American Revolution," *AHR,* 61 (1955), 1–20; idem, "Social Origins of Some Early Americans," in James Morton Smith, ed., *Seventeenth-Century America: Essays in Colonial History* (Chapel Hill, 1959); Edmund S. Morgan, *American Slavery, American Freedom: The Ordeal of Colonial Virginia* (New York, 1975), 62–70.

34. H[eylyn], *Microcosmus,* 242 (and *Cosmographie,* 295–297); ivory dial, Inventory no. 47,973, Museum of the History of Science, University of Oxford; George Peckham, *True reporte* (1583), *NAW,* 3:54, 58; Edward Hayes and Christopher Carleill [1592], "A discourse concerning a voyage," *NAW,* 3:157.

35. Burton, *Anatomy of Melancholy,* 3:260 (quotation), 340–341; [Philip Vincent], *A True Relation of the Late Battell* (London, 1637), [1], 21; Champlin Burrage, ed., *John Pory's Lost Description of Plymouth Colony in the Earliest Days of the Pilgrim Fathers* (Boston, 1918), 28; Richard Whitbourne, *A Discovrse and Discovery of Nevv-Found-land* (London, 1622), 19; [John White], *The Planters Plea* (London, 1630), 1, see also 38.

36. Peter Martyr, *The Decades of the Newe Worlde,* trans. Richard Eden, *Eng. Books,* 87, 104; Crooke, *Microcosmographia,* 194 (lactating men), 262 (dark women), 274 (men's natural heat).

37. Winthrop, *Journal,* 19.

38. Peckham, *True reporte*, 41, 42; Richard Hakluyt the elder, ". . . the voyadge intended" (ca. 1584), *NAW*, 3:62; Cuningham, *Cosmographical Glasse*, 113; Hakluyt, *Discourse of Western Planting*, 73. See Whitbourne, *Discovrse of Nevv-Found-land*, 15, on northeast America's proximity to England.

39. William Vaughan, *The Newlanders Cure* (London, 1630), A5ᵛ; [Vincent], *Late Battell*, 23; Whitbourne, *Discovrse of Nevv-Found-land*, 74, 75 (nurse, mother, and "Sister Land"); [Bradstreet], *Tenth Muse*, 180–181; [White], *Planters Plea*, 33, 34 (mother), 38.

40. Ivan Hannaford, *Race: The History of an Idea in the West* (Washington, D.C., and Baltimore, 1996), 93–96, 122–124; Benjamin Braude, "The Sons of Noah and the Construction of Ethnic and Geographical Identities in the Medieval and Early Modern Periods," *WMQ*, 54 (1997), 103–142; Paul Freedman, *Images of the Medieval Peasant* (Stanford, 1999), chap. 4; Colin Kidd, *British Identities before Nationalism: Ethnicity and Nationhood in the Atlantic World, 1600–1800* (Cambridge, 1999), 9–33, explains the theories of Noachian lineage, but the rest of his work complicates the picture. On custom as a second nature, see Donald R. Kelley, *The Human Measure: Social Thought in the Western Legal Tradition* (Cambridge, Mass., 1990), 168–174.

41. Crooke, *Microcosmographia*, 258–259; J[ohn] B[ulwer], *Anthropometamorphosis: Man Transformed, or, the Artificiall Changling* (London, 1653), 284–285 (inheritance), 446–448 (male seed and female womb), also 515–516.

42. Elizabeth B. Gasking, *Investigations into Generation, 1651–1828* (Baltimore, [1967]), chap. 2 (Harvey, ovist theory), chaps. 3, 4, and 9 (preformation); Laqueur, *Making Sex*, 38–43, 49–52, 54–61, 99–103, 117–121, 142–148; Phillip Sloan, "The Gaze of Natural History," in Christopher Fox, Roy Porter, and Robert Wokler, eds., *Inventing Human Science: Eighteenth-Century Domains* (Berkeley, 1995), 116–117 (preformation); Clara Pinto-Correia, *The Ovary of Eve: Egg and Sperm and Preformation* (Chicago, 1997).

43. Crooke, *Microcosmographia*, 290, 292.

44. Philip Hermanus, *An excellent Treatise teaching howe to cure the French-Pockes* . . . (London, 1590), 1, 61. See also Henry Oldenburg to Richard Norwood, February 10, 1667–68, Oldenburg, *Correspondence*, 4:167. On climate affecting humans even before birth, see Siraisi, *Medieval and Early Renaissance Medicine*, 110–111; Jorge Cañizares Esguerra, "New World, New Stars: Patriotic Astrology and the Invention of Indian and Creole Bodies in Colonial Spanish America, 1600–1650," *AHR*, 104 (1999), 33–68.

45. Crooke, *Microcosmographia*, 280, also 438, 440; B[ulwer], *Anthropometamorphosis*, 3ᵛ (hag), B1ᵛ–V2ᵛ, 8–9, 13, 17–28 (the supposedly monstrous races), 124 (husbands), 135–136 (eunuchs); John Baptista [Giambattista della] Porta, *Natural Magick* (London, 1658), 51 (straightening limbs). See also Rudolph M. Bell, *How to Do It: Guides to Good Living for Renaissance Italians* (Chicago, 1999), chaps. 2–4.

46. Bodin, *Six Bookes,* 568; Martin Pring's voyage, 1603, *NAW,* 3:361; Gabriel Archer, "Discription of . . . Virginia," *NAW,* 5:276; B[ulwer], *Anthropometamorphosis,* 259–273 (painting), 460–461, 465–466 (White's Picts); Karen O. Kupperman, "Presentment of Civility: English Reading of American Self-Presentation in the Early Years of Colonization," *WMQ,* 54 (1997), 193 (Indians' "accidental" characteristics).

47. Martyr, *Decades,* 88, 338; H[eylyn], *Microcosmus,* 382 (quotation); idem, *Cosmographie,* 976.

48. [Della] Porta, *Natural Magick,* 51–55; Burton, *Anatomy of Melancholy,* 1:205–210 (inheritance), 250–252 (imagination).

49. Burton, *Anatomy of Melancholy,* 1:327–330 (quotation 327); H[eylyn], *Microcosmus,* 403 (quotation); idem, *Cosmographie,* 1016; Ralegh, *Historie of the World,* 1:111.

50. B[ulwer], *Anthropometamorphosis,* 467–469.

51. Ibid., 498–499; Josselyn, *Two Voyages,* 129–130.

52. Richard Grenville to Francis Walsingham, October 29, 1585, *NAW,* 3:293; petition to Parliament, 1606, *NAW,* 5:169; Robert Johnson, *Nova Britannia* (1609), *NAW,* 5:235; [White], *Planters Plea,* 1, 12 (Christian migration), 17–20 (English overpopulation).

53. "Briefe motives to maintaine his [majesty's] right unto the River of Amazones . . . ," January 1623, 1/1, CO.

54. Daniel Tucker to Nathaniel Rich, July 14, 1616, in Vernon A. Ives, ed., *The Rich Papers: Letters from Bermuda, 1615–1646* (Toronto, 1984), 8; Winthrop, *Journal,* 86.

55. Hayes and Carleill, "A discourse," 161; Robert Gordon of Lochinvar, *Encouragements . . . for . . . the new plantation of* CAPE BRITON (Edinburgh, 1625), Dᵛ.

56. Ralph Lane to Francis Walsingham, September 8, 1585, *NAW,* 3:292; William Strachey, *The Historie of Travell into Virginia Britania* (1612), ed. Louis B. Wright and Virginia Freund (London, 1953), 44; [Robert Evelin], *A Description of the Province of New Albion* ([London], 1648), 23; Ferdinando Gorges, *America Painted to the Life* (London, 1659), 53.

57. [Nicolás Monardes], *Ioyfull Nevves out of the newe founde World,* trans. Ihon Frampton (London, 1577), 47ᵛ; Josselyn, *Two Voyages,* 56 (masculine nature), 59 (shallow roots).

58. *New Atlantis,* in Bacon, *Works,* 5:379; Strachey, *Virginia Britania,* 40. Raymond Phineas Stearns, *Science in the British Colonies of America* (Urbana, Ill, 1970), 75, discusses Strachey's geology.

59. *NAW,* 3:174, 176.

60. [George Wateson], *The Cvres of the Diseased, in remote Regions* (London, 1598), title page; Hayes and Carleill, "A discourse," 172; Johnson, *Nova Britannia,* 239.

61. George Best, *A True Discourse* (1578), *Frobisher Voyages,* 129, 140; Walter A. Kenyon, ed., "The Canadian Arctic Journal of Capt. Edward Fenton," *Archivaria,* 11 (1980–81), 199; John Brereton, *A Briefe and true Relation*

(1602), *NAW,* 3:351 (height), 352; *Mourt's Relation,* 19, 38; see also 64, 101, 104.

62. Edward Topsell, "The Fowles of Heaven," 31ᵛ–32ʳ, 85ʳ–86ʳ, Ellesmere Ms. 1142, HL; James A. Rosier, *True relation of the most prosperous voyage* (1605), *NAW,* 3:371; Wood, *New England's Prospect,* 123–124.

63. Ralph Lane to Richard Hakluyt, 1585, *NAW,* 3:293; Grenville to Walsingham, 293; *Mourt's Relation,* 103, 136.

64. [John Swan], *Speculum Mundi* (Cambridge, 1643), 439–440; Bernard W. Sheehan, *Savagism and Civility: Indians and Englishmen in Colonial Virginia* (Cambridge, 1980), 72; Order of Council of State, January 30, 1653–54, SP 25/48, PRO; Virginia Company, *True declaration* (1610), *NAW,* 5:254.

65. Rosier, *True relation,* 378; "A valuation of the Commodities . . . in Virginia" [1610], 1/1, CO.

66. "A Reply to the Answeare to the description of Newfound land," September 29, 1639, 109ᵛ, 110ʳ, 1/10, CO.

67. [Vincent], *Late Battell,* [4].

68. Richard Barnes, "A note containing the opinion on Christopher Marley," 185ʳ, 185ᵛ (quotation), Harl. MS., 6848, BL; H[eylyn], *Microcosmus,* 411; Samuel Rowlands, *The Letting of Humovrs Blood in the Head-Vaine* (London, 1600), 17ʳ.

69. John Gerard, *The Herball or Generall Historie of Plantes* (London, 1597), 288; *Winthrop Journal,* 126, 128 (legislation), 263 (Underhill); Edward Hoby, *A Counter-snarle for Ishmael Rabshacheh* (London, 1613), 37 (Underhill); [Robert Hayman], *Quodlibets, Lately Come Over from New Britaniola, Old Newfound Land* (London, 1628), 41. See also Jordan Goodman, *Tobacco in History: The Cultures of Dependence* (London, 1993), 45; [Richard Braithwaite], *The Smoaking Age* (London, 1617).

70. [Swan], *Speculum Mundi,* 260; Vaughan, *Newlanders Cure,* 131; Josselyn, *Two Voyages,* 54–55.

71. Bradford, *Plymouth Plan.,* 26, 143.

72. Martyr, *Decades,* 118; Dionyse Settle, *A true reporte* (1577), *NAW,* 4:212; Gerard, *Herball,* 77 (maize), 780 (potatoes); Thomas Hariot, *A briefe and true report of the new found land of Virginia* (London, 1588), Cʳ.

73. On the early ritual of food gifts, see Bernadette Bucher, *Icon and Conquest: A Structural Analysis of the Illustrations of de Bry's Great Voyages,* trans. Basia Miller Gulati (Chicago, 1981), 65–85; Peter Hulme, *Colonial Encounters: Europe and the Native Caribbean, 1492–1797* (London, 1986), 147–152. Initial native reaction to European food (from Columbus's 1492 voyage) was printed in English in Eden's 1553 translation of Sebastian Munster, *Treatyse of the newe India, Eng. Books,* 28. Quotations from *Mourt's Relation,* 67 (beer), 84; Burrage, *Pory's Lost Description,* 17; Winthrop, *Journal,* 40.

74. Winthrop to Robert Boyle, July 27, 1662, printed in Fulmer Mood, ed., "John Winthrop, Jr., on Indian Corn," *NEQ,* 10 (1937), 125; Henry Wood-

ward, "A Faithfull Relation of My Westoe Voiage," 1674, in Alexander S. Salley, Jr., ed., *Narratives of Early Carolina, 1650–1708* (New York, 1911), 130.

75. [White], *Planters Plea,* 24; "Winthrop on Indian Corn," 130, 131; Thomas Ashe, *Carolina* (1682), in Salley, *Narratives of Carolina,* 146; *Certain Inducements to well minded People . . . to transport Themselves . . . into the West Indies* [London, 1643?], 4.

76. Francis Higginson, *Nevv-Englands Plantation* (London, 1630), B2^r, B3^r; [Edward Waterhouse], *A Declaration of the State of the Colony and Affaires in Virginia* (London, 1622), 5.

77. *The Generall Historie* (1624), in Smith, *Works,* 2:299; Josselyn, *Two Voyages,* 94; *Perfect Description of Virginia,* 5; Wood, *New England's Prospect,* 29.

78. Quotations from Winthrop, *Journal,* 223; John Hammond, *Leah and Rachel, or, the Two Fruitfull Sisters Virginia, and Mary-Land* (London, 1656), 10; John Lawson, *A New Voyage to Carolina* (1709), ed. Hugh Talmage Lefler (Chapel Hill, 1967), 92. See also John Archdale, *A New Description of . . . Carolina* (1707), in Salley, *Narratives of Carolina,* 290–291. On seasoning, see Darrett B. Rutman and Anita H. Rutman, "Of Agues and Fevers: Malaria in the Early Chesapeake," *WMQ,* 1976, 33 (1976), 31–60; John Duffy, "The Impact of Malaria on the South," in Todd L. Savitt and James Harvey Young, eds., *Disease and Distinctiveness in the American South* (Knoxville, Tenn., 1988), 1–21; *The Oxford English Dictionary,* 2d ed., s.v. "season," "seasoned."

79. ". . . prosper in our plantations," 97^v.

80. *Oxford English Dictionary,* s.v. "New England"; Morton, *New English Canaan,* 11 (quotation), 16 (New and old Englands); Wood, *New England's Prospect,* 27, 30; Col. Thos. Temple to Lord Fienes, December 29, 1659, 1/13, CO.

81. [Waterhouse], *Declaration,* 3; Burrage, *Pory's Lost Description,* 17; [Evelin], *New Albion,* 6; Baltimore to King Charles, August 19, 1629, 1/5, CO; Winthrop, *Journal,* 323, 414, 469, 489; James, earl of Marlborough, "Propo. concerning Jamaica," [November ? 1660], 1/14, CO.

82. Richard Eburne, *A Plain Pathway to Plantations* (1624), ed. Louis B. Wright, (Ithaca, N.Y., 1962), 12; [John Mason], *A Briefe Discovrse of the Nevv-found-land* (Edinburgh, 1620), [8]; [White], *Planters Plea,* 29–30; Christopher Levett, *A Voyage into Nevv England* (London, 1628), 25; Hammond, *Leah and Rachel,* 10; [Higginson], *Nevv-Englands Plantation,* C2^v.

83. Higginson, *Nevv-Englands Plantation,* C^r–C^v; Henry Whitfield, *The Light Appearing More and More towards the Perfect Day* (London, 1651), 45; Ashe, *Carolina,* 141.

84. Strachey, *Virginia Britania,* 116; B[ulwer], *Anthropometamorphosis,* 413; *A Relation of Maryland* (London, 1635), 7.

85. ". . . prosper in our plantations," 93^r, 98^v; [Vincent], *Late Battell,* 21.

86. Richard Hakluyt, *Principal Navigations* (London, 1589), 6:197 (suckling child); R. Rich, *Nevves from Virginia* (London, 1610), Bʳ; *Mourt's Relation,* 42, 66; Winthrop, *Journal,* 25, 27, 96; J. Franklin Jameson, ed., *[Edward] Johnson's Wonder-Working Providence, 1628–1651* (New York, 1910), 63.

87. [John Eliot], *New Englands First Fruits* (1643), in Samuel Eliot Morison, ed., *The Founding of Harvard College* (Cambridge, Mass., 1935), 441; Jameson, ed., *Johnson's Wonder-Working Providence,* 100–101; Hammond, *Leah and Rachel,* 17; Ashe, *Carolina,* 141; Gardyner, *Description of the New World,* 99.

88. Sir Edward Hext to Privy Council, November 13, 1618, SP 14/103/87, PRO; copy of affidavit of Thomas Key, June 3, 1609, Ellesmere-Bridgewater MS. 5747, HL; James, earl of Marlborough, "Propo. concerning Jamaica."

5. Death and the Birth of Race

1. Ralph Hamor, *A Trve Discovrse of the Present Estate of Virginia* (London, 1615), 15.

2. J. H. Parry, "Demographic Catastrophe," in Stanley N. Katz and John M. Murrin, eds., *Colonial America: Essays in Politics and Social Development,* 3d ed. (New York, 1983); Alfred W. Crosby, Jr., *The Columbian Exchange: Biological and Cultural Consequences of 1492* (Westport, Conn., 1972), 35–63; idem, "Virgin Soil Epidemics as a Factor in the Aboriginal Depopulation in America," *WMQ,* 33 (1976), 289–299; idem, *Ecological Imperialism: The Biological Expansion of Europe, 900–1900* (Cambridge, 1986), 196–216; William H. McNeill, *Plagues and Peoples* (Garden City, N.Y., 1976), 199–234; Henry F. Dobyns, *Their Number Become Thinned: Native American Population Dynamics in Eastern North America* (Knoxville, Tenn., 1983), esp. 8–45; Sheldon Watts, *Epidemics and History: Disease, Power, and Imperialism* (New Haven, 1997); Noble David Cook, *Born to Die: Disease and New World Conquest, 1492–1650* (Cambridge, 1998).

3. Crosby, "Virgin Soil Epidemics."

4. Compare John M. Murrin, "Beneficiaries of Catastrophe: The English Colonies in America," *The New American History,* rev. ed. (Washington, D.C., 1997), 1–28, and Elizabeth A. Fenn, "Biological Warfare in Eighteenth-Century North America: Beyond Jeffery Amherst," *JAH,* 86 (2000), 1552–80.

5. David D. Smits, "'Abominable Mixture': Toward the Repudiation of Anglo-Indian Intermarriage in Seventeenth-Century Virginia," *VMHB,* 95 (1987), 157–192.

6. See the useful overview by Shelley Fisher Fishkin, "Interrogating 'Whiteness,' Complicating 'Blackness': Remapping American Culture," in Henry B. Wonham, ed., *Criticism and the Color Line: Desegregating American Literary Studies* (New Brunswick, N.J., 1996), 251–290. Most work on "whiteness" has focused on the nineteenth century.

7. See especially Winthrop D. Jordan, *White over Black: American Attitudes to-*

ward the Negro, 1550–1812 (Chapel Hill, 1968), passim (Africans), 13–14, 22, 89, 241–242, 276–277, 477–481, 505, 535 (Indians); Edmund S. Morgan, *American Slavery, American Freedom: The Ordeal of Colonial Virginia* (New York, 1975), chaps. 2–4 (Indians), chaps. 15–16 (Africans); Alden T. Vaughan, "From White Man to Redskin: Changing Anglo-American Perceptions of the American Indian," *AHR*, 87 (1982), 917–953; idem, "The Origins Debate: Slavery and Racism in Seventeenth-Century Virginia," *VMHB*, 97 (1989), 311–354. These analyses trace the accumulation of negative opinions and socioeconomic reasons to denigrate certain visibly identifiable groups. None examines prejudice against Indians on the basis of presumed biological descent before the late eighteenth century.

Iberian discussions of Africans and innate bodily difference (especially related to disease) probably influenced debate over Indians. See Philip D. Curtin, "Epidemiology and the Slave Trade," *Political Science Quarterly*, 83 (1968), 198–211; Peter H. Wood, *Black Majority: Negroes in Colonial South Carolina from 1670 through the Stono Rebellion* (New York, 1975), 88–91. On natural slavery, see Anthony Pagden, *The Fall of Natural Man: The American Indian and the Origins of Comparative Ethnology* (Cambridge, 1986), esp. chap. 3; on creole bodies, see Jorge Cañizares Esguerra, "New World, New Stars: Patriotic Astrology and the Invention of Indian and Creole Bodies in Colonial Spanish America, 1600–1650," *AHR*, 104 (1999), 33–68; on pre-1492 European encounters with populations differently susceptible to disease, see Jerry H. Bentley, *Old World Encounters: Cross-Cultural Contacts and Exchanges in Pre-Modern Times* (New York, 1993), 181–184.

8. Ferdinando Gorges, *America Painted to the Life* (London, 1659), frontis.
9. [Nicolás Monardes], *Ioyfvll Nevves ovt of the newe founde world,* trans. Ihon Frampton (London, 1577), iijᵛ; Nancy Siraisi, *Medieval and Early Renaissance Medicine: An Introduction to Knowledge and Practice* (Chicago, 1990), 1–16.
10. [Anne Bradstreet], *The Tenth Muse Lately Sprung up in America* (London, 1650), 6, 11.
11. William Wood, *New England's Prospect* (1634), ed. Alden T. Vaughan (Amherst, Mass., 1977), 31–32; George Gardyner, *A Description of the New World* (London, 1651), 92; Samuel Wilson, *An Account of the Province of Carolina, in America* (1682), in Alexander S. Salley, Jr., ed., *Narratives of Early Carolina, 1650–1708* (New York, 1911), 169. See also John Canup, "Cotton Mather and 'Criolian Degeneracy,'" *Early American Literature*, 24 (1989), 20–34.
12. See Laurel Thatcher Ulrich, *Good Wives: Image and Reality in the Lives of Women in Northern New England, 1650–1750* (New York, 1982), 135–138, on maternal impressions. Cotton Mather was the first colonist who discussed modern ideas of generation, yet his 1720s writings on this topic, which appeared in his unpublished work "Angel of Bethesda," were idiosyn-

cratic; he referred to maternal impressions and his ideas about inheritance were underdeveloped. See Cotton Mather, *The Angel of Bethesda,* ed. Gordon W. Jones (Barre, Mass., 1972), 30–31, 44, 62, 203; Margaret Humphreys Warner, "Vindicating the Minister's Medical Role: Cotton Mather's Concept of the Nismath-Chajim and the Spiritualization of Medicine," *Journal of the History of Medicine and Allied Sciences,* 36 (1981), 278–295.

13. J. Franklin Jameson, ed., *[Edward] Johnson's Wonder-Working Providence, 1628–1651* (New York, 1910), 132, 133; Winthrop, *Journal,* 253–255 (first quotation from 255), 264–266. See also Anne Jacobson Schutte, "'Such Monstrous Births': A Neglected Aspect of the Antinomian Controversy," *Renaissance Quarterly* 38 (1985), 85–106; Valerie Pearl and Morris Pearl, eds., "Governor John Winthrop on the Birth of the Antinomians' 'Monster': The Earliest Reports to Reach England and the Making of a Myth," *MHS Pro.,* 102 (1990), 21–37.

14. Winthrop, *Journal,* 205–206; [Robert Evelin], *A Description of the Province of New Albion* ([London], 1648), 4.

15. Peter Martyr, *Decades of the Newe Worlde,* trans. Richard Eden, *Eng. Books,* 199; *The Generall Historie of Virginia, New-England, and the Summer Isles* (1624), in Smith, *Works,* 2:441; see also Bradford, *Plymouth Plan.,* 260, 364–365. On the providential view of Indian attrition, see Francis Jennings, *The Invasion of America: Indians, Colonialism, and the Cant of Conquest* (Chapel Hill, 1975), 15–31; Neal Salisbury, *Manitou and Providence: Indians, Europeans, and the Making of New England, 1500–1643* (New York, 1982), 101–109. Bernard Sheehan, *Savagism and Civility: Indians and Englishmen in Colonial Virginia* (Cambridge, 1980), 179–182, has argued that native mortality later brought feelings of guilt and softened opinions on Indians. This may have been the case for the older colonies by the turn of the seventeenth century, but does not describe earlier sentiments nor the views of colonists in newer colonies.

16. Andrew [André] Thevet, *The New found Worlde, or Antarctike,* trans. Thomas Hacket (London 1568), 70^r (manners) 71^v (elements); [Philip Vincent], *A True Relation of the Late Battel* (London, 1637), [3]; Roger Williams, *A Key into the Language of America* (1643), ed. John J. Teunissen and Evelyn J. Hinz (Detroit, 1973), 133; Edward J. Young, "Subjects for Master's Degree in Harvard College from 1655 to 1791," *MHS Pro.,* 18 (1880), 132.

17. Thomas Hariot, *A briefe and true report of the new found land of Virginia* (London, 1588), F^r, F2^r. See also Chapter 1 (Hariot); William R. Newman, *Gehennical Fire: The Lives of George Starkey, an American Alchemist in the Scientific Revolution* (Cambridge, Mass., 1994), 20–32 (Starkey and Wigglesworth).

18. Colin Platt, *King Death: The Black Death and Its Aftermath in Late-Medieval England* (London, 1996), 5; *New Atlantis* (1627), in Bacon, *Works,* 5:363.

19. Richard Ligon, *A True and Exact History of the Island of Barbados* (London, 1657), 1; Wyatt cited in *RVCL*, 4:232; Captain Warner to Secretary Windebank, September 10, 1636, 1/9, CO; Nathaniel Butler to Rich, October 23, 1620, in Vernon A. Ives, ed., *The Rich Papers: Letters from Bermuda, 1615–1646* (Toronto, 1984), 164, 194; Wood, *New England's Prospect*, 28.

20. N. A. M. Rodger, *The Safeguard of the Sea: A Naval History of Britain*, vol. 1, *660–1649* (London, 1997), 317; Governor and Council in Virginia, to Earl of Southampton and Council for Virginia Company, April 3, 1323, 11, CO; Ivor Noel Hume, *The Virginia Adventure: Roanoke to James Towne: An Archaeological and Historical Odyssey* (New York, 1994), 379 (Henrico); *Mass. Records*, 2:237 (quarantine), 280 (lifted the next year); Winthrop, *Journal*, 13, 693.

21. Gabriel Archer cited in *NAW*, 5:286; John Harvey to Viscount Dorchester, Secretary of State, April 15, 1630, 1/5, CO; Winthrop, *Journal*, 92; Virginia Company, *True declaration* (1610), *NAW*, 5:252; Ligon, *History of Barbados*, 20.

22. John West to the Lords Commissioners for Plantations, March 28, 1636, 1/9, CO; Viscount Wimbledon to Secretary Windebank, August 17, 1636, SP 16/330/44, PRO; "Beloved if wee intend to prosper in our plantations . . . ," 96^v–97^r, 1/4, CO.

23. [Monardes], *Ioyfvll Newes*, 11^r; Ligon, *History of Barbados*, 32; [Robert Child], *Samuel Hartlib His Legacie* (London, 1651), 94.

24. Edward Daunce, *A Briefe Discovrse of the Spanish State* (London, 1590), 28 (French), 29 (cannibals); Richard Hakluyt, *A Discourse of Western Planting* (1584), *NAW*, 3:77; Martin Pring, voyage to Virginia, 1603, *NAW*, 3:361; Gardyner, *Description of the New World*, 100.

25. Philip Hermanus, comp., *An excellent Treatise teaching howe to cure the French-Pockes* (London, 1590), 32; prescription, Ellesmere-Bridgewater, Ms. 6180, 1^r, HL; Thomas Harriot, Mathematical Papers, 515^r, Add. MS. 6789, BL.

26. Hermanus, *Excellent Treatise*, 31, 35, 39, 40–63; *Some Observations Made upon the Bermudas Berries* (London, 1694), 4, 5; [Child], *Hartlib His Legacie*, 94; MS. Rawlinson C.406, ff. 79–80, Bodleian.

27. Roger Williams to Henry Vane and John Winthrop, May 1, 1637, in Williams, *Correspondence*, 1:72.

28. Ralph Lane, narrative of Roanoke, 1585–86, *NAW*, 3:301.

29. Archer quoted in *NAW*, 5:276.

30. Winthrop, *Journal*, 403; William Powrey to Archibald Hay, June 13, 1648, Hay of Hayston Muniments, GD 34/834, NAS; William Vaughan, *Newlanders Cure* (London, 1630), A3^r, 99; John Graunt, *Natural and Political Observations . . . Made upon the Bills of Mortality* (London, 1662), 16.

31. Bradford, *Plymouth Plan.*, 114; Governor Argall to Virginia Company of London, March 10, 1618, *RVCL*, 3:92; Winthrop, *Journal*, 108–109, 273, 690.

368 · Notes to Pages 175–180

32. John Josselyn, *New-Englands Rarities Discovered*, 2nd ed. (London, 1675), 46; John Hammond, *Leah and Rachel, or the Two Fruitfull Sisters Virginia, and Mary-Land* (London, 1656), 15; *Publick Good without Private Interest* (London, 1657), 1; "John Clayton's Account of the Medical Practices of the Virginia Indians," *Ethnohistory*, 11 (1964), 3, which discusses Add. MS. 4437, 85ʳ, BL.

33. *Oxford English Dictionary*, 2d ed., s.v. "native"; J[ohn] B[ulwer], *Anthropometamorphosis: Man Transformed, or, the Artificiall Changling* (London, 1653), 2ᵛ.

34. [Robert Hayman], *Quodlibets, Lately Come over from New Britaniola, Old Newfound-Land* (London, 1628), A2ʳ (wits), 19, 31 (elements), 33; Kenneth Silverman, ed., *Selected Letters of Cotton Mather* (Baton Rouge, La., 1971), 398; William Byrd, *Histories of the Dividing Line between Virginia and North Carolina*, ed. William K. Boyd (New York, 1967), 46–57.

35. Joseph [José de] Acosta, *The Naturall and Morall Historie of the East and West Indies*, trans. E[dward] G[rimeston] (London, 1604), 253–260; John Parkinson, *Paradisi in Sole Paradisus Terrestris, or a Garden* (London, 1629), 87; Sarah P. Stetson, "The Traffic in Seeds and Plants from England's Colonies in North America," *Agricultural History*, 23 (1949), 45–56; Joseph Kastner, *A Species of Eternity* (New York, 1978); Richard Drayton, *Nature's Government: Science, Imperial Britain, and the "Improvement" of the World* (New Haven, 2000).

36. William Shakespeare, *The Tempest* (1611), 2.1.31–32. On Indian deaths in Europe, see Alden T. Vaughan, "Trinculo's Indian: American Natives in Shakespeare's England," in Peter Hulme and William H. Sherman, eds., *The Tempest and Its Travels* (London, 2000); Anthony Pagden, *European Encounters with the New World: From Renaissance to Romanticism* (New Haven, 1993), 31–33; Richmond P. Bond, *Queen Anne's American Kings* (Oxford, 1952), 3, 80, 98 (Iroquois).

37. Dionyse Settle, *A True Report of the Last Voyage* (1577), *NAW*, 4:214; MS. Eng. th. c.50, 72ʳ, Bodleian; John Lawson, *A New Voyage to Carolina* (1709), ed. Hugh Talmage Lefler (Chapel Hill, 1967), 172, 173.

38. See Williams, *Language of America*, 243, 244–245; Robert Beverley, *The History and Present State of Virginia* (1705), ed. Louis B. Wright (Charlottesville, Va., 1947), 9, 217, 232.

39. Sherburne F. Cook, "Interracial Warfare and Population Decline among the New England Indians," *Ethnohistory*, 20 (1973), 1–24; John Harvey to Viscount Dorchester, Secretary of State, April 15, 1630, 1/5, CO; [Vincent], *Late Battell*, 17, 20; Peter Heylyn, *Cosmographie in Four Books*, 2d ed. (London, 1657), 1094; Josselyn, *Two Voyages*, 89.

40. Josselyn, *Two Voyages*, 89; Gorges, *America Painted to the Life*, A2ᵛ, 51; Ferdinando Gorges the younger, *A Briefe Narration of the Originall Undertakings of the Advancement of Plantations* (London, 1658), 54.

41. Jameson, ed., *Johnson's Wonder-Working Providence*, 41, 48–49; Edward

Winslow to John Winthrop, May 22, 1637, *Winthrop Papers,* 3:420; Hammond, *Leah and Rachel,* 17.

42. [John White], *The Planters Plea* (London, 1630), 25.

43. William Clowes, *A short and profitable Treatise touching the cure of the disease called (Morbus Gallicus) by Unctions* (London, 1579), Biii^r; Winthrop, *Journal,* 620–621.

44. Platt, *King Death,* 98–101; Paul Slack, *The Impact of Plague in Tudor and Stuart England* (London, 1985), 288–291; Thomas Niccolls to Sir John Wolstenholme, April 2, 1623, *RVCL,* 4:231–232; Champlin Burrage, ed., *John Pory's Lost Description of Plymouth Colony in the Earliest Days of the Pilgrim Fathers* (Boston, 1918), 8–9; Cook, *Born to Die,* 200 (quarantine).

45. *Va. Statutes,* 1:316–317; Hammond, *Leah and Rachel,* 14; town of Providence to Nathaniel Patten, February 12, 1667, in Williams, *Correspondence,* 2:555.

46. Bradford, *Plymouth Plan.,* 270–271; Winthrop, *Journal,* 101, 105.

47. Bradford, *Plymouth Plan.,* 58, 260.

48. Williams to John Winthrop, July 10, 1637, *Correspondence,* 1:94; Winthrop, *Journal,* 105.

49. Edward Maria Wingfield's account, May 1607–May 1608, *NAW,* 5:278; George Best, *True Report* (1578), *Frobisher Voyages,* 143; postmortem report by Dr. Edward Dodding, *NAW,* 4:217; Morgan, *American Slavery, American Freedom,* 100 (poisoning); Roger Williams to [General Court of Commissioners of Providence Plantations?], August 25, 1658, in Williams, *Correspondence,* 2:489.

50. Smith, *Generall Historie,* 2:121; Williams, *Language of America,* 244, 245; Williams to Winthrop, ca. August 1651, in Williams, *Correspondence,* 1:336.

51. *Mourt's Relation,* 123; Sydney V. James, Jr., ed., *Three Visitors to Early Plymouth* (Plymouth, Mass., 1963), 31; Bradford, *Plymouth Plan.,* 271.

52. *Mourt's Relation,* 89 (Samoset), 93.

53. William Shakespeare, *Historie of Henry V* (1590), 3.5.10; Smits, "'Abominable Mixture,'" 181–182; Notes for Ralegh and Cavendish, ca. 1584–85, *NAW,* 3:275 (Roanoke); "Lawes divine, morall and martiall," June 22, 1611, *NAW,* 5:222 (Jamestown); Balthazar Gerbier, *A Sommary Description . . .* ([Rotterdam], 1660), A2^r.

54. Daunce, *Discovrse of the Spanish State,* 9; *Certain Inducements to Well minded People . . . to transport Themselves . . . into the West Indies* [London, 1643?], 13.

55. ". . . prosper in our plantations," 92^v, CO; Smith, *Generall Historie,* 2:257, 262 (quotation); Edward Arber, ed., *Travels and Works of Captain John Smith,* 2 vols. (Edinburgh, 1910), 1:165; *Publick Good without Private Interest,* 1.

56. *Mourt's Relation,* 101, 135; Winthrop, *Journal,* 449, 611.

57. Bradford, *Plymouth Plan.,* 233; Winthrop, *Journal,* 388; Roger Williams to

the General Court of Massachusetts Bay, May 12, 1656, *Correspondence*, 2:451.

58. Peter Hulme, *Colonial Encounters: Europe and the Native Caribbean, 1492–1797* (London, 1986), 147–152; Smits, "'Abominable Mixture,'" 180 (Bermuda); Hume, *The Virginia Adventure* (Dale's proposal), 332; *Mass. Records*, 1:140.

59. *Mourt's Relation*, 129; Winthrop, *Journal*, 56 (quotation); *Mass. Records*, 91 (Dawe's sentence); Josselyn, *Two Voyages*, 90.

60. Israel Stoughton to John Winthrop, ca. June 28, 1637, *Winthrop Papers*, 3:435; Roger Williams to John Winthrop, November 10, 1637, in Williams, *Correspondence*, 1:132.

61. Commonplace book of Thomas Gray, MS. Malone 16, 40, Bodleian; Josselyn, *New Englands Rarities Discovered*, 99, 101; ". . . prosper in our plantations," 98ᵣ.

62. Roger Williams to John Winthrop, January 10, 1637, in Williams, *Correspondence*, 1:126 (child), 140 (quotation); William Coddington to John Winthrop, May 22, 1640, *Winthrop Papers*, 4:247; Wood, *New England's Prospect*, 83; Thomas Morton, *New English Canaan, or New Canaan* (Amsterdam, 1637), 32.

63. James Axtell, "The White Indians of Colonial America," *WMQ*, 32 (1975), 55–88; Brewton Berry, "America's Mestizos," in Noel P. Gist and Anthony Gary Dworkin, eds., *The Blending of Races: Marginality and Identity in World Perspective* (New York, 1972), esp. 194–197; Gary B. Nash, "The Hidden History of Mestizo America," *JAH*, 82 (1995), 941–962. Berry and Nash portray mestizo populations as typical of North America, though the groups they trace only entered the public record in the eighteenth century.

64. Ligon, *History of Barbados*, 12–13, 15–17.

65. Hilary McD. Beckles, *White Servitude and Black Slavery in Barbados, 1627–1715* (Knoxville, Tenn., 1989), 118–121.

66. [Henry Neville], *The Isle of Pines, or, A late Discovery of a fourth Island in Terra Australis, Incognita* (London, 1668), 4 (second quotation), 6; Henri Justel to Henry Oldenburg, July 1668, in Oldenburg, *Correspondence*, 4:564.

67. [George Wateson], *The Cvres of the Diseased, in remote Regions* (London, 1598), B2ᵛ (epidemics), C2ʳ–C2ᵛ (tobacco); Crosby, *Columbian Exchange*, 122–164; Anthony Grafton, *New Worlds, Ancient Texts: The Power of Tradition and the Shock of Discovery* (Cambridge, Mass., 1992), 159–194; Saul Jarcho, *Quinine's Predecessor: Francesco Torti and the Early History of Cinchona* (Baltimore, 1993), esp. chap. 4 (cinchona in England) and 240–244 (fevers as environmentally caused).

68. Raymond Phineas Stearns, *Science in the British Colonies of America* (Urbana, Ill., 1970), 30–31 (Monardes); Charles Webster, "Alchemical and Paracelsian Medicine," in Webster, ed., *Health, Medicine, and Mortality in the Sixteenth Century* (Cambridge, 1979), 326 (quotation), 69n.

69. William Strachey, *The Historie of Travell into Virginia Britania* (1612), ed. Louis B. Wright and Virginia Freund (London, 1953), 113; William Vaughan, *Natvrall and artificiall directions for health* (London, 1600), 66–67, and *Newlanders Cure,* 17 (diet), 44–45; Joyce Lorimer, ed., *English and Irish Settlement on the River Amazon, 1550–1646* (London, 1989), 131–135 (English, quotation on 135), 266 (Irish), 279 (English); Hariot, *Briefe and true report,* B2ʳ.

70. John Duffy, "Medicine and Medical Practices among Aboriginal American Indians," in Felix Martí-Ibanez, ed., *The History of American Medicine: A Symposium* (New York, 1958), 15–33; Richard Harrison Shryock, *Medicine and Society in America, 1660–1860* (New York, 1960), 48. Hariot, *Briefe and true report,* C3ᵛ; Robert Burton, *The Anatomy of Melancholy,* ed. Thomas C. Faulkner, Nicolas K. Kiessling, and Rhonda L. Blair, 3 vols. (Oxford, 1989), 230; Josselyn, *Two Voyages,* 43–44; [Child], *Hartlib His Legacie,* 94; Thomas Ashe, *Carolina* (1682), in Salley, *Narratives of Early Carolina,* 156.

71. John Gerard, *The Herball or Generall Historie of Plantes* (London, 1597), 273, 1357; court minutes, MS. 8200/2, Worshipful Society of Apothecaries of London Archives, Guildhall Library, London.

72. Parkinson, *Paradisi,* 153; *A Relation of Maryland* (London, 1635), 17; Marquis of Lansdowne, ed., *The Petty Papers* (New York, 1967), 2:118; George Alsop, *A Character of the Province of Mary-Land* (1666), ed. John Gilmary Shea (New York, 1869), 64, 65.

73. Morton, *New English Canaan,* 36; Ligon, *History of Barbados,* 65.

74. Wood, *New England's Prospect,* 94.

6. How Improvement Trumped Hybridity

1. Winthrop, *Journal,* 684.

2. On settlement: David Grayson Allen, *In English Ways: The Movement of Societies and the Transferal of English Local Law and Custom to Massachusetts Bay in the Seventeenth Century* (Chapel Hill, 1981); William Cronon, *Changes in the Land: Indians, Colonists, and the Ecology of New England* (New York, 1983); Jack P. Greene, *Pursuits of Happiness: The Social Development of Early Modern British Colonies and the Formation of American Culture* (Chapel Hill, 1988); David Hackett Fischer, *Albion's Seed: Four British Folkways in America* (New York, 1989); Timothy Silver, *A New Face on the Countryside: Indians, Colonists, and Slaves in South Atlantic Forests, 1500–1800* (New York, 1990); James Horn, *Adapting to a New World: English Society in the Seventeenth-Century Chesapeake* (Chapel Hill, 1994). On Indian country: Daniel K. Richter, *The Ordeal of the Longhouse: The Peoples of the Iroquois League in the Era of European Colonization* (Chapel Hill, 1992); Francis Jennings, *The Founders of America* (New York, 1993); Colin Calloway, *The American Revolution in Indian Country: Crisis and Di-*

versity in Native American Communities (New York, 1995). On the Indians' new world: James H. Merrell, *The Indians' New World: Catawbas and Their Neighbors from European Contact through the Era of Removal* (Chapel Hill, 1989); Virginia DeJohn Anderson, "King Philip's Herds: Indians, Colonists, and the Problem of Livestock in Early New England," *WMQ,* 51 (1994), 601–624; Jill Lepore, *The Name of War: King Philip's War and the Origins of American Identity* (New York, 1998), which stresses Indians' anglicization. On middle grounds: Richard White, *The Middle Ground: Indians, Empires, and Republics in the Great Lakes Region, 1650–1815* (New York, 1991); Daniel H. Usner, Jr., *Indians, Settlers, and Slaves in a Frontier Exchange Economy: The Lower Mississippi Valley before 1783* (Chapel Hill, 1992); James H. Merrell, *Into the American Woods: Negotiators on the Pennsylvania Frontier* (New York, 1999).

Some scholars have stressed the hybridity between settlement areas and Indian cultures without explaining the English understanding of this. See James Axtell, "North America without the Indians: Counterfactual Reflections," *JAH,* 73 (1987), 981–996; Jack Weatherford, *Native Roots: How the Indians Enriched America* (New York, 1991); Patrick M. Malone, *The Skulking Way of War: Technology and Tactics among the New England Indians* (Baltimore, 1993); Colin Calloway, *New Worlds for All: Indians, Europeans, and the Remaking of Early America* (Baltimore, 1997).

3. [Francis Higginson], *Nevv-Englands Plantation* (London, 1630), [C4^r].
4. Champlin Burrage, ed., *John Pory's Lost Description of Plymouth Colony in the Earliest Days of the Pilgrim Fathers* (Boston, 1918), 17; John Hammond, *Leah and Rachel, or the Two Fruitfull Sisters Virginia, and Mary-Land* (London, 1656), 10; Christopher Levett, *A Voyage into Nevv England* (London, 1628), 22.
5. Edward Pellham, *Gods Power and Providence: Shewed, In the Miracvlous Preservation and Deliverance of Eight Englishmen, Left by Mischance in Green-land* (London, 1631), A2^r, 3–5 (property), 17–22 (conditions, quotation 20); Francis Kirby to John Winthrop, Jr., November 26, 1631, *Winthrop Papers,* 3:56.
6. *A Commission for . . . New-found-land* (London, 1633), 7–8; Winthrop, *Journal,* 748.
7. John Nicholl, *An Houre Glasse of Indian Newes* (London, 1607), D3^v; Levett, *Voyage into Nevv England,* 4; Jonathan Brewster to John Winthrop, Jr., June 18, 1636, *Winthrop Papers,* 3:270–271.
8. "Occurrents in Newfoundland," 1612–13, *NAW,* 4:162; *Mourt's Relation,* 20 (bow), 22, 34, 37.
9. Winthrop, *Journal,* 227 (booty), 625–626 (tribute); John Underhill, *Newes from America* (1638), *Massachusetts Historical Society Collections,* 3d ser., 6 (1837), 7; Thomas Shepard, *The Clear Sunshine of the Gospel Breaking Forth upon the Indians in New-England* (London, 1648), 41–42; Josselyn, *Two Voyages,* 101, 102.

10. William Strachey, "True Reportory" (1610), *NAW,* 5:295; Winthrop, *Journal,* 40, 41, 43 (English wigwams), 367–368, 740 (boats); *The Generall Historie of Virginia, New-England, and the Summer Isles* (1624), in Smith, *Works,* 2:94, 289; Shepard, *Clear Sunshine of the Gospel,* 7.

11. James Rosier, *A true relation of the Most Prosperous Voyage* (1605), *NAW,* 3:371; Levett, *Voyage into Nevv England,* 8; Williams, *Correspondence,* 1:172 (murder).

12. Nicholl, *Indian Newes,* C2ᵛ, Eᵛ.

13. *Mourt's Relation,* 94, 109–110; Winthrop, *Journal,* 47, 411; Williams, *Correspondence,* 2:496; [Edward Winslow], *The Day-Breaking if not the Sun-Rising of the Gospell with the* INDIANS *in New-England* (London, 1647), 9.

14. Edmund S. Morgan, *American Slavery, American Freedom: The Ordeal of Colonial Virginia* (New York, 1976), 72–75, 81, 86–87, 89–90; *Mourt's Relation,* 21, 30, 64, 100, 115; William Wood, *New England's Prospect* (1634), ed. Alden T. Vaughan (Amherst, Mass., 1977), 89.

15. *A Relation of Maryland* (London, 1635), 9; *Mass. Records,* 1:201; Edward Williams, *Virgo Triumphans: or, Virginia richly and truly valued* (London, 1650), 41; Lion Gardiner to John Winthrop, Jr., November 6, 1636, *Winthrop Papers,* 3:320.

16. Ralph Lane, narrative of Roanoke, 1585–86, *NAW,* 3:301, 302; *Mass. Records,* 1:201; Isaack de Rasieres to Samuel Blommaert, ca. 1628, in Sydney V. James, ed., *Three Visitors to Early Plymouth* (Plymouth, Mass., 1963), 75; Winthrop, *Journal,* 65. See also Lynn Ceci, "Fish Fertilizer: A Native North American Practice?" *Science,* 188 (1975), 26–30; illus. of English medieval fish weirs, in Charles Singer et al., eds., *A History of Technology* (Oxford, 1957), 2:7 596, fig. 543.

17. Martin Pring, voyage to Virginia, 1603, *NAW,* 3:361; *Mourt's Relation,* 100, 137; William Strachey, *The Historie of Travell into Virginia Britania* (1612), ed. Louis B. Wright and Virginia Freund (London, 1953), 130; *Relation of Maryland,* 10, 22–23.

18. Williams, *Correspondence,* 1:234; John Winthrop, Jr., to Robert Boyle, July 27, 1662, printed in Fulmer Mood, ed., "John Winthrop, Jr., on Indian Corn," *NEQ,* 10 (1937), 125–133 (quotations 127, 129); Roger Williams, *A Key into the Language of America* (1643), ed. John J. Teunissen and Evelyn J. Hinz (Detroit, 1973), 101.

19. Winthrop, *Journal,* 478, 601–602 (Castle Island), 732, 734, 735 (plans); [Philip Vincent], *A True Relation of the Late Battell fought in New England* (London, 1637), 13.

20. Strachey, "True Reportory," 293; Joyce Lorimer, ed., *English and Irish Settlement on the River Amazon, 1550–1646* (London, 1989), 343; Winthrop, *Journal,* 149, 340.

21. *NAW,* 3:425–426; Winthrop, *Journal,* 184, 321–322, 391, 517.

22. Nicholl, *Indian Newes,* B3ᵛ, Cʳ; Burrage, *John Pory's Lost Description,* 49; *Mourt's Relation,* 103; Winthrop, *Journal,* 630, 689 (Dobson); Roger Wil-

liams to John Winthrop, Jr., ca. April 7, 1649, Williams, *Correspondence,* 1:279.

23. John Martin, "The Manner Howe to Bringe the Indians into Subiection," December 15, 1622, *RVCL,* 3:704; Jonathan Brewster to John Winthrop, Jr., June 18, 1636, *Winthrop Papers,* 3:270; Winthrop, *Journal,* 179–180; *Mass. Records,* 3:425; Josselyn, *Two Voyages,* 23, also 102. See also Horace P. Beck, *The American Indian as a Sea-Fighter in Colonial Times* (Mystic, Conn., 1959).

24. Williams, *Correspondence,* 1:196, 252; Josselyn, *Two Voyages,* 102. Cf. the account of two Indian women whipped in 1640 "for their insolent carryage, & abusing Mrs Weld," in *Mass. Records,* 1:297.

25. John Winthrop, "A Description of the Artifice and making of Tarr and Pitch in New England," C1.P.III (i), 23ʳ–24ʳ, RS; *Mass. Records,* 2:84–86; *Va. Statutes,* 1:457; John Josselyn, *New-Englands Rarities Discovered,* 2nd ed. (London, 1675), 51, 59–60.

26. Richard Ligon, *A True and Exact History of the Island of Barbados* (London, 1657), 23–24 (pots), 30 (cassava), 42 (bricks), 54 (Indians versus Africans), 118 (drugs).

27. William Hughes, *The American Physitian* (London, 1672), 16, 45, 77 (Spanish and Africans), 65, 90, 92 (Indians).

28. Lewis Hughes to Sir Robert Rich, May 19, 1617, in Vernon A. Ives, ed., *The Rich Papers: Letters from Bermuda, 1615–1646* (Toronto, 1984), 14; Ligon, *History of Barbados,* 15 (wine), 56–59.

29. Ligon, *History of Barbados,* 33, 84 (pineapple), 104 (exchange of pleasures).

30. Ibid., 85.

31. C. H. Firth, ed., *The Narrative of General Venables* (London, 1900), 49 (natives destroyed), 134 (drinking stragglers), 113 (Cromwell's mistake), 148 (Martinique), 156 (Spanish Jamaica).

32. Balthazar Gerbier, *A Sommary Description, Manifesting that greater Profits are to bee done in the hott then in the could parts off the Coast off America* ([Rotterdam], 1660), [A4ʳ], Bʳ (labor); Henry Whistler's "Journal," in Firth, *Narrative of General Venables,* 146.

33. James Parker to John Winthrop, June 24, 1646, *Winthrop Papers,* 5:84; Ligon, *History of Barbados,* 31.

34. Strachey, *Virginia Britania,* 34, 79; Bradford, *Plymouth Plan.,* 87; Thomas Morton, *New English Canaan, or New Canaan* (Amsterdam, 1637), 43; John Winthrop to John Winthrop, Jr., November 16, 1646, *Winthrop Papers,* 5:119.

35. Bradford, *Plymouth Plan.,* 207; Williams, *Language of America,* 235; John Eliot, *A further Account of the Progress of the Gospel amongst the Indians in New England* (London, 1660), 11; George Alsop, *A Character of the Province of Mary-Land* (1666), ed. John Gilmary Shea (New York, 1869), map facing 35; Josselyn, *Two Voyages,* 103–104; J. Franklin Jameson, ed., *[Edward] Johnson's Wonder-Working Providence, 1628–1651* (New York, 1910), 221.

36. [John Eliot], *The Glorious Progress of the Gospel amongst the Indians in New England* (London, 1649), 18; idem, *A Late and Further Manifestation of the Progress of the Gospel Amongst the Indians in Nevv-England* (London, 1655), 1–2; Henry Whitfield, *The Light Appearing More and More toward the Perfect Day* (London, 1651), 35; Hammond, *Leah and Rachel*, 20; [John Eliot], *New Englands First Fruits* (1643), in Samuel Eliot Morison, *The Founding of Harvard College* (Cambridge, Mass., 1935), 423; Shepard, *Clear Sunshine of the Gospel*, 25.

37. [Eliot], *Glorious Progress of the Gospel*, [7–8], 15–16; Whitfield, *Light Appearing*, 39–40.

38. [Henry Whitfield], *Strength out of VVeaknesse . . .* (London, 1652), 3, 4, 14–15, 29–30; idem, *Tears of Repentence* (London, 1653), [C3ᵛ] (fences), 1–2 (meetinghouse).

39. Morton, *New English Canaan*, 53; Josselyn, *Two Voyages*, 67.

40. Williams, *Language of America*, 122; Daniel Gookin, *Historical Collections of the Indians in New England*, ed. Jeffrey H. Fiske (Towtaid, N.J., 1970), 16.

41. Underhill, *Newes from America*, 6; Winthrop, *Journal*, 246; Whitfield, *Light Appearing*, 4, 8; Josselyn, *Two Voyages*, 95; Winslow, *Day-Breaking*, 31; protest of inhabitants of New London, *Winthrop Papers*, 5:124 (New London); Gookin, *Indians in New England*, 40; [Whitfield], *Strength out of VVeaknesse*, 19.

42. [Robert Evelin], *A Description of the Province of New Albion* ([London], 1648), 29; Winthrop, *Journal*, 465, 466 (vines), 644 (Conn.), 732, 733 (sketches).

43. Winthrop, *Journal*, 410; Levett, *Voyage into Nevv England*, 10, 16.

44. Emmanuel Altham to Sir Edward Altham, September 1623, in James, *Three Visitors to Early Plymouth*, 29.

45. Ralph Hamor, *A Trve Discovrse of the Present Estate of Virginia* (London, 1615), 44–45. Powhatan had earlier asked for an English coach and three horses; see Strachey, "True Reportory," 298.

46. Governor and Council in Virginia to Earl of Southampton and Council for Virginia Company, April 3, 1623, 1/1, CO; *Va. Statutes*, 1:396, 455, 481, 546.

47. Williams, *Correspondence*, 1:237–238; Richard Morris to John Coggeshall, ca. May 22, 1647, *Winthrop Papers*, 5:164 (see also 165). On the growth and persistence of an English trade in Indian slaves, see Almon Wheeler Lauber, *Indian Slavery in Colonial Times within the Present Limits of the United States* (New York, 1913), esp. chaps. 4–9.

48. Winthrop, *Journal*, 124.

49. William Allen and Thomas Collough to Lord Protector and Council, September 8, 1657, 1/13, CO; Winthrop, *Journal*, 346, 353, 458; Jameson, ed., *Johnson's Wonder-Working Providence*, 183.

50. Joel Munsell, *Chronology of the Origin and Progress of Paper and Paper-Making* (New York, 1980), 27–31; Dard Hunter, *Papermaking in Pioneer*

America (New York, 1981), 9–10, 20–32; Richard L. Hills, *Papermaking in Britain, 1488–1988: A Short History* (London, 1988), 4–53; D. D. Hogarth, P. W. Boreham, and J. G. Mitchell, *Mines, Minerals, and Metallurgy: Martin Frobisher's Northwest Venture, 1576–1581* (Hull, Quebec, 1994), 83, 85.

51. *Winthrop Papers*, 3:83 (Kirby); 4:29 (Sandbrooke), 135 (Sparhawk); 5:162 (ink).

52. *Va. Statutes*, 1:319; Winthrop, *Journal*, 331, 565; *Mass. Records*, 2:136 (export restrictions); Williams, *Correspondence*, 2:445 (plea for gunpowder).

53. *Mass. Records*, 2:99; John Russell Bartlett, ed., *Records of the Colony of Rhode Island and Providence Plantations* (Providence, 1856), 1:186–187; Whitfeld, *Light Appearing*, 42.

54. Firth, *Narrative of General Venables*, 9; *Va. Statutes*, 1:151.

55. Edward Howes to John Winthrop, Jr., April 18, 1634, *Winthrop Papers*, 3:165.

56. Nicholas Tyacke, "Science and Religion at Oxford before the Civil War," in D. Pennington and Keith Thomas, eds., *Puritans and Revolutionaries* (Oxford, 1978), 73–83; Lorimer, *English and Irish Settlement on the Amazon*, 104–106, 365–366, 385–386; Mea Allan, *The Tradescants, Their Plants, Gardens, and Museum* (London, 1964); Raymond Phineas Stearns, *Science in the British Colonies of America* (Urbana, Ill., 1970), 48–50; Charles Webster, *The Great Instauration: Science, Medicine, and Reform, 1626–1660* (London, 1975), 320.

57. Emmanuel Altham to Sir Edward Altham, September 1623 and June 10, 1625, in James, *Three Visitors to Early Plymouth*, 35, 58 (quotation); John Tinker to John Winthrop, February 26, 1640, *Winthrop Papers*, 4:206; Emanuel Downing to John Winthrop, Jr., November 21, 1632, ibid., 3:93. See also Arthur MacGregor, "'A Magazin of all manner of Inventions': Museums in the Quest for 'Salomon's House' in Seventeenth-Century England," *Journal of the History of Collections*, 1 (1989), 207–212; Paula Findlen, *Possessing Nature: Museums, Collecting, and Scientific Culture in Early Modern Italy* (Berkeley, 1994); Christian F. Feest, "The Collecting of American Indian Artifacts in Europe, 1493–1750," in Karen Ordahl Kupperman, ed., *America in European Consciousness, 1493–1750* (Chapel Hill, 1995); Lorraine Daston and Katharine Park, *Wonders and the Order of Nature, 1150–1750* (New York, 1998), 265–290.

58. Stearns, *Science in the British Colonies of America*, 49–50; Webster, *Great Instauration*, 320; Robert Child to John Winthrop, Jr., June 27, 1643, *Winthrop Papers*, 4:395; Ligon, *History of Barbados*, 63.

59. John Tradescant, *Musaeum Tradescantianum: or, A Collection of Rarities* (London, 1656), 43 (cassava and Drake's trunion), 45 (weapons), 46 (tomahawks and knife), 49 (hatbands and Boleyn's clothing), 51 (wampum).

60. Wait Winthrop to Henry Oldenburg, October 17, 1671, in Oldenburg, *Correspondence*, 8:305.

61. Robert K. Merton, *Science, Technology, and Society in Seventeenth Century*

England (New York, 1970), 112–123; Webster, *Great Instauration*, chaps. 1, 2; J. R. Jacob, *Robert Boyle and the English Revolution: A Study in Social and Intellectual Change* (New York, 1977), 16–38; Charles Webster, *From Paracelsus to Newton: Magic and the Making of Modern Science* (Cambridge, 1982), 15–47; Margaret C. Jacob, *The Cultural Meaning of the Scientific Revolution* (Philadelphia, 1988), 74–76; David D. Hall, *Worlds of Wonder, Days of Judgment: Popular Religious Belief in Early New England* (New York, 1989), 72–77; William R. Newman, *Gehennical Fire: The Lives of George Starkey, an American Alchemist in the Scientific Revolution* (Cambridge, Mass., 1994), 55–58.

62. Webster, *Great Instauration*, 47–51, 57–67, 85–87; Newman, *Gehennical Fire*, 18–20.

63. Newman, *Gehennical Fire*, 41; George Lyman Kittredge, "Dr. Robert Child the Remonstrant," *PCSM*, 21 (1919), 103–108; [Robert Child], *Samuel Hartlib His Legacie: or An Enlargement of the Discourse of Husbandry* (London, 1651), 12, 78–79, 80.

64. [Child], *Hartlib His Legacie*, 32 (grape), 46 (fish in corn), 94 (grandame).

65. Ibid., 24–25. On forest conservation, see Clarence J. Glacken, *Traces on the Rhodian Shore: Nature and Culture in Western Thought from Ancient Times to the End of the Eighteenth Century* (Berkeley, 1967), 484–491; Stearns, *Science in the British Colonies of America*, 122–125; Keith Thomas, *Man and the Natural World: Changing Attitudes in England, 1500–1800* (New York, 1983), 192–212; Richard H. Grove, *Green Imperialism: Colonial Expansion, Tropical Island Edens, and the Origins of Environmentalism, 1600–1860* (Cambridge, 1995), 55–72.

66. [Child], *Hartlib His Legacie*, 53 (kingdoms), 69, 73 (silk), 81.

67. Winthrop, *Journal*, 738–739; Kittredge, "Doctor Robert Child," esp. 4–17, 98–146; Ronald Sterne Wilkinson, "George Starkey, Physician and Alchemist," *Ambix*, 11 (1963), 121–152; Stearns, *Science in the British Colonies of America*, 151–152; Richard S. Dunn, *Puritans and Yankees: The Winthrop Dynasty of New England, 1630–1717* (Princeton, 1962), chap. 4; Newman, *Gehennical Fire*, 14–91.

68. Kittredge, "Doctor Robert Child," 98–131; George H. Haynes, "'The Tale of Tantiusques': An Early Mining Venture in Massachusetts," American Antiquarian Society, *Proceedings*, n.s., 14 (1901), 471–497; William R. Carlton, "Overland to Connecticut in 1645: A Travel Diary of John Winthrop, Jr.," *NEQ*, 13 (1940), 494–510; Stearns, *Science in the British Colonies of America*, 119; Newman, *Gehennical Fire*, 170–208.

69. *Mass. Records*, 1:327 (1641 law); ibid., 2:242 (1648 law); Williams, *Virgo Triumphans*, 5, 6, 17, 35.

70. William Pynchon to Stephen Day, October 8, 1644, deeds of Webucksham and Nonmonshot and of Nodawahunt, October 8 and November 11, 1644, agreement between Thomas King and Winthrop, November 27, 1644, *Winthrop Papers*, 4:495, 496–497, 497; deed of Wobucksham and Wash-

como, January 20, 1645, ibid., 5:4–5; Haynes, "The Tale of Tantiusques," 478.

71. Council of the Virginia Company to the governor and council in Virginia, December 5, 1621, *RVCL*, 3:533; Haynes, "Tale of Tantiusques," 474; Carlton, "Travel Diary of John Winthrop, Jr.," 504, 505; Jonathan Brewster to John Winthrop, Jr., December 1, 1648, *Winthrop Papers*, 5:286; William Berkeley to John Winthrop, Jr., June 25, 1648, ibid., 232; Roger Williams to John Winthrop, Jr., May 22, 1664, Williams, *Correspondence*, 2:527. On "glasses" as chemical equipment, see John Steward to Winthrop, July 22, 1631, *Winthrop Papers*, 3:45–46.

72. Steven Shapin, *A Social History of Truth: Civility and Science in Seventeenth-Century England* (Chicago, 1994), chap. 8; G. Malcolm Lewis, ed., *Cartographic Encounters: Perspectives on Native American Mapmaking and Map Use* (Chicago, 1998).

73. Shepard, *Clear Sunshine of the Gospel*, 37–38.

7. Gender and the Artificial Indian Body

1. [Edward Waterhouse], *A Declaration of the State of the Colony and Affaires in Virginia* (London, 1622), 14.

2. Cf. Elaine Scarry, *The Body in Pain: The Making and Unmaking of the World* (New York, 1985), which focuses on the modern experience of pain yet implies its universal qualities.

3. See Chapter 4, note 6.

4. William Wood, *New England's Prospect* (1634), ed. Alden T. Vaughan (Amherst, Mass., 1977), 93; Roger Williams, *A Key into the Language of America* (1643), ed. John J. Teunissen and Evelyn J. Hinz (Detroit, 1973), 131.

5. Karen Ordahl Kupperman, *Settling with the Indians: The Meeting of English and Indian Cultures in America, 1580–1640* (London, 1980), 60–62; Bernard W. Sheehan, *Savagism and Civility: Indians and Englishmen in Colonial Virginia* (Cambridge, 1980), 93–94; James Axtell, *The Invasion Within: The Contest of Cultures in Colonial North America* (New York, 1985), 151–155; Kathleen M. Brown, *Good Wives, Nasty Wenches, and Anxious Patriarchs: Gender, Race, and Power in Colonial Virginia* (Chapel Hill, 1996), 57–58, 83–88. Wood, *New England's Prospect*, 94–97 (quotation on 94).

6. Winfried Schleiner, "*Divina Virago*: Queen Elizabeth as an Amazon," *Studies in Philology*, 75 (1978), 163–180; [Anne Bradstreet], *The Tenth Muse Lately Sprung up in America* (London, 1650), 202.

7. Jim Bradbury, *The Medieval Archer* (New York, 1985), 152 (Paston), 164–165 (women hunting with bows); James E. Oxley, *The Fletchers and Long-bowstringmakers of London* (London, 1968), 19–20, 135, 137–138; Roger B. Manning, *Hunters and Poachers: A Social and Cultural History of Unlaw-ful Hunting in England, 1485–1640* (Oxford, 1993), 13, 177 (women hunt-

ing with bows). On Tudor men as archers, see [R. S.], *A Briefe Treatise . . . of Archerie* (London, 1596), B2ʳ.

8. J[ohn] B[ulwer], *Anthropometamorphosis: Man Transformed, or, the Artificiall Changling* (London, 1653), 321–322; Schleiner, *"Divina Virago,"* 163–180; Page duBois, *Centaurs and Amazons: Women and the Pre-History of the Great Chain of Being* (Ann Arbor, 1982), 25–48; William Blake Tyrrell, *Amazons: A Study in Athenian Mythmaking* (Baltimore, 1984), xiii–xiv, 40–63; Josin H. Blok, *The Early Amazons: Modern and Ancient Perspectives on a Persistent Myth*, trans. Peter Mason (Leiden, 1995), ix–x, 145–193; Kathryn Schwarz, "Missing the Breast: Desire, Disease, and the Singular Effect of Amazons," in David Hillman and Carla Mazzio, eds., *The Body in Parts: Fantasies of Corporeality in Early Modern Europe* (New York, 1997), 147–169. See also Roger Ascham, *Toxophilus* (1545), facsim. (Menston, 1971), [Uiᵛ].

9. Walter Ralegh, *The Discoverie of the Large, Rich, and Bewtiful Empyre of Guiana* (London, 1596), 101; John Ley cited in Joyce Lorimer, ed., *English and Irish Settlement on the River Amazon, 1550–1646* (London, 1989), 135, 266; *The Proceedings of the English Colony in Virginia* (1612), in Smith, *Works*, 1:235–236 (quotation); *The True Travels* (1630), ibid., 3:226 (lack of Amazons along Amazon River). See also Mario Klarer, "Woman and Arcadia: The Impact of Ancient Utopian Thought on the Early Image of America," *JAS*, 27 (1993), 8–14.

10. Roger Williams, *Actions of the Lowe Countries*, in *The Works of Sir Roger Williams*, ed. John X. Evans (Oxford, 1972), 122; Dianne Dugaw, *Warrior Women and Popular Balladry, 1650–1850* (Cambridge, 1989), 10, 15–42, 45–46.

11. H. K. McIlwaine, ed., *Minutes of the Council and General Court of Colonial Virginia, 1622–32* (Richmond, 1924), 195; Mary Beth Norton, *Founding Mothers and Fathers: Gendered Power and the Forming of American Society* (New York, 1996), 184–197.

12. John Underhill, *Newes from America* (1638), *Massachusetts Historical Society Collections*, 3d ser., 6 (1837), 5; N[icholas] S[altonstall], *The Present State of New-England* (1675), in Charles H. Lincoln, ed., *Narratives of the Indian Wars, 1675–1699* (New York, 1913), 31.

13. [Mary Rowlandson], *The Sovereignty and Goodness of God* (1682), ed. Neal Salisbury (Boston, 1997), 52. On the American frontier as masculine arena, see Richard Slotkin, *Regeneration through Violence: The Mythology of the American Frontier, 1600–1860* (Middletown, Conn., 1973), 22–23, chaps. 6, 7; on puritan viragoes, see Laurel Thatcher Ulrich, *Good Wives: Image and Reality in the Lives of Women in Northern New England, 1650–1750* (New York, 1982), chaps. 9, 10.

14. J. Franklin Jameson, ed., [*Edward*] *Johnson's Wonder-Working Providence, 1628–1651* (New York, 1910), 149. On war and gender in Algonquian societies, see James Axtell, ed., *The Indian Peoples of Eastern America: A Docu-*

mentary History of the Sexes (New York, 1981), 103–104, 141–142; William Scranton Simmons, *Cautantowwit's House: An Indian Burial Ground on the Island of Conanicut in Narragansett Bay* (Providence, 1970), 44–46 (gender-specific burial goods).

15. William Strachey, *The Historie of Travell into Virginia Britania* (1612), ed. Louis B. Wright and Virginia Freund (London, 1953), 64; *Mourt's Relation,* 122; Roger Williams to John Winthrop, July 10, 1637, in Williams, *Correspondence,* 1:96. Winthrop and Boyes are discussed in Chapter 6; on Englishwomen as diplomats in King Philip's War, see Ulrich, *Good Wives,* 207.

16. Charles Best to John Woodall, April 1, 1623, *RVCL,* 4:238; Roger Williams to Henry Vane and John Winthrop, May 1, 1637, in Williams, *Correspondence,* 1:73; John Winthrop to William Bradford, July 28, 1637, *Winthrop Papers,* 3:457; John Winthrop to Uncas, June 20, 1646, ibid., 5:82; *A True Narrative of the Late Rebellion in Virginia by the Royal Commissioners* (1677), in Charles M. Andrews, ed., *Narratives of the Insurrections, 1675–1690* (New York, 1915), 127.

17. Underhill, *Newes from America,* 11; Richard Davenport to John Winthrop, ca. August 23, 1637, *Winthrop Papers,* 3:491. See also Patrick M. Malone, *The Skulking Way of War: Technology and Tactics among the New England Indians* (Baltimore, 1993), 102–125.

18. Waterhouse, *Declaration,* 22.

19. Peter Heylyn, *Cosmographie in Four Books,* 2d ed. (London, 1657), 1029.

20. Strachey, *Virginia Britania,* 113; Thomas Morton, *New English Canaan, or New Canaan* (Amsterdam, 1637), 32; John Lawson, *A New Voyage to Carolina* (1709), ed. Hugh Talmage Lefler (Chapel Hill, 1967), 174.

21. Strachey, *Virginia Britania,* 113, 129; Morton, *New English Canaan,* 32; Williams, *Language of America,* 149.

22. Wood, *New England's Prospect,* 114; Josselyn, *Two Voyages,* 91–92; Lawson, *New Voyage,* 40, 197; Robert Beverley, *The History and Present State of Virginia* (1705), ed. Louis B. Wright (Charlottesville, Va., 1947), 171–172.

23. Edward Maria Wingfield's account, May 1607–May 1608, *NAW,* 5:278; Christopher Levett, *A Voyage into Nevv England* (London, 1628), 21.

24. Wood, *New England's Prospect,* 115; Josselyn, *Two Voyages,* 92, 93. On English belief that Indian parents were indulgent, see Axtell, *Invasion Within,* 56, 209.

25. *The Generall Historie of Virginia, New-England, and the Summer Isles* (1624), in Smith, *Works,* 2:124–125.

26. Isaack de Rasieres to Samuel Blommaert, ca. 1628, in Sydney V. James, Jr., ed., *Three Visitors to Early Plymouth* (Plymouth, Mass., 1963), 78–79; Wood, *New England's Prospect,* 63.

27. Strachey, *Virginia Britania,* 74; Wood, *New England's Prospect,* 82; *A Relation of Maryland* (London, 1635), 25; Winthrop, *Journal,* 207; Josselyn, *Two Voyages,* 104.

28. The Council in Virginia to the Virginia Company, January 1622, *RVCL,* 3:584; Jameson, ed., *Johnson's Wonder-Working Providence,* 168.

29. Wood, *New England's Prospect,* 76; Winthrop, *Journal,* 218–219. On Indian separation of sexual activity and war, see James Axtell, "The White Indians of Colonial America," *WMQ,* 32 (1975), 55–88.

30. *The Present State of New-England,* 28, 30 (rape); N[icholas] S[altonstall], *A New and Further Narrative of the State of New-England* (1676), in Lincoln, *Narratives of the Indian Wars,* 86 (quotation), 98 (rape); [Rowlandson] *Sovereignty and Goodness of God,* 43.

31. P[eter] H[eylyn], *Microcosmus, or A Little Description of the Great World* (Oxford, 1621), 23; Richard Ligon, *A True and Exact History of the Island of Barbados* (London, 1657), 48.

32. B[ulwer], *Anthropometamorphosis,* 396. On African women, see Jennifer L. Morgan, "'Some Could Suckle over Their Shoulder': Male Travelers, Female Bodies, and the Gendering of Racial Ideology, 1500–1770," *WMQ,* 54 (1997), esp. 184–190.

33. "Histoire naturelle des Indes," MA 3900, fol. 107, Pierpont Morgan Library, New York City; Morton, *New English Canaan,* 31, 32.

34. Williams, *Language of America,* 121 (corn), 207; Josselyn, *Two Voyages,* 91–92.

35. Strachey, *Virginia Britania,* 60, 85–86; George Alsop, *A Character of the Province of Mary-Land* (1666), ed. John Gilmary Shea (New York, 1869), 76.

36. Wood, *New England's Prospect,* 76–77, 103; Winthrop, *Journal,* 192–193 (Tilley), 412–413 (lost man).

37. On European atrocities, see James Axtell and William C. Sturtevant, "The Unkindest Cut, or Who Invented Scalping?" *WMQ,* 27 (1980), 451–472; Jill Lepore, *The Name of War: King Philip's War and the Origins of American Identity* (New York, 1998); Ronald Dale Karr, "'Why Should You Be So Furious?': The Violence of the Pequot War," *JAH,* 85 (1998), 879–888.

38. Alsop, *The Province of Mary-Land,* 72.

39. S[altonstall], *A New And Further Narrative,* 83.

40. Ibid., 82–83.

41. Cotton Mather, *Decennium Luctuosum* (1699), in Lincoln, *Narratives of the Indian Wars,* 263–266 (quotation 265). See also Ulrich, *Good Wives,* 167–172.

42. Thomas Mathew, "The Beginning, Progress, and Conclusion of Bacon's Rebellion, 1675–1676," in Warren M. Billings, ed., *The Old Dominion in the Seventeenth Century: A Documentary History of Virginia, 1606–1689* (Chapel Hill, 1975), 232–233.

43. Wood, *New England's Prospect,* 57–58; Winthrop, *Journal,* 218 (Saybrook), 535 (execution); [Philip Vincent], *A True Relation of the Late Battell fought in New England* (London, 1637), [8–9].

44. Roger Williams to John Winthrop, ca. September 9, 1637, in Williams, *Correspondence,* 1:117; William Coddington to John Winthrop, August 5, 1644, *Winthrop Papers,* 4:491.

45. Alsop, *Province of Maryland*, 75–76; Roger Williams to John Winthrop, ca. June 2, 1637, *Winthrop Papers*, 3:427; Winthrop, *Journal*, 225.

46. Petition to Governor William Berkeley, 1676, in Billings, *Old Dominion in the Seventeenth Century*, 267; Increase Mather, *A History of the Warr with the Indians in New-England* (1676), in Richard Slotkin and James K. Folsom, eds., *So Dreadfull a Judgment: Puritan Responses to King Philip's War, 1676–1677* (Middletown, Conn., 1978), 116.

47. Nathaniel Bacon's attack on Susquehannock fort, April 1676, in Billings, *Old Dominion in the Seventeenth Century*, 268, 269; Mather, *Brief History*, 138–139; S[altonstall], *New and Further Narrative*, 90–91. See also Lepore, *Name of War*, 173–180.

48. Roger Williams [to General Court of Commissioners of Providence Plantations?], August 25, 1658, in Williams, *Correspondence*, 2:486.

49. George Best, *A True Discourse* (1578), in *Frobisher Voyages*, 283; for Bernard O'Brien's account of Irish activities in the Amazon, 1621–1624, see Lorimer, *English and Irish Settlement on the Amazon*, 266; Williams, *Language of America*, 216; report of Dr. Edward Dodding, November 8, 1577, *NAW*, 4:217.

50. [Vincent], *Late Battell*, [5]; William Pynchon to John Winthrop, February 19, 1644, *Winthrop Papers*, 4:444; Josselyn, *Two Voyages*, 90; John Winthrop, Jr., to John Winthrop, January 17, 1649, *Winthrop Papers*, 5:304; Henry Whitfield, *The Light Appearing More and More towards the Perfect Day* (London, 1651), 4.

51. Roger Williams to John Whipple, Jr., July 8, 1669, Williams, *Correspondence*, 2:588.

52. Wood, *New England's Prospect*, 75, 110–111; Beverley, *History of Virginia*, 159, 217, 232.

53. Roger Williams [to General Court of Commissioners of Providence Plantations?], August 25, 1658, in Williams, *Correspondence*, 2:488; *Mass. Records*, 3:425. Cf. Peter C. Mancall, *Deadly Medicine: Indians and Alcohol in Early America* (Ithaca, N.Y., 1995), which concentrates on the eighteenth century.

54. Josselyn, *Two Voyages*, 99; Roger Williams to John Throckmorton, July 30, 1672, in Williams, *Correspondence*, 2:675.

55. Daniel Gookin, *Historical Collections of the Indians in New England* (1674), ed. Jeffrey H. Fiske (Towtaid, N.J., 1970), 53–54; John Duffy, *Epidemics in Colonial America* (Baton Rouge, La., 1953), 69–70.

56. Winthrop, *Journal*, 101; Lawson, *New Voyage to Carolina*, 232; *The Four Kings of Canada* (London, 1710), 25; John Josselyn, *New-Englands Rarities Discovered*, 2nd ed. (London, 1675), 3; Kenneth Silverman, ed., *Selected Letters of Cotton Mather* (Baton Rouge, La., 1971), 213–214.

57. Cotton Mather, *The Angel of Bethesda*, ed. Gordon W. Jones (Barre, Mass., 1972), 93, 117.

58. Josselyn, *Two Voyages*, 93.

59. Clarence J. Glacken, *Traces on the Rhodian Shore: Nature and Culture in Western Thought from Ancient Times to the End of the Eighteenth Century* (Berkeley, 1967), 484–491; Anthony Low, *The Georgic Revolution* (Princeton, 1985), esp. 117–167; Max Oelschlaeger, *The Idea of Wilderness: From Prehistory to the Age of Ecology* (New Haven, 1991), 98–103; Keith Thomas, *Man and the Natural World: Changing Attitudes in England, 1500–1800* (New York, 1983), 254–269; Joyce E. Chaplin, "The Meaning of Wildness in Early English Accounts of America," in Mario Materassi and Maria Irene Ramalho de Sousa Santos, eds., *The American Columbiad: "Discovering" America, Inventing the United States* (Amsterdam, 1996).

60. [Waterhouse], *Declaration*, 11, 23.

61. Edward Williams, *Virgo Triumphans: or, Virginia richly and truly valued* (London, 1650), 1; [Charles de Rochefort], *The History of the Caribby-Islands*, trans. John Davies (London, 1666), 22–23; Ligon, *History of Barbados*, 43–44 (plantains).

62. John Graunt, *Natural and Political Observations . . . Made upon the Bills of Mortality* (London, 1662), 31.

63. Daniel Gookin, "An Historical Account of Doings and Sufferings of the Christian Indians in New England," *Transactions and Collections of the American Antiquarian Society*, 2 (1836), 494.

8. Matter and Manitou

1. Linda Welters et al., "European Textiles from Seventeenth-Century New England Indian Cemeteries," in Lu Ann De Cunzo and Bernard L. Herman, eds., *Historical Archaeology and the Study of American Culture* (Winterthur, Del., 1996), 225–228. On Indian grave goods, see William Scranton Simmons, *Cautantowwit's House: An Indian Burial Ground on the Island of Canonicut in Narragansett Bay* (Providence, 1970), esp. 43–47, 68; Susan G. Gibson, ed., *Burr's Hill: A Seventeenth-Century Wampanoag Burial Ground in Warren, Rhode Island* (Providence, 1980), 14, 22–23, 25–33. On English Protestant burials, see Ralph Houlbrooke, *Death, Religion, and the Family in England, 1480–1750* (Oxford, 1998), 343.

2. Peter Dear, "*Totius in verba*: Rhetoric and Authority in the Early Royal Society," *Isis*, 76 (1985), 145–161. On the new connections between science and empire, see Raymond Phineas Stearns, *Science in the British Colonies of America* (Urbana, Ill., 1970); Richard Drayton, "Knowledge and Empire," in P. J. Marshall, ed., *The Oxford History of the British Empire*, vol. 2, *The Eighteenth Century* (New York, 1998), 231–252.

3. Cf. Michael Adas, *Machines as the Measure of Men: Science, Technology, and Ideologies of Western Dominance* (Ithaca, N.Y., 1989), intro. On manitou, see Neal Salisbury, *Manitou and Providence: Indians, Europeans, and the Making of New England, 1500–1643* (New York, 1982), 37, 39.

4. Jill Lepore, *The Name of War: King Philip's War and the Origins of American Identity* (New York, 1998), chap. 1.

5. Charles Webster, *The Great Instauration: Science, Medicine, and Reform, 1626–1660* (London, 1975), 144–153; Clarence J. Glacken, *Traces on the Rhodian Shore: Nature and Culture in Western Thought from Ancient Times to the End of the Eighteenth Century* (Berkeley, 1967), 392–398; Michael Hunter, *Science and Society in Restoration England* (Cambridge, 1981), chap. 7.

6. Christopher Hill, *The Century of Revolution, 1603–1714* (London, 1961); idem, *The World Turned Upside Down* (London, 1972), chap. 14; Keith Thomas, *Religion and the Decline of Magic* (London, 1971), 92–94; David D. Hall, *Worlds of Wonder, Days of Judgment: Popular Religious Belief in Early New England* (New York, 1989), chap. 2; John L. Brooke, *The Refiner's Fire: The Making of Mormon Cosmology, 1644–1844* (Cambridge, 1994), 5–29, 33–58.

7. Hunter, *Science and Society*, 168–170; Steven Shapin and Simon Schaffer, *Leviathan and the Air-Pump: Hobbes, Boyle, and the Experimental Life* (Princeton, 1985), chap. 3.

8. Robert Hugh Kargon, *Atomism in England from Hariot to Newton* (Oxford, 1966); Webster, *Great Instauration*, 145–153; J. R. Jacob, *Robert Boyle and the English Revolution: A Study in Social and Intellectual Change* (New York, 1977), chaps. 3, 4; Margaret C. Jacob, *The Cultural Meaning of the Scientific Revolution* (Philadelphia, 1988), 73–104; Caroline Walker Bynum, *The Resurrection of the Body in Western Christianity, 200–1336* (New York, 1995).

9. Hunter, *Science and Society*, 26–31, chap. 7.

10. Thomas Sprat, *The History of the Royal Society of London* (London, 1667), 62; Stearns, *Science in the British Colonies of America*, 87–101 (Royal Society statutes on 91).

11. Jacob, *Robert Boyle*, 112–118, 159–176; Shapin and Schaffer, *Leviathan and the Air-Pump*, esp. chap. 3. See also William R. Newman, "The Alchemical Sources of Robert Boyle's Corpuscular Philosophy," *AS*, 53 (1996), 567–585.

12. Edward J. Young, "Subjects for Master's Degree in Harvard College from 1655 to 1791," *MHS Pro.*, 18 (1880), 128, 129; William Hughes, *The American Physitian* (London, 1672), 109.

13. James Axtell, *The Invasion Within: The Contest of Cultures in Colonial North America* (New York, 1985), 131–136, 179–182; William Kellaway, *The New England Company, 1649–1776: Missionary Society to the American Indians* (London, 1961), 8–9.

14. Webster, *Great Instauration*, 1–31, 100–115; Hall, *Worlds of Wonder*, chap. 1 (Protestant meanings of literacy); Edward G. Gray, *New World Babel: Languages and Nations in Early America* (Princeton, 1999), chap. 2.

15. Kellaway, *New England Company*, 11–16 (foundation), 96–100 (Eliot and

Mayhew); George Parker Winship, ed., *The New England Company of 1649
. . . Ledger . . . and Record Book* (Boston, 1920), vi–vii, xiv–xix; Ola Elizabeth Winslow, *John Eliot: "Apostle to the Indians"* (Boston, 1968), a hagio-
graphic treatment; Axtell, *Invasion Within*, chaps. 7–10.

16. Kellaway, *New England Company*, 22–27 (pamphlets and other published
accounts), 36–40 (donations); Winship, *New England Company Ledger and
Record Book*, lxviii–lxxxiv (New Model Army contributions on first three
pages), 123–124 (Mowsche).

17. Winthrop, *Journal*, 569 (schools), 682–683 (Eliot); John Eliot, *A Brief Narrative of the Progress of the Gospel amongst the Indians in New-England*
(London, 1671), 3, 4; Axtell, *Invasion Within*, 220–241.

18. Francis Jennings, *The Invasion of America: Indians, Colonization, and the
Cant of Conquest* (New York, 1976), 238–253; Axtell, *Invasion Within*,
159–164; James P. Ronda, "'We Are Well As We Are': An Indian Critique of
Seventeenth-Century Christian Missions," *WMQ*, 34 (1977), 66–82; Alden
T. Vaughan, *New England Frontier: Puritans and Indians, 1620–1675* (Nor-
man, Okla., 1995), 247–249.

19. Richard S. Dunn, *Puritans and Yankees: The Winthrop Dynasty of New
England, 1630–1717* (Princeton, 1962), chaps. 6–8; John Endecott to Robert
Boyle, November 9, 1665, in Thomas Birch, ed., *The Works of the Honour-
able Robert Boyle*, 5 vols. (London, 1744), 1:137.

20. On parallel transatlantic connections, scientific and religious, see Stearns,
Science in the British Colonies of America, 101–116; Kellaway, *New England Company*, passim (see 47 on Boyle's sponsoring scriptural translations);
Jacob, *Robert Boyle*, 148–155; Webster, *Great Instauration*, 78, 94, 95,
501–502 (Oldenburg).

21. Richard Norwood to Henry Oldenburg, November 16, 1668, in Oldenburg,
Correspondence, 4:547–549 (quotations on 548); Oldenburg to Norwood,
July 16, 1668, ibid., 5:172–173; Stearns, *Science in the British Colonies of
America*, 221–225 (Bermuda and Norwood).

22. Kellaway, *New England Company*, 42; Winship, *New England Company
Ledger and Record Book*, 90 (Boyle asked to approach Lord Chancellor in
1662); Jacob, *Robert Boyle*, 148–155; Nicholas Canny, *The Upstart Earl: A
Study of the Social and Mental World of Richard Boyle, First Earl of Cork,
1566–1643* (Cambridge, 1982), on the Boyle family in Ireland; Michael
Hunter, ed., *Robert Boyle by Himself and His Friends* (London, 1994), lxx–
lxxii, 87. After Boyle's death in 1691, his nephew arranged for £5,400 of his
estate to be invested and the profits to go to Indian education at the new College of William and Mary. The money was never so used, however; see
Axtell, *Invasion Within*, 190.

23. Kellaway, *New England Company*, chap. 6; Wolfgang Hochbruck and
Beatrix Dudensing-Reichel, "'Honoratissimi Benefactores': Native American
Students and Two Seventeenth-Century Texts in the University Tradition," in
Helen Jaskoski, ed., *Early Native American Writing: New Critical Essays*

(New York, 1996), 1–14 (which reproduces and translates the texts; quotation on 5); Robert Boyle to John Winthrop, Jr., April 1664, *MHS Pro.*, 5 (1862), 376–377; list of John Winthrop, Jr.'s, gifts to the Royal Society is printed in Stearns, *Science in the British Colonies of America*, quotation on 694; John Winthrop, Jr., to Henry Oldenburg, September 25, 1673, in Oldenburg, *Correspondence*, 9:256–257.

24. Roger Williams, *A Key into the Language of America* (1643), ed. John J. Teunissen and Evelyn J. Hinz (Detroit, 1973), 33–34 (dialogue form), 84 (first quotation), 134 (Anglo-Indian communication), 173 (manitou), 189 (many gods, creation of the universe).

25. John Eliot, *The Indian Grammar Begun* (Cambridge, Mass., 1666), A^r, 8–10.

26. On development of ideas of organicism, see Charles E. Raven, *John Ray, Naturalist: His Life and Works* (Cambridge, 1950); L. J. Jordanova, *Lamarck* (Oxford, 1984), esp. 44–57; Otto Mayr, *Authority, Liberty, and Automatic Machinery in Early Modern Europe* (Baltimore, 1986), 81–92, 187–189; Jacques Roger, *Buffon: A Life in Natural History*, trans. Sarah Lucille Bonnefoi, ed. L. Pearce Williams (Ithaca, N.Y., 1997), 65–75.

27. John Eliot to Robert Boyle, August 26, 1664, in Birch, *Works of Boyle*, 5:548–549; Eliot, *Indian Grammar*, A2^r.

28. [Henry Whitfield], *Strength out of VVeaknesse . . .* (London, 1652); idem, *A Late and Further Manifestation of the Progress of the Gospel Amongst the Indians in Nevv-England* (London, 1655), 22.

29. [John Eliot], *The Glorious Progress of the Gospel amongst the Indians in New England* (London, 1649), dedication by Edward Winslow, [A3^r], [4].

30. Stephen Parmenius, *Thanksgiving Hymn* (1582), trans. from Latin, in David B. Quinn and Neil M. Cheshire, eds., *The New Found Land of Stephen Parmenius* (Toronto, 1972), 153; "Some Physico-Theological Considerations about the Possibility of the Resurrection" (1675), in Boyle, *Works*, 8:99–100.

31. William Strachey, *The Historie of Travell into Virginia Britania* (1612), ed. Louis B. Wright and Virginia Freund (London, 1953), 100.

32. Thomas Morton, *New English Canaan, or New Canaan* (Amsterdam, 1637), 51; William Wood, *New England's Prospect* (1634), ed. Alden Vaughan (Amherst, Mass., 1977), 93; Josselyn, *Two Voyages*, 96; Winthrop, *Journal*, 246; J. Franklin Jameson, ed., [*Edward*] *Johnson's Wonder-Working Providence: 1628–1651* (New York, 1910), 128.

33. Williams, *Language of America*, 135; John Eliot, *Tears of Repentence* (London, 1653), 29; idem, *Late and Further Manifestation*, 14.

34. Morton, *New English Canaan*, 51, 52; Eliot, *Tears of Repentence*, 26–27; [Edward Winslow], *The Day-Breaking if not the Sun-Rising of the Gospell with the* INDIANS *in New-England* (London, 1647), 16.

35. Thomas Shepard, *The Clear Sunshine of the Gospel Breaking Forth upon the Indians in New-England* (London, 1648), 48.

36. Henry Whitfield, *The Light Appearing More and More towards the Perfect Day* (London, 1651), 23; Shepard, *Clear Sunshine of the Gospel*, 48.

37. [John Eliot], *New Englands First Fruits* (London, 1643); Eliot, *Late and Further Manifestation*, [iii].

38. Winthrop, *Journal*, 101, 105.

39. Ibid., 401 (Wequash); Eliot, *Tears of Repentence*, 4, 7, 43, 46, 47; [John Eliot], *A further Accompt of the Progresse of the Gospel amongst the Indians in New-England* (London, 1659), 9, 14–16, 19. See also idem, *A further Account of the Progress of the Gospel amongst the Indians in New England* (London, 1660), 69.

40. [Eliot], *Further Accompt*, postscript; Eliot, *Further Account*, 20, 54; [Eliot], *Glorious Progress of the Gospel*, [6–7], 13.

41. Eliot, *Tears of Repentence*, 21, 27 (Peter), 36; Eliot, *Late and Further Manifestation*, 16; Eliot, *Further Account*, 11–12, 25.

42. *Some Helps for the Indians* (London, 1659), 30.

43. Ibid., postscript; Eliot, *Brief Narrative*, 5.

44. Winslow, *Day-Breaking*, 3, 21; Shepard, *Clear Sunshine of the Gospel*, 20; Eliot to the Commissioners of the United Colonies, July 4, 1671, in John W. Ford, ed., *Some Correspondence between . . . the New England Company in London and the Commissioners of the United Colonies in America* (London, 1897), 44.

45. Winslow, *Day-Breaking*, 14.

46. Ibid., 6.

47. Shepard, *Clear Sunshine of the Gospel*, 19; [Whitfield], *Strength out of VVeaknesse*, 25.

48. Stephen Winthrop to John Winthrop, Jr., July 16, 1649, *Winthrop Papers*, 5:356.

49. Sprat, *History of the Royal Society*, 15–16.

50. Robert Boyle, "The Aretology" and "Of Piety," in John T. Harwood, ed., *The Early Essays and Ethics of Robert Boyle* (Carbondale, Ill., 1991), 73–74 (gugaws), 180 (bell); *The Usefulness of Natural Philosophy* (1671), in Boyle, *Works*, 6:522 (key); *Some Considerations Touching the Usefulness of Experimental Natural Philosophy* (1663), ibid., 3:248 (Indians).

51. Eliot, *Indian Grammar Begun*, 2; Sprat, *History of the Royal Society*, 81.

52. Richard Kemp to Henry Oldenburg, August 18, 1668, 1ᵛ, 2ʳ, and August 29, 1668, Extra Ms. 4, RS. See also Oldenburg, *Correspondence*, 5:19n.

53. Richard Kemp to Henry Oldenburg, August 29, 1668, quotations from 12ʳ, 16ʳ–16ᵛ, 17ʳ–17ᵛ, RS.

54. John Winthrop, Jr., to Robert Moray, August 26, 1668, 1ᵛ, W.3.20, RS; Winthrop to Henry Oldenburg, August 26, 1670, in Oldenburg, *Correspondence*, 7:143.

55. John Winthrop, Jr., to Henry Oldenburg, November 12, 1668, in Oldenburg, *Correspondence*, 5:153; Robert Beverley, *The History and Present State of Virginia* (1705), ed. Louis B. Wright (Charlottesville, Va., 1947), 55.

56. Josselyn, *Two Voyages*, 40, 97; Winthrop discussed in Stearns, *Science in the British Colonies of America*, 122–123, and John Canup, *Out of the Wilderness: The Emergence of an American Identity in Colonial New England* (Middletown, Conn., 1990), chap. 6.

57. Mayhew cited in [Whitfield], *Strength out of VVeaknesse*, 26; Eliot, *Teares of Repentence*, B2ʳ, [B3ᵛ].

58. Eliot, *Glorious Progess of the Gospel*, 11, 25; Whitfeld, *Light Appearing*, 9; Shepard, *Clear Sunshine of the Gospell*, 36–37.

59. *Of the Reconcileableness of Specifick Medicines to the Corpuscular Philosophy* (1685), in Boyle, *Works*, 10:364.

60. Kellaway, *New England Company*, 65, 66 (books of physic); Winship, *New England Company Ledger and Record Book*, lxxix, 35.

61. Mayhew cited in Eliot, *Glorious Progress of the Gospel*, [3–5]; Whitfeld, *Light Appearing*, 4 (Hiacoomes), 31 (smallpox); *Strength out of VVeaknesse*, 1 (profane neighbors).

62. [Whitfield], *Strength out of VVeaknesse*, 1; Eliot, *Brief Narrative*, 6; Shepard, *Clear Sunshine of the Gospel*, 43.

63. Daniel Gookin, *Historical Collections of the Indians in New England*, ed. Jeffrey H. Fiske (Towtaid, N.J., 1970), 21; [Whitfield], *Strength out of VVeaknesse*, 32.

64. Sprat, *History of the Royal Society*, [ii], 86, 87.

65. On the frontispiece, see Hunter, *Science and Society*, 194–197. On Enlightenment truisms about learning and empire, see Anthony Pagden, *European Encounters with the New World: From Renaissance to Romanticism* (New Haven, 1993), chap. 3; David Armitage, "The New World and British Historical Thought: From Richard Hakluyt to William Robertson," in Karen Ordahl Kupperman, ed., *America in European Consciousness, 1493–1750* (Chapel Hill, 1995), 60–70; Drayton, "Knowledge and Empire," 234–237.

66. John Graunt, *Natural and Political Observations . . . Made upon the Bills of Mortality* (London, 1662), dedication. On population theory, see Chapter 1, note 14.

67. Erich Strauss, *Sir William Petty: Portrait of a Genius* (London, 1954), 39–40 (Hartlib circle), 52–53 (Ireland); James H. Cassedy, *Demography in Early America: Beginnings of the Statistical Mind, 1600–1800* (Cambridge, Mass., 1969), chap. 3; James Bonar, *Theories of Population from Raleigh to Arthur Young* (Bristol, 1931), 82–100; Marquis of Lansdowne, ed., *The Petty Papers* (New York, 1967), 1:64–67 (Ireland), 2:115–116 (Pennsylvania); James Kelly, "The Origins of the Act of Union: An Examination of Unionist Opinion in Britain and Ireland, 1650–1800," *Irish Historical Studies*, 25 (1987), 239–240.

68. Lansdowne, *Petty Papers*, 2:118. On the genre of the questionnaire for travelers or foreign informants, see P. J. Marshall and Glyndwr Williams, *The Great Map of Mankind: Perceptions of New Worlds in the Age of Enlightenment* (Cambridge, Mass., 1982), 45–47.

Coda

1. Bernard Romans, *A Concise Natural History of East and West Florida* (London, 1775), 37–38.
2. George Alsop, *A Character of the Province of Mary-Land. . . . Also a Small Treatise on the Wilde and Naked INDIANS (or Susquehanokes) of Mary-Land* (1666), ed. John Gilmary Shea (New York, 1896); Robert Beverley, *The History and Present State of Virginia* (1705), ed. Louis B. Wright (Charlottesville, Va., 1947), 161 (European coats), 204, 211, 229 (European tools), 233.
3. On American degeneracy, see Antonello Gerbi, *The Dispute of the New World: The History of a Polemic, 1750–1900,* trans. Jeremy Moyle (Pittsburgh, 1983), chaps. 1–5; P. J. Marshall and Glyndwr Williams, *The Great Map of Mankind: Perceptions of New Worlds in the Age of Enlightenment* (Cambridge, Mass., 1982), 216–218. On the debate over nature's laws, see Joyce E. Chaplin, "Mark Catesby, a Skeptical Newtonian in America," in Amy R. W. Meyers and Margaret Beck Pritchard, eds., *Empire's Nature: Mark Catesby's New World Vision* (Chapel Hill, 1999), 34–90.
4. Thomas Morton, *New English Canaan, or New Canaan* (Amsterdam, 1637), 23.
5. Russell Thornton, *American Indian Holocaust and Survival: A Population History since 1492* (Norman, Okla., 1987), chaps. 5, 7, 8.

Index

Abandoned settlements: Indian occupation of, 73; scavenging and, 206
Abenaki Indians, 64–65, 69, 100, 101, 208, 226
Absurd transcription: detection of, 27, 28; in Hariot's report on Roanoak, 33–34. *See also* Structural theory
Acclimatization: Arctic explorations and, 47, 52–53, 54–55; bodily humors and, 120–121; as seasoning, 151–152
Acculturation, 222–223
Acosta, José de, 18, 44, 120, 124, 177
"Act for the promoting and Propagating the Gospel of Jesus Christ in the New World," 289
Adams, William, 51
Africa, 43
Africans/African slaves: English explanations of skin color, 52, 139, 140–141; melancholy and, 122; European justifications for slavery, 122–123; English fears of, 131–132; English racial ideology and, 160; English sexual contact and, 191–192, 193; English eroticization of women, 192; English notions of mastery over, 193; English reluctance to provide nursing care to, 193; West Indian slavery, 204, 219–220; Anglo-African hybridity, 219–220;

English accounts of easy childbirth in, 262, 263; Richard Ligon's description of, 278
Agincourt, 86, 89
Agnello, John Baptisto, 48, 50, 57
Agricola (Tacitus), 93, 95
Agriculture: Arctic expeditions and, 49–50; success of crops in America, 151; trade in metal tools and, 203; hybrid practices in, 203, 211–212; West Indies and, 216, 217–218; Robert Child on, 237, 238; Indian women and, 246, 247. *See also* Food; Livestock; Maize; Plantations; Tobacco
Alchemy, 13, 22, 62, 239
Alcohol, 273–274
Alexander, Amir, 30
Algonquian Indians, 108, 257, 261
Algonquian language, 25, 32–33, 308
Allerton, Mary, 155
Almanacs, 13
Alsop, George, 197, 221, 264, 266, 269, 322
Altham, Emmanuel, 226, 232–233
Amazon: gunpowder technology in, 90; mineral cures from, 195; Roger Fry and, 232
Amazons, 248, 249–250
America: early geographic representations,

89; ceremonial associations, 89; notions of manly virtue and, 95–96; Smythe's defense of, 96; positive representations of, 97; early English colonists and, 97–99; Arctic expeditions and, 98, 354; English historical misconceptions regarding, 101; Englishmen shot with Indian arrows, 102; gunpowder shortages and, 230; women and, 248–249. *See also* Indian archers/archery; Longbows

Arctic explorers/exploration: impact of, 39–40, 59; motives for and goals in, 43, 44, 45–47; pre-English reports and accounts, 44–45; Inuit and, 45, 49, 51, 53, 55, 56, 98, 122; gold and, 46–47, 50–51, 56–57; expert advisers for, 47, 48; acclimatization and, 47, 52–53, 54–55; Frobisher's expeditions, 47–50, 51, 52–53, 54, 56–58, 59, 98; use of skilled workers on, 48–49; agricultural experiments, 49–50; Davis's expeditions, 51, 53, 56; technological failures, 56–57; castaways on Kodlunarn Island, 57, 58; Inuit accounts of, 57–58; effect on English perceptions of Indians, 59; images of Elizabeth and, 59; archery and, 98

Arctic regions: cosmographic theory on, 43–44; pre-English reports and accounts, 44–45; acclimatization and, 47, 52–53, 54–55

"Aretology or Ethicall Elements" (Boyle), 307

Argall, Samuel, 174
Argall, Thomas, 188
Aristotelian medicine, 135–136
Aristotle, 40; natural philosophy and, 12; corpuscular theory and, 29
Armillary spheres, 60
Arrows/Arrowheads, 101, 102, 112–113, 235. *See also* Archery; Longbows
Art: images of Indians, 36, 51, 61, 103; Elizabethan icons, 59–60; issues of idolatry and, 60–61
Arte de Navigar (Cortés), 18
Artillery Company of London, 89
Art of Archerie (Markham), 88
Ascham, Roger, 86–87, 88, 95–96, 101
Ashe, Thomas, 150, 154, 156, 196

Ashmole, Elias, 233
Ashmolean Museum, 233
Astrology, 33
Astronomy: Indian, 69, 311; European, 232
Atheism, 30; atomists and, 285
Atomism, 29–31, 285–286. *See also* Corpuscular theory
Axtell, James, 24, 191
Azores, 169

Bacon, Francis, 1–2, 11, 33, 40, 42, 43, 90, 143, 167, 236, 316, 318
Bacon, Nathaniel, 116, 254, 270
Bacon's Rebellion, 90, 244, 254, 268, 269–270
Baffin Eskimo, 45, 53–54. *See also* Inuit
Bahamas, 131
Bainbridge, John, 232
Baker, Alexander, 110
Baker, William, 191
Ballads: on women soldiers, 250–251
Baltimore, Lord. *See* Calvert, George
Barbados, 169, 170, 216–217, 218, 278
Barlowe, Arthur, 42, 72, 99
Barlowe, Roger, 44
Barwick, Humphrey, 92, 96
"Bataille of Agincourt" (Drayton), 86
Bateman, Stephen, 195
Beaver: pelt trade, 147; tame, 224
Beer, 149, 150
Berkeley, William, 241
Bermuda, 113; reports of mines on, 109; number of colonists estimated to sustain, 142; climate of, 153; need for nursing care in, 182; Anglo-Indian marriage in, 189; English views of life in, 205; rats and, 218
Bermudas Berries, 171–172
Best, George, 46, 49, 51, 55, 140, 141, 145, 184
Beverley, Robert, 36, 75, 178, 189, 258, 273, 310, 322
Bible, 286; Book of Ezekiel, 300–301; Book of Matthew, 302–303
Bills of mortality, 129
Biringucci, Vannuccio, 18
Black bile, 121
Black Death, 14, 128–129, 181
Black lead. *See* Graphite mining

on Indians lessened, 205–206; hybrid use of materials by, 206; shipbuilding by, 213
Castle Island, 168, 212
Catholics, 63; Indian idolization and, 65
Cecil, William, 20
Certain Discourses Military (Smythe), 91–92
Charity: nursing care and, 180, 183
Charles II, 89, 287, 316, 318
Chastity: Indian women and, 189–190
"Chauquaquock," 111
Cheeshateaumauk, Caleb, 25, 293, 304
Chemical pharmacology. *See* Mineral pharmacology
Chemistry, 22–23, 239, 309. *See also* Alchemy
Chesapeake Indians, 102
Chesapeake settlements: Indian sailing and, 214; copper mining and, 240–241; female agricultural labor and, 247
Chickahominy Indians, 106, 157
Chiggers, 197
Child, Robert, 170, 172, 196, 233, 236–238, 239, 319
Childbirth: colonists' notions of fertility and, 155–156; Antinomian women and, 164–165; Indian women and, 246, 262, 263–264, 272–273, 314–315; English accounts of easy childbirth in foreigners, 262; narratives of torture and murder, 266–267; Indian body and, 270; notions of wildness and, 278
Childrearing, Indian, 257–260
Children: creole, 155, 164–165; transmission of syphilis to, 181; Anglo-Indian, 191; Anglo-African, 192
Choleric temperament: Indians and, 271, 272
Christianity: magic and, 39, 67–68; concepts of matter and spirit, 286; science and, 286–287; Indian churches, 291. *See also* Indian conversion; Missionaries
Churches: Indian, 291
Cider, 149
Cinchona, 171, 172
Clayton, John, 175
Clendinnen, Inga, 83

Climactic theory, 43–44
Climate: disease and, 116, 151, 168–169; colonists' views of, 116, 151–154; effects on the body and bodily humors, 117, 118, 120–121, 256; national temperaments and, 122–123; warfare over resources and, 128; effects on sexual characteristics, 133–134; English denial of effects from, 176; Indian bodies and, 256. *See also* Acclimatization; Hot climates
Clovell, Eustace, 102
Clowes, William, 181
Cockacoeske, 254
Coddington, William, 191, 269
Cole, Humphrey, 47
Collections, 232–235
Colonies: population theories and, 126, 127; English definitions of, 133
Colonies (Du Bartas), 127
Comenius, Jan, 235
Commentaries (Caesar), 93–94
Company of Bowstringers, 249
Company of Fletchers, 249
Concubinage, 187, 189
Cook, Wequash, 302
Cooke, Edward, 92–93
Copernicus, Nicolaus, 12
Copper: Indian trade in, 109; mining, 240–241
Corn. *See* Maize
Cornmeal, 212
Corporation for the Propagation of the Gospel in New England. *See* New England Company
Corpuscular theory, 29–31, 124, 166–167, 287
Cortés, Martín, 18
Cosmographie in Four Books (Heylyn), 127
Cosmography, 43–44, 118
Cotton, Charles, 88–89
Cotton, John, 155, 164, 165
Cradle boards, 257, 258
Creoles: children, 155, 164–165; identified as "inhabitants," 175; notions of the effects of America on, 176; as natural to America, 178
Creolization, 137

Eden, Richard, 18, 20, 38, 42, 46, 62, 90, 91, 118, 120, 121, 133, 139

Edmonds, Clement, 94

Education: in natural philosophy, 13; in the New World, 22–23; archery and, 88; study of Roman texts, 93–94, 96; medical schools, 163. *See also* Indian education

El Dorado ritual, 63

Eleazar (Indian man), 25

Elfrith, Daniel, 131–132

Eliot, John, 127, 299; *Indian Grammar Begun,* 23, 293, 294–295, 297–298, 308; criticism of Indian technology, 222; praise of Indian carpenters, 223; missionary activities of, 290–291; analysis of Indian languages, 293, 294–295; Robert Boyle and, 295; use of Song of Solomon to explain missionary work, 296–297; preaching of the Book of Ezekiel, 300–301; accounts of Indian conversion and sickness, 303; Indian education and, 304–305; criticism of Indian medicine, 312; on smallpox, 313–314; on mercy in praying Indians, 314; proximity and assistance to Indians, 315

Elizabeth, Queen: images and tokens of, 59–60; Roger Ascham and, 87; as bodily symbol of dominion, 126; as Amazon, 248, 249

Elliott, J. H., 82

Ellis, John, 65

Ellis, Thomas, 71

Elyot, Thomas, 88, 93–94

Endecott, John, 223, 291

England: climactic theory and, 44; piracy and, 44; Elizabethan icons and, 59; study of Roman texts, 93–94; notions of primitivism vs. civility, 94–96; poetic evocation of wilderness, 95; literacy in, 96; Indians in, 97, 177; justifications of slavery, 123; Black Death in, 129, 181; mixed lineage in, 130; papermaking and, 229; forests of, 237–238

"English," 329

English Civil War, 228

English explorers/exploration, 16; natural philosophers as advisers to, 19–20; indecision over capabilities of

technology, 40; notions of experience and discovery, 40; views of difference from natives, 41; Spanish presence and, 41–42; beliefs challenged by, 43. *See also* Arctic explorers/exploration

English navy, 168

Ensenore, 210

Epicurus, 30

Epidemics. *See* Disease

Eroticization: of Indian women, 190–191; of African women, 192

Erysipelas, 194

Eskimo. *See* Baffin Eskimo; Inuit

Ethnography: as military intelligence, 81, 82; poststructural critique of, 82; notions of cultural comparisons and, 82–83; notions of human progress and, 83; nostalgic treatment of archery and warrior ethic, 83–84; in Tacitus's writings, 94

Ethnohistory, 24, 28

Euclid, 39

Evangelization. *See* Indian conversion; Missionaries

Evans, Owen, 156

Evelin, Robert, 143

Evelyn, John, 238

Experience, 40

Experiments, 40

Exploration narratives: ambivalent attitudes in, 41; technology praised in, 42; deification of inventors in, 42–43; criticisms of materialist ambitions, 61–62, 63–64. *See also* America, texts and writings about

Explorers. *See* Arctic explorers/exploration; English explorers/exploration

Fenton, Christopher, 56

Fenton, Edward, 53, 145

Ferryland, 153

Fertility: English views of, 132, 154–156; of American soil, 143, 144

Fire: Indian use of, 223. *See also* Burning

Firearms: English concerns with, 21, 91; Indian acquisition of, 80, 108, 111, 113, 221; limited effectiveness of, 80–81; Richard Eden on, 91; compared to longbows, 91–92; used with longbows,